UTAH FISHING GUIDE

I t's all here! From the Green River and Strawberry Reservoir to 40 lakes on the Boulder Mountains, this first complete fishing guide to the state really fills a void. Hundreds of easy-to-read maps, easy-to-follow tactics, and GPS directions. Gee, even I might be able to catch fish. Hopefully, this will encourage Utah anglers to explore new areas and take some pressure off the over-fished waters.

Reece Stein
KUTV Outdoors

U tah has never been known as a place to come and fish. This book will change a lot of minds.

Byron Gunderson, owner
Fish Tech Outfitters

I feel the Utah Fishing Guide is, without a doubt, the most comprehensible and concise reference to the waters of Utah available. With a free flowing format and world class artwork, it is both extremely informative and enjoyable to read. It is definitely a must for any serious angler!

David Scadden, owner
Anglers Inn

U tah anglers have long-awaited a comprehensive directory to the many diverse and productive fishing waters Utah has. Utah Fishing Guide by Steve Cook more than adequately fills this void. This extensive and exhaustive work is filled with valuable information for all anglers. Residents and visitors alike will find the maps, fishery descriptions, and encompassing details invaluable when planning a trip or researching a new Utah destination. Utah Fishing Guide will be an excellent addition to any angler's library interested in exploring Utah fishing resources.

Steve Schmidt, owner
Western Rivers Flyfisher

I t's about time someone produced a book about fishing in Utah. You have done an excellent job, even if you did give away some of my "secret" holes. I especially enjoy your Tactics about each water; identifying what flies and lures are most productive and when; this will be a great guide for everyone. Letting people know where to go and what USGS maps to use is an excellent idea. Your GPS guide is great.

Wes Johnson, Chairman
Utah Council of Trout Unlimited

publisher:
Bryan Brandenburg
Utah Outdoors
P.O. Box 728
Centerville, UT 84104
tel: (801) 523-1266
www.utahoutdoors.com

contributing editor:
Steve Jackson

editor:
Rita Dickey

contributing writers:
Mike Ferguson
Matt Jackson
Rick Peterson
Tom Pettengill
Dave Webb
Sam Webb

contributing photographers:
Dennis Breer
John Campbell
Bill Furniss
Byron Gunderson
Emmett Heath
James R. Henderson
Brad Nicholson
David N. Olsen
Greg Pearson
Steve Schmidt

artists:
Brett Kennedy / Kennedy Art
Full-color lithographs available.
Call (801) 967-1067.

Greg Pearson

Mike Stidham
Full-color prints available.
Contact the publisher, Utah Outdoors.

maps:
Peter Strohmeyer
Salt Lake City, Utah

cover design:
Cory Maylett
Salt Lake City, Utah

cover photo:
Steve Schmidt
Western Rivers Flyfisher

layout:
Marjo Peltonen
Salt Lake City, Utah

printer:
Publishers Press
Salt Lake City, Utah

©1999 Utah Outdoors

Printed in the USA.

Library of Congress Catalog Card Number: 99-62572
ISBN: 0-9671738-0-9

UTAH
FISHING GUIDE

by Steve Cook

To my parents,
who took us fishing.

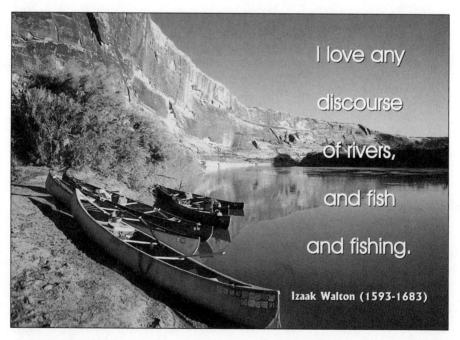

I love any

discourse

of rivers,

and fish

and fishing.

Izaak Walton (1593-1683)

Acknowledgements

T his book is not the work of any single person. Rather it is made up of the contributions of a great many people who share a passion for fishing and the wild and peaceful places of Utah. Our hope is that all these pieces will combine into a unified whole that will exceed the individual parts and bring enjoyment to anglers of all ages and descriptions.

With that said, I would like to thank the Utah Division of Wildlife Resources (DWR) as a whole, as they are the managers and protectors of our fisheries. Without their commitment and service, there would be little value in a book about Utah's fisheries. Many individuals within the DWR provided information included in the following pages. These are Louis Berg (Regional Aquatics Manager, South East Region); Ed Johnson (Regional Aquatics Biologist, North Eastern Region), Mike Ottenbacher (Fisheries Biologist, Southern Region); Charlie Thompson (Regional Aquatics Manager, Central Region); and Kent Sorenson (Regional Aquatics Manager, Northern Region). Laura Milton of the Springville office went out of her way to be helpful. Jim Lamb is a dedicated Conservation Officer II from the Loa District who shared his complete and detailed knowledge of the Boulder Mountain Area. Dr. Chris Wilson of the DWR Fisheries Experiment Station took the time to review our section on whirling disease and Don Archer (Wildlife Program Coordinator) provided and reviewed information on aquatic nuisance species in Utah. Tom Pettengill (Sport Fisheries Coordinator) merits special thanks for his contribution on Fisheries Management in Utah and review of walleye fishing. Much of the information on catch-and-release techniques was also drawn from his writings.

The US Forest Service are custodians of our public lands and deserve our cooperation with road closures and other land use issues. We are grateful to Marvin Turner (US Forest Service District Ranger, Loa and Teasdale Districts) who provided information on road closures on Boulder Mountain. David Palmer of the Vernal Forest Service office answered access questions in the Uinta Mountains.

The project was blessed with the support of Utah's angling fellowships. Thanks go to Wes Johnson and Trout Unlimited; Ray Shelble and Rocky Mountain Anglers; Kenny Kummer and Utah Bass Federation.

Rita Dickey was one of our editors and helped us with perspective. Nick Brandenburg worked on research. Marjo Peltonen, loyal friend, put in many long hours doing layout. Peter Strohmeyer produced the maps for the book while remaining patient and tolerant when we didn't know exactly what we wanted. Teresa Johnson is the clever woman that could do whatever was needed and Jan

Webb proof read when time was short. Sonia Couillard compiled our index. Fred Gruter and Fred Furner of Pre Press Services scanned the art and photos with their usual flexibility and good humor.

Many fine friends in the fishing business have provided input as well. Byron Gunderson (Fish Tech) shared his Uinta photos while Dennis Breer (Trout Creek Flies) gave us the picture of the huge Green River brown. Jake Cleveland (Western Rivers Flyfisher) and John Campbell (The Outdoor Source) contributed information and photos. Bill Furniss offered photos of his many trophy fish. Andy Fitzhugh (Western Rivers Flyfisher) took the time to contribute text while moving into a new home. John "Harley" Jackson and Cory Kapolowski (both of Trout Bum 2) reviewed destinations and gave input regarding accuracy.

No thanks are sufficient for Steve Schmidt and Emmett Heath of Western Rivers Flyfisher. Not only did they both help with the book and provide some of our best photos, but they brought me into the circle of anglers and the influence of both men has changed my life.

Dave Webb (Editor, Utah Outdoors) contributed the wonderful piece on bass fishing. Matt Jackson is a great fishing companion (and up and coming oarsman) who wrote about backcountry travel and clothing for the book. Rick Peterson is the passionate and patient teacher of fly-fishing, and father of three boys, who gave us *Fly-fishing Basics* and *Etiquette*.

We are pleased to have the artwork of Mike Stidham and Greg Pearson in the pages that follow. Both are passionate fishermen and artists. Mike's work is well known and we think Greg's should be also. Cory Maylett (Deseret News) is the talented artist who knocked us over with his design for our cover, and Brett Kennedy's fine lithographs are reproduced in these pages. Kevin Schieffer is a longtime friend who sent us his poem *Tyin' Flies*. Brad Nicholson, James R. Henderson and David N. Olsen came through with pictures in the eleventh hour.

There are four people whose contributions were above and beyond. Bryan Brandenburg (President, Utah Outdoors) had the initial vision for the book and provided a vehicle to bring it to anglers. Sam Webb (General Manager, Utah Outdoors) probably knows Utah's waters better than anyone else. He had incredible patience with the many phone calls and I doubt that the book could have been completed without his input. Stephen Jackson is a contributing editor. The tone and flavor of the book arises in large part from his sense of style and passion for the sport. Last but far from least is Lisa Albertson. She designed the book, coordinated layout, printing, writing and anything else that was needed. In short, she helped to make the project a success. If you find the book appealing, the credit is hers. ◆

Steve Cook

ARTIST: BRETT KENNEDY / KENNEDY ART

Table of Contents

WARMWATER LAKES AND RESERVOIRS

HIGH UINTA LAKES

SOUTHERN UTAH 326

RIVERS AND STREAMS

Dean of the Green

N o book about fishing in Utah would be complete without mentioning Emmett Heath.

Emmett has been a strong, quiet presence in the fishing profession in Utah for the last 30 years. During that time he has touched the lives of thousands of anglers with his guiding, instruction, and slide shows. To recognize his prowess and contributions to the sport, *Fly Rod & Reel* named him "Guide of the Year" in 1992.

One of the first fly-fishing guides on the Green, Emmett has remained a steward and protector of the river by organizing annual cleanups. His care and concern for the fish show in the names he has given them and the stories he tells about their home.

To new guides learning the ways of trout and water, he is an example of not only skill and knowledge, but also of character and deportment. His power and grace at the oars is underscored by his humble manner.

He is a man of large stature — called by some the "Gentle Giant." When his heavy hand rests for a moment on your shoulder, there is a sense of permanence; not necessarily of ourselves, but of the natural world we come in contact with as we pursue our sport. ♦

Emmett pulling on the oars in Red Creek Rapids on the Green River. (PHOTO: STEVE SCHMIDT / WESTERN RIVERS FLYFISHER)

Introduction

O ur intent with this guide is to stimulate your curiosity, rather than satisfy it. A great deal is known about the most popular fishing destinations. Much of it will be presented in the pages that follow. There are other places, less often visited, that still retain a feel of mystery. These obscure destinations appear with some background, directions, and enough tips on tactics to get you started. Adventure lies in the unknown.

Time and space did not allow us to list all the fishing waters of the state so we tried to pick the best. There are still a few waters out there waiting for the angler with the imagination and fortitude to track them down.

We have provided information that will help anglers enjoy water throughout the state to encourage more even distribution of fishing pressure. If you are disappointed to see your favorite out-of-the-way fishing hole in this book, you may be compensated by finding a little more room the next time you visit one of the better known fisheries.

PHOTO: COURTESY UTAH OUTDOORS

We also want to build support for all the fisheries of Utah. When our waters are threatened, it is the people who know and enjoy them best that can be counted on to step forward and act on their behalf.

Fishing conditions are dynamic and many fisheries are quite changeable. The information included in this book is the most recent available. Updated editions will incorporate changing conditions and new regulations, as well as meeting the requests of our readers.

How To Use This Guide

The destination descriptions and *fish species* information will help you decide if a particular water has the qualities you look for when planning a fishing excursion.

Fishing regulations in Utah consist of the *General Season Dates and Bag & Possession Limits*, which you will find listed following this introduction. There are additional provisions for specific waters, which are listed under *Special Regulations* for each fishing destination. The 1999 regulations are listed solely for the convenience of the reader. Anglers should always carry a current Utah Fishing Proclamation and understand it. Look up regulations concerning new waters as part of the trip planning process. The *Utah Fishing Guide* assumes no liability for any violations of laws that might result from misunderstandings arising from use of this publication.

The *tactics* section lists some of the approaches that have been successful for other anglers. You may enjoy experimenting with some of the methods described, or simply employ techniques with which you are already proficient.

The routes described in *How to Get There* start from likely points of origin. The same route is displayed on the map that accompanies each destination. *Accessibility* information will list some facilities available at the destination and indicate public access.

Adventure lies in the unknown

PHOTO: JAMES R. HENDERSON

When to Go points out the best time to visit a particular fishing location based on historic and recent trends. Prime fishing seasons can vary widely, depending on weather, water levels, human impact, and other factors. Choosing the "best time to fish" is somewhat subjective, and should not be confused with the question of "Should I go?" Remember the old saying: "The best time to fish is whenever you can."

With some of the destinations we have also included *services* that you might want to contact for reservations or information before your trip.

GPS coordinates are provided with each destination to aid in navigation. All coordinates are in latitude/longitude format of degrees, minutes, seconds.

The information in the *maps* section references the *Utah Atlas and Gazeteer*. This publication is useful for anglers wishing to find their way to unfamiliar fishing destinations around the state. If you are seeking more detailed maps for backcountry destinations, consider the purchase of *All Topo Maps: Utah* by iGage. This product is a two CD set with all the 7½-minute (1:24000)series topographic maps covering Utah. It will allow you to print your own maps and has many other helpful features. ◆

General Season Dates and Bag & Possession Limits

(From the 1999 Fishing Proclamation, Section IV. R657-13-19)

This section sets forth general provisions. Where a more localized and specific provision is given, it will appear in Special Regulations for each destination. The more specific provision takes precedence.

A. Closed Areas

(1) All waters of state fish raising and spawning facilities are closed to fishing.

(2) State waterfowl management areas are closed to fishing except as posted or as listed in the current proclamation.

B. General Season Dates

The general season for taking fish and crayfish is January 1 through December 31, 1999, 24 hours each day.

C. General Season Bag and Possession Limits

(1) A person may not fish in waters that have a specific bag or size limit while possessing fish in violation of that limit.

(2) Fish not meeting the size, bag or species provisions on specified waters shall be returned to the water immediately.

(3) A person may not take more than one bag limit in any one day or have in possession more than one bag limit of each species or species aggregate regardless of the number of days spent fishing.

(4) A person (resident or nonresident) under 14 years of age may:

(a) fish without a license and take one-half (1/2) a bag and possession limit;

or

(b) purchase a license and take a full bag and possession limit.

ARTIST: GREG PEARSON / WESTERN RIVERS FLYFISHER

(5) The following bag and possession limits apply statewide, except as provided in Section V in the current proclamation.

❏	Bonneville cisco	30 fish
❏	*Bluegill and green sunfish in the aggregate	50 fish
❏	Bullhead	24 fish
❏	*Channel catfish	8 fish
❏	*Crappie	50 fish
❏	Crayfish	No limit
❏	*Largemouth and smallmouth bass in the aggregate	6 fish
❏	Nongame species	No limit
❏	*Northern pike	6 fish
❏	*Tiger muskellunge (hybrid)	I over 40"
❏	Sacramento perch	10 fish
❏	Striped bass	No limit
❏	*Trout, including salmon, grayling and hybrids in the aggregate, except no more than two shall be lake trout/mackinaw	8 fish
❏	*Walleye	6 fish
❏	*Whitefish	10 fish
❏	White bass	No limit
❏	Wiper (hybrid white bass x striped bass)	2 fish
❏	*Yellow perch	No limit

*On some waters, specific bag or size restrictions apply. (See Section V in the current proclamation.)

Utah 1999 Licensing Fees

License	Age	Fee
Residents		
☐ Combination license	12 and over	$28
☐ Season (Annual)	*14 - under 65	$20
☐ 65 years of age or older		$9
☐ *1-day . . . . (Wildlife Habitat Authorization not required)	14 and over	$6
☐ *7-day	14 and over	$11
☐ *Wildlife Habitat Authorization	14 and over	$6
Nonresidents		
☐ Season (Annual)	*14 and over	$42
☐ *1-day (14 years of age or older) . . . . (Wildlife Habitat Authorization not required)		$7
☐ *7-day	14 and over	$17
☐ 1-day fishing stamp . . . . (used to extend 1 or 7-day license — Wildlife Habitat Authorization not required)		$5
☐ Wildlife Habitat Authorization	14 and over	$6
*A license may be purchased by a person 13 or under wanting to take a full bag and possession limit.		
Reciprocal Fishing Stamp (Nonresidents Only)		
☐ Flaming Gorge Reservoir . . . . (for use with Wyoming resident and nonresident license)		$10
☐ Lake Powell . . . . (for use with Arizona resident license)		$8

Using GPS

by Michael Ferguson

R apidly increasing numbers of outdoor enthusiasts are purchasing Global Positioning System (GPS) receivers. These units now sell for as little as $100 and have become much more user friendly. There is still a learning curve for users, but the time spent is well invested as GPS offers huge benefits to anyone who spends time in the outdoors. GPS is just a tool, but a powerful one. It will give you the opportunity to go farther with greater comfort, and allow you to focus more of your attention on why you are outdoors in the first place.

How GPS Works

Your GPS receiver depends on a constellation of 24 satellites. Each satellite constantly transmits a stream of radio messages. Your receiver uses those messages to calculate its (your) position. It does this by determining its distance from several satellites (3 or more) in known positions. Your receiver can only calculate a position in 2-D mode with 3 satellites. It then has to depend on the last known elevation to generate a solution. In mountainous terrain this can induce error exceeding one mile. Make sure you can determine if your receiver is in 2-D mode and don't rely on it at such times. Satellite coverage has greatly improved in recent years and you can usually acquire the necessary 4 satellites for 3-D operation. Getting out in the open will help or simply wait for better coverage as satellites move overhead.

Selective Availability

Messages from GPS satellites have intentionally-induced error called Selective Availability (SA). This results in normal accuracy for consumer-grade receivers of about 20-30 meters. Error introduced by SA will cause your position to move around when you are standing still and it affects elevation as well. The constant random movement of your position makes displayed speed and direction of travel inaccurate at speeds under 12 miles per hour. SA is scheduled to be turned off sometime between the year 2000 and 2006. When that happens, your receiver will instantly become three to five times more accurate.

Land Navigation With GPS

The Global Positioning System is the most significant development in land navigation since the invention of the compass. GPS fundamentally changes the way you use a map. The coordinate system on the map was essentially irrelevant to the land navigator. Now, with GPS, coordinates are everything. Coordinates you read on the display of your receiver can be used to pin-point your position on the map, and coordinates you obtain from the map or some other source (such as this guide) can be entered into your receiver so it can guide you to that location. It's safe to say that the key to unlocking the full potential of your GPS receiver is knowing how to work with coordinate systems. Make sure your GPS receiver is set to the same datum/format as the coordinates you are entering.

If coordinates are the key to GPS, distance and direction are the treasure. Once you have coordinates stored in your receiver's memory you're ready to navigate. Distance and direction are the foundation of GPS-based navigation.

A GPS receiver is in navigation mode when it has been told to "GoTo" a stored waypoint. There are many items of information associated with navigation mode, but distance and direction are easily the most important of these. Quite simply, they give you the exact distance and direction as the crow flies to the destination you selected. If there is a river between you and your destination you may not be able to literally follow the directions provided by your receiver. However, if you know the location of a bridge you can use it as an intermediate "GoTo" destination, then switch the "GoTo" to your final destination upon reaching the bridge. Obviously, this requires that you have two waypoints stored in your receiver: one for the final destination, and one for the bridge.

A more advanced way to deal with this scenario is to link the two waypoints into a route. A route is just several waypoints that have been linked into legs. Routes can be used to order waypoints so that a complicated path of travel is easier to follow. Also, most receivers automatically switch their "GoTo" to the next waypoint as you pass the current waypoint. A convenient touch.

Using A Compass With GPS

There are two distinct reasons compasses are important to GPS users. One reason is that although GPS receivers are very good at telling you the exact direction to your destination, they are very lousy at telling you what that direction is on the ground. Your GPS receiver will tell you it's 1.23 miles and a bearing of 312 degrees to the bridge, but it's your compass that will show you the real-world direction that is 312 degrees. When using a compass to follow the directions provided by your GPS receiver you need to make sure your GPS receiver and your compass are set for the same "type" of north.

A compass needle naturally aligns with the direction known as magnetic north, which is different than true (geographic) north. The difference between true north and magnetic north is known as magnetic declination. Some compasses can be adjusted for magnetic declination to display true north based directions. Almost all GPS receivers have the option of providing direction readouts as either true directions or magnetic directions. The important thing is that you make sure both your receiver and your compass are set to give the same type of reading.

Very often when you perform a "GoTo" with your receiver you will not be able to actually see the destination you are "going to." A handy trick in this situation is to use your compass to find some visible distant landmark that is on the path to your destination. Now you can put both your compass and GPS receiver away until you reach that intermediate destination. Once you're there, haul out your receiver and compass and repeat this process.

The second reason compasses are an important accessory for a GPS user is more traditional. You guessed it, a compass also serves as a backup in case you lose the use of your GPS receiver. Whether it's due to a malfunction, drained batteries, your horse stepped on it, or whatever, when your GPS receiver stops working you need to know how to use just a map and compass to find your way. There's a saying among old mariners: "Never rely on a single navigation method." That's how they became old mariners. Hopefully, when the time comes to rely on those traditional navigation skills they will serve you well. It will take more effort (after all, saving effort is what GPS is all about), but those traditional skills can and should bail you out. In fact, quite a few GPS users have commented that using GPS has allowed them to improve their map and compass skills. That's because GPS provides instant feedback and verification, thereby allowing rapid gains in their confidence levels. ◆

Michael Ferguson is the author of GPS Land Navigation *and* GPS Waypoints.

This is Utah

U tah's first human inhabitants are believed to have been hunter/gatherers known as Paleo Indians, arriving around 11,000 B.C. As the climate changed over centuries, the landscape evolved into a high desert of basin and range. As agriculture developed, nomadic groups were able to establish the more permanent settlements associated with the Fremont and Anasazi cultures.

These early cultures were eventually replaced by the Goshute, Paiute, Ute, Shoshone and Navajo tribes who were present in Utah when Spanish explorers first visited the area. Utah owes its name to the Ute Tribe.

The first expedition of Europeans to reach Utah was lead by Father Francisco Atanasio Dominguez and Father Silvestre Velez de Escalante. They came looking for gold and a safe route from Santa Fe to the California Missions. They found neither, but their explorations encouraged others to venture into the mountain ranges and vast canyon desert country.

The mighty Green. (PHOTO: BRAD NICHOLSON)

Mountain Men were the next group to make their way to Utah. General William H. Ashley lead a party of trappers, including Jim Bridger, to the Cache Valley in 1811. General Ashley initiated the practice of an annual rendezvous where trappers could socialize and trade their furs.

Brigham Young arrived in Utah in 1847 with the first group of Mormon settlers. Upon first viewing the Salt Lake Valley he declared "This is the right place." They called their territory the State of Deseret and settled a series of industrious communities that are still symbolic of the beehive that became the state seal. Utah became the 45th state in 1896.

The Green and Colorado, Utah's largest rivers, remained unexplored until a Civil War veteran by the name of Major John Wesley Powell proposed a bold journey into this unknown territory. Major Powell began his expedition on the Green River in 1869 with nine men and four boats "staunch and firm." He emerged from the Grand Canyon of the Colorado three months later with three boats and six of his companions.

Utah Now

The organization and community spirit of the original settlers is still apparent in Utah today. Most towns are laid out in a grid with streets running north-south or east-west. Streets are numbered sequentially from the center of town, making navigation simple. People are generally friendly and helpful to visitors.

Willard Bay. (PHOTO: BRYAN BRANDENBURG)

Utah has the youngest population as well as the most educated workforce in the nation. It is one of the fastest growing states in the U.S. Seventy percent of Utahns are Mormon (members of the Church of Jesus Christ of Latter-day Saints).

Utah is a land of great geographic diversity. Most of the state's population lives in the cities along the Wasatch Front. The desert of the Great Basin lies to the west and includes the Bonneville Salt Flats, where many land speed records have been set. Northeastern Utah has the highest mountains with a myriad lakes and forests. The striking red-rock canyons of the Colorado Plateau make up the southeastern portion of the state. Visitors will recognize Monument Valley as the setting for many classic Western movies.

Most of Utah is above 4,000 feet elevation with the highest point in excess of 13,000 feet. Changes in elevation greatly affect climate, and it is possible for visitors to ski in the morning then drive to a lower elevation and golf (or fish) in the afternoon. Most of Utah experiences four seasons, but the southwest near St. George has very mild winters. Visitors should be prepared for a variety of conditions. Refer to the section on *Dressing for Utah Weather* on page 34.

Recreational opportunities abound in the state. In addition to great fishing, Utah is a very popular ski destination, and will host the 2002 Olympic Winter Games. There are more than a dozen downhill ski areas and numerous cross-country areas. Mountain biking is also extremely popular. Cyclists can find everything from heart-pounding mountain trails and super steep slick-rock to easy and scenic rides that will appeal to the whole family. Opportunities to hike or backpack are everywhere. Choose the solitude found in the desert or climb up to a mountain peak. Whitewater enthusiasts float the Green River, Westwater and Cataract Canyons of the Colorado River, and many smaller but equally challenging rivers.

If sightseeing or auto-touring appeals to you, than visit the landscapes preserved in Utah's five national parks, seven national monuments, and two national recreation areas. These include Arches, Canyonlands, Bryce Canyon, Capitol Reef and Zion National Parks. You will also find Cedar Breaks, Dinosaur, Grand Staircase, Hovenweap, Natural Bridges, Rainbow Bridge, and Timpanogos Cave National Monuments. Flaming Gorge and Glen Canyon National Recreation Areas both offer wide-open water for boating and some excellent fishing.

Residents of Utah show a great deal of support for the arts. When looking for entertainment, consider the Utah Symphony, Ballet West, the Utah Opera Company, and Repertory Dance Theatre. There are also many community theatres around the state. Don't forget the Utah Shakespearean Festival held in Cedar City each summer, the Sundance Film Festival in January, or one of the many rodeos or community celebrations that celebrate the diversity and culture of Utah's past and present.

Whether fishing is your main reason for being in Utah, or one of many options you are considering, enjoy the adventure and entertainment of this "pretty, great state." ♦

ARTIST: GREG PEARSON / WESTERN RIVERS FLYFISHER

Sharing Water

by Steve Jackson

ll water in Utah forces us to share. None of the water in this guide was designed to withstand the trampling it now receives from anglers — not to mention boats, vehicles, highways, hikers and other recreationists.

Finding a piece of water with no one in casting distance or lurking around the next bend is becoming more rare along the walkable stretches of the Green, the highway water on the Provo, and most of the Ogden and Logan — even on weekdays.

Those with stamina will find solitude on the lonelier drainage lakes and streams coming off the south slopes of the Uintas, the tributaries of the Sevier, or perhaps the Boulder waters up on the Aquarius Plateau.

Because most of the popular water is crowded enough with family and friends, we must devise new methods (beyond what equipment will do) to mitigate the impact of more people on the water: approach the water with stealth, practice patience — wait, be tolerant, of yourself and others. Ask rather than assume.

The less-crowded water away from paved roads can be covered by splitting up and fishing separate sections; a popular approach which allows for temporary solitude with the chance to compare stories later. Some rivers can be fished by stalking fish in side eddy pools, taking turns casting and leapfrogging along the bank. Some water allows anglers to fish on both banks or along the same shore.

Sometimes it's the size of the water, not the presence of people, that encourages us to share. On the smaller upper mountain meadow and canyon waters, try taking turns on the next good hole that comes into view. Three casts and you're out.

And while it is hard to watch the cast of someone we do not know, it is a pleasure to watch one of someone we like. Someone who shares our passion for catching and keeping or letting go.

There are many anglers in Utah. Some natives, some transplanted, like many of the fish. Some anglers will be just as dismayed to see you upriver as you are to see them. There is room for a few more of us on the water — as long as everyone stays at least casting distance away, asks about a piece of water "in between," and we treat each other as gracefully as the fish we pursue. ♦

Etiquette

by Rick Peterson

There are rules of conduct or etiquette that every angler should be aware of and observe. A critical aspect of this conduct is the responsibility to show respect for the land, both public and privately owned. Every year we lose precious access to more water because of the irresponsibility of a few anglers. The remaining open waters must absorb the pressure which brings with it many negative results. We need to be aware of the critical importance of asking for permission to enter posted land, and then when given such permission, be good caretakers of the land we've been allowed to access.

We must also be aware of the need to respect fellow anglers. Give others their space and maintain an appropriate distance. Overcrowding and encroachment on someone's fishing hole many times results in poor fishing success as well as frayed nerves.

Excess noise such as yelling back and forth amongst your party can be irritating to those that have come out for some peace and quiet. This is especially annoying when a person seeks to loudly verbalize their success to everyone else on the water. It's great to be excited about your success, but inappropriate to boast of it to all around you.

Share your expertise and knowledge with those you meet that would like a little help or advice. Be careful not to force yourself onto others in an effort to help, where it may not be needed or wanted.

Appreciation of our natural environment should be a constant as we venture out on each fishing experience. All of us need to be cognizant of the fact that these resources are finite and in many cases very fragile. Again it's a matter of responsibility for our own actions, and the realization that we impact the environment we interact with while fishing.

There should be no mistake in assuming that as long as a particular action is legal then it is ethical as well. Some anglers engage in activities that may not be contrary to state or federal laws, but are a serious breach of the type of ethical behavior or code that anglers should value. In the vast majority of these instances our natural resources bare the brunt and suffer the most from these actions.

If you practice good etiquette, fishing will come to mean more to you for all the right reasons. There are still mysteries to be solved, challenging casts to be made, and elusive fish that deepen the respect we hold for the quarry and the sport. ◆

Travel in Utah

Many of Utah's early settlers pushed handcarts loaded with all their possessions across the plains and through the mountain canyons to get here. Today, traveling to and around the state is much easier. Modern roads and services are available throughout Utah, but there are remote areas where services are non-existent and travelers may have to rely on their own preparedness and resources.

For anglers desiring to reach fishing destinations around the state, driving yourself is the only practical way to get around. A vehicle with high clearance and/or 4-wheel-drive is necessary to drive to some of the destinations listed in this guide, but most can be reached by passenger vehicles.

An early traveler to the Green leaves his mark. (PHOTO: BRAD NICHOLSON)

Steep mountain roads can place extra demands on cooling and braking systems. Snow tires are required on roads to many ski areas from November to March. Make sure that your vehicle is equipped with adequate food, water, blankets or clothing, and a first-aid kit.

Much of Utah is rural and services can be widely spaced. Plan ahead for fuel, water and other necessities, especially when traveling in remote areas.

Major Interstate and U.S. Roadways

If you are driving to Utah there are four major interstate freeways to speed your journey. I-80 passes through Utah going east and west from Wyoming to Nevada. I-70 provides access from Colorado to the east. Utah can be reached from Idaho to the north on I-84 and I-15. Visitors arriving from Las Vegas or Arizona can enter southwest Utah on I-15.

U.S. roadways are not always the fastest way to get to and through Utah, but they offer scenic vistas that make the time and miles worth the drive. US 89 enters Utah from Arizona and winds up through the heart of Utah, eventually leaving Utah in Wyoming. US 40 will take you west of Colorado, across the Green River,

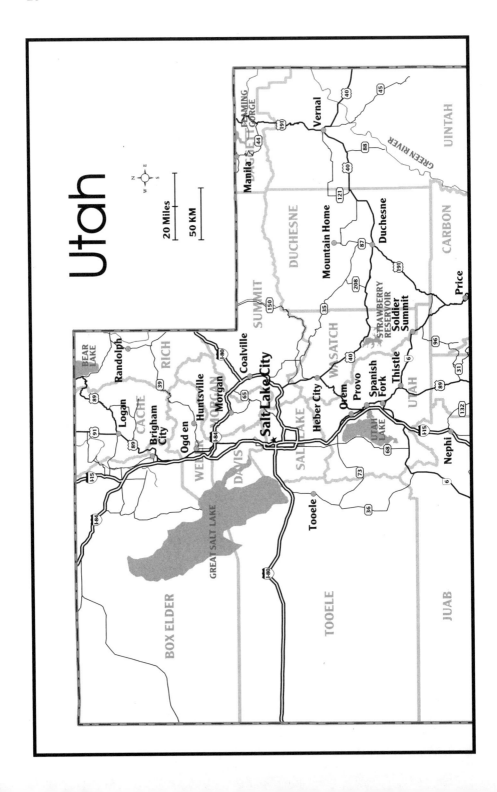

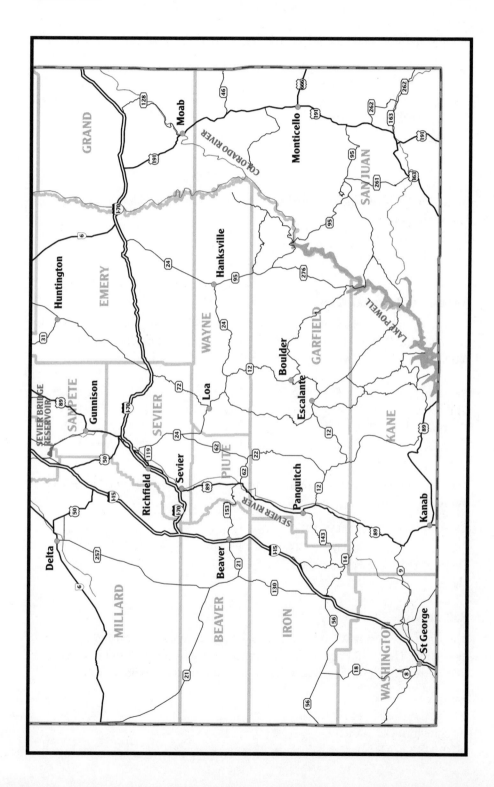

and into the Uintah Basin, eventually connecting with I-80 near Park City.

There is major roadway construction underway in Utah, and it is likely to continue up until the Olympics in 2002. The largest project affects I-15 in Salt Lake County. If you are planning to use this route you may use the contacts listed below for further information:

I-15, Salt Lake Area	(888) INFO I-15 www.i15.state.ut.us

For information on other roadway construction, contact the Utah Department of Transportation.

Utah D.O.T.	(800) 492-2400 www.dot.state.ut.us

Airlines and Rental Cars

Almost all visitors arriving in Utah by air will do so through Salt Lake International Airport. There are daily flights from many different cities in the US and Canada. Airlines with service into Salt Lake are listed below:

America West	(800) 235-9292	Northwest	(800) 225-2525
American	(800) 433-7300	Skywest	(800) 453-9417
Continental	(800) 525-0280	TWA	(800) 221-2000
Delta	(800) 221-1212	United	(800) 241-6522

You will find most major car rental companies conveniently located at Salt Lake International Airport.

Avis	(800) 331-1212	National	(800) 227-7368
Budget	(800) 527-0700	Payless	(800) 729-5377
Dollar	(800) 800-4000	Thrifty	(800) 367-2277
Hertz	(800) 654-3131		

Rail Service

The Amtrak's Desert Wind runs from Los Angeles to Chicago with a stop in Salt Lake City. The California Wind has service from Chicago to San Francisco with several stops in Utah. For schedules or more information, write or call:

Amtrak
400 N. Capitol Street NW
Washington, DC 20001
(800) USA-RAIL

Backcountry Travel

by Matt Jackson

here are some great fishing destinations in Utah's backcountry. Some of these remote areas are very beautiful and not often visited by others. Anglers can find peace and solitude, along with uneducated fish.

We have all learned the skills we need to get around in the towns or cities that we live in. Here are some of the things you should know to travel safely in the backcountry and minimize your impact while there.

Common Sense

Common sense is the most important thing to take with you into the backcountry. Panic only complicates an emergency situation. Pause and make a mental list of what is most important, then plan your actions accordingly. If you spend much time in remote areas, first-aid training can be invaluable. Take the time to tell someone where you are going and when you plan to return, or leave a note at your vehicle.

Personal Gear

Carry a first-aid kit — including moleskin and adhesive tape, any required medication, sunglasses, insect repellent, toilet paper in a ziploc bag, a pocket knife, a bandana, a lighter or waterproof matches, and a flashlight (with spare batteries). You can make a small emergency kit weighing a pound or two. Get in the habit of taking it with you whenever you leave the road behind.

Water

When traveling in the backcountry, you must choose whether to carry your water with you, or to filter your water as needed. Assume that all water must be treated, either chemically or with a filter, before it is safe to drink.

Dehydration

Thirst will not protect us from dehydration. It is possible to lose fluid so quickly that the normal thirst mechanism is overwhelmed or overridden. Once thirst is felt we are usually dehydrated already. Drink before you are thirsty. The rate of water loss from the body will vary according to activity levels, air temperature, humidity and altitude. Limit caffeine, which is a diuretic and will contribute to dehydration.

Combating Heat

- ☐ Stay well-hydrated and eat salty snacks.
- ☐ Maintain a reasonable pace.
- ☐ Rest often, out of the sun.
- ☐ Wear clothing that allows evaporation.
- ☐ Wear a brimmed hat or cap.
- ☐ Take a nap during the hottest part of the day.

Heat Exhaustion

This is a condition caused by water and electrolyte loss. Heat exhaustion is not a life-threatening illness. Little or no rise in body core temperature will be noted. Symptoms include fatigue, exhaustion, nausea, lightheadedness, and possibly heat cramps. Heat exhaustion usually comes on several hours after exertion and dehydration. The individual may have replaced the lost fluids, but not the electrolytes. Give heat exhaustion patients lots of water with a teaspoon of salt per liter. With enough rest and water, heat exhaustion is self-correcting.

Heatstroke

Heatstroke occurs when a person's body core temperature rises to dangerous levels. The skin will be red and hot. Without proper care, heatstroke victims will most likely die. Death can occur in as little as 30 minutes. As the brain overheats, the individual may become disoriented, combative, argumentative, and may hallucinate. Heatstroke treatment should begin immediately in the backcountry, and the person taken to the emergency room as soon as possible. Cool heatstroke patients as rapidly as possible. Douse with water, fan, and massage extremities. Rehydrate them as their condition allows. Evacuate as soon as possible.

Animals

There are black bears and mountain lions in Utah, yet they are rarely seen. It is very unlikely that you will have a negative encounter with these animals, but here are a few suggestions to reduce the odds:

- ☐ Be alert, especially early morning or at dusk.
- ☐ Carry a deterrent device within easy reach.
- ☐ Go in a group and stay together.
- ☐ Stay on trails where possible.
- ☐ Hike in the middle of the day.
- ☐ Make noise while hiking.
- ☐ Keep a clean camp.
- ☐ Cook and hang food 200 feet away from sleeping areas.

Snakes

Rattlesnakes will try to avoid you if possible. In most instances they will only strike when threatened. If you are in rattlesnake territory:

- ❐ Wear solid boots or waders if practical. No sandals.
- ❐ Step on, not over obstacles (logs or large rocks) in your path.
- ❐ Stop if you hear a snake rattle. Locate the snake before backing away.

If someone is bitten, use the following first-aid:

- ❐ Wash the wound.
- ❐ Immobilize the affected part.
- ❐ Seek medical help as quickly as possible.
- ❐ Apply a constricting band if medical treatment is more than 30 minutes away.

Insects

As Utah has a dry climate, insects are less of a problem than in many other states. However, in some places, particularly after a wet and warm spring, they can make you very uncomfortable. Wet areas protected from the wind and cattle grazing areas are often the worst areas.

BEES, HORNETS, AND WASPS. Trees and logs are favorite nesting areas, but you can also find them entrenched in trail shelters and even underground. Wearing flowery scents while hiking should generally be avoided. If you are bitten, wash the bite with soap and water. Apply something cool to the bite. An oral antihistamine like Benadryl will also help. If you're allergic, make sure you carry a sting kit whenever you hike.

BLACKFLIES, DEERFLIES, AND GNATS. These insects love running water, so camp well away from where they muster. You'll want a tent with a fine mesh netting on its windows and doors. DEET in a 30% solution works best at repelling these insects. Protect your head with a bandanna or hat and keep collars, cuffs, and sleeves tightly closed. Treat by washing the bite with soap and water. Antihistamines will help reduce the swelling and itching.

MOSQUITOES. These airborne attackers love stagnant water. Camp in an open and even breezy area. Long-sleeved shirts and long pants give extra protection. DEET in a 30% solution does wonders toward fending off their attacks. Bites will disappear quickly if not scratched.

TICKS. These "hitchhikers" can be picked up from branches and boughs of trees, but are most common in grassy areas — especially in cattle country. Stick to the middle of trails and avoid long grass when possible. Wear long pants tucked into your socks. Apply a permethrin-based repellent to clothing in tick territory. It takes about four hours for a tick to firmly implant itself, so check yourself periodically. Once a tick is fully attached, it is best to convince them to back out so the head is not left in the wound. Coat them with nail polish or Vaseline so they can't breathe. Lyme disease and Rocky Mountain spotted fever are both serious diseases that are carried by ticks. Note the date if you are bitten and save the tick to aid diagnosis if you develop flu-like symptoms.

Waste

Garbage is the number one problem cited by backcountry visitors. The no-trace response to litter follows the time-tested notion that if you "pack it in, pack it out." To this we add: "Pick up what others have left behind."

Proper Disposal of Human Waste

1. Carry a small trowel or shovel, toilet paper and hand cleaner.

2. Find an out-of-the-way site in stable soils at least 200 feet from surface water.

3. Make sure the site is at least 200 feet from established campsites, trails, and other centers of human activity.

4. Look for a site with an active layer of organic topsoil. The ground should be moist and fairly easy to dig in.

5. Dig a hole six to eight inches deep. Keep the sod lid intact if possible.

6. Burn toilet paper, or better yet, pack it out. Cover waste completely.

7. Clean hands. Pre-packaged hand wipes are compact and can easily be packed out.

As more people go into the backcountry, we should consider packing out human waste. Boaters can easily carry portable latrines (these are required now on many stretches of river, including overnight trips on the Green River below Little Hole). Lightweight, collapsible containers are also available for hikers and backpackers. Be sure to dispose of the waste properly when you exit the backcountry.

Deserts

Winter is the best season for desert hikes, and spring and fall can be temperate as well. You'll find more water, fewer tourists and more human-friendly temperatures. It's unwise to backpack through much of Utah's desert canyon country in summer. Severe and sudden thunderstorms accompanied by flash flooding are most common from June through August.

Wear sunglasses that offer protection from both UVA and UVB rays and shield against light coming in from the sides.

Use sunscreen (including lip protection with sunscreen) with an SPF of at least 15 to protect areas not covered by clothes.

Bring warm clothes, such as a pile jacket and pants, for chilly desert nights. Although daytime highs can reach triple digits, desert nights can typically dip to half of the daytime high.

Keep extra water in your car. A 5-gallon jug of water stashed in the car will help if you get back to the trailhead low on fluids or if you have car trouble getting to and from the trailhead.

Summary

Utah's backcountry is a great place to escape the pressures of town and city life while catching a few fish. With a sensible attitude and some preparation, your experience can safely preserve you and your soul, and the backcountry that both need to survive. ◆

"Dressed-to-kill" on the Green. (PHOTO: EMMETT HEATH / WESTERN RIVERS FLYFISHER)

Dressing for Utah Weather

by Matt Jackson

S taying comfortable, safe and warm while traveling in Utah's varied climate will help you focus more on fishing. Take into account these clothing basics:

❏ Layering is the key to getting maximum comfort with minimum weight. Versatile layers of clothing can be mixed and matched to create the right amount of insulation, ventilation, and weather protection. Layers can be divided into the base layer, which is next to your skin; insulation layer, which goes over the base layer; and the shell, which covers the insulation layer in windy or wet conditions.

❏ Layering in the proper order will trap warm air while allowing moisture to be conducted away from your skin. The choice of garments must be versatile enough to adapt to your activity level and variations in the weather. Add or remove layers as comfort and temperature dictate. Use your hat, gloves, and zippers for slight adjustments that can make a big difference.

❏ Protection from the sun is important, especially at higher elevations. Water will reflect UV rays, increasing your exposure while fishing. Brimmed hats, long sleeves and long pants will protect your skin in addition to sunscreens.

❏ Remember that temperatures in Utah's backcountry can change drastically in a short amount of time. Early morning temperatures may start in the mid-thirties and reach the mid-seventies by the afternoon. It is not that unusual to have snow in May or October. At high elevations, you may experience extreme weather any month of the year.

Below are two suggested clothing lists, which can be combined or adapted to fit the best and worst scenarios of any forecast.

❏ Lightweight synthetic or
   silk long underwear
❏ Thick wool or polypropylene
   socks (no cotton!)
❏ Thin synthetic wicking socks
❏ Fleece or pile pants
❏ Fleece or pile shirt
❏ Synthetic pile jacket

❏ Storm shell with full hood
❏ Shell pants
❏ Neoprene waders
❏ Wool, synthetic,
   or neoprene gloves
❏ Synthetic liners
❏ Fleece or wool hat
❏ Thin balaclava

Warm Weather Clothing

- Long-sleeved, light-colored, loose-fitting cotton shirt
- Light-colored, loose-fitting cotton pants or shorts
- Silk, synthetic, or cotton underwear
- Fleece jacket or vest
- Lightweight synthetic or silk long underwear
- Lightweight rain shell
- Lightweight rain pants, hip boots, or Gore-Tex Waders
- Light-colored, well-ventilated cotton or nylon hat with brim
- Bandannas (cotton or silk)
- Extra socks
- Footwear

Cold Weather Clothing

Choose fishing footwear just like you would hiking boots. Try the boots on with the socks you will actually use. Try a thin pair under a medium pair, or a medium pair under a heavy pair (comfort is the rule). The two sock system will provide for maximum wicking of moisture, allow for ventilation, and prevent blisters. Long lasting, high quality socks are worth the investment.

Waders

Stocking-foot waders, combined with a sturdy but flexible fishing boot, will help you be more comfortable if walking longer distances or wading rocky rivers. Neoprene waders have some stretch for freedom of movement and insulate you from cold water. They are also somewhat safer as they are more form fitting and provide some buoyancy if you should go for a swim.

A boot-footed wader is generally a bit warmer in cold weather. Some models have felt liners or other insulation in the boot. These are really a bonus during freezing or icy conditions — no laces to fumble with.

The relatively new breathable waders (made of Gore-Tex® and similar fabrics) are very comfortable in warmer weather or during long walks to the water.

Accessories

Sunscreen and lip balm (with SPF ratings for your skin type), polarized glasses, clippers, knife, hemostats or forceps, pliers, insect repellent, camera and film, matches, wader repair kit, first-aid kit. ◆

36

Conservation

T he verb conserve implies action, "to keep from harm or loss, for future use." Utah has many thriving fisheries that provide recreation and relaxation to many. If we, as anglers, are to keep them from harm, prevent their loss, and preserve them for the future, we must all take action.

The following section describes conservation issues that can have a large effect on Utah's fisheries:

❑ **Whirling disease** is the most imminent threat. If we are to keep it from spreading throughout the state, all anglers will need to act. Share the information.

❑ **Catch-and-release fishing** is becoming more important as we look to the future. If you are going to release a fish, do it with care.

❑ **Unwanted exotic species** can have a negative effect on our fisheries. If you travel outside the state, be sure to clean boats and equipment thoroughly before launching in Utah waters.

Whirling Disease

T he microscopic fish parasite responsible for whirling disease was accidentally introduced to the United States from Europe in 1958. Its initial impact was primarily felt at fish hatcheries, but it can now be found in 22 states and is considered a major threat to wild trout fisheries throughout the Rocky Mountains.

The recent population collapse of rainbow trout in Montana's Madison River above Ennis Lake (from 3,300 rainbows per mile to 300 per mile) demonstrates the devastating effect whirling disease can have. Research in Colorado showed whirling disease was present in 13 of 15 river systems. Rainbow populations in highly-infected areas crashed.

Young cutthroat trout have also proven to be susceptible to whirling disease. Recent research indicates that all species of cutthroat trout may be threatened or endangered in the next century unless human impact (including the spread of whirling disease) on their habitats is reduced.

Whirling disease was likely introduced to Utah in the late 1980s. It was first discovered in a series of private hatcheries and adjacent waters in the Fremont River drainage in 1991.

Humans are not affected by whirling disease.

What is Whirling Disease?

Whirling disease is a condition that affects trout and salmon. It is caused by a microscopic parasite known as Myxobolus cerebralis. The parasite attacks the cartilage tissue of a fish's head and spine. Young fish may develop symptoms such as whirling behavior, a black tail, or even death. If they survive, fish may develop head deformities or twisted spines.

Fish biologists believe there are other harmful effects, such as making fish more susceptible to predation and environmental disturbances, as well as impairing their ability to feed and reproduce.

The parasite exhibits a complex life cycle. One stage is hosted by small aquatic worms which are common to most waters. Host worms release the more fragile parasitic stage that must infect a trout within a few days or die. Infected trout develop very persistent spores which can survive in moist places for years. When an infected fish dies, these spores are released into the environment. The spores can be transferred to other waters on muddy boots or other fishing equipment.

Rainbow trout are the most susceptible of Utah's game fish, followed by kokanee salmon, golden, cutthroat, brook, brown trout and splake. Whitefish and grayling can be infected as well. Lake trout may be immune; other game fish species such as bass, bluegill, perch or walleye do not get whirling disease.

There is currently no known treatment or cure for fish infected with the parasite. Whirling disease can be controlled in hatchery environments. Its effects on wild fish cannot be controlled.

What is Being Done?

The DWR initially attempted to eradicate the parasite by removing fish from the affected waters. This was unsuccessful, and whirling disease spread to other drainages.

Current DWR efforts are directed towards containment and control of whirling disease:

☐ Barriers are installed to prevent the spread of infected fish.

☐ Stocking policies have changed from the less-resistant rainbow trout to the more-resistant brown trout in contaminated streams.

☐ State hatcheries are tested every 6-12 months to ensure they remain free of the parasite.

☐ State hatcheries near affected streams are closed to visitors, except by appointment.

❏ The DWR's Fisheries Experiment Station continues to conduct ongoing research.

The DWR and Trout Unlimited have launched a campaign to educate the public about whirling disease.

Signs will be installed beginning spring 1999, indicating if particular waters test positive or negative for whirling disease.

What Can You Do?

Thoroughly clean mud from all equipment before going to other waters. This includes moving above barriers such as dams on the same water. Waders, boots, anchors, boats and boat trailers should all be carefully cleaned. Thoroughly dry equipment in the sun, if possible, before reuse. If you are traveling directly to other waters, clean your equipment with a 10% solution of chlorine bleach or use another set of equipment.

Do not clean fish in any body of water other than the one in which the fish were caught. Adult fish can carry whirling disease without showing any deformities. In particular, the heads of infected fish contain the resistant spores. Do not dispose of fish parts in other waters.

It is illegal to transport live fish. Upstream spread of whirling disease can be blocked by dams and diversions. Moving fish above these barriers can allow this disease to spread.

Call the DWR if you observe the symptoms of whirling disease in fish, or observe illegal stocking. Contact your local conservation officer directly or call the poaching hotline at 1-800-662-3337.

Help to educate other anglers that you know or meet afield. We all have to work together if whirling disease is to be controlled.

Where is Whirling Disease Found in Utah?

The parasite responsible for whirling disease is currently found in 8 Utah drainages. Clean equipment thoroughly if fishing in these waters:

Utah state hatcheries are tested twice a year. Whirling disease has never been found in any of these facilities. ♦

Affected Drainages	And Affected Reservoirs
Fremont River	Mill Meadow Reservoir
Little Bear River	Porcupine Reservoir and Hyrum Reservoir
Weber River and Beaver Creek	Rockport Reservoir
South Fork of the Ogden	Causey Reservoir
Otter Creek	Otter Creek Reservoir
Beaver River	Minersville Reservoir
Geyser Ditch	
Blacksmith Fork	

Catch-and-Release Fishing

As more pressure is placed on our fisheries, by increased angler use and environmental changes, catch and release is becoming an increasingly important fisheries management tool. It allows more anglers to enjoy a higher quality angling experience from the same resources.

Why do anglers release fish? Fishing regulations require release of certain sizes of fish on different waters. You may choose to release fish to extend your day's sport, or just for the thrill of watching a live creature leave your hand and swim away to freedom.

It only makes sense to release fish that will survive. Unless prohibited by regulation, you should keep and utilize fish that are likely to die.

Fish caught on bait are much less likely to survive release. Over 60% of deeply hooked fish die after release. If you must release a deeply hooked fish, cut the line instead of removing the hook.

In most cases, 9 out of 10 fish caught on artificial lures and flies will survive after release.

When fishing water deeper than 30 feet, most fish (lake trout are an exception) will not survive release. Puncturing the swim bladder does not aid recovery. If you are fishing in deep water, you should keep legal-sized fish and quit when you have reached your limit.

Warm water and low oxygen content add to the stress fish experience when caught. Trout are particularly susceptible in lower elevation waters during July and August. Consider keeping fish or limiting the numbers you release under these conditions.

Spawning trout are vulnerable to infection. Anglers who pursue these fish increase stress levels and disrupt an activity that sustains our fisheries. Limit your impact on spawning fish, even if it means giving the fish a rest.

To increase the survival of fish you release:

❏ Fish with flies or lures. Bend down the barbs on your hooks. Replace treble hooks with single hooks.

❏ Land the fish as quickly as possible. Wet your hands before handling fish.

❏ Keep the fish in the water and use a pair of forceps or needle-nosed pliers to remove the hook.

❏ Handle the fish as little as possible.

Tiger muskies require special care for handling and release. When targeting these big, strong fish, be sure to carry a large landing net, long-nosed pliers, heavy-duty wire cutters, and jaw spreaders:

❏ Do not bring fish into the boat.

❏ Grip fish over top of the gill plates without squeezing too hard. Do not grab the fish's gills.

❏ Keep the fish in the water.

❏ Use jaw spreaders to hold open the mouths of deeply hooked fish.

❏ Cut hooks with wire cutters if removal is likely to injure the fish. ◆

Aquatic Nuisance Species

W hen a new species is introduced into an ecosystem where it has no pred- ators, it can sometimes increase unchecked and upset nature's balance. There are a variety of species that could have a negative affect if they gain access to Utah's fisheries.

In the late 80s, Zebra Mussels were unknowingly introduced into the Great Lakes. This mussel is native to Asia and has slowly spread through 21 states and provinces of North America. Though only 1 to 1.5 inches long it develops into massive colonies that clog water pipes and attach to any solid object. These colonies can filter tremendous volumes of water while collecting microscopic organisms for food. In Lake Erie, the visibility has been increased from three feet to 30 feet. Food and nutrients needed to support the food chain of native species are consumed by Zebra Mussels. The Zebra Mussel is now spreading throughout the Missouri and Mississippi river drainages and across most of the Eastern Seaboard.

In Utah, water is our state's limiting resource, and we have created massive water development projects. These water-use facilities are susceptible to blockage by the mussels and an invasion would be devastating and virtually unstoppable. Recreational boating is the most likely mode of transfer. Our most vulnerable waters happen to be our most popular ones, such as Lake Powell and Flaming Gorge.

Utah already has one potentially devastating plant species, the Eurasian Watermilfoil. It has become established in Fish Lake and Otter Creek Reservoir, where it is choking shorelines and marinas with its extremely dense growth.

When boaters transport their boats from infested waters into unaffected waters, a new invasion is likely to occur if they have not taken precautions to rid their boat of all living aquatic plants or animals. So the solution to protect Utah's waters is quite simple:

❏ Keep your boats clean.

❏ Do not transport water or any aquatic plants/animals/fish

   from one water body to another.

❏ When leaving a lake, stream or reservoir, it is imperative

   that you clean all vegetation from your watercraft and trailer.

❏ Also, remember to drain your live well and bilge water.

Two or three days of drying will kill any living organisms attached to your boat, trailer or motor. If you are going directly to another body of water, the DWR strongly advises you to carefully inspect your equipment and thoroughly wash it down with hot water to eliminate the potential of transferring harmful organisms.

Programs are currently being developed to monitor incoming boats from the eastern states and to intercept any potential carriers of Zebra Mussels. Western states are implementing a major boat inspection program along a line west of areas that are known to be infested.

The Utah DWR is currently working to develop an extensive public education program and prevention/management program, with focus on establishing a comprehensive monitoring program to detect the early introduction of Zebra Mussels. All we can do is collectively attempt to stop the introduction and spreading of Zebra Mussels and other harmful species into and throughout the state.

An additional concern is the illegal transportation of live fish and their introduction into Utah waters. Per the 1999 proclamation, "a person may not transport live fish or crayfish away from the water where taken." Fishing with any live fish as bait is also prohibited. These regulations are designed to stop the spread of undesirable rough fish (often used as bait) and to keep new species from changing the balance of our carefully managed fisheries.

Once an undesirable species is established in a particular water, it is difficult to impossible to completely remove it from the system. The best and most effective measures are prevention. To effectively deal with this threat, everyone must participate. It only takes one careless, indifferent person to undo all of our efforts. ♦

ARTIST: GREG PEARSON / WESTERN RIVERS FLYFISHER

Fishing Techniques

he following chapter is intended to help anglers new to Utah find success in their trips afield. If you are already an experienced Utah angler, you may still find some tips useful.

Rick Peterson is a guide and has been teaching fly-fishing and fly-tying in Utah for 15 years. In his contribution on fly-fishing basics, he shares with us his love and knowledge of the sport.

A passionate bass fisher and editor for *Utah Outdoors* Magazine, Dave Webb imparts his knowledge of bass, their habits, and how they can best be caught in Utah waters.

Fly-Fishing Basics

by Rick Peterson

Fly-fishing is an exciting way to catch fish. It's a very active method that totally involves and focuses the participant. Such concentration gives your mind an opportunity to relax. Fly-fishing's appeal to many, is the challenge it offers and the never-ending source of learning opportunities it provides.

Developing a patient attitude is essential. Your success and enjoyment of fly-fishing will reflect the degree of patience that you bring to the water.

Proper presentation of the artificial fly is a critical factor for success. Good casting skills are key to enjoying fly-fishing.

Some basic points to remember when casting are to relax, with your arm comfortably at your side. Hold the rod handle as you would a tennis racquet, with your thumb on top. In contrast to spin-casting where the weight of the lure carries out the line, in fly-fishing the weight of the fly line delivers the fly to the waiting fish. It's critical that the wrist be kept stiff and rigid, bending the elbow in order to properly transfer power from the shoulder/arm region to the rod and line. Stopping the rod at the proper point on the forward and backcasts (basically 11:00 to 1:00 o'clock) will help maintain a smooth properly shaped loop, and help keep your line and fly in the air until you're ready to present it to the fish.

Get casting help from a more experienced friend, or better yet, take a lesson from a professional.

PHOTO: EMMETT HEATH / WESTERN RIVERS FLYFISHER

A good basic knowledge of insects (entomology) is helpful in determining which fly to select for a particular situation. Use nymphs or wet flies fished below the surface to imitate stages of the insects found underwater. Dry flies float on the surface to imitate the adult stages of insects. Take the time to observe both insects and fish and think about how they interact.

A fish's life is a critical balance between the amount of food it takes in and the amount of energy it expends to catch that food. This natural law governs where and how the fish will feed. Your understanding of this principle will help you learn where and when to locate fish.

Fish have three basic needs for their survival. It is important to note that these needs are intrinsically tied to the aforementioned natural law. First is food, then shelter or protection while resting from threats, and of course, comfort. Fish are no different than we are when it comes to seeking out areas where it will be comfortable; water temperature and shade are examples.

In moving water — rivers and streams — fish will move into *feeding lies*, where food is most readily available. Often these feeding lies are shallower areas of water that offer little or no cover.

At various times of the day, fish will use *shelter lies* — an area where the fish can retreat for rest or when startled by a predator, be it natural or human. These areas can be undercut banks, snags, submerged trees or logs, or deep regions of a pool — basically any place the fish can hurry to in the event of a threat.

A *prime lie* is where the fish may feed while feeling secure in the fact that it has shelter or cover nearby. Many times a prime lie will be where the moving currents can conduct food to the fish along the edge of a sheltering lie. A good example would be an undercut bank, where the fish can hang out into the edge of the current, feeding on what the current brings its way, and then quickly darting under the security of the bank structure.

Again with regards to moving water in any of these three discussed lies, there are what we call edges. A good example of an edge in moving water would be the interface between fast and slow currents. This is one of the most commonly looked for edges where fish will hold in the slow current and conserve energy, while allowing the faster current to bring food to them. Other good edges where fish can be found are logs, rocks and banks — areas where the current speed is broken and interrupted allowing the fish to post up in the broken current while looking for feeding opportunities.

Reading water is a process that requires time, observation, and experience. If you venture out with the right attitude — not just to catch fish, but to learn — then you'll learn it more completely. Look for lies and edges regardless of whether there is a rod in your hand or not. Your ability to read water will come quicker and you'll find those fish. ◆

Bass Fishing

by Dave Webb

Some of the fastest and most enjoyable fishing I've ever experienced has come pursuing smallmouth bass at Lake Powell and Flaming Gorge. They are feisty fish that hit aggressively and fight hard. Pound for pound, I think they are tougher than trout. They fight with finesse, dancing on their tails and shaking their heads as they try desperately to throw a hook. During the spring, smallmouth come into shallow, rocky areas to spawn. It is easy to locate and catch fish at that time. There are days when you can catch 30 fish in a few hours. Good bass fishers often catch many more than that.

Now that's fun. Cast out, reel in a bit, then. . . pow! There will be times when you catch fish almost every cast.

Smallmouth action becomes very good in southern Utah during the last half of April, and gets even better in May. Fishing slows a bit as the heat of summer sets in, but it usually stays pretty good through August, then becomes good again in September and October. In the north, fish spawn in June, and that's when action is fastest. Success is usually excellent during the spawn, then very good through the summer and into fall, finally tapering off in October.

Bass have adapted well to our desert environment. Our lakes don't have many lily pads or stumps or weed patches. Instead, broken rock serves as the key structure for bass. Find a place where broken rocks extend into the water and you will find smallmouth. That usually occurs in the bays and coves, and toward the backs of canyons.

The best way to fish for smallmouth is from a boat or float tube cruising slowly along the shoreline. Stay offshore as far as you can, but close enough that you can cast into water just inches deep. Then work your lure slowly into deeper water, allowing it to settle into the rocks at each new level.

Smallmouth will often pick up a jig as it is falling, making it difficult to detect a strike. Sometimes you'll know you have a fish on when you no longer feel the weight of the lure. Other times it will feel like you've snagged a rubber band, as the fish pulls back on the jig. A light graphite rod really helps when you are fishing for bass.

If you feel anything different, pop your rod upward and see if you hook a fish.

Bill Furniss with a big Lake Powell largemouth. (PHOTO: COURTESY BILL FURNISS)

Bass Facts

Crayfish are a major food item for Utah smallmouth. Lures and jigs that imitate crayfish are very effective. Double-tail grubs, tube jigs and lizards in greens, browns and purples work very well. Crankbaits also take fish. During the spawn the fish sometimes hit anything that comes into their territory, including spinners and trout lures. Night crawlers, can also be effective. Other important food items include other fish, insects, frogs, tadpoles, worms and fish eggs. Smallmouth almost never eat dead food. Making the lure or bait appear to be alive is essential to ensure fishing success.

Smallmouth spawn in late spring when water temperatures climb to between 61 and 65 degrees. Males build nests in shallow water with sandy or gravelly bottoms.

The nests are usually built close to some kind of structure like rock piles, brush piles, logs, etc. The male defends the nest vigorously and will attack any fish or lure that enters his territory. This defensive behavior makes for some extremely fast and fun fishing during the spawn, which usually lasts from between 7 to 10 days. Of course any bass caught during this time should be immediately released so they can continue their spawning activity.

Smallmouth prefer water temperatures between 68 and 80 degrees. However, they begin to feed aggressively when the water temperature climbs above 47 degrees. Below 47 degrees feeding slows and the bass become less active. When the water temperature climbs above 80 degrees, smallmouth also become inactive.

Smallmouth like areas with lots of rocks and with a sandy bottom. They are generally not found in areas with lots of aquatic plants or areas with muddy bottoms.

Largemouth bass generally grow bigger than smallmouth and can withstand higher water temperatures (up to about 90 degrees). They spawn when the water temperature reaches 59 degrees, and while they do build nests much like smallmouth, they do not defend them as vigorously. The fry will hatch in 5 to 6 days.

Largemouth are not commonly found in the rocky areas preferred by smallmouth. They like areas with muddy bottoms and lots of aquatic vegetation. Largemouth feed aggressively and will readily take crayfish, other fish, worms, frogs mice and even snakes and small ducklings. Common lures used when bass fishing include crankbaits, plastics (singletail grubs, worms, crawfish imitations), night crawlers and various jigging lures that can be worked down into the rocks. During the summer, when the bass are aggressively feeding, top-water lures can be extremely effective and fun to use. ♦

Walleye Fishing

W alleye (*Stizostedion vitreum*) are members of the freshwater perch family and are very good table fare. Their most obvious feature is their large reflective pupils. The walleyes excellent vision in low light combined with a highly developed lateral line system makes them effective predators in the dark or in cloudy, turbid waters. They feed primarily on small fish.

Walleye spawn in the spring when water warms to around 45 to 50 degrees. Rather than make a nest, they spread their eggs on hard bottoms of gravel, sand or rock. They prefer some water movement, seeking river currents or shallow areas with wave action to lay their eggs. In Utah, walleyes can spawn as early as February in the south, continuing to April in the north at higher elevations.

After spawning, male fish will remain in the area if food is available. Females will usually head for deeper water for a while before moving into shallows as water warms. There is often a lull in feeding activity after spawning. Fishing heats up as water temperatures hit the 60 to 70 degree range. As a result, May and June are the best months for walleye fishing in Utah, with many waters continuing strong through July. Fish will move to deeper water as fall approaches.

In Utah, forage species include yellow perch, threadfin shad, Utah chubs, white bass and gizzard shad. Crayfish and insects become important if there is not adequate food. The population dynamics of the walleye's food have a large effect on fishing success. When there are many baitfish available, angler success declines, but size and condition of fish improves. Lakes with little food may have high catch rates for smaller fish.

Walleyes are nomadic and anglers can't count on finding fish in the same locations each time they visit a particular water. A good first step is to gather information. The Utah

Anglers like Bill Furniss know where the big walleyes live. (PHOTO: COURTESY BILL FURNISS)

DWR website — ww.nr.state.ut.us/dwr/%21aquati.htm — is a good source and includes "Statewide fishing reports for anglers by anglers" with up-to-date tips. Joining a club like Rocky Mountain Anglers (see appendix) can also give you access to great information. Hydrographic maps will help you pick likely structures such as points, ledges, and mid-lake humps to begin your search. Also keep your eyes open for rocky shorelines or rip-rap. Fish will usually orient to structure, except when walleyes pursue a forage fish like gizzard shad (Willard Bay) in open water. Use your fish finder to look for baitfish while trolling 1.5 to 3 miles per hour until you locate feeding fish. Increase your speed as water temperatures warm.

Trolling is an effective tactic when walleyes are widely dispersed. Favorite lures for trolling are crankbaits and spinner rigs. Bottom bouncers with a crawler harness are also a good choice. Use trolling boards to spread lures. You will be able to cover more area and reach fish that have not been disturbed by the passing of the boat. Vary trolling speeds and make gentle turns. If you are getting more action on the lures to the ouside of turns, try trolling faster, or go slower if inside lures are more productive. Get lures to the depth that you are marking most fish, usually near the bottom.

Jigs work well when fishing vertically or casting. They are far more effective when fished on the bottom where the fish are. Use a jig heavy enough to "feel" the bottom, but remember that walleyes gently suck a bait into their mouths. Experiment until you find the right weight for conditions. Use light and /or bright colored jigs in dirty water, such as chartreuse, yellow or orange. Clear waters call for dark and/or natural colors like black or purple. Jigs can be fished with a variety of plastic bodies or a night crawler. If fish are aggressive, pop the jig up off the bottom a foot before letting it settle back. When fish are more docile, slower movement is the key. Try simply dragging the jig along the bottom. Good jig fishing requires careful attention. Watch your line closely where it enters the water. High visibility line is helpful. Set the hook if you see the slightest movement.

Crankbaits are popular lures for walleye and work well when trolling or casting. They are available in a dazzling array of sizes, shapes, colors, and diving abilities. Like jigs, use light and/or bright colors in turbid waters, dark and/or natural colors in clear water. Try to match size and color of the main forage fish that walleyes feed on. Depth control is key. Keep track of the length of line you use when trolling, so you can return to the same depth after landing a fish. Vary speed of retrieve or adjust the amount of weight above the bait to fine tune depth. Crayfish imitating crankbaits should bump along the bottom. Baits with rattles are good at attracting fish in turbid waters. Adding a night crawler to the front hook will give your crankbait that special flavor.

Look a walleye in the eye and you will quickly understand why they feed heavily at night. They are the owls of the underwater world and darkness gives them an extra edge over their prey species. If you plan to go night fishing, you should scout likely areas in daylight. Fish will often move into shallower water under cover of darkness. Points that hold fish in daylight will have even more hungry walleyes at night. Make good use of your sonar to spot fish and help you keep track of where you are. Walleye bite softly at night so keep lures a couple feet off the bottom. This will allow you to strike at the slightest bump.

Utah waters hold some very large walleyes, with a state record in excess of 15 pounds. If you want to go hunting a trophy, take the time to hone your skills with electronics to find fish. Develop the sensitive touch that tells you of the softest bites. Do your homework before going to the water and be prepared with hydrographic maps, etc.

Please remember to practice safety. Only keep fish that you will use. Walleye are at their best when fresh, so you are encouraged to only harvest enough for a meal or two, rather than taking home a limit after every outing. If you plan to release fish, handle them carefully. Fish caught from depths below 30 feet will not likely survive if released. ◆

Trolling for Trout

xceptionally good trollers seem to have a sixth sense about fish. Their powers of observation and knowledge of trout and their habits combine to the point where they seem to anticipate a fish biting before it happens.

The most important part of their knowledge is where the fish will be found. This question needs to be answered in terms of where in the lake and at what depth. There are a variety of edges that will attract and hold trout. These include drop offs, weed lines, brush, rocky ledges and surface ice. Other less tangible edges are current from streams and rivers entering the lake, the edge of wind riffle or storms and temperature changes like the thermocline. Learn the lake you are fishing by talking with other anglers and studying hydrographic maps. If you have the opportunity to visit favorite reservoirs when they are at very low levels, you can easily locate structures that are normally hidden and record them on maps or GPS. A good fish finder is invaluable for locating structure as well as concentrations of fish.

In springtime, trout are drawn to the surface, and often close to shore by abundant food and comfortable water temperature. Trollers can reach fish easily and deep trolling equipment is unnecessary. Side planers can be helpful to pull lures out to the sides away from motor noise. They can also present lures closer to shore while the boat is kept farther out to avoid spooking trout cruising the shallows.

As summer heat warms the surface waters, trout move to deeper cooler water. This is the time when most people like to fish and depth control techniques come into their own. Downriggers allow anglers to troll deep with light tackle and lure depth can be precisely controlled. Lead line is simple to use and is usually color coded so if fish are hooked it is easy to return to the same depth. Effective use of electronics is often the best way to determine the depth at which fish are concentrated.

Afternoon breezes are common in summer. Anglers can use the wind as motive power for silent trolling. This allows you to fish shallow areas with little disturbance. The surface riffle created by wind helps trout to feel more secure in near shore waters.

Cold nights in autumn cool surface water and, as freshwater is most dense at 39 degrees, this causes "turn over" as surface waters settle to the bottom and nutrients from the bottom are brought to the surface. Trout come again at this time, feeding strongly in preparation for the winter to come.

Now let's assume that you have located the fish, determined their depth, and have your tackle selected for proper delivery. It is time to choose a lure. A set of flashers or pop gear with a worm is a popular setup. Select a flasher that does not create excessive resistance when trolling. Thread one half of a night crawler onto your hook, leaving about 1½ inch loose to wiggle seductively. Popular spoons include Needlefish, Triple Teaser, Little Cleo, and Kastmaster. Spinners like Panther Martin, Mepps and Roostertail work well. Plugs by Rapala, Rebel and Flatfish round out a good selection.

Trolling speed should match the lure used. Flashers and pop gear work best at slow speeds, just fast enough to keep the blades tumbling. Test your lures a short distance behind the boat and adjust boat speed until the action looks right. Try trolling in slow curves or vary speeds as you search for the right combination.

After you hook a fish, review the strike in your mind. Where was your lure when it was intercepted? Had you adjusted speed? Were you turning? Careful attention to detail will help you build on your successes.

Your methods should take into account the species of trout you are pursuing. Lake trout are most likely to go deep and can only be found near the surface for fairly short periods early and late in the season. They are fall spawners and can be found on shallow bars and humps when the urge to reproduce strikes. Splake (a cross between lake trout and brook) will also be found in deep water in summer. These colorful fish respond well to bait and you may greatly improve your catch rate by adding dead minnows or sucker meat to trolled lures. Small amounts of bait will give the required scent with out greatly hampering lure action. Brown trout are fall spawners as well and slowly trolled crankbaits can be very effective when they are the target. Rainbows and cutthroat seem to prefer flashy lures. These fish tend to stay closer to the surface and sometimes respond well to slightly faster trolling speeds. Brook trout often find small spinners irresistible, especially when tipped with a small piece of worm.

Whatever species of trout you pursue, trolling can be an effective and relaxing way to fish. Lures spend more time in the water and you can cover large areas in less time than with other fishing methods. Trollers can also use lures and rigs that are too large to be cast easily, increasing their chances to catch the trophy fish of a lifetime. ◆

Fishing Utah's Private Waters   *by Sam Webb*

I f you are looking for fast fishing, big fish, help with your fly-fishing skills, or a place to take the kids or grandkids, then it's time to look at Utah's private waters. These destinations vary greatly — amenities, cost, size and numbers of fish, fishing techniques allowed, guides, distance from major population centers — are all factors when planning a trip.

One of LC Ranch's resident rainbows poses with Mark "Bortis" Bennion. (PHOTO: WESTERN RIVERS FLYFISHER)

Private fishing waters can be broadly placed into two categories: catch-out ponds and trophy catch-and-release ponds. The management style and philosophy of these two kinds of fisheries are completely different, although both have their place.

Catch-out ponds are generally stocked heavily with cacheable-size rainbows. Fishing is almost always fast and furious and the fish are easy to catch. Most any bait or lure is allowed; however all fish caught must be kept and purchased.

Generally there is a fee based on the number of pounds of fish caught. These ponds are generally located near the major population centers and are popular places to take younger anglers. They are often crowded on weekends.

Trophy ponds are managed so that the fish remain in the water and have an opportunity to grow big and fat. A limited number of anglers are allowed to fish the ponds each day. This keeps the fish from being stressed and allows them to grow rapidly. Only barbless hooks are allowed and fish are carefully released. Spin-fishing is generally not allowed and bait-fishing is never allowed.

Paradise Pond Busy catch-out pond, just off I-15 in American Fork. Most people fish with bait and keep the fish they catch (fee is by the pound), although a few anglers practice catch-and-release fly-fishing and are charged an hourly rate.
tel: (801) 756-7821

Bear River Lodge Trout Ponds is located on SR 150 (Mirror Lake Highway) on the north slope of the Uinta Mountains, about 30 minutes south of Evanston, Wyoming. Ponds are located next to the Bear River in an alpine setting. The fish cost $3.50 per pound for catch-out anglers. Catch-and-release fly-fishing is allowed for $15 per hour or $25.00 per half day.
tel: (800) 559-1121
website: www.bearriverlodge.com

Ruby's Inn Pond is just down the road from Bryce Canyon National Park. This big, beautiful pond is next to the Ruby's Inn complex, and fishing is for guests at Ruby's Inn only (no additional fee). Catch-and-release spin or fly-fishing with single barbless hooks. No bait allowed. Ice-fishing is allowed.
tel: (435)-834-5341

Stevenson's LC Ranch is just north of the town of Altamont, nestled in the juniper foothills of the south slope of the Uinta Mountains. This wonderful lodge and cabin resort is adjacent to over a dozen private trout ponds. Guided catch-and-release fly-fishing. The limited number of anglers per day protects the fishery and allows anglers to find solitude, serenity, and plenty of monster rainbows, hard-fighting steelhead, and wild browns.
tel: (435)-454-3750 / website: www.lcranch.com / e-mail: lcranch@ubtanet.com

Road Creek Ranch features trophy trout ponds full of big rainbows, brook trout, browns, and steelhead, as well as a classy lodge and a wonderful restaurant in the town of Loa. Guided or non-guided, catch-and-release fly-fishing. Barbless hooks only. The record rainbow is a 16-pound monster. An added bonus is the half mile of stream fishing. Hunting for upland game (pheasant, chukar, and quail) and a sporting clays course are also available.
tel: (800)-388-7688 / website: www.roadcreekranch.com

Deseret Land and Livestock and Tom Land of Wild Country Outfitters offer Utah's premier wildlife and cattle ranch one hour from Salt Lake City. The 200,000-acre ranch is a beautiful backdrop for 9 mountain lakes and ponds with 13 miles of a pristine high mountain stream. Float or wade fish for rainbows ranging from 14 to 35 inches. The stream is populated with native Bonneville cutthroat that reach 20 inches. They feature guided or hosted, one or multi-day trips customized to fit anyone's needs. Lodging is available. Catch-and-release fly-fishing only. Barbless hooks.
tel: (801) 479-1194 / website: www.wildcountryoutfitters.com

The Lodge at Red River Ranch Magnificent lodge nestled among cottonwoods just outside of Capitol Reef National Park. The ranch boasts a five-mile stretch of the Fremont River and a trophy trout pond. A stunningly beautiful area at the foot of Boulder Mountain. Guided or hosted fly-fishing. Catch and release only with single, barbless hooks.
tel: (800) 20 LODGE / website: www.thelodge@redriverranch.com

Mountain West Outfitters offers great fishing on a two-and-a-half mile stretch of Lost Creek and on several private ponds with monster rainbows. Fly and spin-fishing are both allowed. Catch and release only, artificial fly and lure only with a single barbless hook. All trips are guided. Only 45 minutes from SLC, near the town of Croydon.
tel: (801) 394-2769

Larry Knight releases another fine rainbow at the LC Ranch. (PHOTO: DAVE N. OLSEN / WINDOW ON WILDLIFE)

Willow Valley Ranch This unique fishery has six miles of meandering spring creeks, 9 still water ponds, and 2.5 miles of freestone river (the Little Bear), all nestled into a 12,000-acre ranch that is home to deer, elk, and upland game. Guided and hosted fly-fishing. Catch and release only. Single barbless hooks.
tel: (435) 755-6800

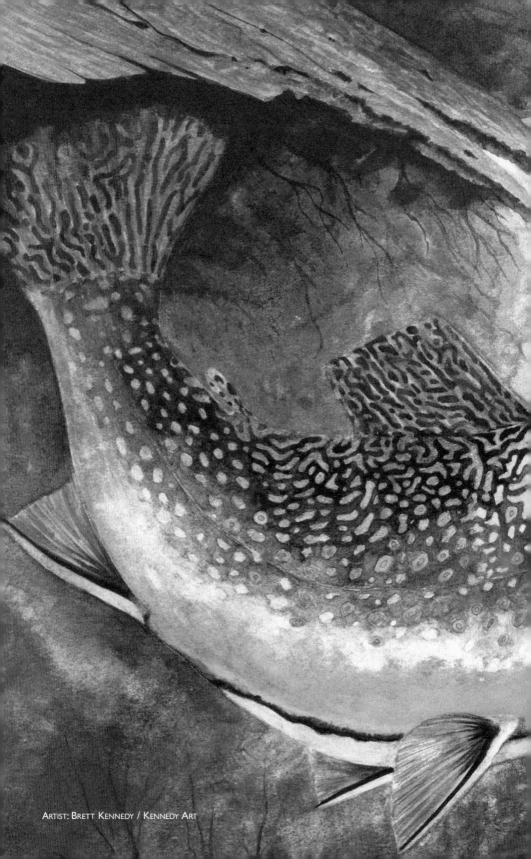

Fishing Destinations

Northern Utah

T he fisheries of northern Utah are incredibly diverse. They range from the large and powerful Green River to tiny Thistle Creek, and from the semi-industrial Utah Lake to the remote and pristine waters of the High Uintas.

Many of these waters are within two hours drive of the state's major population centers, and can be easily reached by urban anglers.

PHOTO: STEVE SCHMIDT / WESTERN RIVERS FLYFISHER

The following four chapters describe fishing destinations in the northern half of Utah. They are divided as follows:

☐ Rivers and Streams

☐ Coldwater Lakes and Reservoirs

☐ Warmwater Lakes and Reservoirs

☐ High Uinta Lakes

Coldwater Lakes and Reservoirs include waters where coldwater species (trout and kokanee salmon) are the primary target. In *Warmwater Lakes and Reservoirs*, anglers are more apt to pursue bass, walleye, pike, perch and bluegills. ◆

American Fork Creek

T he lower portion of the canyon is on the scenic Alpine Loop, a beautiful drive from American Fork to Provo, passing around the east side of Mount Timpanogos.

Timpanogos Cave National Monument is on this route. If you would like to take a tour of the cave, you will need to make a reservation in advance. See their web site at www.nps.gov/tica/ or call (801) 756-5238 in the summer and (801) 756-5239 in the winter. Cave tours are $6 for ages 16 and older, $5 for ages 6 to 15, and $3 for 5 and younger.

Fish Species

Rainbow, cutthroat, brown, and brook trout.

Special Regulations

American Fork Creek east from Utah Lake to I-15:

❏ Walleye limit, 2; but only 1 over 20 inches.

❏ **Closed** between 7 p.m. and 7 a.m., March 1 through 7 a.m. the last Saturday of April (April 24, 1999). During this period anglers may only use lures with 1 single hook. The single hook must be able to pass through a 9/16 inch opening. The distance between the point of the hook and the shank on a single hook may not exceed 9/16 inch. A person may not possess hooks or lures with hooks that exceed 9/16 inch.

Tactics

This is a small narrow water with a lot of brush in many spots. Much of it is best suited to spin-fishing. Try the smallest sizes of spinners or drift salmon eggs and worms through the deeper holes.

Fly-fishers will find more open water immediately above and below Tibble Fork Reservoir. Cast attractor type dry flies in late summer.

How to Get There

From I-15 near American Fork, take Exit 287 and go east on SR 92.

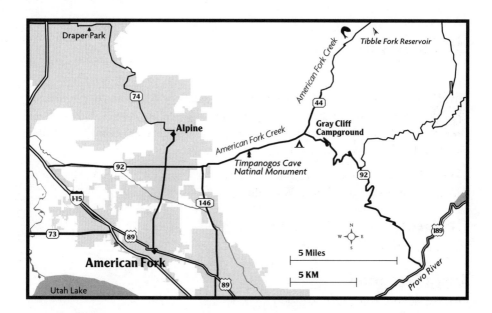

Accessibility

SR 92 runs up American Fork Canyon and follows the stream for several miles. Access to the upper portion of American Fork Creek is on SR 144 near the South Fork Ranger Station.

Visitors wishing to drive the Alpine Loop (SR 92) must pay a $3 entrance fee.

GPS Coordinates

Timpanogos Cave National Monument	N 40° 26′ 24″ W 111° 42′ 32″
Gray Cliff Campground	N 40° 26′ 59″ W 111° 40′ 28″
Tibble Fork Reservoir	N 40° 28′ 56″ W 111° 38′ 39″

Maps

USGS 1:24000   Pelican Point, Lehi, Timpanogos Cave

Utah Atlas and Gazetteer   Page 53

When to Go

July through October. ◆

Bear River

S ummer days on a Uinta stream like the Bear River are hard to beat. Families will enjoy the easy access and many campgrounds. Hiking trails provide additional recreation and access to many lakes that you will find listed in the High Uinta Lakes chapter of this guide.

Note: The guide refers only to the Bear River on the North Slope of the Uinta Mountains before it passes into Wyoming.

Fish Species

Rainbow, cutthroat, and brook trout.

Special Regulations

General season, bag, and possession limits apply.

Tactics

These are simple, unsophisticated trout. The largest individuals are often found in beaver ponds. The East Fork and Hayden Fork have several ponds that are generally in swampy, brushy areas. Either wear waders or be prepared to get wet and dirty.

Small nymphs and terrestrials are effective in this area. Yellow humpies in size 14 or 16 can be very productive. Bead head prince nymphs and weighted damselfly nymphs are a good bet for fooling fish in the beaver ponds.

Small spinners work well, especially with the addition of a small worm. Ultralight spinning tackle will cast one half of a night crawler without any additional weight, providing a fairly quiet presentation in the still waters of beaver ponds.

How to Get There

From Kamas, take SR 150 northeast past Mirror Lake. The Hayden Fork of the Bear River follows the road north to its confluence with the Stillwater Fork, near Stillwater Campground, and the East Fork by East Fork Campground.

Accessibility

This portion of the Bear River and its tributaries are mostly in the Wasatch-Cache National Forest, and access is excellent.

SR 150 gives access to the Hayden Fork and the Bear River below the other two main forks. There are six campgrounds along this stretch of SR 150, including

Hayden Fork and Stillwater Campgrounds.

FR 057 (Stillwater Road) goes up to Christmas Meadows Campground, where you will find good access to the Stillwater Fork. There is good fishing in the meadow areas above here. TR 098 provides easy access above the campground.

The East Fork can be reached by taking FR 058 east from SR 150, then turning north on FR 059. Access the upper reaches of the East Fork on TR 151.

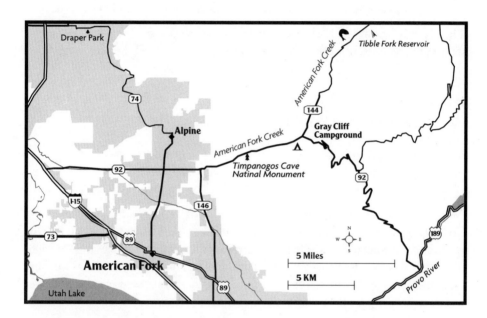

GPS Coordinates

Hayden Fork Campground	N 40° 49′ 47″ W 110° 51′ 11″
Stillwater Campground	N 40° 52′ 06″ W 110° 50′ 04″
Christmas Meadows Campground	N 40° 49′ 28″ W 110° 48′ 04″
East Fork Bear River Trailhead	N 40° 51′ 32″ W 110° 45′ 14″

Maps

USGS 1:24000   Deadman Mountain, Whitney Reservoir,
                       Christmas Meadows, Red Knob

Utah Atlas and Gazetteer   Pages 54, 55

When to Go

Expect stream flows to subside to fishable levels in July, depending on snow pack and weather. Fishing continues through September. ◆

Blacksmith Fork   CACHE COUNTY

T his small stream has the potential to produce very large fish. A Utah State University biologist trapped a 33-pound monster here in the early 1980s. While it is not likely that this fish is still alive, it is possible that other trophies still hide in Blacksmith Fork's deep holes and undercut banks.

The river is known to harbor whirling disease. Please see the whirling disease section in the guide for precautions to ensure that you don't help to spread this disease.

Fish Species

Rainbow, cutthroat, and brown trout; whitefish.

Special Regulations

General season, bag, and possession limits apply.

Tactics

This small stream is one of the few waters in Utah with a salmonfly hatch. This hatch usually coincides with high water in June. If you arrive while water is high, or shortly afterwards, you can have some great fishing on sofa pillows or any salmonfly patterns. If the water remains high, concentrate your efforts on slower waters next to the bank.

The stream will fish well during summer with caddis imitations. In the fall, shift to blue-winged olives. Black stonefly nymphs and prince nymphs can be effective throughout the season and may produce bigger trout.

Spinning rod enthusiasts can try crankbaits that resemble the rainbow trout that are stocked here, and that are the preferred food of any oversized browns.

How to Get There

From Brigham City, take US 89 north 17 miles toward Logan. Turn onto SR 101 and go east. SR 101 will take you through Hyrum and you will reach the river in about 7 miles.

Accessibility

There is quite a bit of private water in the main Blacksmith Fork. Respect this private property. The Left Hand Fork of the Blacksmith Fork has plenty of easy access.

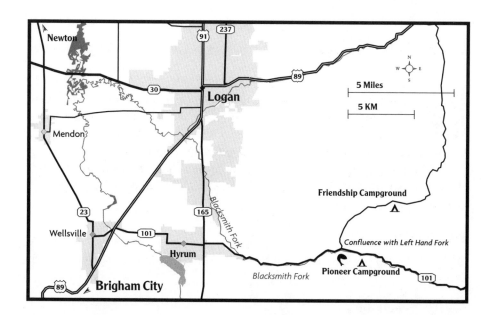

GPS Coordinates

Pioneer Campground	N 41° 37' 42" W 111° 41' 41"
Confluence with Left Hand Fork	N 41° 37' 50" W 111° 42' 27"
Friendship Campground	N 41° 39' 41" W 111° 39' 49"

Maps

USGS 1:24000   Logan, Paradise, Porcupine Reservoir,
                           Logan Peak, Hardware Ranch

Utah Atlas and Gazetteer   Pages 60, 61

When to Go

If you can time it to be on this river during the salmonfly hatch when the water is not too high, count yourself fortunate. Mid-June should be about right, but the hatch is short-lived and flows may still be quite high. A local contact is invaluable.

Fishing is generally good from July through October. Look for big browns to spawn in the fall. Do not step on spawning redds. ♦

Currant Creek

This delightful creek seems designed for fly-fishers. Because it is dam-controlled and regulated as part of the Central Utah Project, it rarely runs high and water stays clear most of the year. It has many interesting beaver ponds and some very respectable trout for such a small body of water. Dense brush shields the angler from road traffic, but there are many points where the stream approaches the road or where open areas keep access to the waters from being much of a problem.

Fish Species

Although brown trout are the main species, there are also cutthroat and rainbow trout.

Special Regulations

Water Hollow Creek upstream to headwaters, including all tributaries to Currant Creek Reservoir, but not the reservoir itself:

❐ Artificial flies and lures only.

❐ Trout limit, 2.

Tactics

The fish here mainly key on aquatic insects. Couple this information with the "Artificials Only" regulation and fly-fishing quickly becomes the method of choice. There are several good insect hatches here. The best mayfly species to imitate is the pale morning dun, a pale yellow mayfly ranging from 14 to 18 that is present much of the summer. One will also find blue-winged olives early and late in the season, as well as a few green drakes. Bead head nymphs, prince nymphs, and hare's ears are productive underneath. In late summer, grasshopper patterns can generate exciting surface action.

Pay special attention to the beaver ponds on this creek. They often hold the largest fish. Small wooly buggers and damselfly nymphs will work well. Spin-fishers would do well to try spinners in these pond areas.

There are many spots where there is little room to cast. A short rod can be an advantage, because shorter rods allow greater accuracy. On the other hand, longer rods can allow you to lift your backcast above streamside brush.

How to Get There

Take US 40 east 40 miles from Heber City. About 8 miles past the Soldier Creek Dam turnoff (the last place that you will see Strawberry Reservoir), turn north at the sign for Currant Creek Reservoir onto Currant Creek Road. If you are arriving from the east, turn north 3.8 miles west of Fruitland.

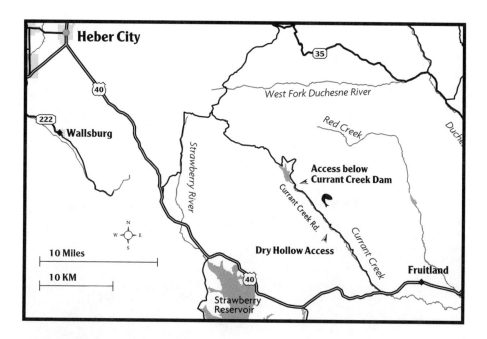

Accessibility

If you are not willing to wade, this is a difficult place to fish.

The best water begins about 5 miles north of US 40 and runs up to Currant Creek Dam. The bottom section is private, and it gets quite a bit of sediment from the drainages above, so it often runs dirty. Above Water Hollow, there are several turnouts and access sites. Heavy brush along the stream is not too much of a problem if you stay in or near the stream. **Caution:** A friend fell and broke an ankle here. He was alone and it took him two hours to crawl back to his car. Wear appropriate footwear and move slowly in brushy areas. Always watch where you step.

GPS Coordinates

Access below Currant Creek Dam	N 40° 19′ 31″ W 111° 02′ 42″
Dry Hollow Access	N 40° 16′ 40″ W 110° 59′ 17″

Maps

USGS 1:24000   Fruitland, Deep Creek Canyon,
                      Raspberry Knoll, Jimmies Point

Utah Atlas and Gazetteer   Pages 54, 46, 47

When to Go

This creek is open all year. If the road is passable, the resourceful fisher can find fish in any month. The best time is June through September. The best chance to find green drakes is in July. Flows are generally consistent then, so this is a good choice when most other small streams are high and off color. ◆

Big, handsome brown. (PHOTO: STEVE SCHMIDT / WESTERN RIVERS FLYFISHER)

Diamond Fork Creek   UTAH COUNTY

T his is a very pretty stream especially in the fall. It is convenient to Salt Lake City and Provo and has good camping facilities. There are several nice hikes in the area and you will not soon forget an afternoon soaking in the hot spring.

Diamond Fork below Three Forks is used to carry water to Utah Valley, causing high flows most of the summer. Anglers cannot fish effectively here for much of the year. Officials are considering linking the Syar Tunnel with another tunnel at Monk Hollow. If this project is undertaken, it could be completed by the year 2003. Diamond Fork would receive consistent flows from Strawberry Reservoir and conditions for fishing would be greatly improved.

Fish Species

Brown, cutthroat, and rainbow trout.

Special Regulations

Diamond Fork Creek (Utah County) — including all tributaries from Springville Crossing to the headwaters:

❏ Artificial flies and lures only.

❏ **Closed** to the possession of cutthroat or trout with cutthroat markings.

❏ All other trout species, limit 8.

Tactics

Fishing this creek during high water is not recommended, as it is both difficult and more hazardous at this time. If you must fish during high water, look for fish in slow eddies along the bank. Use tackle strong enough to lift fish out of the water.

Caution: The velocity and power of high water should never be underestimated.

When the water drops, this is a beautiful stream to wade up in search of trout. The stretch right below Three Forks is well treed and lush. You will think you've left the arid West.

Casting a royal Wulff or elk hair caddis straight upstream is very rewarding on Indian summer days. The usual nymphs will work well in the deeper holes. Spin-fishers will do well with spinners.

How to Get There

From I-15 at Spanish Fork, take Exit 261and go east 4 miles on SR 214. Continue on US 6 southeast about 7 miles. Turn north at the sign for Diamond Fork. If you are coming from the east, this will be 4 miles west of the junction where US 6 and US 89 separate near the flooded town of Thistle.

This road parallels the creek for most of its length.

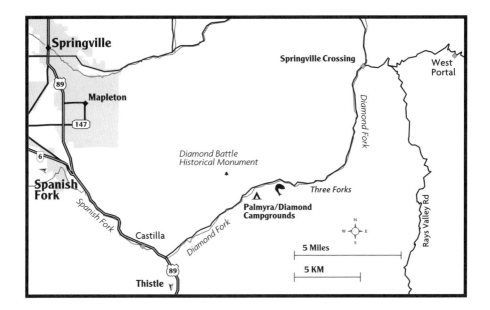

Accessibility

The best fishing and easiest access begins above the Palmyra and Diamond camp-grounds and continues to Three Forks. Above Three Forks the stream is much smaller, but there are still fish in the deeper holes all the way to the junction at Springville Crossing.

Three Forks is a trailhead at the confluence of Diamond Fork, Sixth Water Creek, and Cottonwood Canyon. If you go up Sixth Water Creek and then cross the bridge and continue up Fifth Water Creek, you will come to a beautiful hot spring at the base of a waterfall. It is a great place to soak your bones at the end of the day.

Note: There is some controversy over what to wear while soaking. Some wear nothing at all. If you are not prepared for this, you might want to avoid this area.

GPS Coordinates

Palmyra / Diamond Campgrounds	N 40° 04' 24" W 111° 25' 35"
Three Forks	N 40° 05' 04" W 111° 21' 15"
Junction Springville Crossing	N 40° 09' 18" W 111° 19' 50"

Maps

USGS 1:24000   Spanish Fork Peak, Billies Mountain, Rays Valley, Two Tom Hill

Utah Atlas and Gazetteer   Page 46

When to Go

This stream is subject to very high flows during summer as it is the main conduit for the Central Utah Project to bring water from Strawberry Reservoir to Utah Valley. Therefore, the best time to fish here is after the water drops in September. ◆

The falls above the hot springs. (PHOTO: BRAD NICHOLSON)

Duchesne River   WASATCH AND DUCHESNE COUNTIES

T he Duchesne River is a surprisingly large drainage for the small amount of attention it receives. By the time it reaches the town of Duchesne, the river drains 660 square miles. There are over 80 miles of fishable water between the North and West Forks and the main Duchesne River.

There are good camping facilities on the North Fork. Lodging is available at Defa's Dude Ranch on this fork and at lodges in Hanna and Tabiona.

Easily accessible from the Wasatch Front, this area is approximately two hours from Salt Lake City and Provo.

Services

National Forest Campgrounds:

tel: (877) 444-6777
or (800) 280-2267

Hades
Aspen Grove
Iron Mine
South Fork

Lodging:

Defa's Dude Ranch
Hanna, UT 84031
tel: (435) 848-5590

The Sagebrush Inn
Tabiona, UT 84072
tel: (435) 848-5637

MAIN DUCHESNE RIVER

This stretch can get quite dirty when there is substantial runoff. When it is clear, it has a reputation for producing some large brown trout.

Fish Species

Rainbow, cutthroat, and brown trout.

Special Regulations

General season, bag, and possession limits apply.

Tactics

Fly-fishers will do well imitating grasshoppers in July and August. Muddler minnows are favored by knowledgeable local anglers and can score on the bigger fish.

How to Get There

From Duchesne, go north on SR 87 and cross the Duchesne River on the edge of town. Continue north on SR 87, and then turn west on SR 35 toward Hanna. This road runs along the Duchesne all the way to the confluence of the North and West Forks. Anglers from Salt Lake City can take I-80 to US 40, and then turn north on SR 208 (about 7 miles past Fruitland) to reach SR 35 near Tabiona.

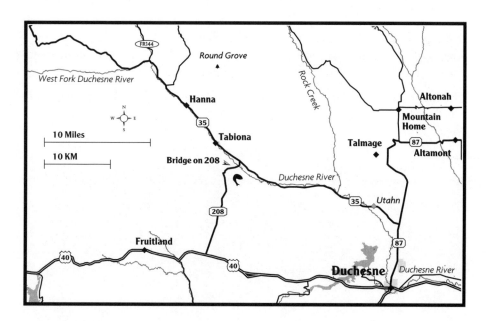

Accessibility

This stretch is predominantly private. Anglers wishing to fish here should secure permission from landowners. Please respect private property.

GPS Coordinates

Bridge on 208	N 40° 19' 27" W 110° 40' 19"

Maps

USGS 1:24000   Hanna, Farm Creek Peak, Tabiona, Blacktail
                      Mountain, Talmage, Duchesne.

Utah Atlas and Gazetteer   Pages 47, 54, 55

When to Go

This stream is a good choice in late summer and fall. Anglers can sometimes find good conditions before the runoff begins in the spring. This stretch of the river can turn muddy with any substantial rainfall.

For the most part, this is a fun and simple stream to fish. There are rainbows and some browns in the lower stretches of the river. The upper portion is home to many bright and unsophisticated brook trout.

If you park at the end of the road and fish upstream, you will seldom see other anglers. The fish make up in numbers what they lack in size. The short, steep canyon walls on this stretch are unusual and interesting.

The lower stretches receive more pressure and are stocked with rainbows. The DWR added 12,000 catchable rainbows to the river on the last day of May in 1998.

Bud "R.F." Murray and friend on the Duchesne River (PHOTO: GREG PEARSON / WESTERN RIVERS FLYFISHER)

NORTH FORK DUCHESNE

Fish Species

Rainbow, cutthroat, brown, and brook trout.

Special Regulations

General season, bag, and possession limits apply.

Tactics

Favorite fly patterns are stimulators, elk hair caddis, and royal Wulffs in summer, and blue-winged olives in fall. Cased caddis and hare's ears work well underneath.

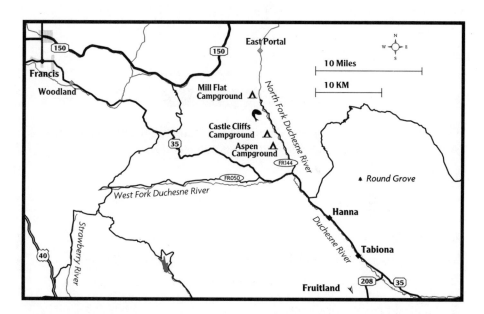

How to Get There

From Salt Lake City, take I-80 to US 40 and then turn north on SR 208 (about 7 miles past Fruitland) to reach SR 35 near Tabiona. Then turn west and follow the Duchesne to the confluence. Turn north onto FR 144 about 0.2 mile past the Stockmore Ranger Station.

Accessibility

FR 144 follows the North Fork of the Duchesne from its confluence to Mill Flat Campground. There is some private property here, but there are several campgrounds and plenty of good access.

GPS Coordinates

Aspen Campground	N 40° 29' 49" W 110° 50' 46"
Castle Cliffs Campground	N 40° 30' 48" W 110° 51' 19"
Mill Flat Campground	N 40° 33' 30" W 110° 53' 11"

Maps

USGS 1:24000   Hanna, Grandaddy Lake, Iron Mine Mountain, Mirror Lake

Utah Atlas and Gazetteer   Page 54

When to Go

High water usually recedes in late June. Expect good fishing from July through October. ◆

WEST FORK DUCHESNE

The West Fork is a small brushy stream. The cutthroat in the upper stretches can be particularly willing adversaries on a warm summer day.

Fish Species

Cutthroat and brown trout.

Special Regulations

From the confluence with North Fork to headwaters, including Wolf Creek:

❏ Only 2 trout may be cutthroat trout or trout with cutthroat markings.

❏ Artificial flies and lures only.

❏ **Closed** January 1 through 6 a.m. on the second Saturday of July (July 10, 1999).

Note: The special regulations here should help to reduce angling pressure compared to the North Fork.

Tactics

This stream has a good population of cutthroat trout. They will eagerly take dry flies such as stimulators and royal Wulffs. There is a fair amount of brush on the banks, so the best approach is to get in the creek when necessary and fish upstream.

How to Get There

From Salt Lake City, take I-80 to US 40 and turn north on SR 208 (about 7 miles past Fruitland), where you will reach SR 35 near Tabiona. Then turn west and follow the Duchesne to the confluence. Go 3.5 miles west from Stockmore Ranger Station, then turn west onto FR 050. This will take you to the West Fork of the Duchesne in about 7 miles.

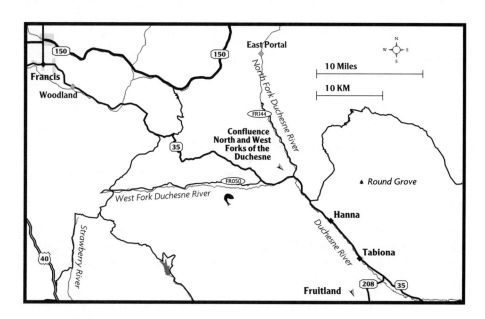

Accessibility

The lower portion of this creek was previously controlled by a sportsmen's group, and is private. There is good public access further up the stream.

GPS Coordinates

Confluence N. & W. Forks of the Duchesne	N 40° 27' 44" W 110° 49' 57"

Maps

USGS 1:24000   Hanna, Wolf Creek, Wolf Creek Summit, Heber Mountain

Utah Atlas and Gazetteer   Page 54

When to Go

This stream will begin to fish well in mid-July, when it opens, and continue through October. ◆

East Canyon Creek   MORGAN COUNTY

T his is very productive water close to the Salt Lake Valley, but it is almost all privately controlled. There are only a few short sections of water open to the public. Anglers who can obtain access to private water would be advised to do so. There have been water quality problems here in the past.

Fish Species

Rainbow, cutthroat, and brown trout.

Special Regulations

East Canyon Creek from Whites Crossing (approximately 2 miles upstream from Porterville) upstream to the East Canyon Reservoir Dam:

❏ **Closed** January 1 through March 31 and November 1 through December 31.

Tactics

This stream supports a good population of insect life. There are blue-winged olives in the spring and caddis flies in the summer. One can find large numbers of grasshoppers here into the fall and hopper imitations are probably a fly-fisher's best bet to land a larger fish.

Small and even medium-sized spinners work well here. Try gold-bladed Mepps or Panther Martin spinners, particularly in the autumn months.

How to Get There

From Salt Lake City, take I-80 east to Exit 134 and go north 13 miles on SR 65. This will bring you to East Canyon Creek about 2 miles above the reservoir.

An alternate route is to continue east up I-80 to the Jeremy Ranch Exit (143) and then go north to the frontage road. Turn west, then turn north on Lariat. When you reach the bottom of the golf course, take the dirt road (Jeremy Road) through the gate.

Accessibility

Jeremy Road follows East Canyon Creek from the Park City area to SR 65, which continues north along the creek to East Canyon Reservoir. SR 66 parallels the stream from the reservoir to Morgan.

There is public access only in a few places; the rest of the stream is private and most is posted. Please respect private property and get permission before entering.

There is nearly a mile of accessible water from Mormon Flats down to where Schuster Creek enters East Canyon Creek. This stretch has a variety of water types, including beaver ponds. Private land along the stream is posted above and below here.

There is also access to a short section on state park lands at River Edge Campground, located on the upper end of East Canyon Reservoir. The water above here is controlled by East Canyon Resort.

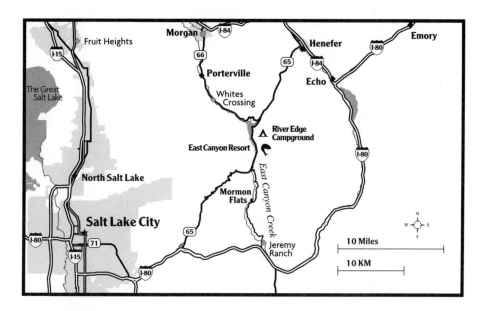

GPS Coordinates

Mormon Flats	N 40° 48′ 52″ W 111° 35′ 04″
East Canyon Resort	N 40° 52′ 15″ W 111° 35′ 02″
River Edge Campground	N 40° 52′ 35″ W 111° 34′ 53″

Maps

USGS 1:24000   Park City West, Big Dutch Hollow, East Canyon Reservoir, Porterville, Morgan

Utah Atlas and Gazetteer   Pages 53, 61

When to Go

Expect clear water and normal flows by July in most years. September brings very good hopper fishing below Mormon Flats. Cold weather will normally halt fishing in December. Flows below the reservoir may be erratic due to irrigation demand. ♦

East Fork Little Bear River   CACHE COUNTY

his small river holds plenty of nice fish and gets very little pressure. Porcupine Reservoir on the East Fork of the Little Bear was drained in 1998. No adverse effects to the river are anticipated.

This river is known to harbor whirling disease. Please see the whirling disease section in this guide for precautions to ensure that you don't help to spread this disease.

Fish Species

Rainbows, cutthroat, and brown trout. Kokanee salmon can move out of the reservoir into the river.

Special Regulations

East Fork Little Bear River and its tributaries upstream from Porcupine Reservoir:

❑ **Closed** August 15 through September 30.

East Fork Little Bear Porcupine Dam downstream to the Avon-Paradise County Road, second stream crossing below reservoir:

❑ Artificial flies and lures only.

❑ Trout and salmon limit, 2.

Tactics

The river above the reservoir fishes well with attractor flies like renegades and royal Wulffs; caddis imitations are also a good choice.

Below the reservoir, glo-bugs and San Juan worms work well in the early season before runoff. During the summer months, caddisflies and terrestrials should work well.

How to Get There

From Brigham City, take US 89 north 16 miles to SR 101. Go east 4.9 miles through Hyrum and take SR 165 south 8.1 miles to Avon. South of Avon SR 165 becomes SR 162. Turn east on La Plata Road just past the East Fork of the Little Bear River.

Accessibility

La Plata Road follows the river up to Porcupine Reservoir. The road goes around to the north and comes back to the East Fork above the reservoir.

There is good access on DWR lands below Porcupine Reservoir.

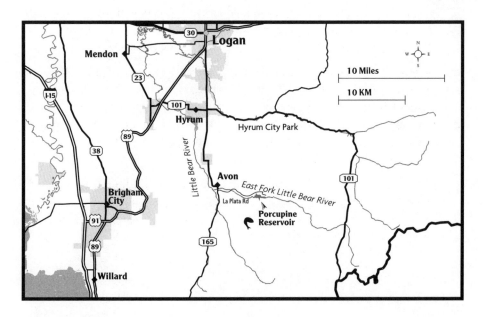

GPS Coordinates

Porcupine Reservoir	N 41° 31' 09" W 111° 44' 15"

Maps

USGS 1:24000   Porcupine Reservoir, Paradise

Utah Atlas and Gazetteer   Pages 60, 61

When to Go

High water normally recedes in late June. Expect good fishing from July through October. Remember that the stream above the reservoir is closed from August 15 to September 30. ◆

Green River
DAGGETT COUNTY

T he Green is Utah's most famous trout river. A world-class fishery in an incredible setting, its clear emerald green waters flow through steep red-rock canyons lined with ponderosa pines. This is big country, with a history that includes Butch Cassidy and Major John Wesley Powell.

The Flaming Gorge Dam was completed in 1962. But the river did not begin to reach its true potential until 1978 when changes were made that allowed temperature control of water leaving the dam. Introduction of special regulations was the final step toward preserving the fish populations of the Green River. It now has all the attributes of a large spring creek, an abundance of large fish, clear water, and prolific insect hatches.

It is a large, powerful river that lends itself to floating and fishing from a variety of watercraft. Well-maintained trails also give the wading angler good access to much prime water. The large number of fish, together with water clarity, give the angler a great opportunity to watch trout behavior and observe how they react to different flies and lures.

The section of the river from Flaming Gorge Dam to the Colorado State Line is a Class 1 trout fishery. This is the only section of the Green River referred to in this guide.

Fish Species
Brown trout are the dominant species, with a 29 lb. 12 oz. monster having been caught by Don Brown in December 1996. The brown trout population is self-sustaining. Rainbow numbers stay up as the result of a good stocking program and some natural reproduction. There are still fair numbers of cutthroat trout with their beautiful gold and crimson coloration. Hybrid rainbow/cutthroat often reach a truly impressive size in the Green River, and their strength and fighting abilities are second to none.

Special Regulations
From the Colorado state line in Brown's Park upstream to Flaming Gorge Dam; including Gorge Creek, a tributary entering the Green River at Little Hole:

❏ Artificial flies and lures only.

❏ **Closed** to fishing from a boat with a motor.

❏ Licensed anglers, trout limit is 3 (2 under 13 inches and 1 over 20 inches).

❏ Unlicensed anglers 13 years of age or younger, trout limit is 2 (2 under 13 inches or 1 under 13 inches and 1 over 20 inches).

Tactics

To float or not to float is the question on the Green. There is good access for anglers either walking or wading on the northeast bank of the river from the dam to just above Red Creek, and this approach simplifies logistics. However, floating greatly increases the amount of water that can be effectively fished. Fly-fishers will appreciate the incredibly long drag-free drifts that are possible from a boat traveling at the speed of the current. Floating anglers can access the southeast bank of the river, which gets less pressure, and can cover many more river miles in a day than their wading counterparts.

If you decide to float, be sure your equipment and skills are up to the challenge, or consider booking a trip with one of the many licensed guides who row the river regularly.

The Green has some very good hatches. As a result, the average trout feeds almost entirely on insects, and fly-fishing is the method of choice. There are a great number of guide services on the river to help everyone from beginner to expert get the most out of the time on the water. A chart of the main hatches that the fly-fisher can imitate is on page 86.

The blue-winged olive is probably the most important hatch of the year on the river. It has the most insects and can span three months in the spring. There are places where, on a good afternoon, one can see hundreds of trout all feeding on blue-winged olives. Use leaders of at least 9 feet, tippet down to 5x or finer. Parachute Adams, comparaduns, and thorax patterns in sizes 16 to 20 are all effective. For difficult fish, a Quigley Cripple can be the answer.

In late May, experienced anglers begin listening with anticipation for a buzzing in the trees. This is usually the first sign that the cicadas have begun to hatch. The large, clumsy terrestrial insects can cause big trout to throw caution to the wind when the hatch is really on. This is the best chance to catch really big fish on a dry fly. Cicadas have cyclic populations, so insect numbers can vary widely from one year to the next. The most popular patterns have bodies of black foam with calf tail wings sizes 6 to 10, and are good floaters.

Nymph fishing is very popular and effective on the Green. Tungsten bead head nymphs have been very successful since they were introduced. One popular technique is to fish a "Dry and Dropper." This is most commonly a cicada or another large, good-floating dry fly with a bead head nymph hanging 18 to 48 inches below. Tying tippet to the bend of the hook on the large dry fly does not seem to compromise its hooking ability.

Spin-fishers do well with Rapalas and jigs. Minnow plugs can work especially well after stocking has occurred. Floating and fishing small 1/8 oz. rubber-tailed jigs bounced along on the bottom is also effective.

The largest fish in the river feed on other fish. If you would like to catch a real trophy and are willing to put in the time, use streamer flies or minnow-type plugs 8 inches or longer.

How to Get There

Anglers from out of state will most likely fly into Salt Lake City. Rental cars are easy to obtain and it is a 3 to 3 1/2-hour drive to Dutch John from the airport. Skywest Airlines has regular service to Vernal. However, Vernal is still an hour from Flaming Gorge Dam, and additional transportation is necessary. One can fly a private charter to the Dutch John Airport as well.

The following shuttle services are available in the area:

❏ Green River Outfitters, P.O. Box 200, Dutch John, Utah 84023
   tel: (435) 885-3338

❏ Flaming Gorge Lodge, Dutch John, Utah, 84023 tel: (435) 889-3773

The direct route from Salt Lake City is I-80 east 110 miles to Exit 34 at Fort Bridger, Wyoming. Follow SR 414 through town and turn right at Lyman at the 4-way stop. Pass through Mountain View and continue southeast. Wyoming SR 414 will become Utah SR 43 and continue to Manila, Utah. Turn south onto SR 44 in Manila and climb up into the Uinta Mountains, eventually turning east onto US 191. This will bring you to the Flaming Gorge Lodge, and then over Flaming Gorge Dam to the town of Dutch John.

An alternate route is to take I-80 East to US 40, and continue east to Vernal. From Vernal, head north on US 191 to the junction with SR 44.

Accessibility

There are three main sections of the Green River between Flaming Gorge Dam and the Colorado border. The "A Section" consists of 7 miles of water from the dam to the access site at Little Hole. The "B Section" refers to the 8 miles of river from Little Hole to the boat ramp at Indian Crossing in Brown's Park. The "C Section" is approximately 17 miles of river from Indian Crossing to the Utah/Colorado State Line.

A Section: This section has the highest density of fish, consistently clear water, and the easiest access. Not surprisingly, it has most of the fishing pressure as well as the vast majority of recreational boaters. If you would rather not share the river with others, plan your trip for off-season (October to March), fish mid-week, or

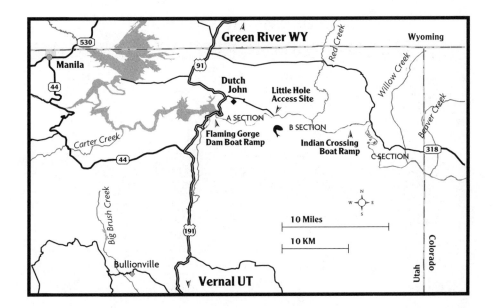

plan to be on the water either earlier or later than the majority of anglers.

About one quarter of a mile east of Flaming Gorge Dam a paved road leads to a parking area and boat ramp. A maintained foot trail goes from here to the next access at Little Hole, a distance of 7 miles. The trail can be reached from the south end of the upper parking area or from the boat ramp.

If you are launching a watercraft, prepare everything in the upper parking area, as there is a limited amount of room at the boat launch. Make sure you have necessary safety equipment, such as a spare oar or paddle, bail bucket or pump, and an approved Personal Flotation Device (PFD) type 3 or better for all passengers plus a spare. There are several large Class II to III rapids on this section of the river. Make sure that your skills and your watercraft are adequate.

B Section: The "B Section" still has a strong population of fish and considerably fewer anglers. The water will be clear for the first 3 miles, but after Red Creek it may be too muddy to fish, depending on runoff. Floating anglers can make a full day of these first 3 miles, but all the fishers in this section will be concentrated here if Red Creek is known to be running.

To reach Little Hole and the beginning of the B Section, from US 191 turn east on Little Hole Road, 0.1 miles north of the turnoff to Dutch John. Six miles of paved road will take you to the access site. The foot trail from the dam continues down river another 2.7 miles to Trails End.

There are three boat ramps here, but it is still a good idea to rig your watercraft as completely as possible before backing down to the water. Most rapids on this

Green River Fly Selection

INSECT	DRY FLY	NYMPH	SIZE
Ants and Beetles	CDC Ant Black Fur Ant Parachute Ant	None	10 to 24
Blue-Wing Olive (Mayfly)	Parachute Adams Comparadun No Hackles Quigley Cripple	Hare's Ear Pheasant Ear WD-40 RS-2	18 to 22
Caddisfly	Hemingway Caddis Goddard Caddis	Brassie Sparkle Pupae	
Cicada	Mutant Ninja Cicada Chernobyl Ant Madam X Hopper Patterns	None	6 to 12
Cranefly	Double Ugly	Sandy Translucent	2 to 8 x-long
Hoppers	Daves Hopper Para-Hopper Chernobyl Ant	None	10 to 4 x-long shank
Midge	Griffith's Gnat Grizzly Midge Double Hackle Fuzz Ball	Brassie Midge Emergers Serendipity	18 to 28
Pale Morning Dun (Mayfly)	Comparadun (light) Sparkle Dun No Hackle (lt. yellow)	Hare's Ear Pheasant Tail Floating Nymph	16 to 20
Scuds	None	Olive Grayish/Olive Sand & Orange	14 to 24
Trico (Mayfly)	Black Spinner Harrop's Emerger Quigley Cripple	Pheasant Tail WD-40	20 to 26

Courtesy of Emmett Heath and Western Rivers Flyfisher

section are Class I, but Red Creek is Class III. If you are not prepared to negotiate a large, powerful rapid with many rocks and obstacles, or line your craft around it, you should avoid this section. Once you have safely passed Red Creek Rapids, you may remove your PFD.

Note: While this section is only 8 miles by river, the shuttle route is over 40 miles, much of it dirt that requires 4-wheel-drive in wet weather and can become impassable in extreme weather. Also, any substantial flow in Red Creek can make the last 4 miles of this section unfishable.

C Section: The fishing in Brown's Park is the most variable. On a good day here you can catch many fish that will average even larger than those in the upper portion of the river and you may not see another angler. A bad day might mean few if any trout to catch or land while fighting wind and dirty water.

Brown's Park Road parallels this section and there are several access points along it. From Dutch John, go north on US 191, go right at the turnoff marked "Clay Basin" and "Brown's Park." It is about 26 miles to the river from here. There are several turns and forks; just stay on the main road. There is a newly paved section, but most of the road is dirt and Clay Basin is aptly named. When wet, the road becomes slick quickly and 4-wheel-drive is a must. Travel here should be avoided in extremely wet conditions.

One can also reach Brown's Park from Vernal by way of Diamond Mountain. From US 40 in Vernal, turn north onto US 191 (Vernal Ave.). Turn right at the sign for Diamond Mountain and Brown's Park. Stay left at the junction that appears in about 3 miles, stay left at the Y, another 4.5 miles ahead. It will be about 25 miles before you reach the left turn to Brown's Park. Stay on this road through Crouse Canyon and cross into Colorado before crossing the Green on Swinging Bridge. Turn left at the junction to cross back into Utah.

GPS Coordinates

Flaming Gorge Dam Boat Ramp	N 40° 54′ 45″ W 109° 25′ 14″
Little Hole Access Site	N 40° 54′ 42″ W 109° 18′ 45″
Indian Crossing Boat Ramp	N 40° 53′ 48″ W 109° 11′ 02″

Maps

USGS 1:24000   Dutch John, Goslin Mountain, Clay Basin, Warren Draw, Swallow Canyon

Utah Atlas and Gazetteer   Page 57

*Greg Pearson
with a big hybrid
that chased down
an 8-inch
streamer.*
(PHOTO: STEVE COOK)

When to Go

The blue-winged olive hatch is the first really productive hatch of the year. It generally starts at the end of March. By April, the hatch is becoming fairly consistent, with any overcast or rainy afternoon producing excellent dry fly-fishing from Secret Riffle to Washboard Rapid. When the blue-wings start to fade in late May, the cicadas begin to show up and can be very important through June. These large terrestrial insects have a cyclic population, so they can vary a great deal from year to year. The dog days of July and August can find the Green a bit slower; but afternoon hatches of caddis on the A section, midmorning PMDs in Brown's Park, and hopper and ant fishing down the entire river can all be rewarding.

Flows above 4,000 CFS can be difficult for wading anglers and the bridge at Indian Crossing (C section) can be impassable to anglers floating the river. Fishing can be difficult for one to three days after a major change in flows. In recent years, an effort has been made to change flows gradually, as abrupt changes are detrimental to fishing. When flows are stable, fishing can be good at a wide range of levels. ◆

Services

National Forest Campgrounds:

tel: (877) 444-6777 or (800) 280-2267
Greendale
Dripping Springs

Guides & Outfitters —
Permittee Ashley National Forest:

Anglers Inn
2292 S. Highland Drive
Salt Lake City, UT 84106
tel: (801) 466-3921 / (888) 426-4466
www.anglersfly.com

Big Foot Fly Shop
38 N 400 W
Vernal, UT 84078
tel: (435) 789-4960
(fly-fishing equipment only)

Green Rivers Outfitters
P.O. Box 200
Dutch John, UT 84023
tel: (435) 885-3338
fax: (435) 885-3370
www.utah-greenriver.com
e-mail: greenriver@cisna.com

Old Moe Guide Services
P.O. Box 308
Dutch John, UT 84023
tel and fax: (435) 885-3342
www.quickbyte.com/oldmoe
e-mail: gwerning@union-tel.com

Spinner Fall Fly Shop
2645 East Parley's Way
Salt Lake City, UT 84109
tel: (801) 466-5801 / (800) 959-3474
fax: (801) 466-3029
www.spinnerfall.com

Trout Creek Flies
P.O. Box 247
Dutch John, UT 84023
tel: (435) 885-3355 / (800) 835-4551
fax: (435) 885-3356
www.fishgreenriver.com
e-mail: info@fishgreenriver.com

Western Rivers Flyfisher
1071 East 900 South
SLC, UT 84105
tel: (801) 521-6424 / (800) 545-4312
fax: (801) 521-6329
www.wrflyfisher.com
e-mail: westriv@xmission.com

Lodging:

Flaming Gorge Lodge
155 Greendale, US 191
Dutch John, UT 84023
tel: (435) 889-3773
fax: (435) 889-3788
www.fglodge.com
e-mail: lodge@fglodge.com
(guide service, fly shop)

Red Canyon Lodge
790 Red Canyon Rd.
Dutch John, UT 84023
tel: (435) 889-3759
fax: (435) 889-5106

Green River Hatch Chart

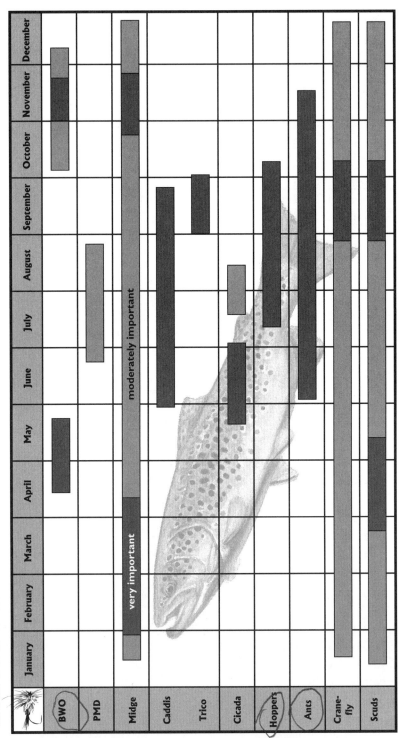

	January	February	March	April	May	June	July	August	September	October	November	December
BWO												
PMD												
Midge		very important					moderately important					
Caddis												
Trico												
Cicada												
Hoppers												
Ants												
Crane-fly												
Scuds												

Courtesy of Emmett Heath and Western Rivers Flyfisher

Ring-side seating. (PHOTO: EMMETT HEATH / WESTERN RIVERS FLYFISHER)

A fish of a lifetime. (PHOTO: DENNIS BREER / TROUT CREEK FLIES)

Huntington Creek   EMERY COUNTY

T his is a rich and productive stretch of water with a wide variety of opportunities for the fishing family. Several nearby reservoirs provide good fishing. There are many streams in the area, some larger, some smaller, and there are also different regulations from fly-only to bait-fishing. With the addition of several campgrounds, this locale is a trout angler's paradise.

The fairly strict trophy regulations on the upper section below the dam are designed to help this small stream produce some large trout. Harvest of fish under 12 inches is an important part of the DWR's management plan. Fly-fishers on the stretch from Flood and Engineers Canyons upstream to Electric Lake Dam are encouraged to keep a legal limit of fish.

This is one of the few sections in the state where the regulations are artificial flies only. "Artificial fly" means a fly made by the method known as fly-tying. "Artificial fly" does not mean a weighted jig, lure, spinner, attractor blade, or bait. Spinning rods may still be employed; the regulation refers to the terminal tackle.

As SR 31 from Fairview to Huntington is kept clear all year, this is a good winter destination. Driving up on a sunny winter's day and catching handsome brown trout in chest-deep snow is one of the best ways to combat cabin fever.

Fish Species

Brown trout are predominant, especially below Electric Lake. There are rainbows and cutthroat as well. The Left Fork has some larger cutthroat, especially in its lower reaches.

Special Regulations

Right Fork (from Flood and Engineers Canyons upstream to Electric Lake Dam):

❑ Artificial flies only.

❑ All trout 12 to 20 inches must be released immediately.

❑ Only 1 trout over 20 inches.

Tributaries to Electric Lake (streams only; this excludes Boulger Reservoir):

❑ Artificial flies and lures only.

❑ **Closed** January 1 through 6 a.m. on the second Saturday of July (July 10, 1999).

❑ Trout limit, 4; all trout over 12 inches must be released immediately.

Left Fork (from the top of USFS Campground, near confluence with Right Fork to headwaters, including all tributaries — Scad Valley Creek, Rolfson Creek, Lake Creek, Staker Creek, Millers Flat Creek, Paradise Creek, and Spring Creek):

❏ Artificial flies and lures only.

❏ Closed to the possession of cutthroat trout or trout with cutthroat markings.

❏ All other trout species limit, 8.

Tactics

The first mile of Huntington Creek below Electric Lake provides some nice midge fishing through the winter. There is some deep, slow water immediately below the dam that fishes well with small wooly buggers and other streamer patterns. Be prepared for some large fish here. Farther down you'll find some faster water, which will fish well with attractors and caddis during the summer months when water levels are reasonable.

The Left Fork is primarily a summer stream. Expect good results with stimulators and trudes. In the meadow areas farther up, terrestrials such as ants and hoppers should be effective in late summer. This section also has some very large October caddis in the fall.

Spin-fishers can use weighted nymphs drifted along the bottom of pools in the fly-only stretch. A muddler minnow fished with a split shot above can be a deadly tactic when used by experienced anglers. Bait-fishing is allowed from Engineers Canyon downstream. Drifted salmon eggs and half night crawlers are favorites. Look for fish in the bigger pools.

How to Get There

From Spanish Fork, take US 6 & 89 east to the junction near the flooded town of Thistle. Continue south 29 miles on US 89 to Fairview, and then east 22 miles on SR 31 towards Huntington. You will pass Huntington and Cleveland Reservoirs before reaching Huntington Creek just below the dam at Electric Lake.

One can also reach Huntington Creek from the town of Huntington, by traveling northwest on SR 31.

Accessibility

As Huntington Creek follows SR 31 down the canyon, access is very easy with several handy turnouts. There is some private land farther down the canyon.

The Left Fork of Huntington is best accessed from the Forks of Huntington USFS Campground about 10 miles down the canyon from Electric Lake Dam. There is a well-maintained trail that goes up along the creek.

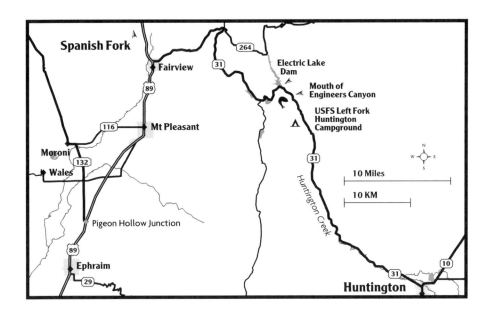

GPS Coordinates

Electric Lake Dam	N 39° 36' 02" W 111° 12' 39"
Mouth of Engineers Canyon	N 39° 33' 42" W 111° 10' 29"
USFS Left Fork Huntington Campground	N 39° 30' 03" W 111° 09' 35"

Maps

USGS 1:24000   Candland Mountain, Huntington Reservoir, Scofield, Rilda Canyon, Hiawatha, Red Point, Huntington

Utah Atlas and Gazetteer   Page 38, 46

When to Go

Good fishing can be found here most of the year if you are willing to brave the elements. Electric Lake is above 8,500 feet elevation, so be prepared for changeable weather and cold nights.

We have been fishing here in near blizzard conditions in winter and the road crews do an incredible job of keeping the road clear. Make sure you park where you will not hinder their work.

Late April and early May, depending on weather, will be the peak of runoff with the worst water conditions. As there are several small drainages entering Huntington Creek just below the dam, one might fish other tailwaters at lower elevations until the water here has had time to clear. ▼

Jones Hole Creek   UINTAH COUNTY

T here is good fishing, with a chance for really large fish, a good hiking trail, and a chance to view ancient Indian rock art. The scenic canyon is narrow with high, sheer walls and massive sandstone panels. The stream rises from springs at the hatchery and is crystal clear and cold most of the year. Shade trees in the canyon and the babbling waters make for peaceful, pleasant afternoons.

Anglers will be interested in the U.S. Fish & Wildlife Service fish hatchery at the head of the stream. Visitors are invited to walk among the outside raceways and visit the main hatchery building.

Fish Species

Rainbow, brown, brook, and cutthroat trout. Some very large trout occasionally move into the creek from the Green River.

Special Regulations

❏ Artificial flies and lures only.

❏ Trout limit, 2; no more than 1 may be a brown trout larger than 15 inches.

Tactics

Jones Hole Creek is small, with clear water and a rapid flow. Trout are spooky and only the stealthy angler will be rewarded. As the trail passes close to the stream in many spots, it's not a bad idea to get on the water early before there is much foot traffic.

There are few pools — it's mainly riffle and pocket water fishing. Effective spin-fishing is difficult. Large terrestrials or weighted nymphs cast into the slack behind rocks or next to the bank can be effective. Cicadas can be found here in May of some years and will encourage trout to let down their guard. Hoppers and large ants work well as summer advances.

Early season will find a few large rainbows up from the Green River to spawn. Look for them just above the confluence and in the Green itself, where Jones Hole Creek dumps in.

Most of the fish in this creek are from 10 to 14 inches, but there are always some large browns in residence.

How to Get There

Jones Hole Creek is located about 30 miles east of Vernal. From downtown Vernal, take US 191 north to 500 North Street, then drive east 3 miles on 500 North Street. Take the left (north) fork of Brush Creek Road and go northeast 21 miles. Go east 11 miles on Jones Hole Road to the hatchery. When in doubt just follow the main road; it is rough in spots, but still suitable for a passenger car. The route takes you up over Diamond Mountain.

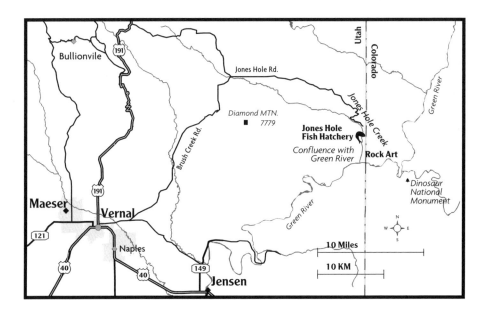

Accessibility

Most of the stream is just inside Dinosaur National Monument, on the Utah side of the Utah/Colorado border. The trail begins at the lower end of the hatchery and is easy to spot. Just follow the water, walking past the hatchery runways. Dogs are not allowed in the hatchery or the canyon. There are about 4 miles of stream before it enters the Green River.

Rock art panels are located about 2 miles down the trail below the hatchery, near the mouth of Big Draw. They are on the west side of the canyon. Look for them immediately after the wooden bridge where the trail crosses the stream. Signs and well-used side trails lead the way. There is also an overhang where there was an ancient structure. The art is mostly in the form of pictographs — figures painted onto the rock. These pictographs represent the work of several cultures over a long time period. Some figures are faded and barely visible. Others are bold, vivid, and easy to see.

GPS Coordinates

Jones Hole Fish Hatchery	N 40° 35' 16" W 109° 03' 23"
Confluence with Green River	N 40° 32' 25" W 109° 03' 35"

Maps

USGS 1:24000   Jones Hole

Utah Atlas and Gazetteer   Page 57

When to Go

The road to the hatchery is generally open during the winter, but may close for periods after storms. Spring and summer are ideal times to explore this area. Summer days are hot, but most hiking is in the shade along the stream and is pleasant even during warm weather.

Jones Hole Creek is primarily spring-fed, and normally runs clear. Water levels will rise and discoloring occurs during periods of high snow melt or after heavy rains. Fishing should be good from May through October, with May being the best month. ◆

Services

Camping:

Red Fleet State Park
Vernal
tel: (435) 789-4432
Reservations: (800) 322-3770
(In Salt Lake City, call 322-3770)

Guides & Outfitters:

Big Foot Fly Shop
38 N 400 W
Vernal, UT 84078
tel: (435) 789-4960

Lake Fork River   DUCHESNE COUNTY

ake Fork is a high Uinta river that has its descent interrupted by Moon Lake, a man-made reservoir. Moon Lake Lodge provides comfortable, rustic accommodations for visitors who don't wish to camp.

The river below Moon Lake Dam is subject to very high flows in summer, often followed by extremely low or no water release in the fall, greatly reducing its potential as a fishery.

Fish Species

Rainbow, cutthroat, brown, and brook trout.

Special Regulations

General season, bag, and possession limits apply on public lands.

The lower portions of Lake Fork are on the Uintah and Ouray Indian Reservation. A fishing permit is $50.00/season or $10.00/day plus a $10.00 conservation stamp. Regulations are subject to frequent change, so contact the tribal office at (435) 722-5511 before you make plans to fish tribal lands. The *Utah Atlas and Gazetteer* displays reservation boundaries.

Note: The Ute Plaza Supermarket in Fort Duchesne sells fishing permits for Ute Tribal Lands. They can be reached at (435) 722-3282.

Brown Duck Basin (Duchesne County) Uinta Mountains — all streams in the Brown Duck Basin and the outlet of Clements Reservoir to its confluence with Lake Fork Creek:

❏ **Closed** January 1 through 6 a.m. on the second Saturday of July (July 10, 1999).

Tactics

The trout above Moon Lake have a short season in which to feed and grow. They are generally happy to eat what is put in front of them as long as they have not been spooked.

Fly-fishers will find yellow stimulators effective in the early season as there are usually some small golden stoneflies hatching at this time. Grasshoppers, royal Wulffs, renegades, humpies and gray-hackle-yellows are all good patterns. A Moser is an unusual local wet fly with a black acetate body.

Small spinners are a good choice, as are drifting worms or Power Bait in the deeper holes. Small spoons tipped with dead minnows may produce a splake or two in the holes just above Moon Lake.

When the river below Moon Lake is fishable, grasshoppers are capable of producing big brown trout. Try muddler minnows, spinners, or worms as well.

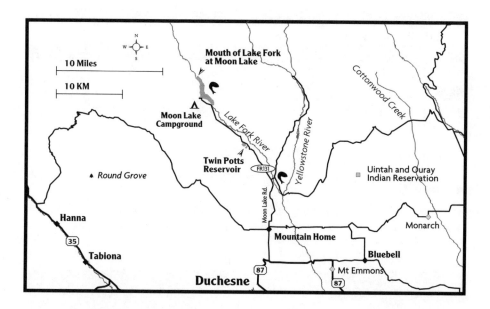

How to Get There

From Mountain Home, go north on Moon Lake Road, which becomes FR 131.

Accessibility

Access to the river above Moon Lake is by trail from the Moon Lake Campground or by boat. It is 3 miles to the mouth of Lake Fork, where it enters Moon Lake. The entire river above the lake lies within the boundaries of Ashley National Forest.

Below the reservoir are national forest lands, private land (Fisher Ranch), and tribal lands (see **Special Regulations**). Access is from Moon Lake Road. The dam at Moon Lake is operated for irrigation, meaning there are high flows during the growing season and virtually no water released the rest of the year. For these reasons, this section of the river is fishable only in the fall and you need to be far enough below the dam (6 miles or more) for other drainages to provide sufficient water to sustain fish. In the past, some large brown trout have been caught below the confluence with Yellowstone Creek on tribal lands.

You will pass Twin Potts, which is a popular lake fishing destination on tribal lands. Just north of the national forest boundary and east of the road are some beaver ponds that can provide some nice fishing.

GPS Coordinates

Moon Lake Campground	N 40° 34' 09" W 110° 30' 33"
Mouth of Lake Fork at Moon Lake	N 40° 35' 57" W 110° 31' 07"
Twin Potts Reservoir	N 40° 30' 34" W 110° 25' 53"

Maps

USGS 1:24000   Oweep Creek, Kidney Lake, Lake Fork Mountain, Mountain Home

Utah Atlas and Gazetteer   Page 55

When to Go

Above Moon Lake, good fishing can be had from July through September. Water below the reservoir is fishable only from mid-September through October. ◆

Summertime on Lake Fork River. (PHOTO: STEVE SCHMIDT / WESTERN RIVERS FLYFISHER)

Logan River

L ogan River drains over 200 square miles and provides roughly 30 miles of easily accessible roadside trout fishing. Many years ago this river produced a 37¾ pound brown trout from the First Dam Reservoir. While there are no guarantees that fish this big are currently living in the system, there are still some large fish to be had.

This is also a good side trip for families vacationing at Bear Lake. There are numerous recreational opportunities at the lake such as sailboating, scuba diving, jet skiing, golfing, and more fishing. It is only 16 miles from Bear Lake to the Franklin Basin Road on US 89.

Fish Species

Rainbow, cutthroat, brown, and brook trout.

Special Regulations

From Card Canyon Bridge downstream to Cutler Marsh including all 3 impoundments:

❏ Trout limit, 4.

Card Canyon Bridge upstream to the highway bridge at Red Banks Campground, including all tributaries in between:

❏ Artificial flies and lures only.

❏ For licensed anglers, the limit for any combination of trout and whitefish is 3 (2 fish under 12 inches and 1 over 18 inches) and only 1 trout may be a cutthroat, rainbow, or their hybrid cross. All other fish must be released immediately.

❏ For unlicensed anglers 13 years of age or younger, the limit for any combination of trout and whitefish is 2 (2 under 12 inches, or 1 under 12 inches and 1 over 18 inches), and only 1 trout may be a cutthroat, rainbow, or their hybrid cross. All other fish must be released immediately.

From the highway bridge at Red Banks Campground upstream to the Idaho state line, including all tributaries:

❏ **Closed** January 1 through 6 a.m. on the second Saturday of July (July 10, 1999).

❑ For licensed anglers, the limit for any combination of trout and whitefish is 3 (2 under 12 inches and 1 over 18 inches), and only 1 trout may be a cutthroat, rainbow, or their hybrid cross. All other fish must be released immediately.

❑ For unlicensed anglers 13 years of age or younger, the limit for any combination of trout and whitefish is 2 (2 under 12 inches, or 1 under 12 inches and 1 over 18 inches), and only 1 trout may be a cutthroat, rainbow, or their hybrid cross.

It is unclear if the cutthroat trout in the Logan River are the original Bonneville strain or Yellowstone, which are believed to have been stocked. Both strains are being considered for protection under the Endangered Species Act. It is important for the DWR to show that native cutthroat are being protected or the federal government could take over control of the river if these strains are granted protection under the Endangered Species Act.

Tactics

The impoundments in the extreme lower canyon, called 1st, 2nd, and 3rd dams, are stocked with rainbows throughout the summer. Fishing there can be fast.

Note: The DWR released more than 40,000 catchable rainbow trout into the Logan River on the last day of June 1998. This program is likely to be repeated each year, making the Logan a good place to take your young anglers for Memorial Day or the Fourth of July holiday. The Logan above the impoundments is basically a wild-trout fishery. Both browns and cutthroat reproduce well in the stream, making stocking unnecessary.

Look for good fishing on caddis patterns beginning in mid-July. You should find large numbers of fish that will eat elk hair caddis and stimulator patterns, particularly in the Franklin Basin area. Caddis make up the bulk of the fish's diet and imitations produce strikes long after the naturals are no longer available. The fish are so accustomed to seeing caddis that they will take imitations almost year-round.

Blue-wings and midge patterns also work well, even when the weather turns cold. Standard pheasant tail and chamois caddis nymphs and cased caddis are particularly good.

Fall is one of the best times to go after big browns in the Logan River because browns spawn in the late fall and early winter. They become aggressive and readily attack minnow-imitating flies and lures. Look for the largest fish in the lower third of the river. Muddlers, zonkers, wooly buggers and other large patterns are very effective.

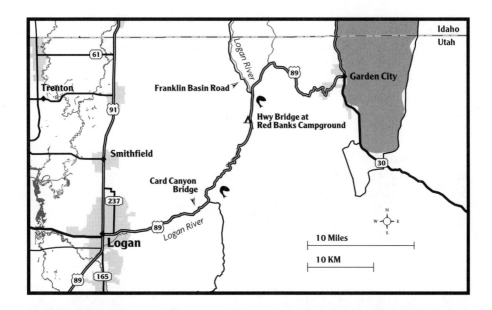

Panther Martins and other spinners also work well. Cast them upstream and reel them quickly through holes. Small Rapalas and other minnow plugs can be effective as well.

How to Get There

From Logan, go northeast on US 89.

Accessibility

US 89 follows the river for most of its length. It is easily accessible from the several campgrounds, picnic areas, and turnouts. Where US 89 departs the Logan River, the Franklin Basin Road continues up to the Idaho state line.

GPS Coordinates

Card Canyon Bridge	N 41° 45′ 57″ W 111° 39′ 58″
Hwy Bridge at Red Bank Campground	N 41° 53′ 49″ W 111° 33′ 50″
Franklin Basin Road	N 41° 55′ 60″ W 111° 33′ 57″

Maps

USGS 1:24000   Logan, Logan Peak, Mount Elmer, Temple Peak, Tony Grove Creek

Utah Atlas and Gazetteer   Pages 60, 61, 63

When to Go

The best time to fish here is after runoff as the water starts to recede. This is mid-June in most years. You should find good fishing throughout the summer. September and October are the best months. ◆

Services

Camping:

Beaver Mountain RV Park
Logan Canyon - US 189
tel: (435) 753-0921
fax: (435) 753-0975

Riverside RV Park/Campgrounds
Logan, 1 mi S on US 89
tel: (435) 245-4469

Lodging:

Beaver Creek Lodge
11808 N US 89
P.O. Box 277
Logan, UT 84028
tel: (800) 946-4485
www.beavercreeklodge.com

Cutthroat trout. (PHOTO: EMMETT HEATH / WESTERN RIVERS FLYFISHER)

Lost Creek   MORGAN COUNTY

T here are good numbers of fish here, but access is very restricted due to adjacent private land. Lost Creek Reservoir was drained so repairs can be made to the dam. This resulted in an increase in stream flow sediment and may have adversely affected the fishery.

The best fishing is on the accessible portion just above the reservoir. There is a subspecies of native Bonneville cutthroat trout here.

Fish Species

Rainbow and cutthroat trout.

Special Regulations

Lost Creek (Morgan County) — the entire drainage upstream, beginning at the bridge (culvert) approximately .25 mile above Lost Creek Reservoir, except Squaw Creek:

❑ Artificial flies and lures only.

❑ Catch and release only.

Lost Creek Reservoir:

❑ **Closed** 1999.

Tactics

Anglers should do well with most dry-fly patterns for smaller fish. Small spinners and jigs should also prove effective.

Try caddisfly and stonefly imitations immediately below the reservoir — these were successful patterns before the reservoir was drained.

How to Get There

From I-84 take Exit 117 and go northeast on North Lost Creek Road to Lost Creek Reservoir.

Accessibility

There is a half-mile section open to the public above the reservoir. Above this section, there is no public access as the land is owned by the Deseret Land and Livestock Company. The road going to the upper end of the reservoir is currently closed until the future of the state park is decided.

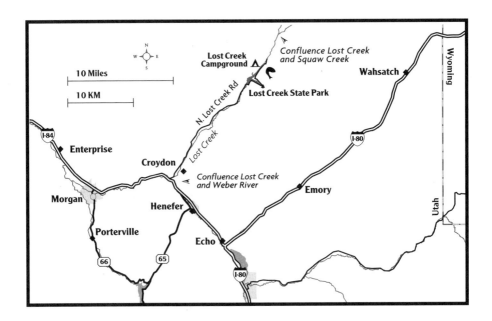

There is also public access immediately below the dam. Beyond this section, the remainder of the creek is private. Be sure to get permission before crossing private property.

GPS Coordinates

Confluence Lost Creek and Weber River	N 41° 03' 37" W 111° 32' 19"
Lost Creek State Park	N 41° 11' 09" W 111° 22' 52"
Lost Creek Campground	N 41° 12' 47" W 111° 22' 00"
Confluence Lost Creek and Squaw Creek	N 41° 14' 32" W 111° 20' 47"

Maps

USGS 1:24000   Peck Canyon, Francis Canyon, Lost Creek Dam, Henefer, Devils Slide

Utah Atlas and Gazetteer   Page 61

When to Go

July to October. ♦

Ogden River

Weber County

his is a productive river with large numbers of brown trout. The DWR estimates there may be as many as 5,000 trout per mile in Ogden Canyon. This section of river would benefit from some harvest.

The downside of fishing here is the difficult access, as there are many summer homes in the canyon quite close to the river. There really isn't any place to fish the Ogden in solitude, but there are some nice fish.

This river is known to harbor whirling disease. Please read the whirling disease section on page 36 to ensure that you don't help to spread this disease.

Fish Species

Rainbow, cutthroat, brown trout, and whitefish.

Special Regulations

Ogden River from the first bridge on Canyon Road (SR 39, mouth of Ogden Canyon) downstream to the confluence with Weber River:

❐ Trout limit, 4.

Ogden River from Pineview Dam downstream to the first bridge (about 0.5 mile):

❐ **Closed.**

Tactics

Fly-fishers can have good success with blue-winged olive patterns in April and May if water levels are not too high. There can be good midge hatches in the canyon in February and March, but snow makes parking and moving up and down the river even more difficult.

Fishing with egg imitations in November is effective, but it is also stressful to fish at a time when they are already vulnerable. There was a small fish kill in the fall of 1998 due to spawning stress. If you fish for spawning fish, consider keeping what you catch. There is not much point in catching and releasing large numbers of fish, only to have many of them succumb to stress later.

How to Get There

From I-15 just north of Ogden, take Exit 347 and go east 5 miles on SR 39.

To reach the Ogden River Parkway, turn south on Monroe from SR 39 (3.3 miles east of I-15). Turn into the park on your left just after the bridge.

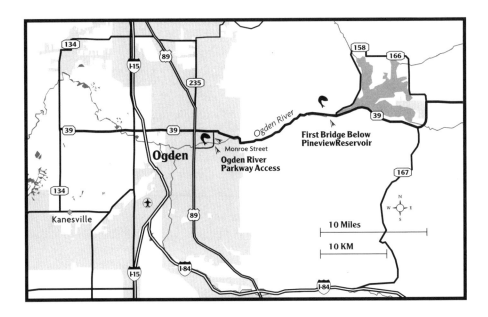

Accessibility

SR 39 follows the Ogden River up Ogden Canyon. There is much private property and limited access to the river. Once you find a spot to get in the river, you will have to stay in. Please remember to be considerate, as the river runs through the backyards of others.

The Ogden River Parkway follows the river through town and anglers can walk up and down the river easily on this paved trail. If you decide to fish here in town, expect an urban angling experience. Quite a bit of work has been done adding structures to the river, which provide holding water for some nice fish.

GPS Coordinates

First Bridge below Pineview Reservoir	N 41° 15' 13" W 111° 50' 58"
Ogden River Parkway Access	N 41° 14' 07" W 111° 57' 12"

Maps

USGS 1:24000   Huntsville, North Ogden, Ogden

Utah Atlas and Gazetteer   Pages 60, 61

When to Go

High water will normally occur in May, but the river level can vary with power demands. Best time to fish here will be in the autumn and early winter. ♦

Price River (Lower Fish Creek)   CARBON AND UTAH COUNTIES

O ne of my first fishing trips in Utah was in late September on this section of the Price River below the dam. The overall quality of the fishing experience was unbeatable. Being alone in this lovely canyon except for the ducks and deer is something every fisher should be exposed to. The fishing that day was great as trout after trout slammed my small spinner with abandon. Repeat trips to the area have confirmed that, more often than not, fishing here will live up to one's expectations.

This is a great place to fish because of the access. If you park at the dam, it is a pleasant stroll down the railroad tracks to the area you want to fish. With no roads or traffic in the canyon it is a very peaceful place.

There are also some very large fish here. A friend caught a brown trout below the dam that he estimated at 12 pounds.

The Price River may be negatively impacted by implementation of the proposed Narrows Reservoir Project. Winter flows will likely be reduced below current levels. The Division of Wildlife Resources (DWR) is trying to guarantee minimum flows by purchasing water rights.

Fish Species

Brown trout are predominant with rainbows and cutthroat as well.

Special Regulations

From the bridge approximately one mile below Scofield Reservoir Dam downstream to the confluence with the White River:

◻ Artificial flies and lures only.

◻ Trout limit, 4.

Tactics

With no special regulations on the first mile of the river, this is a good place to take children. There are always snakes to catch and other adventures to be had if young anglers tire of fishing.

The first mile is mostly slow water. You will see some fish feeding on top here, but small streamer flies or spinners are often the best offering.

As you walk downstream past the first railroad bridge, the river changes character abruptly. It begins to twist and turn with many riffles and pools. Where the river runs up against the railroad grade you will find large rocks and other interesting structures.

Below the confluence of the White River and US 6, much of the river is too steep for fish to find much holding water. Where the current is slow enough for them, they will be concentrated.

Grasshoppers and caddis imitations work well in summer here. In October, there can be some incredible concentrations of fish in some of the pools 100 yards or so below the first railroad bridge 1 mile east of the dam.. Hare's ear nymphs and orange scuds work very well at times like this.

On sunny fall days, the smallest sizes of Panther Martin or Mepps spinners can move a surprising number of fish in this river.

If you are in the first mile below the dam or below the White River, bait offerings of salmon eggs, night crawlers or Power Bait will not likely be ignored. Use a float to keep bait off the bottom in the weedy sections of the river.

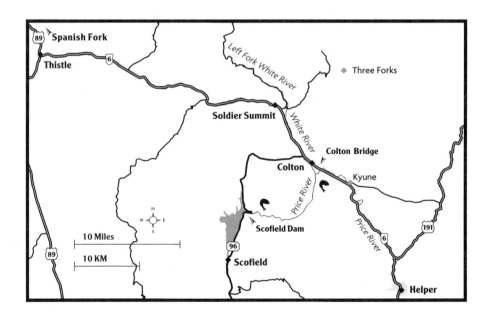

How to Get There

From Spanish Fork, take US 6 southeast towards Price. Turn south on SR 96 just past Soldier Summit at the sign for Scofield Reservoir. Continue about 13 miles to reach the dam and use the parking area just below it.

You can also continue along US 6 until you cross the Price River just below its confluence with the White River.

Accessibility

The best access is below the dam. From here, the Denver and Rio Grande Railroad runs through the canyon and follows the river, which makes for easy walking up and down the canyon. The best fishing is after the first mile.

Anglers can also come up from the bridge where US 6 crosses the Price River. Watch for the signs for DWR access south of the Colton Bridge.

There are several places to reach the river from US 6 as it parallels the Price River through the canyon. Much of the river is very steep here. Look for areas with lower gradient, where fish will be very concentrated. Much of this section is on private property, but access to unposted areas doesn't seem to be a problem. Be sure to respect private property and ask for permission if you have any doubts.

Some habitat improvements have been made at the Helper Parkway (where the river flows through Helper). Fish densities are up to 1,100 fish-per-mile. Access to this water is very easy and few anglers take advantage of it.

GPS Coordinates

Scofield Dam	N 39° 47′ 12″ W 111° 07′ 09″
Colton Bridge (US6 and Price River)	N 39° 50′ 38″ W 110° 59′ 46″

Maps

USGS 1:24000   Colton, Kyune, Standardville, Helper

Utah Atlas and Gazetteer   Page 46

When to Go

This river fishes well from June through October. Even November can be great when the weather stays warm. Scofield Dam is at about 7,600 feet elevation and so weather can change quickly while you are in the canyon. Make sure you are prepared before you leave your vehicle. ◆

Provo River

SUMMIT, UTAH AND
WASATCH COUNTIES

T his river is relatively short — approximately 50 miles from its headwaters until it enters Utah Lake. However, its high quality fishing and proximity to Salt Lake City and Provo make it one of the state's most important fisheries.

There are three distinctly different sections of the Provo River. This guide divides them as follows:

The Upper Provo River begins in the Uinta Mountains as a small freestone stream. Its character changes gradually until it reaches Heber Valley.

Jordanelle Reservoir momentarily stops the river's descent, and when it leaves the dam as the Middle Provo, it has a new look. It runs through agricultural and grazing lands. The riverbed has been altered by numerous diversions for irrigation. This does not detract from the river's visual appeal or fishing quality.

The river pauses again in Deer Creek Reservoir before making its final run to Utah Lake as the Lower Provo. The river must compete with US 189 for space, and consequently, a lengthy road construction project can cause delays and distractions from the natural beauty of the canyon. The river then flows through Provo, enroute to Utah Lake.

Services

Camping:

Deer Creek Park Campground
Provo Canyon US 189
tel: (801) 225-9783

Jordanelle State Park
Hailstone — tel: (435) 645-9540
(12 N on US 40, Mayflower Exit)
Rock Cliff — tel: (435) 783-3030
(Francis, 2 mi W off SR 32)

Wasatch Mountain State Park
Midway tel: (435) 654-1791
For state park reservations —
tel: (800) 322-3770
(In Salt Lake City, call 322-3770)

Lodging:

Sundance Resort
RR 3 Box A-1
Sundance, UT 84604
tel: (435) 225- 4107 / (800) 892-1600
fax: (435) 226-1937
e-mail: sales@sundance-utah.com
website: www.sundance-utah.com

Guides & Outfitters:

Anglers Inn
2292 S. Highland Drive
Salt Lake City, UT 84106
tel: (801) 466-3921 / (888) 426-4466
www.anglersfly.com

Fish Tech
6153 Highland Dr.
Salt Lake City, UT 84121
tel: (801) 272-8808
fax: (801) 272-6935

Spinner Fall Fly Shop
2645 East Parley's Way
Salt Lake City, UT 84109
tel: (801) 466-5801 / (800) 959-3474
fax: (801) 466-3029
www.spinnerfall.com

Trout Bum 2
4343 N SR 225, Suite 101
Park City, UT 84098
tel: (435) 645-6611 / (877) 878-2862

Western Rivers Flyfisher
1071 East 900 South
SLC, UT 84105
tel: (801) 521-6424 / (800) 545-4312
fax: (801) 521-6329
www.wrflyfisher.com
e-mail: westriv@xmission.com

LOWER PROVO RIVER

Fish Species

Provo Canyon is still primarily a brown trout fishery with some rainbow and cut-throat. This section of the river also holds some very large mountain whitefish. Walleyes are found in the lowest reaches of the river during their spawning period.

Special Regulations

East from Center Street Bridge (entrance to Utah State Park) to I-15:

❑ Walleye limit, 2; only 1 over 20 inches.

❑ **Closed** to taking non-game fish by methods other than angling.

❑ **Closed** between 7 p.m. and 7 a.m. March 1 through 7 a.m. on the last Saturday of April (April 24, 1999).

❑ During this period, anglers may only use lures with one single hook. The single hook must be able to pass through a 9/16" opening.

Upstream from Olmstead Diversion Dam to Deer Creek Reservoir:

❑ Artificial flies and lures only.

❑ Brown trout limit is 2 under 15 inches.

❑ **Closed** to possession of cutthroat and rainbow trout. All rainbows and cut-throat trout and their hybrids must be released.

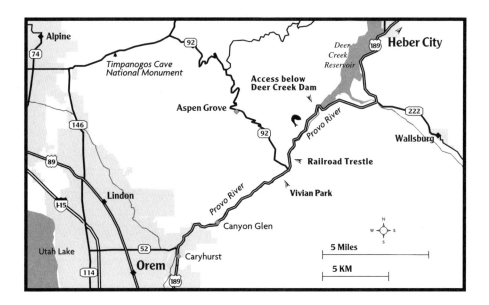

Tactics

The Lower Provo produces fish by a variety of methods. Fly-fishers can look for morning midge hatches beginning in February. Griffith gnats and mating midge patterns in sizes 18-20 fished on long, light leaders can bring up fish. Nymphing with hare's ears, pheasant tails, and sowbugs can also work well in the early season. March brings the blue-winged olive hatch. Parachute Adams and other dry and emergent mayfly patterns work well from mid-morning to mid-afternoon. Nymphing continues to be effective during this period.

Flows generally increase in May, and fishing/wading gets more difficult. Pale morning duns hatch in July and August, and flows usually taper down for the return of blue-winged olives in September. October and November are spawning months for the brown trout here.

Fish typically create spawning redds in shallow graveled areas and tail outs. These redds appear as light-colored circles on the bottom. Dead drifting glow bugs can be extremely effective, but it is very disruptive to spawning fish. **Avoid walking or fishing in these spawning areas.**

Spin-fishers use nymphs effectively on the Provo with a technique called "the bounce." One or two nymphs can be attached on droppers with the weight fastened at the bottom. The weight is bounced along the bottom on a tight line. The nymphs appear to drift suspended off the bottom and travel at roughly the speed of the current. Spinners and Rapala types of plugs are also effective here, especially as fall approaches. Bait-fishing is allowed below the Olmstead Diversion, and salmon eggs are a favorite.

How to Get There

Take I-15 to Orem, and take Exit 275 to US 189 to Provo Canyon. Continue east through town. This will put you on the Provo Canyon section of the Lower Provo. You can also reach this water from Heber City, traveling west on US 189.

Accessibility

There are a number of turnouts and parking areas on this section of the river. Some areas, particularly around the Deer Creek Campground, are posted. Respect private property. On-going road construction can create delays.

GPS Coordinates

Access below Deer Creek Dam	N 40° 24' 07" W 111° 31' 46"
Railroad Trestle	N 40° 22' 33" W 111° 33' 16"
Vivian Park	N 40° 21' 21" W 111° 34' 22"

Maps

USGS 1:24000   Provo, Orem, Bridal Veil Falls, Aspen Grove

Utah Atlas and Gazetteer   Page 53

When to Go

This is a great early season fishery if you can stand the cold. It fishes well from February until the water comes up, usually in May. Anglers willing to deal with high water can find success through the summer. As water is taken out at the Olmstead Diversion, the river is a little more manageable below here in the summer months. Fall colors combined with lower water make this a great place to fish in the fall. ◆

MIDDLE PROVO RIVER

Fish Species

In this section below Jordanelle Dam are mostly brown trout, with more rainbows as the river approaches Deer Creek Reservoir. In late fall through early spring, fish move up from the reservoir for spawning and there are more rainbows and some very large browns.

Special Regulations

From Charleston Bridge just above Deer Creek Reservoir upstream to the Jordanelle Dam, including the Valeo Diversion, the Wasatch Diversion and the streams that return flows from these diversions directly to the Provo River:

❒ Artificial flies and lures only.

❒ Brown trout limit is 2 under 15 inches.

❒ **Closed** to the possession of cutthroat and rainbow trout. All rainbow and cutthroat trout and their hybrids must be released.

Tactics

With the completion of Jordanelle Reservoir, this section is now a tail-water fishery, and, as a result, flows, water clarity, and temperature are all more consistent. The aquatic insects in the river have responded well, and with this larger food base, the fishing has improved markedly.

The "artificial only" regulation and some great hatches mean this section of river is well suited to the fly-fisher. Nymphing in the early season can be good, with a good chance of finding some large fish up from Deer Creek Reservoir.

In late June and early July, one can find golden stoneflies and green drakes hatching in good numbers and some very large fish feeding on the surface. This time period corresponds with fairly high flows, so exercise caution when wading.

One can find caddis hatches on summer evenings, but larger fish will generally be caught on nymphs. Tungsten bead head nymphs, size 12 and 14, in brown and olive are good choices. As fall approaches, look for blue-winged olive hatches in the afternoon. Good streamer fishing can also be had at this time. Try zonkers, articulated leaches, and wooly buggers.

Spin-fishers can do well using the bounce method described in the Lower Provo tactics. Minnow-type plugs and spinners become increasingly effective as pre-spawn fish become more territorial.

How to Get There

To reach the Middle Provo from Salt Lake City, take I-80 east to US 40. Go east on US 40 until you pass Jordanelle and cross the Provo River. A left turn on SR 32 and another quick left takes you to Jordanelle Dam. If you turn right from US 40, you will parallel the river on your way to Midway. You can also take US 189 from Provo or Heber and turn off to Midway, reaching the Middle Provo at Charleston Bridge.

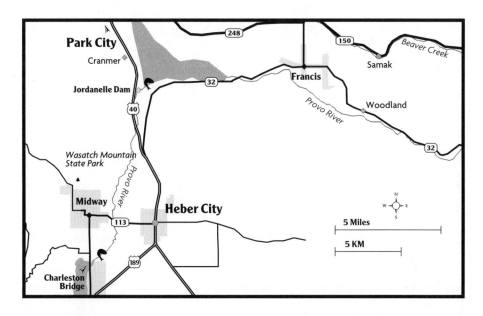

Accessibility

Much of this section has levees down both sides with two-track road on top, so walking up and down the river is very pleasant. Just make sure you leave all gates as you found them and respect private property. You can get on the river at Jordanelle Dam, the sports access between US 40 and the dam, and at the turnout where US 40 crosses the Provo. Also, where SR 113 crosses the Provo between Heber City and Midway, there is an access site next to a red barn on Casperville Road and at Charleston Bridge.

When to Go

If you are willing to brave the cold of the Heber Valley, this area is a good choice from February through April. You will want to avoid the high water that usually occurs from May to mid-June. This is a great destination for late summer fishing, and it is a beautiful place to stroll along the river, rod in hand, on an autumn day.

GPS Coordinates

Charleston Bridge	N 40° 28' 39" W 111° 28' 16"
Jordanelle Dam	N 40° 35' 49" W 111° 25' 28"

Maps

USGS 1:24000   Charleston, Heber City

Utah Atlas and Gazetteer   Page 54

UPPER PROVO RIVER

Fish Species

Brook, brown, rainbow, and cutthroat trout can all be found on this section of the Provo from headwaters in the Uintas to Jordanelle Reservoir.

Special Regulations

From Jordanelle Reservoir upstream to the confluence of the South Fork Provo River:

☐ Artificial flies and lures only.

☐ Brown trout limit is 2 under 15 inches.

☐ **Closed** to the possession of cutthroat and rainbow trout and their hybrids. All rainbow and cutthroat and their hybrids must be released.

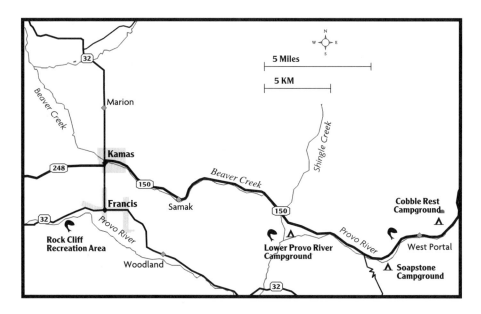

Tactics

This is the kind of simple fishing that many of us grew up with. The fly-fisher need only attach an attractor fly or caddis and cast upstream while wading. Look for fish in the heads and tails of pools.

Spin-fishers will do well with their favorite small spinner. Bait-fishing is allowed in much of this section, and salmon eggs or night crawlers drifted through the deeper pools are effective.

How to Get There

The Mirror Lake Hwy. (SR 150) follows the Upper Provo for several miles. From Salt Lake City, take I-80 east to US 40. Go east on US 40 to the turnoff for SR 248 to Kamas. At the stop in Kamas, take a left, then right onto SR 150, or go right at the stop and reach the Upper Provo at Francis.

Accessibility

For good access, try Rock Cliff Recreation Area on the Jordanelle Reservoir going upstream. There is quite a bit of private water around Francis. Respect private property. In the Soapstone area, the river is in the Wasatch Cache National Forest and the river parallels the Mirror Lake Hwy., so access is easy. This area is above the South Fork Provo, so bait-fishing is also allowed.

GPS Coordinates

Lower Provo River Campground	N 40° 35' 36" W 111° 06' 57"
Soapstone Campground	N 40° 34' 42" W 111° 01' 37"
Cobble Rest Campground	N 40° 35' 40" W 110° 58' 28"
Rock Cliff Recreation Area	N 40° 36' 17" W 111° 20' 45"

Maps

USGS 1:24000   Francis, Woodland, Soapstone Basin,
                      Iron Mine Mountain, Mirror Lake

Utah Atlas and Gazetteer   Page 54

When to Go

The best times on this stretch of river are from July, when water levels drop, to October. ◆

Rock Creek

T his stream is the perfect size for summer fly-fishing in shorts and wading boots. Very restrictive regulations on the tribal-controlled portions of Rock Creek will be relaxed somewhat in 1999, giving anglers a chance at water that has seen very little pressure in recent years.

There are some ponds by Lower Stillwater on Forest Service lands that can produce some large fish.

Fish Species

Rainbow, cutthroat, brown, and brook trout.

Special Regulations

General season, bag, and possession limits apply on public lands.

The lower portions of Rock Creek are on the Uintah and Ouray Indian Reservation. The length of Rock Creek on tribal lands will again be open to fishing in 1999. You will need a $10.00/day permit plus a $10.00 conservation stamp (season licenses will not be valid here). Regulations are subject to frequent change, so contact the tribal office at (435) 722-5511 before you make plans to fish tribal lands. The *Utah Atlas and Gazetteer* displays reservation boundaries.

Note: The Ute Plaza Supermarket in Fort Duchesne sells fishing permits for Ute Tribal Lands. They can be reached at (435) 722-3282.

Tactics

Summer is terrestrial time at Rock Creek with grasshopper imitations as the fly of choice. Stimulators, elk hair caddis, and royal Wulffs are all effective dry-fly patterns. Streamer fishing is most productive in September and October with muddler minnows and wooly buggers.

Rock Creek reportedly has giant salmon flies, which are believed to hatch in June; but high water makes fishing this hatch impractical in most years.

Spin-fishers use spinners and small spoons to advantage. Casting muddler minnow flies with a BB or 3/0 split shot above can also work well in the autumn.

How to Get There

From Mountain Home, go 15 miles northwest on Rock Creek Road (FR 134) to reach Rock Creek at the national forest boundary.

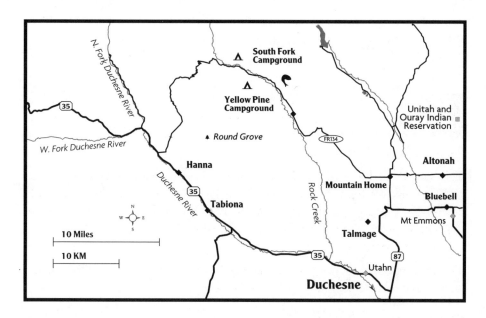

Accessibility

Access is quite good on Forest Service lands. Lower Stillwater is just north of the national forest boundary and has 12 ponds. Restrooms are available. The Robbins Ranch is only about a mile upriver and has private ponds. Be sure to respect their property and do not trespass. There are three Forest Service campgrounds on Rock Creek: South Fork, Yellow Pine, and Miners Gulch.

While all of Rock Creek on tribal lands is intended to be open for 1999, much of the surrounding areas will be closed. Be sure to get a copy of the regulations. Remember that you are a guest on their lands.

GPS Coordinates

Yellow Pine Campground	N 40° 32′ 10″ W 110° 38′ 10″
South Fork Campground	N 40° 32′ 56″ W 110° 41′ 40″

Maps

USGS 1:24000   Tworoose Pass, Kidney Lake, Dry Mountain, Blacktail Mountain, Talmage

Utah Atlas and Gazetteer   Page 55

When to Go

Anglers should find Rock Creek in fishable condition from July to September. In years with low or early runoff, try fishing the salmonfly hatch in June. ◆

Sixth Water Creek   UTAH COUNTY

T his unique freestone creek ran quite small until the opening of the Strawberry Tunnel. As part of the Central Utah Project, Sixth Water Creek became a conduit to carry water from the Uinta Basin to the Provo Valley, and ran at high flows all summer.

The Syar Tunnel is now completed. A malfunctioning valve has been repaired and the bulk of the irrigation water will enter the streambed about 2.5 miles downsteam (south) from the bridge on the Rays Valley Road. This will leave the upper seven miles (from the Strawberry Tunnel to the Syar Tunnel) as a tailwater with consistent year-round flows.

This change, combined with the special regulations initiated by the DWR, should allow this quality fishery to reach its true potential.

Fish Species

Brown trout. The occasional rainbow or cutthroat comes down from Strawberry Reservoir.

Special Regulations

❏ Trout limit, 4.

Tactics

The creek is small, with steep banks in most places. Wading and fishing upstream is by far the best option.

Flyfishers will want to use high floating dry flies — a stimulator or yellow humpy.

This area experiences a good hatch of cicadas in some years. If you hear or see numbers of these loud insects, try small (size 10 or 12) cicada patterns for some fast fishing.

Nymping can be effective if you adjust your technique to the conditions. Using weighted nymphs, flip them into pockets behind rocks or drop them into pour overs. Keep a tight line by lifting your rod tip as they float back to you.

How to Get There

Go east from Spanish Fork on US 6 and 89. Turn north on to Diamond Fork Canyon Road. Follow this road for about 28 miles to Springville Crossing, and then turn east on Rays Valley Road (FR 029). Once you get on top, the road forks; take the left fork to go to Dip Vat Creek and the West Portal and the right fork (FR 051) to get to the bridge.

Other options are to continue farther up US 6 / 89 and take the Rays Valley Road (FR 029) all the way in from the highway. If coming west on US 40 from Strawberry Reservoir, turn south on FR 131 on the west side of the reservoir, then head west on FR 029.

Another option is to hike up from Three Forks Trailhead, located on the Diamond Fork Canyon Road. This is not a recommended route as the canyon is very rough and there are fewer fish in that section.

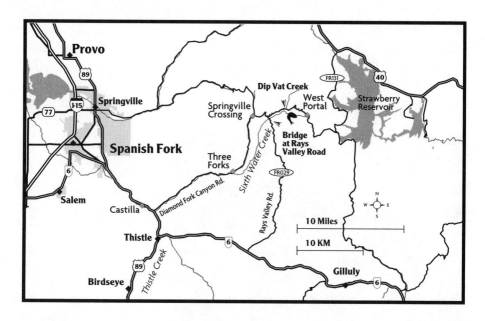

Accessibility

All approaches to this creek, with the exception of the Three Forks Trailhead, are on dirt roads with a lot of clay. You do not want to be here if it is wet or threatening rain. You need 4-wheel-drive **and chains**. Plan your trip for dry weather and leave immediately if it starts to rain heavily.

Once you reach the creek be prepared for rough wading. If the water is high, it can be very dangerous and you should consider going elsewhere.

The best fishing is up or down from the bridge on Rays Valley Road. The scenic canyon above Dip Vat Creek held many fish before Strawberry Reservoir was treated with rotenone in 1990, but the steepness of the canyon has slowed the repopulation of this section from below. You can hike up from Dip Vat Creek and walk back on the road, but this is a very strenuous hike.

GPS Coordinates

Confluence with Dip Vat Creek	N 40° 09' 49" W 111° 16' 33"
West Portal	N 40° 09' 40" W 111 14' 38"
Bridge at Rays Valley Road	N 40° 09' 04" W 111° 18' 01"

Maps

USGS 1:24000   Rays Valley, Two Tom Hill

Utah Atlas and Gazetteer   Page 46

When to Go

With the expected changes here, the top seven miles should be at good fishable levels thoughout the year. Access will be the largest factor. Depending on weather, the road in should be passable from May through October. If the drainage is still experiencing runoff or has had significant rain, you should avoid this road.◆

Sixth Water Creek looking upstream at West Portal. (PHOTO: STEVE COOK)

South Fork Ogden River

his is a pretty tailwater fishery only 20 minutes from downtown Ogden. It holds a self-sustaining brown trout population and gets supplemental plantings of rainbow trout.

There are several good campgrounds in close proximity to Pineview Reservoir, which allows visiting anglers to pursue both warm and cold water species of game fish.

This river is known to harbor whirling disease. Please see the whirling disease section in the guide for precautions to ensure that you don't help to spread this disease.

Fish Species

Rainbow, cutthroat and brown trout, also whitefish.

Special Regulations

South Fork Ogden River (Weber County) — downstream from Causey Dam to Pineview Reservoir:

❏   Trout limit, 8; only 2 brown trout.

Tactics

Fly-fishers have a variety of hatches to look forward to. There are blue-winged olives in the spring and fall, and caddisflies and pale morning duns in the summer months. Look for golden stoneflies and large salmonflies in June.

Suggested dry-fly patterns are parachute Adams, elk hair caddis, stimulators, cream colored comparaduns and deer hair salmonflies. Effective nymphs include pheasant tails, cased caddis, prince nymph, golden stoneflies, and large black stoneflies.

Spin-fishers will find medium-sized gold bladed spinners effective, especially when cast upstream in the fall. Small minnow plugs such as Rapalas can be effective, particularly in the pool below the spillway.

How to Get There

From I-15 at Ogden, take Exit 347 and follow SR 39 up Ogden Canyon and past Pineview Reservoir. SR 39 makes a hard right turn at Huntsville, then continues up along the South Fork of the Ogden.

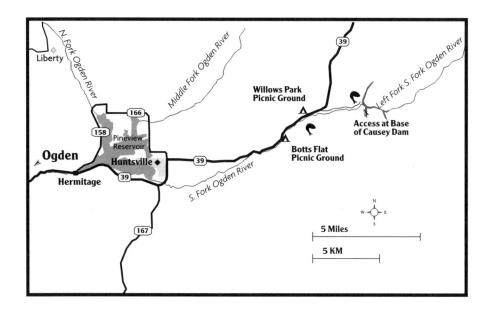

Accessibility

There are several picnic grounds on the first seven miles of river below Causey Reservoir, so access is very easy. Solitude is, however, in shorter supply. But if you are willing to walk away from the immediate vicinity of the campgrounds, you can usually find some elbow room. There is also a road going to Causey Dam that gives good access to the river.

Note: The pool at the bottom of the spillway has often held some large fish.

GPS Coordinates

Access at Base of Causey Dam	N 41° 17' 52" W 111° 35' 21"
Willows Park Picnic Ground	N 41° 17' 31" W 111° 37' 59"
Botts Flat Picnic Ground	N 41° 16' 38" W 111° 39' 25"

Maps

USGS 1:24000   Causey Dam, Browns Hole, Huntsville.

Utah Atlas and Gazetteer   Page 61

When to Go

High water normally recedes some time in June and the river is fishable through the fall and winter until runoff returns in April. September and October provide good fishing to aggressive fish preparing to spawn. The salmonfly hatch in June is probably the best time to catch a very large fish. ◆

Strawberry River

WASATCH AND DUCHESNE COUNTIES

T his river runs through such a unique and beautiful canyon that the Nature Conservancy has seen fit to purchase and protect 15 miles of it. The chalky cliffs that border the river near the Strawberry Pinnacles are awe-inspiring, giving off an eerie white effect under a full moon. Those seeking solitude will find it here in this very rugged remote section of Strawberry River.

Fish Species

Brown, cutthroat, and brook trout.

Special Regulations

From the confluence with Red Creek near Pinnacles, upstream Soldier Creek Dam:

❐ Artificial flies and lures only.

❐ No overnight camping on division land.

From Soldier Creek Dam downstream to the confluence with Willow Creek (approximately 1 mile):

❐ Artificial flies and lures only.

Tactics

This is a small stream with low flows and relatively little deep water. The angler who uses a very stealthy approach and careful presentation will find more success.

Fly-fishers will find success imitating the blue-winged olive hatch in spring and fall. Pale morning duns will start in July along with golden stoneflies. July and August have caddis hatches as well as good terrestrial action (hoppers and ants). There are a few green drakes just below the dam in early July. There is also some good nymph fishing.

One good approach in the steeper sections is to use a heavily weighted bug like the CK nymph. You can add shot as large as BB. While fishing upstream, flip your fly into holes and plunge pools, and drag it back downstream at the speed of the current. This technique works well with spinning or fly tackle.

How to Get There

Take US 40 east 33 miles from Heber City. Pass Strawberry Reservoir and then turn right at the sign for Soldier Creek Dam. There is access below the dam.

To reach the river in the Pinnacles section, from Fruitland, go east 3.3 miles on US 40. Turn south and go 6 miles on this road, which parallels Red Creek, and you will reach its confluence with the Strawberry River. Turn left onto Strawberry River Road, going past the rock pinnacle.

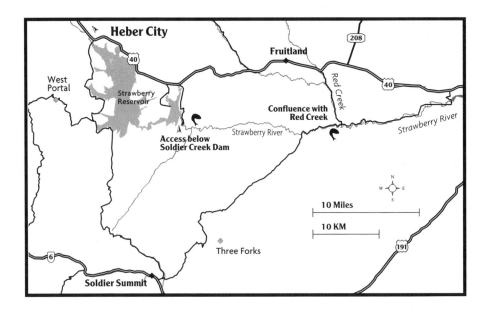

Accessibility

The best water on Strawberry River is from Soldier Creek Dam to the confluence with Red Creek, which carries a heavy sediment load and muddies the water below here. The Nature Conservancy has protected over 15 miles of this river. Thanks to their efforts, most of the water is accessible to the public. There is access below the Soldier Creek Dam, and a trail goes downstream for about 2 miles, after which it's very rugged. There is public access for the first 8 miles below the dam. Private property begins 0.3 miles west of Beaver Canyon.

Anglers can reach the lower part of this section from the junction with Red Creek and then follow the road up along the river. Public access ends at the gate. Please respect private property.

GPS Coordinates

Access below Soldier Creek Dam	N 40° 07' 39" W 111° 01' 24"
Confluence with Red Creek	N 40° 07' 39" W 111° 01' 24"

Maps

USGS 1:24000   Duchesne, Rabbit Gulch, Strawberry Pinnacles, Fruitland, Avintaquin Canyon, Strawberry Peak, Deep Creek Canyon, Strawberry Reservoir SE, Strawberry Reservoir NE

Utah Atlas and Gazetteer   46, 47

When to Go

Consistent flows are usually found on Strawberry River from July until winter sets in. The best hatch activity is usually in July, with good fishing to be expected throughout the summer months. This stream seems to be affected more than most by fishing pressure. Try to fish mid-week, if possible. ◆

Strawberry River below Soldier Creek Dam. (PHOTO: EMMETT HEATH / WESTERN RIVERS FLYFISHER)

Thistle Creek   UTAH COUNTY

T his small creek is surprisingly rich and productive in some stretches. The lower section of Thistle Creek was heavily impacted when a large landslide downstream from the town of Thistle dammed the Spanish Fork River and flooded back up through the canyon below Billies Mountain.

Fish Species

Rainbow, cutthroat and brown trout.

Special Regulations

General season, bag, and possession limits apply.

Tactics

This is a lovely small stream to cast dry flies during the warmer months, although things can be slow during mid-day in hot weather. A parachute ant works well here as do caddis imitations and hopper patterns.

Aquatic vegetation and changing water depths make nymphing difficult on much of this stream, but hare's ears and other mayfly nymphs work well if they can be presented properly.

There are some nice beaver ponds that fish well with midge imitations in the late season.

How to Get There

From US 6 between Spanish Fork and Price, take US 89 south to the flooded town area.

Accessibility

US 89 follows Thistle Creek for about 15 miles, with the best water beginning about one mile above the flooded town of Thistle and continuing 5.5 miles south to the town of Birdseye.

The creek flows across private lands — some of it is posted. If you are not sure about access, ask permission of land owners.

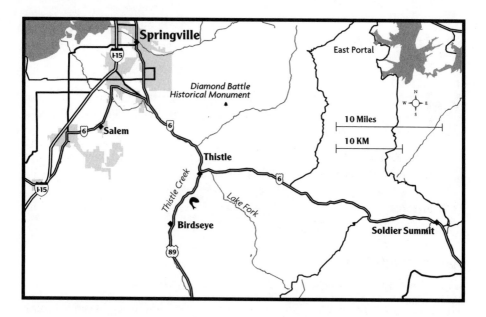

GPS Coordinates

Thistle	N 39° 59' 29" W 111° 29' 51"
Birdseye	N 39° 55' 28" W 111° 32' 56"

Maps

USGS 1:24000   Thistle, Birdseye

Utah Atlas and Gazetteer   Pages 45, 46

When to Go

After runoff in June, the summer months through fall fish best. Good fishing into November when the weather stays warm. ◆

Uinta River

 his is a large river for the South Slope of the Uintas. It drains seven major basins in the high country and has Kings Peak (Utah's highest mountain at 13,528 feet) at its head.

The U-Bar Ranch on the Uinta River has cabins for rent and also offers pack trips to high lakes in the High Uinta Wilderness area.

Fish Species

Rainbow, cutthroat, brown, and brook trout.

Special Regulations

General season, bag, and possession limits apply on public lands.

The lower portions of the Uinta River are on the Uintah and Ouray Indian Reservation. A fishing permit is $50.00/season or $10.00/day plus a $10.00 conservation stamp. Regulations are subject to frequent change, so contact the tribal office at (435) 722-5511 before you make plans to fish tribal lands. The *Utah Atlas and Gazetteer* displays reservation boundaries.

Note: The Ute Plaza Supermarket in Fort Duchesne sells fishing permits for Ute Tribal Lands. They can be reached at (435) 722-3282.

Tactics

Dry flies such as grasshoppers, renegades, and humpies work well, as they do on other rivers and streams dropping out of the High Uintas.

The deeper waters and higher flows make nymphing much more practical in the Uinta River than in other South Slope streams. Try bead head prince nymphs, CK nymphs, hare's ears, and stonefly imitations.

How to Get There

From Roosevelt, go north 10 miles on SR 121 to Neola, then continue north 7 miles. Go north another 5.7 miles on Uinta Canyon Road then turn north onto FR 118 after crossing the Uinta River.

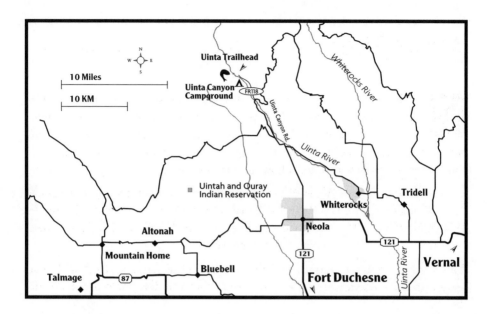

Accessibility

Best access on national forest lands is to go to Uinta Canyon Campground on FR 118 and fish upstream or go to the trailhead by Wandin Campground and hike up the canyon before fishing. **This is a powerful river, so use caution when wading.**

You can find lodging at The U-Bar Ranch: (435) 645-7256 or (800) 303-7256.

GPS Coordinates

Uinta Canyon Campground	N 40° 37' 24" W 111° 08' 35"
Uinta Trailhead	N 40° 37' 54" W 110° 09' 08"

Maps

USGS 1:24000   Pole Creek Cave, Heller Lake, Bollie Lake.

Utah Atlas and Gazetteer   Pages 55, 56

When to Go

High water can continue into July. The best time to plan a trip here is from late July to early October. ♦

Weber River
SUMMIT, MORGAN, WEBER AND DAVIS COUNTIES

Man has made a heavy impact on this large river system. Stream bed alterations were made to facilitate power production, make room for the freeway, and control flooding. Two large reservoirs and several diversions control water for agriculture with little regard to fishing quality. Finally, much of the river is privately controlled, allowing no public access.

In spite of these factors, Weber River still produces reasonable fishing for the public in some areas. The DWR stocks the river extensively to maintain fishing. In 1998, more than 150,000 trout were released into the Weber, and 50,000 of these were the more expensive 10-inch catchable size.

This river is known to harbor whirling disease. Please see the whirling disease section in the guide for precautions to ensure that you don't help to spread this disease.

Fish Species

Rainbow, cutthroat, brown trout and whitefish. There are also brook trout in the higher sections above Peoa.

Special Regulations

General season, bag, and possession limits apply.

Tactics

The water near Ogden at the mouth of the Weber Canyon holds brown trout, and is routinely stocked with rainbows. Try fly-fishing here with caddis and stimulators in the summer time, and with blue-winged olives in the fall. Standard nymphs such as cased caddis and pheasant tails will work. If you get them right on the bottom, you will likely be rewarded with some whitefish as well.

If you are lucky enough to gain access to the river above Rockport Reservoir, there is good caddis fishing on most summer evenings from July into August. Attractor patterns like royal Wulffs and trudes also work well here.

In the fall, look for large browns preparing to spawn throughout the river. Try the water around Wanship and just above Echo and Rockport Reservoirs. Big streamer flies and glo-bugs work as well as spinners and small crankbaits.

Rockport has been producing some very large browns in recent years. Look for these fish to move up into the Weber above the reservoir when the procreative urge strikes them in October and November.

The Weber has a large number of whitefish. Fishing for them from late fall into early spring can be very fast. Nymphs bounced right on the bottom are the ticket, whether cast with fly rod or spinning gear. Favorite patterns are red serendipity, prince nymph, and light-colored stoneflies and hare's ears. These fish are good eating and can easily sustain the harvest. They are particularly good when smoked.

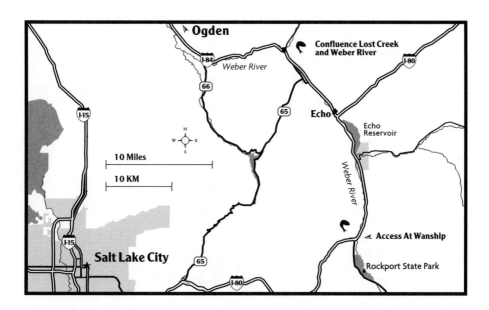

How to Get There
The lower Weber River is accessible just off of US 89 on the south edge of Ogden. It follows I-84 from Ogden to the junction with I-80 near Echo Reservoir. The river parallels I-80 from this junction to the town of Wanship.

Accessibility
Access is very difficult on much of the Weber River, particularly on the upper sections.

Thousand Peaks Ranch controls a large stretch of the upper river. As permits become available, they can be had on a lottery basis. Contact Jans Mountain Outfitters at (435) 649-4949 for details.

The remainder of the river from Thousand Peaks to Rockport Reservoir is mostly private. Get permission before entering private property.

There is access to the river at Wanship near the Spring Chicken Inn. There is also access in the Croyden area where Lost Creek enters the Weber River.

In Ogden, at the mouth of Weber Canyon, there is access from US 89 going up the canyon to the power plant.

GPS Coordinates

Confluence with Lost Creek	N 41° 03' 37" W 111° 32' 18"
Access at Wanship	N 40° 48' 48" W 111° 23' 57"

Maps

USGS 1:24000   Ogden, Snow Basin, Peterson, Morgan, Devils
                                Slide, Henefer, Coalville, Wanship, Crandall
                                Canyon, Kamas, Hoyt Peak, Hidden Lake,
                                Slader Basin, Whitney Reservoir

Utah Atlas and Gazetteer   Pages 54, 60, 61

When to Go

Summer and fall can be good times to fish here. Brown trout will be actively spawning in the fall. Whitefish can provide good action throughout the winter as they congregate in the deeper, slower holes at this time. ◆

Upper Weber River. (PHOTO: EMMETT HEATH / WESTERN RIVERS FLYFISHER)

Whiterocks River

DUCHESNE AND UINTAH COUNTIES

T he Whiterocks River emerges from the Uintas by way of a spectacular gorge. Hardy and prepared anglers can find fish and solitude in an incredible setting if they are willing to put forth the effort to get into the gorge. You will not likely find big fish, but you should find many trout that are brightly colored and willing to dispute ownership of your fly.

Fish Species

Rainbow, cutthroat, and brook trout.

Special Regulations

General season, bag, and possession limits apply on public lands.

The lower portions of the Uinta River are on the Uintah and Ouray Indian Reservation. A fishing permit is $50.00/season or $10.00/day plus a $10.00 conservation stamp. Regulations are subject to frequent change, so contact the tribal office at (435) 722-5511 before you make plans to fish tribal lands. The *Utah Atlas and Gazetteer* displays reservation boundaries.

Note: The Ute Plaza Supermarket in Fort Duchesne sells fishing permits for Ute Tribal Lands. They can be reached at (435) 722-3282.

Tactics

Proper footwear may be more important here than the right fly. Use good supportive wading boots over stocking foot waders or under a pair of shorts in warm weather. It cools off quickly when the sun drops behind the shoulder of the canyon, so bring some extra clothing.

Fly patterns used on other Uinta streams work well here. Offer the trout grasshoppers, stimulators, elk hair caddis, royal Wulffs and renegades. Much of this water is also suitable for nymphs such as bead head prince, hare's ear or chamois caddis.

Small spinners and worms are favored by spin-fishers.

How to Get There

From Roosevelt, go east 7.9 miles on US 40. Between Fort Duchesne and Gusher, turn and go north 4.4 miles on Lapoint Hwy. Go west 1.1 miles on SR 121, then turn north on Tridell Hwy. and go 7.7 miles. Continue north 4 miles on Whiterocks Loop Road, then take Whiterocks Canyon Road north along the river. This road becomes FR 492.

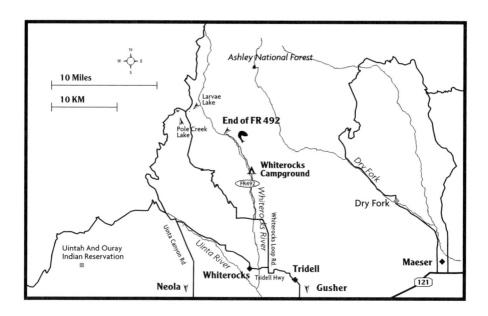

Accessibility

There is good access to the river above and below Whiterocks Campground. If you follow FR 492 to its end, a trail continues upstream another 1.5 miles. Progress above this point is slow and difficult and you will need to wade in spots. You can force your way up to waters that are seldom fished.

There are reports of anglers descending into this narrow canyon from around Larvae Lake. The exact route used is unclear and is believed to be very rugged. Anglers inclined to attempt this approach to the river should be prepared to assume the risks associated with route-finding on mountainous terrain.

GPS Coordinates

Whiterocks Campground	N 40° 37′ 11″ W 109° 56′ 32″
End of FR 492	N 40° 38′ 47″ W 109° 58′ 28″

Maps

USGS 1:24000   Whiterocks, Ice Cave Peak, Paradise Park, Rasmussen Lakes

Utah Atlas and Gazetteer   Page 56

When to Go

Expect high water to continue into July. The best fishing in the Whiterocks is from late July to early October. ◆

Yellowstone Creek   DUCHESNE COUNTY

 his smaller South Slope stream is particularly pretty and offers some nice fishing as well. The creek gets its name from the Yellow Ledges that can be seen about one-half mile west of the road near Crystal Ranch.

There are five national forest campgrounds along the Yellowstone, so it makes a good destination for weekend camping and fishing trips.

Fish Species

Rainbow, cutthroat, and brook trout in the higher sections with a few brown trout near the confluence with Lake Fork on tribal lands.

Special Regulations

General season, bag, and possession limits apply on public lands.

The lower portions of the Uinta River are on the Uintah and Ouray Indian Reservation. A fishing permit is $50.00/season or $10.00/day plus a $10.00 conservation stamp. Regulations are subject to frequent change, so contact the tribal office at (435) 722-5511 before you make plans to fish tribal lands. The *Utah Atlas and Gazetteer* displays reservation boundaries.

Note: The Ute Plaza Supermarket in Fort Duchesne sells fishing permits for Ute Tribal Lands. They can be reached at (435) 722-3282.

Tactics

This is a very pleasant stream for dry-fly fishing in summer. Yellow humpies are a favorite fly, along with hoppers and royal Wulffs. An adult damselfly can be very effective when dapped along the edges in summertime. Small muddler minnows in sizes 10 and 12 work well when fished downstream with a BB or 3/0 shot pinched onto the leader 6 inches above the fly.

How to Get There

From Mountain Home, go north 5.5 miles on Moon Lake Road (FR 131). Cross Lake Fork, turn north, then turn northeast on FR 119 to reach Yellowstone Creek.

Accessibility

The lower stretch of the creek is on tribal lands. Once north of the national forest boundary, there are two private ranches.

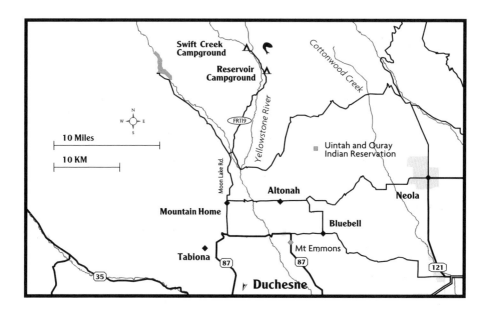

There is good access from Reservoir Campground upstream. At Swift Creek Campground, TR 057 follows the Yellowstone up into the High Uintas.

GPS Coordinates

Swift Creek Campground	N 40° 36' 04" W 110° 20' 50"
Reservoir Campground	N 40° 34' 30" W 110° 19' 27"

Maps

USGS 1:24000   Altonah, Burnt Mill Spring, Lake Fork Mountain, Garfield Basin

Utah Atlas and Gazetteer   Page 55

When to Go

Stream flows normally drop to fishable levels in early July. Fishing continues to be good until the end of September. ◆

Bear Lake

RICH COUNTY

his 172-square mile lake is often called the "Caribbean of the Rockies" due to its incredible cobalt blue waters. The color is caused by sunlight reflecting off suspended limestone particles.

It is believed that the lake has been isolated for 8,000 years by earthquake activity. This isolation led to the development of the Bear Lake strain of cutthroat and several unique fish species.

A wide variety of recreational opportunities is available to families visiting the area. Watersports include swimming, sailing, wave runners, jet skiing, water skiing, and scuba diving. One can also golf, hike, or visit some of the area's caves.

Bear Lake is famous for its raspberry crop, which is celebrated every year during Bear Lake Raspberry Days the first week of August. There are fireworks, a parade, and a rodeo.

Fish Species

Cutthroat (Bear Lake strain) and lake trout.

Bonneville cisco, Bonneville whitefish, and Bear Lake whitefish are all species unique to Bear Lake. They are found nowhere else in the world.

Special Regulations

Note: This is an interstate water. Consequently, the holder of a valid Utah or Idaho fishing or combination license may fish within both the Utah and Idaho boundaries of Bear Lake. However, only one bag limit may be taken and held in possession even if licensed in both states.

❑ Trout limit, 2.

❑ Cutthroat trout and trout with cutthroat markings with all fins intact must be released immediately. Only cutthroat that have one or more healed fins clipped may be kept.

❑ Cisco may be taken with a hand-held dip net January 1 through February 13. Net opening may not exceed 18 inches in any dimension. When dip-netting through the ice, the size of the hole is unrestricted.

❑ When ice-fishing for fish other than cisco, the size of the hole may not exceed 18 inches.

Big Spring Creek from Lamborn Diversion (approximately 500 yards below SR 30) out into the lake as buoyed or posted:

❑ **Closed** April 15 through 6 a.m. the second Saturday of July (July 10, 1999).

Big Spring Creek from Lamborn Diversion (approximately 500 yards below SR 30) downstream to Bear Lake:

❑ Catch and release only and artificial flies and lures only [January 1 through April 14 and from 6 a.m. the second Saturday of July (July 10, 1999) through December 31]. All fish must be released immediately.

Swan Creek and the area extending from its mouth into the lake 2,000 feet or as buoyed:

❑ **Closed** April 15 through 6 a.m. the second Saturday of July (July 10, 1999).

Swan Creek from Bear Lake to its headwaters spring:

❑ Catch and release only and artificial flies and lures only [January 1 through April 14 and from 6 a.m. the second Saturday of July (July 10, 1999) through December 31]. All fish must be released immediately.

Tactics

Bear Lake has a smooth, sandy bottom, so anglers cannot count on finding fish at particular locations from one trip to the next. A fish-finder is highly recommended for this lake as the only reliable way to locate your quarry and determine the depth that most of the fish are occupying.

Trolling with Flatfish and Rapalas is one of the most popular ways to catch cutthroat and lake trout. Fish can be found in shallower water in April. Later in the year, anglers will need lead line or downriggers to take lures to where the fish are. Trout range widely here, but two particularly good places to try for them are off creek mouths at North Eden and South Eden. The deepest water in the lake (208-foot maximum) is located on the east side of the lake, with South Eden at its center.

Jigging for lake trout is another productive method. Modern electronics allow anglers to present these fast sinking lures at the proper depth and location to greatly improve their success. Try the Gus Rich Point area with this technique.

How to Get There

From Salt Lake City, the quickest route is to take I-80 to Evanston, Wyoming, then turn north on Wyoming SR 89, which becomes Utah SR 16 . Take a left onto SR 30 at Sage Creek Junction. You will reach the shore of Bear Lake in 13 miles.

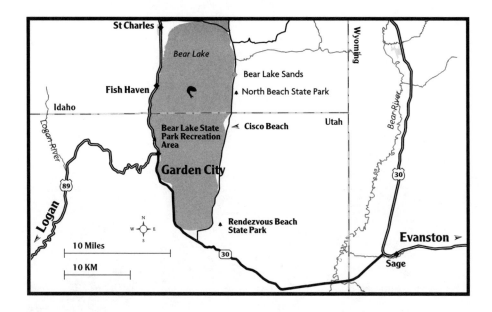

Accessibility

There are many campgrounds and boat ramps around the lake where the angler can gain access to these deep blue waters. There is much private property on the south and west sides of the lake. Shore access is best on the east side of the lake.

GPS Coordinates

Bear Lake State Park Recreation Area	N 41° 57' 56" W 111° 23' 58"
Rendezvous Beach State Park	N 41° 50' 46" W 111° 20' 32"
Cisco Beach	N 41° 58' 42" W 111° 16' 12"

Maps

USGS 1:24000   Garden City, Bear Lake South, Laketown

Utah Atlas and Gazetteer   Page 63

When to Go

Trout fishing is best in spring and fall. Fish are in shallow water and there is not as much recreational activity on the lake at these times. Fish are generally in deeper water during mid-summer, but there are many activities for the visiting family to enjoy, and the angler can find success in surrounding waters, such as the Logan River.

Cisco fishing occurs in mid-January. Water temperatures will be very cold. Ice, if present, can be very thin, so **use caution.** ♦

Services

Camping:

Bear Lake State Park
Marina and Eastside
Garden City
tel: (435) 946-3343
Reservations: (800) 322-3770
(In Salt Lake City, call 322-3770)

Bear Lake KOA
485 N. Bear Lake Blvd
Garden City
tel: (800) 562-3442

Fish overboard. (PHOTO: COURTESY BILL FURNISS)

Big Sand Wash Reservoir

DUCHESNE COUNTY

 his reservoir has mostly fair-sized rainbows, but it does produce some very large brown trout on occasion. Fishing is generally good in this productive body of water, and as a result, angler use is heavy.

The DWR plants smaller rainbows in the fall and allows them to grow in the reservoir, producing catchable-sized fish in the spring at a lower cost.

Fish Species

Rainbows, brown trout, and whitefish.

Special Regulations

❑ January 1 through May 21 (1999), trout limit, 4.

❑ May 22 through December 31 (1999), trout limit, 8.

Tactics

Many anglers prefer to troll Big Sand Wash with spinners trailed by a worm. Still fishing with your favorite trout bait should also prove effective.

How to Get There

From Roosevelt, go west 5 miles on US 40, then drive west 10 miles on SR 87.

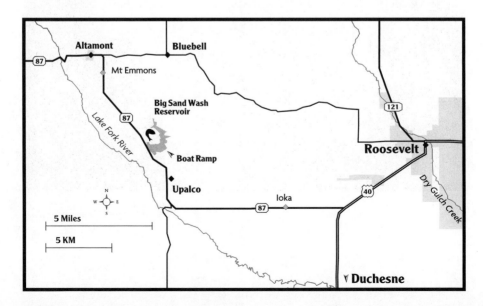

Accessibility

There is some access around the reservoir on dirt roads, and a boat ramp at the south end.

GPS Coordinates

Boat Ramp	N 40° 17' 47" W 110° 13' 15"

Maps

USGS 1:24000   Bluebell

Utah Atlas and Gazetteer   Page 55

When to Go

Can be good ice-fishing in January and February; be sure to check ice conditions. The ice usually comes off in late March. May and early June generally provide the best action. ♦

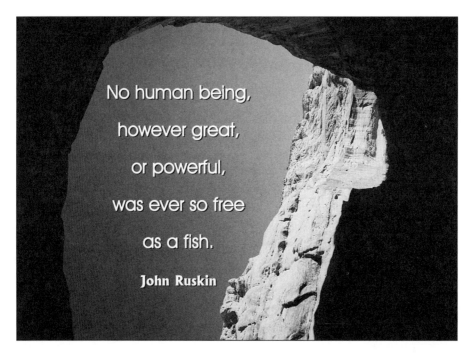

No human being,

however great,

or powerful,

was ever so free

as a fish.

John Ruskin

PHOTO: BRAD NICHOLSON

Birch Creek Reservoirs RICH COUNTY

hese two small bodies of water are 9.5 miles west of Woodruff, and about 8 miles north of Woodruff Reservoir. Fishing pressure is very light, so anglers looking for solitude may enjoy a day here.

Fish Species
Rainbow and cutthroat trout.

Special Regulations
General season, bag, and possession limits apply.

Tactics
These are good reservoirs for float tubers. The cutthroat will respond well to flies like wooly buggers and damselfly nymphs. Spinners and small spoons are also good choices.

How to Get There
From Ogden, go east on SR 39 for 49 miles then turn west about 1.5 miles to the reservoirs. SR 39 is closed in winter, but usually opens up anywhere from Memorial Day through the Fourth of July. If SR 39 is still closed you may be able to get in from the town of Woodruff which is northwest of Evanston, Wyoming, on SR 16.

Accessibility
The road runs past the lower reservoir and anglers can walk up to the upper reservoir. There is a campground just 1.5 miles north.

GPS Coordinates

Lower Birch Creek Reservoir	N 40° 30′ 23″ W 111° 18′ 48″
Upper Birch Creek Reservoir	N 40° 30′ 22″ W 111° 19′ 29″

Maps
USGS 1:24000   Birch Creek Reservoirs

Utah Atlas and Gazetteer   Page 61

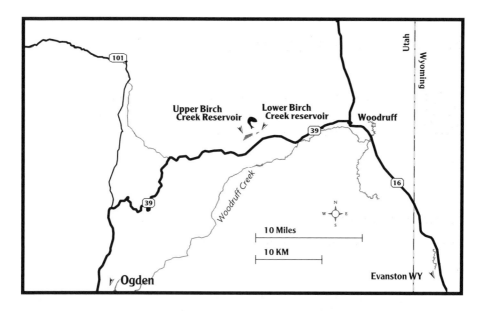

When to Go

Anglers will likely find open water and good fishing from April to October. There is little ice-fishing pressure as winter access is by snowmobile only. ♦

▼ Bottle Hollow Reservoir

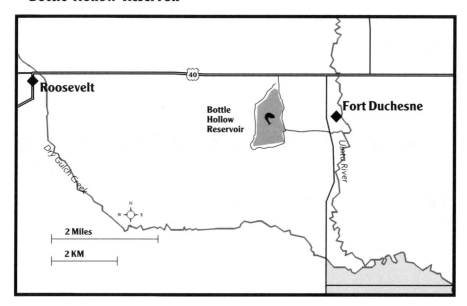

Bottle Hollow Reservoir

 B ottle Hollow is a productive and easily accessible water. It is often a good, if not consistent, producer of good-sized trout. Remember that you are a guest on Ute Tribal Lands and are subject to their regulations.

Fish Species

Rainbow, cutthroat, brown, and brook trout.

Special Regulations

Bottle Hollow is open to fishing year round.

❏ Daily bag limit, 3; 16 inches and under, one 16 inches or over.

A season fishing permit is $50.00 and a one day permit is $10.00. You will also need a conservation stamp which is $10.00. For restrictions on fishing hours, contact the tribal office at (435) 722-5511. The Ute Plaza Supermarket in Fort Duchesne (435-722-3282) sells fishing permits for Ute Tribal Lands.

Tactics

Most anglers still-fish with baits such as worms and Power Bait.

How to Get There

From Roosevelt, go west on US 40 about 6 miles.

Accessibility

Bottle Hollow is just south of the highway and there is a boat ramp and dock at the north end of the reservoir.

GPS Coordinates

Bottle Hollow Reservoir	N 40° 17' 25" W 109° 52' 07"

Maps

USGS 1:24000   Fort Duchesne

Utah Atlas and Gazetteer   Page 56

When to Go

Water is open from April to November. There is some ice-fishing as well. ◆

Calder Reservoir

T his is a productive and rich body of water that grows large, healthy trout. This small reservoir is between Matt Warner and Crouse Reservoir. It has been known to winterkill so you may want to contact the Vernal office of the DWR at (435) 789-3103 before planning a trip here. As of the fall of 1998, there has not been a fish kill in several years, so conditions are good.

Fish Species

Rainbow and cutthroat trout.

Special Regulations

Calder Reservoir:

❑ Trout limit, 4.

Pot Creek (Uintah County) — *including tributaries*:

❑ Trout limit, 4.

Tactics

Fly-fishers should try stripping wooly buggers and damselfly nymphs. Intermediate or slow sinking fly lines work well in the shallows. Float tubes allow for better access and maneuverability on the water.

Trollers find spinners and pop gear effective here.

Bait-fishing from shore can be effective. Using a combination of a worm and a marshmallow on a slip sinker rig will suspend your bait just above the weeds.

How to Get There

From Vernal, go north on US 191 for 25 miles. Then go east 8.8 miles on the Diamond Mountain Road. Then turn north and go 6 miles (toward Matt Warner Reservoir), then go east another 6.5 miles.

Accessibility

There is a boat ramp here at the west end of the reservoir. The county is usually able to keep the road open through the winter.

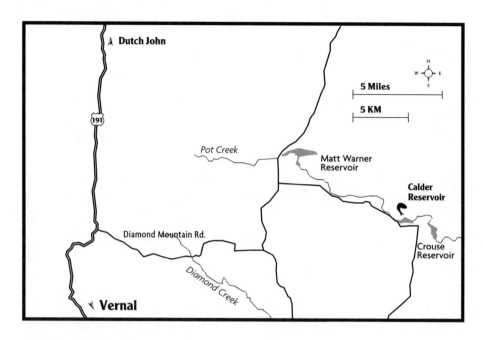

GPS Coordinates

Calder Reservoir	N 40° 43' 48" W 109° 12' 29"

Maps

USGS 1:24000   Crouse Reservoir

Utah Atlas and Gazetteer   Page 57

When to Go

Expect good fishing from April to October, with May and June the best months. Ice-fishing is good from January to March. Always check ice conditions. ♦

Causey Reservoir

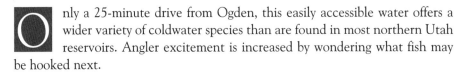 nly a 25-minute drive from Ogden, this easily accessible water offers a wider variety of coldwater species than are found in most northern Utah reservoirs. Angler excitement is increased by wondering what fish may be hooked next.

Slake (a cross between lake trout and brook trout) are the newest species of game fish in Causey Reservoir and they have the potential to grow quite large as they feed on other fish.

This reservoir is known to harbor whirling disease. Please see the whirling disease section in this guide for precautions to ensure that you don't help to spread this disease.

Fish Species

Kokanee salmon, rainbow, cutthroat, brown, brook, and splake trout.

Special Regulations

Causey Reservoir:

❒ January 1 through May 21, trout limit, 4.

❒ **Closed** to the possession of kokanee salmon with any red color from August 15 through September 30.

Causey Reservoir tributaries:

❒ **Closed** January 1 through 6 a.m. on the second Saturday of July (July 10, 1999).

❒ **Closed** August 15 through September 30.

Tactics

Splake are doing quite well here and many anglers are targeting these hard-fighting predators. Spoons and jigs can be effective, but success increases greatly if lures are tipped with dead minnows or sucker meat. These fish like to spend a good part of the year in the depths, so effective use of a fish-finder can greatly increase your catch.

This lake is a popular ice-fishing destination.

How to Get There

From I-15 at Ogden, take Exit 347 and follow SR 39 up Ogden Canyon and past Pineview Reservoir. SR 39 makes a hard right turn at Huntsville, then continues ascending alongside the South Fork of the Ogden. Turn right at Causey Road by Red Rock Ranch.

Accessibility

Roads run north and south from the dam and give good access to the west side of the reservoir. The remainder of the shoreline and the tributaries can be accessed from hiking trails. Small boats, canoes, or other small watercraft provide the best access as there is no boat ramp. Boats must be carried to the water.

GPS Coordinates

Causey Reservoir Dam	N 41° 17′ 54″ W 111° 35′ 12″

Maps

USGS 1:24000 Causey Reservoir

Utah Atlas and Gazetteer Page 61

When to Go

If splake are your target, then ice-fishing from January to March is the best time to go. There should be open water and good fishing from April to November. ♦

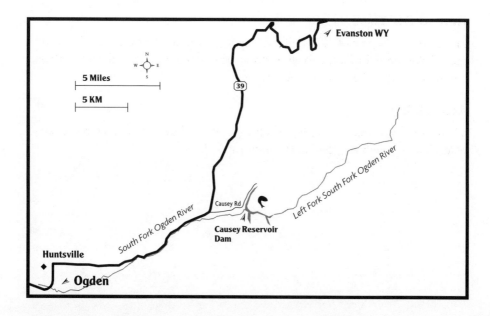

Cottonwood Reservoir UINTAH COUNTY

 his small reservoir has become a very good smallmouth bass fishery, with fish up to 5 pounds being caught. This water receives only light fishing pressure, and anglers can camp in the area.

Fish Species

Smallmouth bass and rainbow trout.

Special Regulations

❏ Bass limit, 6; only 1 of which may be larger than 12 inches.

Tactics

Smallmouth will be found along rocky shorelines and points. Large boulders always hold fish. Favorite lures are jigs with plastic tails or tipped with a night crawler. Crankbaits that mimic crayfish are effective.

Smallmouth like to spawn in 2 to 4 feet of water. During May and June, anglers should position their boat or float tube so that they can cast to the shore, then bounce lures down the bottom descending into deeper water. Concentrate your efforts around large rocks and boulders. After spawning, the fish will move into water from 10 to 25 feet deep. Make sure your offering is reaching the bottom.

How to Get There

From Roosevelt, go east on US 40 for 9 miles to the town of Gusher. Go north 1 mile. Take the right fork, and go north another 0.9 miles. Take the left fork and continue another 3.5 miles to the reservoir.

Accessibility

There is no boat ramp here, but a solid shoreline allows the launching of larger boats. There is public access to the entire shoreline.

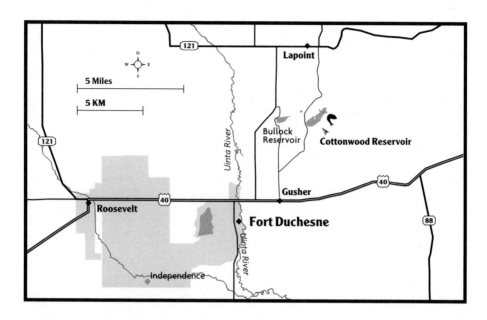

GPS Coordinates

Cottonwood Reservoir	N 40° 21' 19" W 109° 47' 14"

Maps

USGS 1:24000   Fort Duchesne

Utah Atlas and Gazetteer   Page 56

When to Go

There should be open water from March through October, with May and June providing the fastest fishing for smallmouths when they spawn. ◆

Crouse Reservoir   UINTAH COUNTY

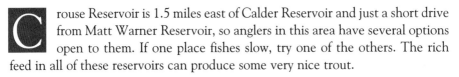 rouse Reservoir is 1.5 miles east of Calder Reservoir and just a short drive from Matt Warner Reservoir, so anglers in this area have several options open to them. If one place fishes slow, try one of the others. The rich feed in all of these reservoirs can produce some very nice trout.

This reservoir is subject to winterkill, so you may want to contact the Vernal office of the DWR at (435) 789-3103 before planning a trip. As of the fall of 1998, there has not been a kill in several years, so conditions are good.

Fish Species
Rainbow trout.

Special Regulations
Crouse Reservoir:

❐ Trout limit, 4.

Pot Creek (Uintah County) — including tributaries:

❐ Trout limit, 4.

Tactics
Fly-fishers should try stripping wooly buggers and damselfly nymphs. Intermediate or slow sinking fly lines work well in the shallows. Float tubes allow for better access.

Trollers find spinners and pop gear effective.

Bait-fishing from shore can be effective. Using a combination of a worm and a marshmallow on a slip sinker rig will suspend your bait just above the weeds.

How to Get There
From Vernal, go north on US 191 for 25 miles. Then go east 8.8 miles on the Diamond Mountain Road. Turn north and go 6 miles (toward Matt Warner Reservoir), and then turn east and go another 9.5 miles, about 1.5 miles past Calder Reservoir.

Accessibility
There is a new boat ramp by the dam. The county is usually able to maintain access through the winter.

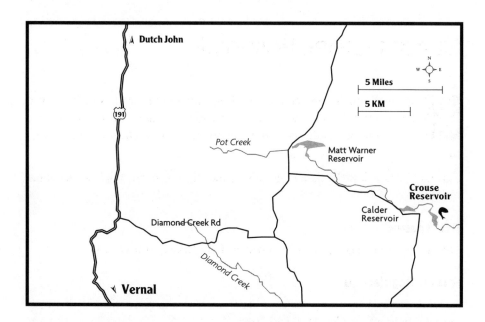

GPS Coordinates

Crouse Reservoir	N 40° 43' 28" W 109° 10' 58"

Maps

USGS 1:24000   Crouse Reservoir

Utah Atlas and Gazetteer   Page 57

When to Go

Expect good fishing from April to October, with May and June the best months. Ice-fishing is good from January to March. Always check ice conditions. ◆

Currant Creek Reservoir   WASATCH COUNTY

T his reservoir is only about a 1.5 hour drive from Salt Lake City. It is a good option for anglers that want to avoid crowds on nearby Strawberry Reservoir and still have the opportunity to catch some very large cutthroat.

Currant Creek below the dam is also a very nice fishery, giving anglers here some variety.

Fish Species

This fishery is managed primarily to sustain Bear Lake cutthroat trout.

Special Regulations

General season, bag, and possession limits apply in the reservoir, but there are special provisions for Currant Creek itself.

Currant Creek (Wasatch County) — from Water Hollow Creek upstream to head-waters, including all tributaries to Currant Creek Reservoir, but not the reservoir itself:

❑ Artificial flies and lures only.

❑ Trout limit, 2.

Tactics

Trollers can employ the same techniques they would use at Stawberry Reservoir. Effective lures include Strawberry wobblers, Rapalas, or Flatfish. Pop gear and a worm works well. Anglers who effectively combine fish-finders and downriggers will greatly increase their chances of taking big fish.

The tributary streams have good fishing and you can find fish concentrated near the stream mouths early in the season.

How to Get There

From Heber City, go east 16 miles on US 40, then turn north onto FR 083, which will follow Currant Creek up to the reservoir for 16 miles.

Accessibility

There are both a boat ramp and a Forest Service campground adjacent to the reservoir. Access on the gravel road in the winter is variable and can be difficult in wet weather.

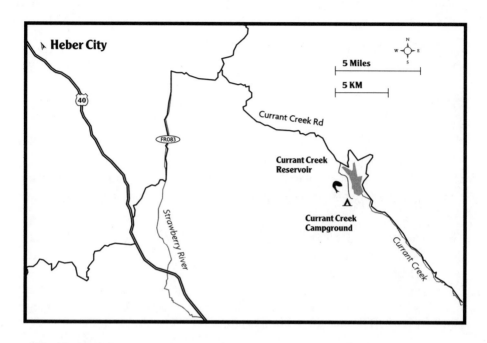

GPS Coordinates

Currant Creek Dam	N 40° 19′ 59″ W 111° 03′ 07″
Currant Creek Campground	N 40° 19′ 44″ W 111° 04′ 08″

Maps

USGS 1:24000   Jimmies Point

Utah Atlas and Gazetteer   Page 54

When to Go

Expect good fishing from ice-off in April until freeze- up in November. Best time is just as the ice is coming off (access may be difficult to impossible) and May and June.

There should be good ice-fishing January through March. Check ice conditions yourself before venturing out. ◆

Deer Creek Reservoir

eer Creek Reservoir is easily reached from the Provo-Orem area and has good recreational facilities, including restaurants, boat rentals, and so forth. Predictable canyon winds make this lake popular with windsurfers.

The reservoir was formerly a good rainbow trout fishery, but the population balance has been upset by the illegal introduction of walleye. There is little protection for young forage fish, and over predation by walleyes caused a decline in the early 1990s.

The Utah Division of Wildlife Resources (DWR) has instituted new regulations protecting yellow perch and rainbow trout. Rainbows being stocked are 10 inches in length. In October 1998, 80,000 catchable rainbows were stocked here. Perch numbers have rebounded in response to the new regulations. Anglers should be allowed a daily limit of 10 perch in the year 2000. Walleye are stabilizing at good levels along with their forage fish.

Fish Species

Rainbow and brown trout, largemouth and smallmouth bass, walleye, and yellow perch.

Special Regulations

- ❑ Trout limit, 4.
- ❑ Walleye limit, 6; but only 1 over 20 inches.
- ❑ Bass limit, 4; but only 1 over 15 inches. All bass between 12 and 15 inches must be released immediately.
- ❑ **Closed** to the possession of yellow perch.

Tactics

Deer Creek has a good population of walleyes. Studies estimate that there are 6,000 of them 14 inches and larger in the lake. The state record was caught in the Provo River just above Deer Creek in 1991 by Jeffrey Tanner. His fish was 31¾ inches long and weighed 15 lb. 9 oz. Perch numbers appear to be increasing, and walleye growth is good. Each year anglers catch walleyes up to 10 pounds. The best fishing is in the upper half of the reservoir. Try perch or rainbow trout imitating crankbaits or night crawler tipped jigs along the shoreline.

Bass fishers will find smallmouth along rocky shorelines and near brush at the north end of the lake. Jigs with plastic bodies or night crawlers are top producers.

Trout trollers do well with pop gear and night crawlers. Fly-fishing from float tubes with wooly buggers near Charleston and during "ice out" around the island can both be good. In the spring, try dead drifted cranefly larvae in the river channel as it enters the lake.

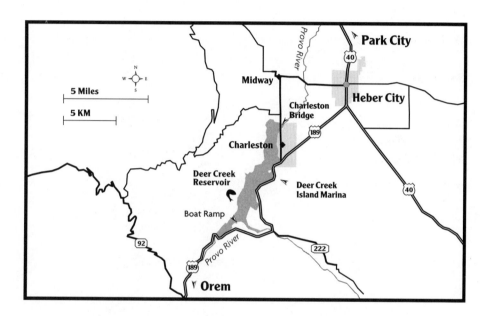

How to Get There

From I-15 near Orem, take Exit 275 to US 189 and go east. It is 11 miles up Provo Canyon to reach the dam on Deer Creek Reservoir. Anglers coming from Salt Lake City may prefer to take 1-80 to US 40, turning south on US 189 in Heber City.

Accessibility

Best access is along the east side of the reservoir. There are a number of facilities just off of US 189. There is no road access to the west side of the lake.

When to Go

The best months for walleye, trout, and smallmouth bass are May and June. Look for walleye and trout to be concentrated around the mouth of the Provo River in the spring. Fly-fishing with wooly buggers for rainbows is good during "ice out." ♦

GPS Coordinates

Deer Creek State Park Boat Ramp	N 40° 24' 57" W 111° 30' 26"
Deer Creek Island Marina	N 40° 26' 45" W 111° 28' 38"
Charleston Bridge	N 40° 28' 38" W 111° 28' 16"

Maps

USGS 1:24000   Aspen Grove, Charleston

Utah Atlas and Gazetteer   Pages 53, 54

Services

Camping:

Deer Creek Park Campground
Provo Canyon US 189
tel: (801) 225-9783

Deer Creek State Park
Heber
tel: (435) 654-0171

Wasatch Mountain State Park
Midway
tel: (435) 654-1791

For state park reservations:
(800) 322-3770
(In Salt Lake City, call 322-3770)

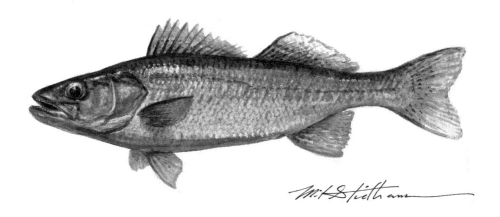

Walleye. (ARTIST: MIKE STIDHAM)

East Canyon Reservoir   MORGAN COUNTY

his 680-acre reservoir is easily accessible from Salt Lake City and Ogden. It receives fairly heavy usage due to its proximity to the major population centers of the state.

Upstream development has had an adverse effect on the reservoir's water quality. Flows into the reservoir have been steadily reduced over the years and water that reaches East Canyon is warmer. During the heat of summer, trout are restricted to the thermocline area as the water above is too warm and the water below does not hold enough oxygen. The stress keeps fish from surviving year round in the reservoir.

Because of stress, the fish in this reservoir have been affected by a parasitic anchor worm which can cause sores. Although this mars the appearance of the trout, there is no hazard to humans.

Fish Species
Rainbow trout.

Special Regulations
☐ Trout limit, 4.

Tactics
Ice-fishers have success with jigs and teardrops tipped with mealworms and Power Bait. Most anglers here still-fish with bait for the stocked rainbow trout. Worms and Power Bait are favored.

How to Get There
From Salt Lake City, take I-80 east to Exit 134 and then go north 14 miles on SR 65. If you are coming from Ogden, take I-84 east to Morgan at Exit 103. Take SR 66 south 13 miles to East Canyon Reservoir.

Accessibility
The state park campground is at the north end of the reservoir. There is a large cement boat ramp, as well as modern restrooms and showers. There are also boat rentals, a convenience store, and a refreshment stand.

The small and primitive River Edge Campground is at the south end of the reservoir.

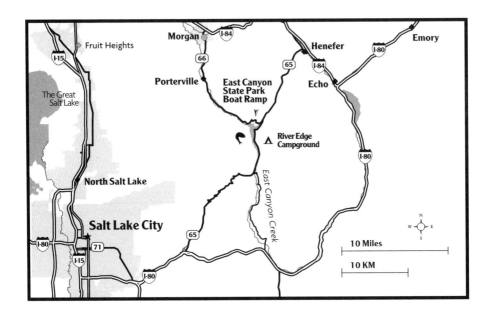

GPS Coordinates

East Canyon State Park Boat Ramp	N 40° 55′ 17″ W 111° 35′ 29″
River Edge Campground	N 40° 52′ 35″ W 111° 34′ 53″

Maps

USGS 1:24000   East Canyon Reservoir

Utah Atlas and Gazetteer   Page 53

When to Go

Best fishing is generally May and June. The majority of rainbows are stocked in the end of September to allow them to grow over the winter. This provides some ice-fishing activity. ◆

Services

Camping:

East Canyon State Park
Morgan
tel: (801) 829-6866
Reservations: (800) 322-3770
(In Salt Lake City, call 322-3770)

Echo Reservoir

Summit County

 ess than 1 hour from Salt Lake City, this reservoir is a popular destination for water sport enthusiasts. If you want to combine some fishing with waterskiing this is a good choice.

This reservoir is known to harbor whirling disease. Please see the whirling disease chapter in this guide for precautions to ensure that you don't help to spread this disease.

Fish Species

Rainbow and brown trout, channel catfish, crappie, and smallmouth bass.

Special Regulations

❏ Minimum bass size 12 inches; all bass less than 12 inches must be immediately released.

❏ Dead yellow perch may be used as bait.

Tactics

Crappie can be found near the brush at the upper end of the reservoir during their spring spawning period. Small jigs cast right into thick cover are best. Fishing them under a bobber lets you stay in the strike zone longer.

Though not plentiful, there are some large brown trout in the reservoir. The best way to target these trophy fish is to troll large crankbaits.

Smallmouth bass can be taken with jig/grub combinations in the brushy upper end of the reservoir. Casting crankbaits to points and rocky areas can produce some nice smallmouth and an occasional large brown trout.

Stocked rainbows can be taken by trolling or still-fishing with bait.

How to Get There

From Salt Lake City, go east 40 miles on I-80 to Exit 164 at Coalville. Go east into Coalville, then turn north on Main Street, which will turn into Echo Dam Road.

Accessibility

Echo Dam Road gives access to the east side of the reservoir. There is a resort here with camping, picnicking, and a boat ramp.

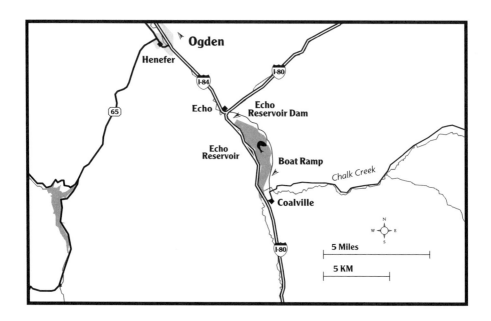

GPS Coordinates

Echo Reservoir Dam	N 40° 57′ 57″ W 111° 25′ 51″

Maps

USGS 1:24000   Coalville

Utah Atlas and Gazetteer   Page 54

When to Go

Best trout fishing is May and June, as it gets too warm in late summer. Crappie fishing is best during their spawn in May and June. ◆

Electric Lake

T his is an attractive reservoir at fairly high elevation (8,500 feet), with several other fishing destinations in close proximity. Lower Gooseberry Reservoir, Fairview Lakes, Huntington Reservoir, Cleveland Reservoir, and Huntington Creek are all within 10 miles. Scofield Reservoir is only about 15 miles to the north.

This reservoir is home to Utah's brood stock of Yellowstone cutthroat trout.

Fish Species

Cutthroat trout.

Special Regulations

Electric Lake (Emery County):

❑ Artificial flies and lures only.

❑ Trout limit, 4; all trout over 12 inches must be immediately released.

Electric Lake Tributaries (Emery and Sanpete Counties) — streams only, this excludes Boulger Reservoir but includes those streams flowing into Boulger Reservoir):

❑ **Closed** January 1 through 6 a.m. on the second Saturday of July (July 10, 1999).

❑ Artificial flies and lures only.

❑ Trout limit, 4; all trout over 12 inches must be immediately released.

Tactics

This reservoir is a good destination for fly-fishers and their float tubes. Look for midge hatches at evening time. Try Griffith gnats and blood midges.

Cutthroat will respond well to spinners and small spoons.

How to Get There

From Provo, go south on I-15 to Exit 261 and then go east on US 6. Turn south on US 89 to Fairview. Go east on SR 31 about 8.3 miles, then southeast 5.2 miles on Skyline Drive (SR 264). This route brings you to the upper end of the reservoir. If you stay on SR 31 you will come to the dam and the lower end of the reservoir.

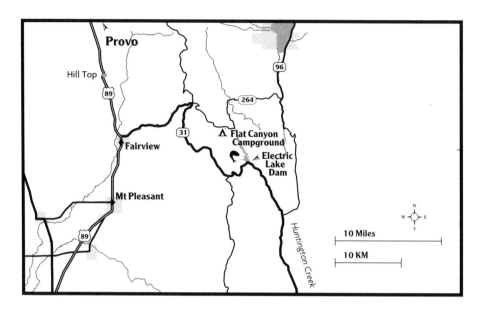

Accessibility

Flat Canyon Campground is only 1.5 miles away from the water. In addition to the access at the north and south ends of the reservoir, there are Forest Service roads that reach the lake on the east and west shore. There is a boat ramp on the east side of the reservoir.

GPS Coordinates

Electric Lake Dam	N 39° 36′ 03″ W 111° 12′ 41″
Flat Canyon Campground	N 39° 38′ 44″ W 111° 15′ 33″

Maps

USGS 1:24000   Fairview Lakes, Scofield, Candland Mountain

Utah Atlas and Gazetteer   Page 46

When to Go

June and July are the best months, but you can expect good success through October. ◆

Fairview Lakes

T hese small reservoirs are subject to winterkill and fairly heavy harvest. As a result they are primarily put-and-take fisheries, with catchable rainbows stocked at the start of the season and harvested by fall. The DWR's stocking efforts provide good fishing through the summer months.

Fish Species

Rainbow trout.

Special Regulations

Fishing from a boat with a motor of any kind is prohibited on Fairview Lakes.

Tactics

Most anglers still-fish from the banks with their favorite trout baits.

Fly-fishers can do well fishing from float tubes with adult damselfly patterns cast near the shore. Wooly buggers and damselfly nymphs are effective under the surface.

How to Get There

From Provo, go south on I-15 to Exit 261 and then go east on US 6. Turn south on US 89 to Fairview. Go east on SR 31 about 8.3 miles, then southeast on Skyline Drive (SR 264) for 2.2 miles. Continue south on Skyline Drive to FR 187, which continues to the lakes.

Accessibility

There is road access to the north and east sides of the reservoir. Toilets are available.

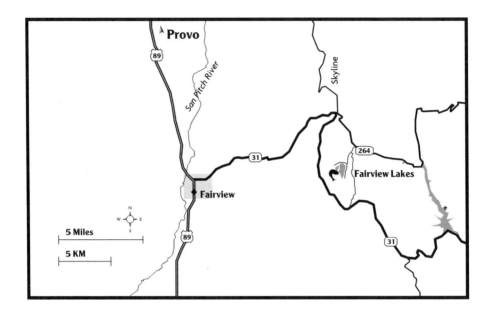

GPS Coordinates

Fairview Lakes	N 39° 38′ 31″ W 111° 18′ 32″

Maps

USGS 1:24000   Fairview Lakes

Utah Atlas and Gazetteer   Page 46

When to Go

These lakes open as soon as the hatchery trucks can get in, usually in late May. Many local anglers prefer to fish later in the season as trout grow quickly and are considerably larger by fall. ◆

Flaming Gorge Reservoir

DAGGETT COUNTY

T his large reservoir is nearly 90 miles long with water depths to 400 feet near the dam. Much of the reservoir extends up into Wyoming, but the Utah waters include most of the visually striking canyon area of the reservoir. Flaming Gorge is an appropriate name, the orange and red cliffs glowing in the fading fire of the setting sun.

This reservoir has produced more than its share of huge fish over the years. Below is a list of the Utah state fishing records that were set by fish pulled from Flaming Gorge waters:

Current Angling Record Fish				
Lake Trout	1988	51 lb. 8 oz	45 ⅛ in.	Curt Bilbey
Brown Trout	1977	33 lb. 10 oz	40 in.	Robert Bringhurst
Rainbow Trout	1979	26 lb. 2 oz	—	Del Canty
White Sucker	1992	2 lb. 8 oz	19 ¼ in.	Ray Johnson
Current Catch-and-Release Record Fish				
Lake Trout	1998	52 lb. 1 oz.	45 ½ in.	Ray Johnson
Rainbow Trout	1997	—	23 ¾ in.	Jolene Johnson
Kokanee Salmon	1997	—	23 ¾ in.	Lisa Johnson
Smallmouth Bass	1997	—	17 ¼ in.	Ray Johnson
Carp	1997	—	29 ½ in.	Ray Johnson
White Sucker	1997	—	19 in.	Kirk Ray Johnson
Utah Chub	1997	—	14 ¼ in.	Sue McGhie Troff

As you can see from the list, this is the place to go in search of a truly huge fish. You will note that Ray Johnson's 52 lb. 1 oz. lake trout was caught in 1998. There is a very good chance that this record can be broken again in the years to come.

Anglers vacationing here can find a variety of other fishing options close by. The Green River, Jones Hole Creek, Steinaker, and Red Fleet Reservoirs are just a few of the choices. Families will be interested in touring Flaming Gorge Dam, where one can feed trout over 20 pounds. Dinosaur National Monument, one hour from Vernal, is a fascinating display of fossils and well worth a visit.

Fish Species

Rainbow, brown, lake trout; kokanee, channel catfish, and smallmouth bass.

Special Regulations

Note: This an interstate water.

The purchase of a reciprocal fishing stamp allows a person to fish across the state boundaries of interstate waters.

Any person possessing a valid Wyoming fishing license and a Utah reciprocal fishing stamp for Flaming Gorge is permitted to fish within the Utah waters of Flaming Gorge Reservoir.

❑ Licensed anglers, limit 6 trout or kokanee salmon in the aggregate. No more than 3 may be kokanee salmon, and no more than 3 may be lake trout/mackinaw. Only 1 lake trout may exceed 28 inches.

❑ Unlicensed anglers 13 years of age or younger, limit 3 trout or kokanee salmon in the aggregate. No more than 2 may be kokanee salmon, and no more than 2 may be lake trout/mackinaw. Only 1 lake trout may exceed 28 inches.

❑ Catfish limit, 6.

❑ Smallmouth and largemouth bass in the aggregate, limit 10.

❑ No line may have more than 3 baited hooks or artificial flies in series or more than 3 lures.

❑ Possession of a gaff while fishing is unlawful.

❑ When ice-fishing, the hole size may not exceed 18 inches.

Tactics

Spring is a good time to go in search of big lake trout. Fish are spread out, feeding actively, and can be found nearer the surface. Lake trout over 2 pounds feed almost entirely on other fish. Large lures that imitate bait fish, such as Rapalas, Flatfish, and big spoons are all effective.

In summer these big trout will descend to the cooler depths. They prefer water of 60 degrees or cooler. Fish-finders are invaluable to locate fish at this time. Vertical jigging to graphed fish can work well. Downriggers will also allow anglers to present trolled lures at the proper depths.

Lake trout spawn in the fall and early winter. Look for rocky shoals in 5 to 20 feet of water. Fish concentrate in small areas at this time of year and fishers often do too. If you are having trouble finding fish, pay attention to the location of other anglers.

Smallmouth bass spawn in May and June and fishing can be very fast. These fish prefer rocky shorelines and points. Large boulders always hold fish. Favorite lures are jigs with plastic tails or tipped with a night crawler. Crankbaits and rubber worms are also good. Crawfish are a preferred food of smallmouth, so lures that represent them work well.

If you are fishing from a boat, position it so your cast can reach the shore. Bounce lures down to the bottom into deeper water. Concentrate your efforts around large rocks and boulders. Keep in close touch with your lures or bait. Be prepared to set the hook on very subtle takes.

When smallmouth bass spawn, the males arrive first, followed by the females. Fish spawn at temperatures from 60 to 65 degrees on gravel and rock, usually in 2 to 4 feet of water.

Flaming Gorge Reservoir. (PHOTO: COURTESY UTAH OUTDOORS)

After spawning, they are fairly easy to catch, as well as being great table fare. The best tactic is to use a fish-finder to locate schools of fish, then troll small flashy lures past them using downriggers. Try small spoons and spinners. These fish will congregate near stream mouths in August, before they spawn in September. Fish will move into water from 10 to 25 feet deep. Make sure your offering is reaching the bottom.

The cold water in Flaming Gorge keeps smallmouth from growing quickly, so search shallower, warmer areas of the reservoir for the biggest fish.

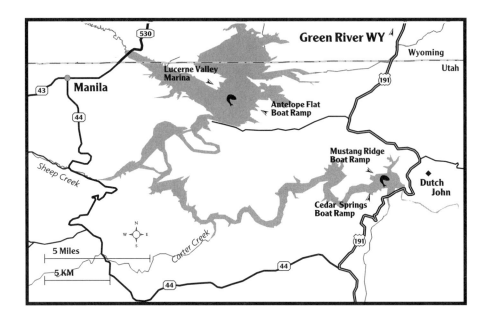

There is an abundance of smallmouths here. Feel free to take fish to eat. Reasonable harvest will actually help the fishery.

Kokanee are considered fairly easy to catch, as well as being great table fare. The best tactic is to use a fish finder to locate schools of fish, then troll small flashy lure past them using downriggers. Try small spoons and spinners. These fish will congregate near stream mouths in August, before they spawn in September.

How to Get There

The direct route from Salt Lake City is I-80 east 110 miles to Exit 34 at Fort Bridger, Wyoming. Follow SR 414 through town and turn right at Lyman at the 4-way stop. Pass through Mountain View and continue southeast. Wyoming SR 414 will become Utah SR 43 and continue to Manila.

An alternate route is to take I-80 east at US 40 and continue east to Vernal, then turn north onto SR 191.

Accessibility

SR 44 runs around Flaming Gorge Reservoir on the west and south sides. US 191 crosses the dam and runs up along the east side of the reservoir. All the facilities that access the lake in Utah can be easily reached from these two roads.

GPS Coordinates

Lucerne Valley Marina	N 40° 59′ 05″ W 109° 35′ 04″
Cedar Springs Boat Ramp	N 40° 54′ 45″ W 109° 26′ 49″
Sheep Creek Bay Boat Ramp	N 40° 55′ 19″ W 109° 40′ 28″
Mustang Ridge Boat Ramp	N 40° 55′ 25″ W 109° 26′ 46″
Antelope Flat Boat Ramp	N 40° 57′ 49″ W 109° 33′ 23″

Maps

USGS 1:24000   Flaming Gorge, Manila, Dutch John

Utah Atlas and Gazetteer   Pages 56, 57

When to Go

Spring has the best success for lake trout and smallmouth bass, but there is good fishing here from early spring to late fall. Just adjust your tactics to the prevailing conditions. Ice-fishing can be popular here, but ice conditions are quite variable. Use caution. ◆

Ice-fishers can score big on good ice years. (PHOTO: COURTESY UTAH OUTDOORS)

Services

Camping:

Flaming Gorge KOA
Campground and RV Park
SR 43 and 3rd West
Manila, UT 84046
tel: (435) 784-3184

Guides & Outfitters —
Permittee Ashley National Forest

Old Moe Guide Services
P.O. Box 308
Dutch John, UT 84023
tel and fax: (435) 885-3342
www.quickbyte.com/oldmoe
e-mail: gwerning@union-tel.com

Triangle G Fishing Service
P.O. Box 271
Manila, UT 84046
tel: (435) 784-3265
winter: (435) 882-1076
www.3gfish@aros.com

Lodging:

Red Canyon Lodge
790 Red Canyon Rd.
Dutch John, UT 84023
tel: (435) 889-3759
fax: (435) 889-5106

Flaming Gorge Lodge
155 Greendale, US 191
Dutch John, UT 84023
tel: (435) 889-3773
fax: (435) 889-3788
www.fglodge.com
e-mail: lodge@fglodge.com
(guide service, fly shop)

Marinas:

Cedar Springs Marina
P.O. Box 337
Dutch John, UT 84023
tel and fax: (435) 889-3795
(boat rentals, slips, lodging, convenience store)

Lucerne Valley Marina
P.O. Box 10
Manila, UT 84046
tel: (435) 784-3483
fax: (435) 784-3433
(boat rentals, slips, RV camping and tours)

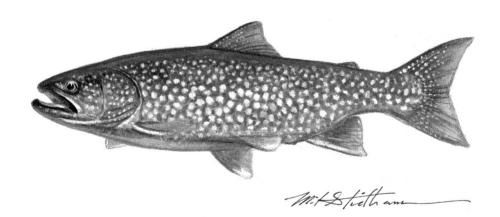

Lake trout. (ARTIST: MIKE STIDHAM)

Gooseberry Reservoir (Lower)   Sanpete County

T his reservoir has become more popular in recent years. Scofield Reservoir is only about 20 miles away. Gooseberry currently has problems with winterkill. Rainbows have difficulty surviving low oxygen levels in winter. If the proposed Narrows Reservoir Project takes place, inflow during the winter months will be reduced. This may make it impossible for the cutthroat trout to overwinter here as well.

Fish Species

Rainbow and cutthroat trout.

Special Regulations

Gooseberry Reservoir Tributaries (Sanpete County):

☐ **Closed** January 1 through 6 a.m. on the second Saturday of July (July 10, 1999).

☐ Trout limit, 4, when open.

Tactics

Most anglers pursue stocked rainbow trout by still-fishing with worms and Power Bait.

You can increase your chances of catching the larger holdover cutthroats by using spinners, minnow plugs, or wooly buggers.

How to Get There

From Fairview, go east 8.4 miles on SR 31, then turn north on Skyline Drive for 0.2 miles. Go northeast on FR 124 for 3 miles to the reservoir.

Accessibility

There is road access to the west side of the reservoir. The Gooseberry Campground is about 1.5 miles south of the reservoir.

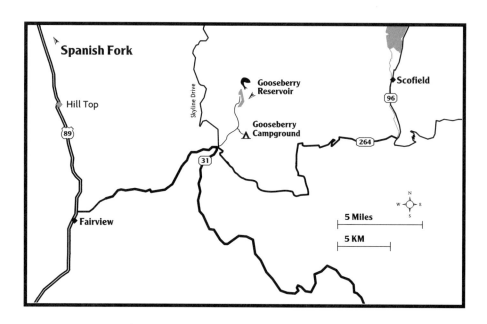

GPS Coordinates

Lower Gooseberry Reservoir	N 39° 42' 37" W 111° 17' 28"
Gooseberry Campground	N 39° 41' 15" W 111° 17' 49"

Maps

USGS 1:24000   Fairview Lakes

Utah Atlas and Gazetteer   Page 46

When to Go

Fall is probably the best time of year for fishing at Gooseberry, although July is also good. This reservoir sits at 8,400 feet and fishes fairly well through the heat of summer. ◆

Huntington Reservoir

 his small reservoir is only 4.5 miles from Electric Lake, and is home to tiger trout. Huntington Reservoir holds fish that could beat the current catch-and-release record tiger trout of 16¼ inches.

Fish Species

Cutthroat and tiger trout (a hybrid cross between a male brown trout and a female brook trout).

Special Regulations

Huntington Reservoir:

❏ Trout limit, 4.

❏ **Closed** to the possession of cutthroat trout and trout with cutthroat markings.

Huntington Reservoir Tributaries:

❏ Artificial flies and lures only.

❏ Trout limit, 4.

❏ **Closed** January 1 through 6 a.m. on the second Saturday of July (July 10, 1999).

❏ **Closed** to the possession of cutthroat trout and trout with cutthroat markings.

❏ Anglers are encouraged to harvest tiger trout.

Tactics

Tiger trout have a reputation for being aggressive. They take spinners and small spoons, as well as streamer flies, and wooly buggers. Bait-fishing can also be effective.

How to Get There

From Fairview, go east 18 miles on SR 31 to Huntington Reservoir.

Accessibility

There are no facilities here.

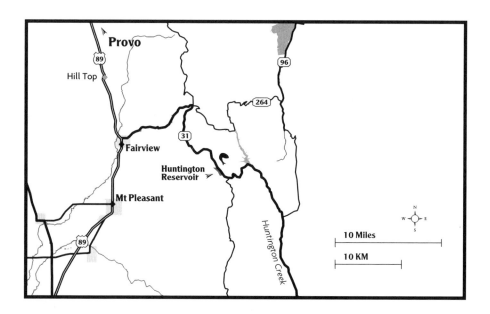

GPS Coordinates

Huntington Reservoir	N 39° 35' 25" W 111° 15' 58"

Maps

USGS 1:24000   Huntington Reservoir

Utah Atlas and Gazetteer   Page 46

When to Go

July to October. ♦

Hyrum Reservoir
CACHE COUNTY

 his is a large reservoir at 450 acres. It is just minutes from Logan and gets fairly heavy recreational use. Hyrum State Park provides easy access for anglers and their families.

This reservoir is known to harbor whirling disease. Please see the whirling disease chapter in this guide for precautions to ensure that you don't help to spread this disease.

Fish Species

Rainbow and brown trout, largemouth bass, bluegill and yellow perch. Splake were added to the reservoir in 1998.

Special Regulations

☐ Minimum bass size is 15 inches.

☐ Dead yellow perch may be used as bait.

Tactics

Trolling is popular with trout anglers at Hyrum Reservoir. Pop gear with a worm trailer is the most common method. This reservoir fills up and then spills most years and it is believed that many fish are lost over the spillway.

Bass anglers pursue their quarry with traditional tactics, casting crankbaits, jig and pigs, and plastic worms.

Large perch in Hyrum Reservoir — some reaching 12 inches — feed on the smaller members of their own species and so they help to regulate themselves. Ice-fishing with teardrops tipped with mealworms or perch eyes is effective.

How to Get There

From Logan, go south 6 miles on SR 165 to Hyrum, then west 2 miles on SR 101. Turn south on 400 west to reach the reservoir. If coming from the south (Brigham City) take US 89 to SR 101.

Accessibility

Hyrum State Park has a campground, boat launch, modern restrooms, and a sandy beach area.

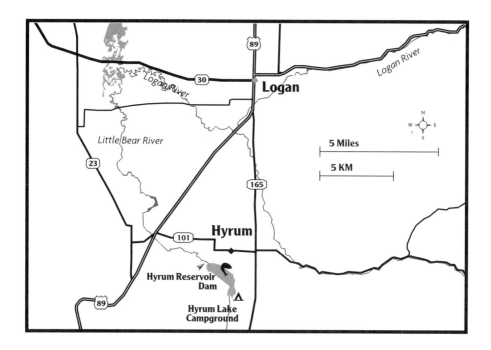

GPS Coordinates

Hyrum Reservoir Dam	N 41° 37' 28" W 111° 52' 22"
Hyrum Lake Campground	N 41° 36' 16" W 111° 51' 08"

Maps

USGS 1:24000   Paradise, Logan

Utah Atlas and Gazetteer   Page 60

When to Go

Expect good fishing from June to October. Angler success is reduced during high water periods. Bass should be in pre-spawn staging areas by late April and move into the shallows as they warm. Ice-fishing commences sometime after the first of the year, and continues into March most years. Be sure to check ice conditions before going out. ♦

Services

Camping:

Hyrum State Park
tel: (435) 245-6866
Reservations: (800) 322-3770 (In Salt Lake City, call 322-3770)

Jordanelle Reservoir

T his attractive reservoir covers 3,300 acres and is a popular recreation area due to its proximity to Salt Lake City and Provo. There is a great deal of watersports activity on this reservoir, so mid-week trips are a good idea. The drive is short enough to make trips after work a good option for valley dwellers.

Families will find a variety of things to do in the area, and Park City, with all of its attractions, is just 11 miles away. The Nature Center at Rock Cliff State Park is very interesting. There is a trail connecting the two State Parks for use by hikers, mountain bikers, equestrians, and cross-country skiers in winter.

Fish Species

Smallmouth bass; rainbow, brown, and cutthroat trout. Most of the trout are rainbows.

Special Regulations

❏ Trout limit, 4.

❏ **Closed** to the possession of bass. All bass must be released immediately.

Tactics

This can be a good place to get rid of your cabin fever with "ice out" fishing. Look for concentrations of rainbows in the old river channel just off the mouth of the Provo River. Black or olive wooly buggers fished slowly on sinking lines are suggested.

Bass anglers will enjoy the emerging smallmouth bass fishery. Brushy coves hold fish, and jig/grub combinations or plastic worms can be used effectively in this heavy cover. For larger fish, concentrate your efforts on small points and rocky stretches of bank. Casting with crankbaits can move the big boys.

Ice-fishers can find success here when there is enough ice. Try the Upper Provo Arm, using ice flies tipped with mealworms or Power Bait.

How to Get There

Jordanelle is located just off of US 40 about 7 miles from Heber City. Anglers traveling from the Salt Lake area, take I-80 east to US 40 and continue going east. It is 8 miles to the reservoir. SR 32 runs along the south edge of the reservoir.

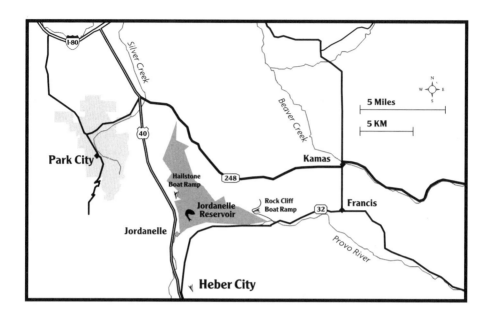

Accessibility

Access is at Hailstone State Park. Take the Mayflower exit from US 40 and follow the signs. There is an excellent boat launch and marina here. You can also use Rock Cliff State Park, reached by turning east onto SR 32 from US 40. Turn left just after crossing the Provo River above the reservoir. Rock Cliff has very good handicapped access to camping and picnic areas along the Provo River. The boat ramp here is the old roadbed and only suitable for smaller boats.

A $5 fee is charged to park at the reservoir recreation areas.

There is a limit of 300 vessels on the reservoir. If that level has been reached, you will be asked to visit other boating areas.

GPS Coordinates

| Hailstone Boat Ramp | N 40° 37' 23" W 111° 25' 07" |
| Rock Cliff Boat Ramp | N 40° 36' 13" W 111° 21' 06" |

Maps

| USGS 1:24000 | This new reservoir does not yet appear on USGS Maps. |
| *Utah Atlas and Gazetteer* | Page 54 |

When to Go

Jordanelle Reservoir is a very popular destination for watersports such as water skiing, jet skiing, and sailing. Anglers may wish to avoid peak use periods such as summer weekends. Spring and fall are the best times. Just after "ice out," you will find rainbows staging off the mouth of the Provo River in preparation for the spawn. Ice-fishers may find good ice from February to March. Always check ice conditions and use caution before venturing out on frozen lakes. ♦

Services

Camping:

Jordanelle State Park

Hailstone — tel: (435) 645-9540
(12 N on US 40, Mayflower Exit)

Rock Cliff — tel: (435) 783-3030
(Francis, 2 mi W off SR 32)

Reservations: (800) 322-3770
(In Salt Lake City, call 322-3770)

A pretty cutthroat — and angler — at Jordanelle Reservoir.
(PHOTO: COURTESY UTAH OUTDOORS)

Lost Creek Reservoir

This reservoir was drained in 1997, to make repairs to the dam. It is expected to be refilled in 1999, but it is still listed as a closed water to allow stocked fish to grow.

The entire reservoir is expected to be under a "wakeless" restriction in the future.

Fish Species

Will be restocked with Bear Lake cutthroat trout and rainbows when it is re-opened in the year 2000.

Special Regulations

Lost Creek Reservoir:

☐ **Closed 1999.**

Lost Creek — the entire drainage upstream, beginning at the bridge (culvert) approximately 0.25 miles above Lost Creek Reservoir, except Squaw Creek:

☐ Artificial flies and lures only.

☐ Catch and release only.

Tactics

Expect this reservoir to provide good fishing for rainbows and some larger cutthroat when it reopens. Trolling should be effective for cutthroats, while rainbows are more susceptible to bait-fishing.

The north end of the lake near the inlet was productive in the past and should be again when the reservoir reopens.

How to Get There

From Ogden, go east on I-84 to Exit 117. Go northeast on North Lost Creek Road to Lost Creek Reservoir.

Accessibility

The road to the upper end of the reservoir is currently closed, but is expected to reopen. The State Park will reopen as well. It will have a boat ramp and campground.

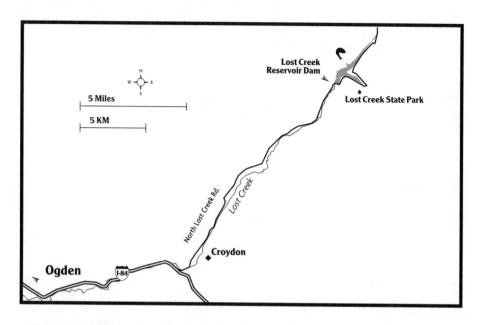

GPS Coordinates

Lost Creek Reservoir Dam	N 41° 11' 04" W 111° 23' 52"
Lost Creek State Park	N 41° 11' 10" W 111° 22' 52"

Maps

USGS 1:24000   Lost Creek Dam, Francis Canyon

Utah Atlas and Gazetteer   Page 61

When to Go

It has provided good fishing from April to October in the past. ♦

Services

Camping:

Lost Creek State Park
Morgan
tel: (801) 829-6866
Reservations: (800) 322-3770
(In Salt Lake City, call 322-3770)

Mantua Reservoir   BOX ELDER COUNTY

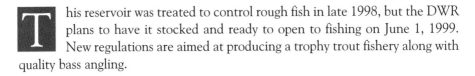

his reservoir was treated to control rough fish in late 1998, but the DWR plans to have it stocked and ready to open to fishing on June 1, 1999. New regulations are aimed at producing a trophy trout fishery along with quality bass angling.

Fish Species

Rainbow trout, largemouth bass, and bluegill.

Special Regulations

❑ Artificial flies and lures only.

❑ Trout limit, 2.

❑ **Closed** to fishing January 1 through May 31.

❑ **Closed** to the possession of bass.

Tactics

This lake has extensive weed growth which makes boating difficult from late June until the weeds die back in the fall. This weed growth makes trolling nearly impossible much of the year.

The best approach is to cast into open pockets in the weeds. Trout anglers can do this effectively with spinners or wooly buggers on fly tackle. Bass fishers will have no difficulty using this approach with their favorite lures.

How to Get There

From Brigham City, go east on US 89 about 3 miles up the canyon. Turn east onto 500 North to reach the reservoir.

Accessibility

There is a road around the entire reservoir, and a boat ramp at the southwest corner. The DWR and Brigham City plan to build a new boat ramp with a parking area and restrooms in the next 2 years.

The Box Elder Campground is about 0.5 miles southwest of the reservoir next to the town of Mantua.

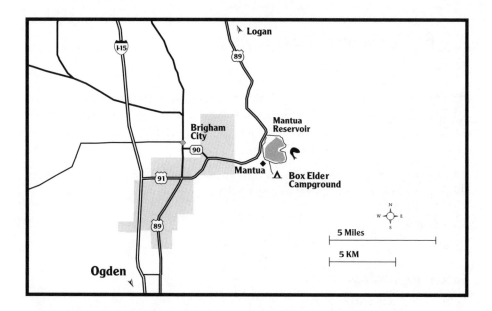

GPS Coordinates

Mantua Reservoir	N 41° 30' 13" W 111° 55' 51"
Box Elder Campground	N 41° 29' 40" W 111° 56' 60"

Maps

USGS 1:24000   Mantua, Mount Pisgah

Utah Atlas and Gazetteer   Page 60

When to Go

Early spring and late fall are the best times to fish here when weed growth is not so much of a problem. ♦

Services

National Forest Campgrounds:
tel:(877) 444-6777 or (800) 280-2267
Box Elder
Willard Basin

Camping:
Mt. Haven RV Park
130 N Main
Mantua, UT 84324
tel: (435) 723-7615

Matt Warner Reservoir   UINTAH COUNTY

T his reservoir is close to Calder and Crouse Reservoirs. All three are impoundments on Pot Creek and all can suffer from winterkill in harsh winters. It is recommended that you contact the Vernal office of the DWR at (435) 789-3103 before planning a trip here.

Of this group of three reservoirs, Matt Warner is the largest, receives the most fishing pressure, and provides the fastest fishing.

Fish Species

Rainbow trout.

Special Regulations

Matt Warner Reservoir:

❏ Trout limit, 4.

Pot Creek (Uintah County) — including tributaries:

❏ Trout limit, 4.

Tactics

Fly-fishers should try stripping wooly buggers and damselfly nymphs. Intermediate or slow sinking fly lines work well in the shallows. Float tubes allow great access.

Trollers find spinners and pop gear effective.

Baitfishing from shore can be effective. Using a combination of a worm and a marshmallow on a slip sinker rig will suspend your bait just above the weeds.

How to Get There

From Vernal, go north on US 191 for 25 miles. Then go east 8.8 miles on Diamond Mountain Road. Then turn north and go 7 miles to arrive at Matt Warner Reservoir.

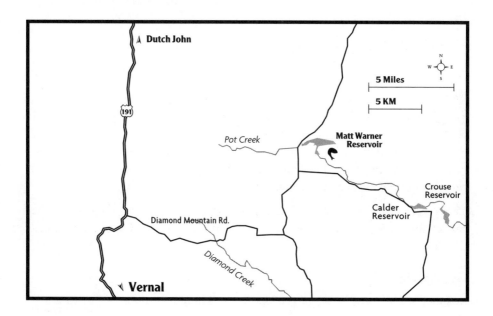

Accessibility

There are roads around the reservoir except for the southeast side. There is a boat ramp and toilets.

The road into Matt Warner Reservoir is not kept open in winter, so access for ice-fishers is by snowmobile. Four-wheel-drive vehicles are recommended, especially if the road is wet.

GPS Coordinates

Matt Warner Reservoir	N 40° 46′ 23″ W 109° 17′ 50″

Maps

USGS 1:24000   Jackson Draw

Utah Atlas and Gazetteer   Page 57

When to Go

Expect good fishing from April to October, with May and June the best months. Ice-fishing is good from January to March. Always check ice conditions. ◆

Porcupine Reservoir CACHE COUNTY

Porcupine Reservoir was drawn down to low levels in the fall of 1998 so repairs could be made to the dam. It will be refilled in spring of 1999. It is not clear how much effect this drawdown will have on the Porcupine Reservoir fishery in the immediate future. The kokanee populations were on the verge of overpopulation. They are the main forage species, so there is reason to believe negative impact will be minimal.

This reservoir is known to harbor whirling disease. Please see the whirling disease chapter in this guide for precautions to ensure that you don't help to spread this disease.

Fish Species
Kokanee salmon, cutthroat, brown, splake, and rainbow trout.

Special Regulations
☐ **Closed** to the possession of kokanee salmon with any red color from August 15 through September 30.

☐ See East Fork Little Bear River on page 80.

Tactics
Trolling with small flashy lures is the most effective way to catch kokanee. Anglers who use a fish-finder to locate schools of fish, and then present lures at the correct depth, will have greater success.

For splake (predatory fish that feed on the kokanee), try using heavy spoons or jigs tipped with dead minnows.

This reservoir is home to a few very large brown trout — some exceeding 10 pounds. Try trolling large crankbaits for these over-sized fish. Look for them near schools of kokanee, particularly in the fall near the inlet. You will likely need to invest a great deal of time to capture one of these trophies.

How to Get There
From Logan, go south on US 89 to SR 165 (at the south edge of town). Go south 14 miles on SR 165 to the town of Avon. Go south 0.3 miles on SR 162. Turn east on La Plata Road and continue about 4 miles to the reservoir.

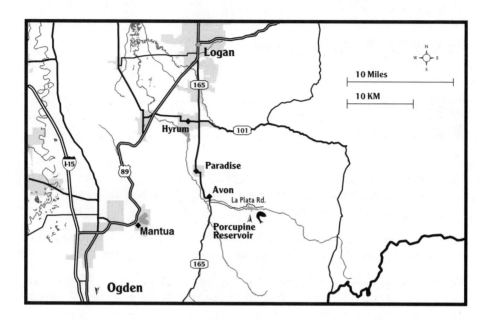

Accessibility

There are no facilities here.

GPS Coordinates

Porcupine Reservoir	N 41° 31' 09" W 111° 44' 12"

Maps

USGS 1:24000   Porcupine Reservoir

Utah Atlas and Gazetteer   Page 61

When to Go

Expect good fishing from April through October. Kokanee fishing will peak in late summer and early fall, but see the Special Regulations above.

Splake are readily caught through the ice. In most winters, ice will be adequate by mid-January. Be sure to check it yourself. ◆

Rockport Reservoir   SUMMIT COUNTY

 his 1,000-acre reservoir is nestled between the Wasatch and Uinta Mountains at 6,000 feet. There are five campgrounds around the lake and it is popular for waterskiing, swimming, and sailing, as well as fishing.

The quality of fishing here has steadily improved over the last few years. There is good success on smallmouth bass and rainbow trout. Perch here are large, running 10 to 12 inches and brown trout over 10 pounds are occasionally caught.

This reservoir is only a 45-minute drive from the Salt Lake Valley, making it perfect for those times when one has only a few hours to get outdoors.

This reservoir is known to harbor whirling disease. Please see the whirling disease section in the guide for precautions to ensure that you don't help to spread this disease.

Fish Species
Rainbow, cutthroat, and brown trout and smallmouth bass.

Special Regulations
- Minimum bass size, 12 inches.
- January 1 through May 21, trout limit is 4.
- Dead yellow perch may be used as bait.

Tactics
Fly-fishers should consider float tubing here. Wooly buggers on sink tip and full sinking lines will take both rainbows and smallmouth bass. Rainbows will be near the river mouth in the spring.

Smallmouth have come on strongly in this reservoir. Look for them along rocky shorelines and points. Good spots are just south of the boat ramp and the east shoreline near the dam. Jigs with plastic bodies or tipped with night crawlers are best, followed by crankbaits.

Perch will be found in shallow spawning areas shortly after "ice out." Jigs tipped with perch meat or night crawlers work well. Consider fishing your jig under a bobber as you would for crappie once you have located fish. You will be able to keep your lure in the productive area for a longer time without casting.

This reservoir is becoming a popular ice-fishing location. Be sure to check ice conditions before venturing out. Taking your fish locator out onto the ice will help narrow your search. Some large trout are being taken through the ice, so be sure your tackle is up to the challenge.

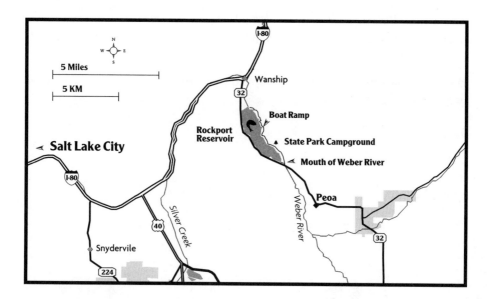

How to Get There

From Salt Lake City, take I-80 east to Exit 156 at Wanship. Turn south on SR 32 and you will reach the dam in about 1.5 miles.

Accessibility

Anglers can access the lake directly from SR 32 or continue past the lake, and turn north 0.5 mile after crossing the Weber River. This will bring you around to the east side of the lake to the state park campground and the boat ramp.

GPS Coordinates

State Park Boat Ramp	N 40° 46′ 30″ W 111° 23′ 25″
State Park Campground	N 40° 46′ 57″ W 111° 23′ 37″
Mouth of Weber River	N 40° 45′ 12″ W 111° 22′ 23″

Maps

USGS 1:24000   Wanship, Crandall Canyon

Utah Atlas and Gazetteer   Page 54

When to Go

Ice-off is prime time for trout anglers; rainbows will be feeding well. Cast to the ice once water opens up along the shore.

Perch spawn just after "ice out" and will be shallow at that time, remember these are school fish; where you find one there are probably more.

Smallmouth bass fishing will be good during the spawn in May and June and still continue strong until cold weather in the fall.

Look for brown trout to begin staging at the mouth of the Weber in September preparatory to spawning. ♦

Services

Camping:

Rockport State Park
Wanship
tel: (435) 336-2241
Reservations: (800) 322-3770 (In Salt Lake City, call 322-3770)

Winter action at Rockport Reservoir. (PHOTO: COURTESY UTAH OUTDOORS)

Scofield Reservoir

CARBON AND UTAH COUNTIES

T his 2,800-acre reservoir, with good camping and boat launching facilities, is only two hours from Salt Lake City. It is above 7,600 feet in a beautiful, mountainous area. Dense stands of pine and aspen around the reservoir provide habitat for deer, elk, and black bear.

Campers staying here are close to the good stream fishing on the Price River below the dam or on Fish Creek above the reservoir.

The scenic Skyline Drive is just to the west. One can make a loop from Scofield Reservoir north to US 6, then turn west to the Tucker Rest Area, where Skyline Drive follows Clear Creek Ridge and climbs to over 9,000 feet to the top of the Wasatch range. You will come to SR 264 near Gooseberry Reservoir, about 28 miles from US 6. A left turn here and another left on SR 96 will return you to Scofield Reservoir.

Grazing practices in the watershed already have had an adverse effect on the fishery. Increased phosphorous levels have caused fish kills in the fall of 1997 and 1998. Scofield Reservoir may experience further negative impact by implementation of the proposed Narrows Reservoir Project. Winter flows into the reservoir will likely be reduced. The amount of water stored by the reservoir could decrease by as much as 26%.

Fish Species
Rainbow and cutthroat trout.

Special Regulations
Scofield Reservoir:

❏ Trout limit, 4.

Scofield Reservoir Tributaries (streams only, this excludes Gooseberry Reservoir and Bench's Pond, but includes those streams flowing into Gooseberry and Bench's Pond):

❏ Trout limit, 4.

❏ **Closed** January 1 through 6 a.m. on the second Saturday of July (July 10, 1999).

Tactics
Scofield is a good choice for bank fishers. The water generally stays cool enough that fish stay near shore all summer. Casting spinners and small spoons out from

shore can be effective, as are wooly buggers. Keep bait offerings just off the bottom. Adding a marshmallow for flotation is a good technique. The shore near the dam is easily accessible and a popular place for bank anglers.

Look for the heaviest concentrations of larger fish in the coves and bays on the west side of the reservoir, particularly between Fish Creek and Madsen Bay. Float tubes, kick boats, and canoes can be used to work these areas quietly. Wooly buggers and damselfly nymphs are good choices, as are Panther Martin and Mepps spinners.

Trollers have had good success over the years with pop gear and night crawlers. Fish-finders can greatly improve your success by pinpointing concentrations of fish. Try Flatfish just below the surface in the fall for some fast fishing.

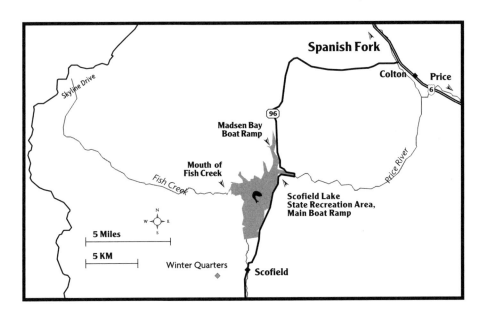

How to Get There

From Spanish Fork, take US 6 southeast 44 miles towards Price. Turn south on SR 96 at the sign for Scofield Reservoir. Continue about 13 miles to reach the dam.

Accessibility

There are two state recreation areas and good access around the lake for bank fishing. Late season drawdowns can make it difficult to reach the water in some places.

GPS Coordinates

Scofield Lake SRA, Main Boat Ramp	N 39° 47' 25" W 111° 07' 44"
Mouth of Fish Creek	N 39° 46' 37" W 111° 10' 34"
Madsen Bay Boat Ramp	N 39° 48' 22" W 111° 08' 24"

Maps

USGS 1:24000   Colton, Scofield Reservoir, Scofield

Utah Atlas and Gazetteer   Page 46

When to Go

Fall is the best time of year for fishing here at Scofield Reservoir. Trout are concentrated and hungry. Because of the elevation, water temperatures don't usually drive fish into deeper water, making this a good choice in mid-summer as well. ◆

Services

Camping

Scofield State Park
tel: (435) 448-9449
winter: (435) 637-2732

Lazy Anchor Campground
Scofield (19 mi S on SR 96)
tel: (435) 448-9697

Strawberry Reservoir   Wasatch County

trawberry is a very large and beautiful high-alpine reservoir. It is at an elevation of 7,600 feet and covers as much as 17,000 acres. That translates into a lot of fishing opportunity.

There are two excellent recreation complexes here: Strawberry Bay Recreation Complex and Soldier Creek Recreation Complex. Both offer fishing access with boat ramps and a marina with fuel services. Camping and picnic areas are also available. Strawberry Bay has a café, as well.

In 1990, the DWR treated Strawberry Reservoir with rotenone to remove rough fish from the ecosystem. Reintroduced trout have done very well in this rich lake, with some very large fish being caught. The year 1998 saw the best kokanee fishing in the reservoir's history and 1999 is expected to be even better.

Fish Species

Rainbow and cutthroat trout; kokanee salmon.

Special Regulations

Strawberry Reservoir:

❑ Trout and kokanee salmon in any combination — limit 4. Only 1 rainbow or cutthroat trout or rainbow-cutthroat hybrid over 18 inches. Anglers are encouraged to voluntarily release rainbow and cutthroat trout.

Strawberry Reservoir Tributaries:

❑ **Closed:** Indian Creek and all tributaries to Indian Creek, Squaw Creek, Strawberry River from Strawberry Reservoir upstream to USFS Road 124 (Bull Springs Rd.), Co-op Creek from confluence with Strawberry River upstream to US 40, and the Central Utah Project Canal (commonly known as the "steps" or "ladders") from U.S. 40 to Strawberry Reservoir as posted.

Strawberry River and its tributaries upstream from USFS Road 124 (Bull Springs Rd.) to its headwaters, Co-op Creek and its tributaries upstream from US 40 to its headwaters, Soldier Creek, Coal Canyon, Cow Hollow, Trout Creek, Sage Creek, Chicken Creek, Little Co-op Creek, Clyde Creek, Mud Creek, Bryants Fork, Horse Creek, Chipman Creek, Trail Hollow, Broad Hollow, Badger Hollow and Road Hollow:

❑ **Closed** May 15 through 6 a.m. on the second Saturday of July (July 10, 1999) and September 1 through 6 a.m. on the second Saturday of October (October 9, 1999).

- Catch and release only (all fish must be immediately released; fishing with fish in possession is illegal).

- Artificial flies and lures only. (Use or possession of bait while fishing is illegal).

Tactics

Anglers here wade or fish from shore, float tubes, and boats. All approaches work well, with float tubers having a slight edge, as they can access most water and can be very quiet.

Waders and float tubers can do well by finding old stream channels at the very heads of the bays with inlet streams. Casting along these channels with black or olive wooly buggers and small muddler minnows is often rewarded.

Fall is the time when kokanee salmon spawn. Look for schools of these tasty fish in front of tributaries beginning in September. Small flashy lures or flies will work best. If you catch a kokanee, remember there are probably more close by.

Trollers can find success with Strawberry wobblers, Rapalas, or Flatfish. Pop gear and a worm are an old standard that still works well. A great deal of Strawberry Reservoir is deep water and anglers who combine fish-finders and downriggers effectively can consistently take big fish.

Note: Do not fillet fish at the reservoir. Conservation officers can't tell size or species when filleted!

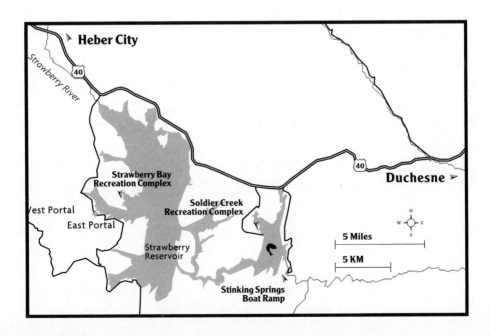

How to Get There

From Salt Lake City, take I-80 to US 40 and travel east. Go through Heber City and continue another 24 miles to reach Strawberry Reservoir.

Accessibility

US 40 runs along the north side of the reservoir and gives access to the Chicken Day-Use Areas. Many anglers also use access at the "ladders" where a Central Utah Project canal emerges from a tunnel and empties into the lake next to US 40. Turning south onto the road at the visitor center will bring you to Strawberry Bay Recreation Complex and the Haws Point Day-Use Area. Turning south on the road at the east edge of Strawberry leads you to Soldier Creek Dam and the Aspen Grove Campground at Stinking Springs. The turnoff for Soldier Creek Recreation Complex is clearly marked on US 40 as well.

GPS Coordinates

Strawberry Bay Recreation Complex	N 40° 10' 53" W 111° 10' 02"
Soldier Creek Recreation Complex	N 40° 09' 20" W 111° 03' 08"
Stinking Springs Boat Ramp	N 40° 07' 43" W 111° 02' 06"

Maps

USGS 1:24000	Strawberry Reservoir NE Strawberry Reservoir NW Strawberry Reservoir SW Strawberry Reservoir SE
Utah Atlas and Gazetteer	Pages 54, 46

When to Go

This reservoir generally fishes well from ice-off (April) to "freeze-up" (November). One of the best times is just when the ice is partially gone. Flies or lures are cast to the ice edge and allowed to sink. Early mornings in July and August can also be especially productive.

Ice-fishers can practice their sport at Strawberry Reservoir from January to March most years. Always check ice conditions before venturing out on to the lake. ◆

Services

Lodging:

Daniels Summit Lodge
US 40, Daniels Summit Pass
P.O. Box 490
Heber City, UT 84032
tel: (435) 548-2300 / (800) 519-9969
fax: (435) 548-2982
www.danielssummit.com

Strawberry Bay Marina and Lodge
Strawberry Bay
tel: (435) 548-2500 — lodge

Marinas:

Soldier Creek Marina
Soldier Creek
tel: (435) 548-2696

Strawberry Bay Marina and Lodge
Strawberry Bay
tel: (435) 548-2261 — store

Emmett Heath Sr. with a Strawberry Reservoir rainbow. (Photo: Emmett Heath / Western Rivers Flyfisher)

Woodruff Reservoir

 A pproximately 11 miles southwest of Woodruff, and 8 miles from Birch Creek Reservoir, this small water is underutilized. Anglers can escape from crowds found elsewhere.

The angler that takes the time to visit Woodruff Reservoir will find some very respectable cutthroat trout waiting for a fly or lure to go past.

Fish Species

Cutthroat trout, whitefish.

Special Regulations

General season, bag, and possession limits apply.

Tactics

Trolling spinners or pop gear can be very effective in this small reservoir. Float tubes are another good way to fish this neglected water. The usual assortment of still-water offerings are effective on this lake.

There is also a good population of whitefish in the lake for those who have the inclination to pursue them. Try small jigs and teardrops or bead head nymphs.

How to Get There

From Ogden, go northeast 57 miles on SR 39 up past the Monte Cristo Ranger Station, then through Walton Canyon, and eventually turn southwest onto Woodruff Creek Road and go 4 miles to the reservoir. SR 39 is closed in winter, but usually opens up anywhere from Memorial Day weekend through the Fourth of July. If SR 39 is still closed, you may be able to get in from Woodruff which is north of Evanston, Wyoming, on SR 16.

Accessibility

There is a gravel boat launch for smaller vessels. Camping is available at Birch Creek Campground 9 miles to the north and 1.5 mile north of the Birch Creek Reservoirs.

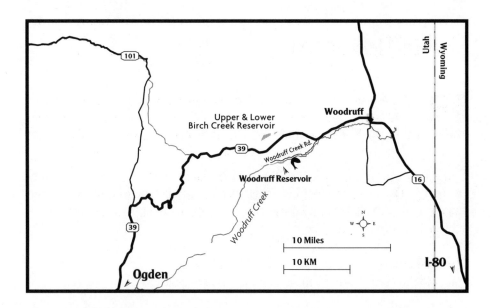

GPS Coordinates

Woodruff Reservoir	N 41° 27' 52" W 111° 19' 35"

Maps

USGS 1:24000   Woodruff Reservoir

Utah Atlas and Gazetteer   Page 61

When to Go

April to October. There is little ice-fishing pressure as winter access is by snow-mobile only. ♦

Cutler Reservoir

T his is one of the most underutilized and underrated warmwater fisheries in the state. There are very extensive shallow areas that can be productive if anglers adjust their tactics. Sand bars and shallows also create navigational hazards for boaters. Operate your vessel with safety in mind.

Cutler Reservoir is a long, narrow reservoir operated by Utah Power to generate electricity. The main channel has some current, and it functions like a riverine aquatic system. Back bays and areas away from the main channel are more typical lake environments.

Fish Species

Largemouth bass, channel catfish, crappie, and bluegill.

Special Regulations

General season, bag, and possession limits apply.

Cutler Reservoir is open to the use of two poles by anglers purchasing a second pole permit for $10.00 along with their regular fishing or combination license (see current proclamation).

Tactics

As this lake is underutilized, there is not much angler experience to draw on for information. The extensive shallows, mixed with more river type of habitat, challenge anglers to adapt to this unusual body of water.

Some anglers recommend spinnerbaits or buzzbaits as effective lures in the shallow water areas of this reservoir.

How to Get There

From Logan, go west 4 miles on SR 30, then north 3.1 miles on 3200 West Street. Go west 2.5 miles, passing through Benson to reach the reservoir.

Accessibility

The Benson Marina (boat ramp only) is the main launch site and is just west of the town of Benson. There is a boat ramp by Cache Junction where SR 23 crosses the reservoir. The Valley View Ramp is where SR 30 crosses the Little Bear River about 6 miles west of Logan.

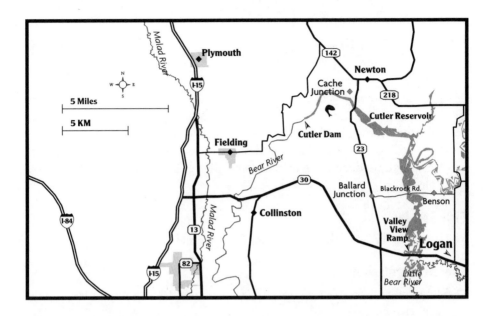

GPS Coordinates

Cutler Dam	N 41° 50′ 12″ W 112° 02′ 51″

Maps

USGS 1:24000   Cutler Dam, Newton

Utah Atlas and Gazetteer   Page 62

When to Go

The bass will be in their pre-spawn period by late April, but turbid water in the early season can make for difficult fishing. Best success will be in late summer and fall.

There is little ice-fishing pressure, and the current through the reservoir makes for variable ice conditions. ◆

Newton Reservoir

T his reservoir has had tiger muskies for about three years, so anglers may begin to see some legal-size fish by mid-August of 1999. Tigers were stocked to control pan fish, which have been numerous but small in the past. The average size of panfish should slowly increase over the next several years as tiger muskies reduce their numbers and the remaining fish have more food available.

Fish Species

Yellow perch, largemouth bass, tiger muskie, channel catfish, and rainbow trout.

Special Regulations

❑ Minimum bass size is 15 inches. All bass less than 15 inches must be immediately released.

❑ Tiger muskie limit, 1. All tiger muskies less than 40 inches must be immediately released.

❑ Dead yellow perch may be used as bait.

Newton Reservoir is open to the use of two poles by anglers that purchase a second pole permit for $10.00 along with their regular fishing or combination license (see regulations).

Tactics

There are good numbers of bass in Newton, but many of them are just under the 15-inch limit. Normal bass tactics are effectively used here.

There is a very large population of smaller perch. This is a good destination to bring young anglers with a short attention span. Worms and dead minnows generate fast action during the warmer months. If ice-fishing, try using ice flies or teardrops tipped with a mealworm or perch eyes.

How to Get There

From Logan, go north 5 miles on US 91, then west 8.8 miles on SR 218. Go west 0.7 miles on SR 23 into the town of Newton and turn north on 6400 West. Travel 3.3 miles, then turn east onto 9000 North, which will pass below the dam, and then turn north at 5800 West.

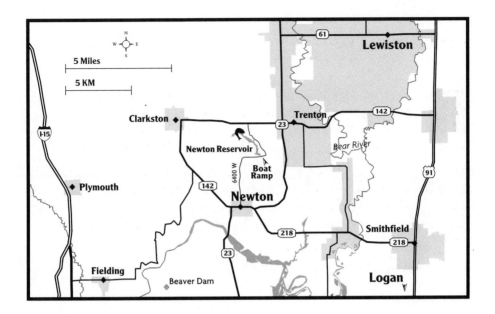

Accessibility

There is a boat ramp at the southeast corner of the reservoir.

GPS Coordinates

Newton Reservoir	N 41° 54' 27" W 111° 59' 03"

Maps

USGS 1:24000   Trenton, Clarkston

Utah Atlas and Gazetteer   Page 62

When to Go

Anglers can look forward to good fishing from April to October.

This is usually one of the first lakes to have safe ice. Hardwater anglers can start ice-fishing before Christmas most years. Be sure to exercise caution and check the ice. ◆

Pelican Lake

The rich wetlands and tulles surrounding Pelican Lake are breeding habitat to a wide variety of birds. Yellow-headed blackbirds and coots serenade the angler here in the spring. With luck, you may see tall and graceful sandhill cranes shepherd their ungainly youngsters back out of your view.

This lake is certainly the best bluegill fishing in the state. Fish are very large for the species and can be found in good numbers, especially in the spring while spawning. This is a great place to get youngsters hooked on fishing. These flat-sided fish put up quite a fight, are colorful and beautiful in the hand, and delicious on the table.

Bass anglers will also appreciate Pelican Lake.

Fish Species

Exceptionally large bluegills and some good bass.

Special Regulations

❏ Bluegill and green sunfish in the aggregate, limit 10.

❏ Bass limit, 6; only 1 bass larger than 16 inches.

Tactics

If you are here for the bluegills, remember that they have small mouths; use small baits and lures.

Quiet wading during spawn can be very exciting, with fish on nearly every cast when you find a concentration of these colorful fighters. Float tubes and small boats will get to the fish as well.

Spawners will be gathered in open areas up inside the tulles in about 3 feet of water. Fly-fishers can use foam-bodied dry flies, but small woolly buggers or damselfly nymphs often work better. Small jigs and spinners are also effective. A small piece of night crawler under a bobber is a great way for young fishers to get started, particularly if it is attached to a cane pole. This simple tackle is easy to operate and will keep frustration to a minimum.

When spawning is past, look for fish in slightly deeper water on the edge of the tulles. Bluegills will be more scattered at this time, so keep moving.

In April or May, when good bass fishing can be found, try casting minnow plugs along the edge of the tulles.

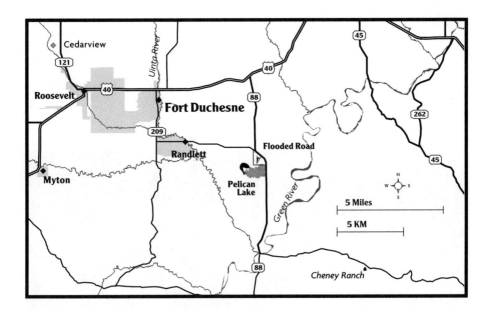

How to Get There

From Vernal, travel west on US 40 about 14 miles to SR 88. Turn south and go 7 miles. Take a left turn on SR 88, which will put you on the west side of the lake.

Accessibility

A flooded road on the north side of the lake makes good access for waders. Small boats and float tubes can also be launched here. Keep in mind that water levels can fluctuate.

From the junction just north of Pelican Lake there is a road just to the west that goes south to the lake. Go 1.1 miles down this road and turn left onto the flooded road. If you park here, don't block the road for others. From the junction you can also go southeast on SR 88 for 1.9 miles and turn left onto the flooded road.

There is a launch area in the southeast corner of the lake, which is accessible from SR 88. Follow the signs.

GPS Coordinates

Flooded Road	N 40° 12' 13" W 109° 40' 24"

Maps

USGS 1:24000	Pelican Lake
Utah Atlas and Gazetteer	Pages 48, 56

When to Go

The best time of year is spring during spawning. Fish should be found in the shallows during the month of May and early June. Good fishing can be expected throughout the summer. Things slow down when water cools in the fall. This is a popular waterfowl hunting area, so you might want to avoid it once hunting season opens. ◆

Dave Champion releases a tiger muskie to fight again another day. (Photo: Bill Furniss)

Pineview Reservoir

T his attractive and easily accessible reservoir has come into its own since the DWR began to manage it for perch and tiger muskie. It gives anglers a chance for a real trophy only 15 minutes from Ogden. The big pike keep perch and crappie from overpopulating, thereby keeping up the average size of these fish.

Remember that tiger muskie are a sterile hybrid and populations are only maintained by stocking. Management of perch and crappie is dependent on harvest by anglers. Taking these fish for food helps to prevent overpopulation and stunting.

Pineview perch and crappie can keep young anglers interested and enthusiastic about fishing. Simple tackle and techniques will help them to feel successful.

Fish Species

Crappie, yellow perch, and tiger muskie are the most pursued fish here. There are also channel catfish, largemouth and smallmouth bass, and bluegill. Rainbow, cutthroat, and brown trout round things out.

Special Regulations

❏ Minimum bass size is 15 inches.

❏ Tiger muskie limit, 1; all tiger muskie less than 40 inches must be released.

❏ **Closed** inside buoys by spillway near the dam.

❏ Dead yellow perch may be used as bait.

Tactics

Tiger muskies are a big draw here. Patrick Benton, Jr. landed a 45 ¼ inch fish here in 1997. As these fish are still relatively new to Pineview, there is every reason to believe that larger ones will be taken in the future. These big predators feed on perch and crappie. Look for them near structure in areas frequented by schools of their forage fish. Casting large crankbaits and spoons is effective. Lures that mimic the colors of perch are recommended.

Perch provide good fishing most of the year. Ice-fishers use wax worms, mealworms, and strips of perch meat fished within 6 inches of the bottom. These fish move in schools, so expect fast action when they move through. These guys spawn in the early spring and you will find them in the shallows as soon as the ice comes off.

Crappie fishing is a great spring activity. Look for these good-eating fish up in the shallows in May and June. You will find them back in the sticks and weeds at this time. Don't be afraid to cast your lure right into the thick stuff. Mini-jigs are the lure of choice. They can be used on light spinning gear or can be cast with a fly-rod. Fishing them under a bobber is most effective, as it allows the angler to stay in the prime locations longer. Fly-fishers can also score with poppers and spiders in chartreuse or wooly buggers underneath. Once the spawn is over, you will find crappie suspended in deeper water near shallow brushy areas where they feed in the evenings.

Smallmouth can be found along rocky and brushy shorelines here, with crankbaits and jigs being the favorite offerings.

Catfishing can be very good here as well. It is easy to get a mess of small fish by sinking a worm to the bottom. Look for them in the same areas where you find crappie.

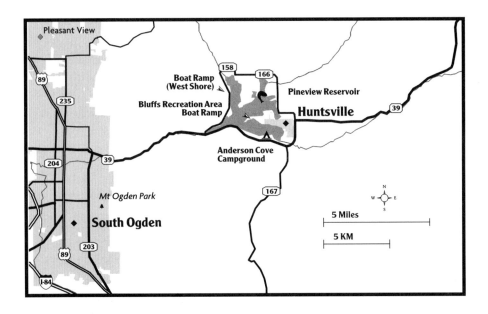

How to Get There
From I-15 in Ogden, take Exit 347 and go east on SR 39. You will reach the dam in about 10 miles.

Accessibility
SR 39 brings you to the south and east sides of the reservoir. Turning left and driving through the town of Huntsville will bring you to Bluffs Recreation Area.

You can also turn left at the dam and follow SR 162 around the west side of the reservoir. SR 166 takes you around the north and east sides and joins SR 39 by Huntsville.

The several day-use areas and the Bluffs Recreation Area combine to provide good access for anglers.

GPS Coordinates

Bluffs Recreation Area Boat Ramp	N 41° 15' 44" W 111° 47' 36"
Anderson Cove Campground	N 41° 15' 05" W 111° 47' 17"
Boat Ramp (West Shore)	N 41° 16' 36" W 111° 49' 05"

Maps

USGS 1:24000   Huntsville, Snow Basin

Utah Atlas and Gazetteer   Pages 60, 61

When to Go

This reservoir can fish well throughout the year, but spring has the most activity. April, May, and June have the perch and crappie spawning, with tigers in shallow water to feed on them.

This is a good ice-fishing destination with perch providing enough activity to keep anglers warm.

Caution: Always check ice conditions before venturing out onto frozen lakes. ▼

Services

National Forest Campground:

tel: (877) 444-6777 or (800) 280-2267
North Fork

Lodging:

Jackson Fork Inn
7345 E 900 S
Huntsville, UT 84317
tel: (801) 745-0051 / (800) 255-0672

Red Fleet Reservoir

ust 15 minutes north of Vernal and surrounded by incredibly vibrant red slickrock, Red Fleet has some big bass as well as good rainbow fishing. There is also a large population of small bluegills to entertain anglers.

The Utah Field House of Natural History State Park is located in Vernal, and Dinosaur Quarry Historic Site is just 20 minutes east. Both will capture the imagination of children and adults alike. A dinosaur trackway has also been discovered near the reservoir.

Fish Species

Largemouth bass, smallmouth bass, bluegill, rainbow, and a few brown trout.

Special Regulations

General season, bag, and possession limits apply.

Tactics

Traditional bass tactics work well here for the largemouth bass. Crayfish are an important source of food so try crankbaits and jigs that imitate them.

Smallmouth have only recently appeared in Red Fleet, and are expected to flourish along the rocky shoreline.

Still-fishing with bait for rainbows is a common and effective method.

How to Get There

From Vernal, drive north 12 miles on US 191, then turn east to the park.

Accessibility

Red Fleet State Park has camping, modern restrooms, a boat ramp, and a beach area.

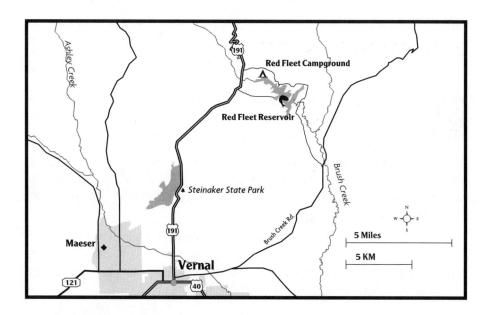

GPS Coordinates

Red Fleet Campground	N 40° 36' 47" W 109° 24' 15"
Red Fleet Reservoir	N 40° 34' 41" W 109° 25' 00"

Maps

USGS 1:24000   Donkey Flat (the reservoir does not appear on currently available USGS Maps)

Utah Atlas and Gazetteer   Pages 56, 57

When to Go

June is probably the best month for bass fishing; rainbows are very active in May and June. Anglers can find open water from April to November. ◆

Services

Camping:

Red Fleet State Park
Vernal
tel: (435) 789-4432
Reservations: (800) 322-3770
(In Salt Lake City, call 322-3770)

Starvation Reservoir

DUCHESNE COUNTY

he appearance of this reservoir seems to fit its name, as thin fingers of the lake reach up into dry, rocky gulches. The bare ridges have a scratchy cover of pinion and juniper over wrinkled sandstone.

The name is also appropriate for small walleyes in this reservoir. Large walleyes and smallmouths eat all the "young of the year" chubs, leaving scant food for little fish. Small walleye grow less than 1 inch per year. Anglers can help the fishery by keeping some of these fish.

This body of water is home to some very large walleye and brown trout. Walleye often exceed 10 pounds. The exciting thing about fishing here is that there are three great species of sport fish and, as their habitat and foods are basically the same, you never know which might challenge you next.

Fish Species

Brown trout, smallmouth bass, and walleye.

Special Regulations

❏ Walleye limit, 10; but only 1 may be over 20 inches.

Tactics

Walleye fishing is easier here through most of the year than in many other waters. July, August, and September can be fast fishing, particularly for smaller fish. The spawning period in spring can be more difficult to fish. Start fishing in the early season with night crawlers. Artificials will work better as water warms and fish are more aggressive. Try slow trolling a night crawler harness or Rapala behind a walking sinker. The area off of Saleratus Wash is a good choice. Jigs and plastic worms work well on rocky shorelines.

Big brown trout can be found in Rabbit Gulch and Saleratus Wash. They will take the same lures and baits as walleyes, so anglers can pursue both at the same time. Look for these fish to stage off the mouth of the Strawberry River starting in September as they prepare to spawn.

There are smallmouth here, as well. They feed on crayfish and insects once the chub populations are depleted. Jigs and crankbaits cast to rock piles and points should provide good action beginning in May and June.

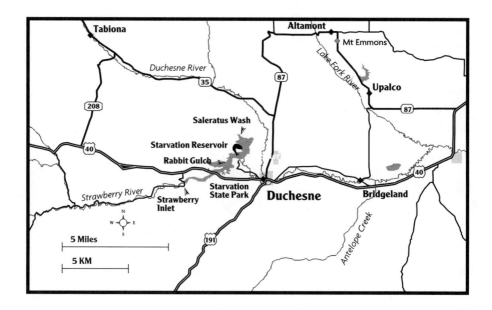

How to Get There

From the Salt Lake Valley, take I-80 east to US 40. Go east 81 miles. You will cross Starvation Reservoir 5 miles west of Duchesne.

Accessibility

There is reasonable access around the lake on dirt roads. The size of the lake (3,500 acres) and its rugged surroundings give boaters a big advantage. Float tubing can also work well and there are many protected bays and coves if the wind kicks up. Camping available at Starvation State Park (tel: 435-738-2326).

GPS Coordinates

Starvation State Park	N 40° 11' 23" W 110° 27' 10"
Strawberry Inlet	N 40° 09' 27" W 110° 32' 42"
Saleratus Wash	N 40° 13' 15" W 110° 26' 50"
Rabbit Gulch	N 40° 11' 08" W 110° 30' 05"

Maps

USGS 1:24000   Duchesne, Rabbit Gulch

Utah Atlas and Gazetteer   Pages 47, 55

When to Go

This reservoir will fish from ice-off until late fall. With the walleye spawn being a little more difficult, late summer may be the best time to fish here. ◆

Steinaker Reservoir

 his 750-acre reservoir is 130 feet deep in places. The facilities at the state park make this water a great base for families vacationing in Dinosaurland.

Dinosaur National Monument and the Utah Field House of Natural History State Park both help visitors to see what the area was like when dinosaurs ruled the landscape.

There are many fishing destinations in the area: the famous Green River, Red Fleet Reservoir, Flaming Gorge Reservoir, and the Ashley Creek Drainage of the Uinta Mountains, just to name a few.

A burst canal upstream on Dry Fork brought a large amount of sediment into the reservoir. While this had a negative effect on the rainbow trout fishery, it is expected to be fully recovered by the year 2000.

Fish Species

Rainbow and brown trout, largemouth bass and bluegills.

Special Regulations

❑ Bass limit, 6; only 1 may be larger than 15 inches.

Tactics

Common bass tactics are employed here. Like nearby Red Fleet Reservoir, Steinaker bass feed heavily on crayfish. Try appropriate crankbait and jig imitations. Some bass as large as 8 pounds have been caught here and 4 pounders are not uncommon.

This reservoir produces a few very large brown trout, some in excess of 10 pounds. Trolling large crankbaits is the most effective way to capture one of these trophy fish.

Rainbow trout are effectively caught by fishing with baits such as worms and Power Bait.

How to Get There

From Vernal, go north 6 miles on US 191.

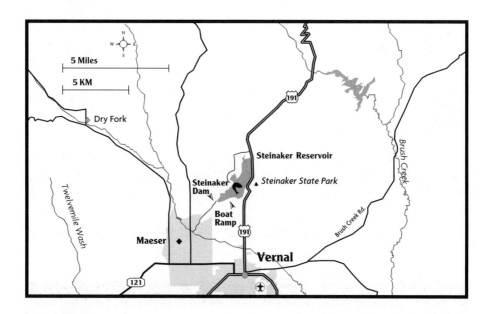

Accessibility

Steinaker State Park has camping, modern restrooms, a beach and swim area, a nature trail, boat ramp and docks. A road accesses most of the reservoir.

GPS Coordinates

Steinaker Dam	N 40° 30′ 13″ W 109° 33′ 09″
Boat Ramp	N 40° 30′ 57″ W 109° 32′ 20″

Maps

USGS 1:24000   Steinaker Reservoir

Utah Atlas and Gazetteer   Page 56

When to Go

Timing here is much the same as nearby Red Fleet. The bass spawn in May and June is probably the best time to catch them. Rainbows are very active in May and June as well. Anglers can find open water from April to November. ◆

Services

Camping:

Steinaker State Park   Reservations: (800) 322-3770
Vernal   (In Salt Lake City, call 322-3770)
tel: (435) 789-4432

Utah Lake

his large natural lake covers 96,000 acres that in historic times was a coldwater trout fishery. Land management and agriculture have greatly altered the water quality of the lake.

Utah Lake's close proximity to the major population centers of the state make this a good target for those short fishing trips when the angler has only a few hours to spare. There are boat launch areas all around the lake to launch and recover boats quickly.

While most anglers don't think of Utah Lake as the place to go for trophy fish, it has produced the state records for catfish and white bass.

Current Angling Record Fish					
White bass	1970	4 lb.	1 oz	—	John R Weckler
Channel catfish	1978	32 lb.	8 oz	39 ¾ in.	Leroy Mortenson
Current Catch-and-Release Record Fish					
White bass	1997	—		13 ¼ in.	Ray Johnson
Channel catfish	1997	—		33 ½ in.	Wesley Scheider

Fish Species
Channel cats, bullheads, white bass, largemouth bass, bluegills, and walleye.

Special Regulations
Utah Lake:

❏ Walleye limit, 6; but only 1 over 20 inches.

Geneva Bubble-up:

❏ **Closed** to fishing between 7 p.m. and 7 a.m. January 1 through 7 a.m. the last Saturday of April (April 24, 1999) in the area starting from the southwest corner of the Linden Marina Dike, south to an intersection with a line running west from the south dike of the Geneva Pond Dike, as posted.

❏ Dead white bass may be used as bait only in Utah Lake.

Tactics

Bass congregate in brushy areas. The shoreline near Saratoga can be particularly good. Spinnerbaits can be cast right into the brush, yet seldom hang up. Jigs and plastic worms rigged "weedless" are also effective in these situations.

The best walleye fishing is in the spring from March to April. Chartreuse and yellow jigs are effective, as are Rapalas and other crankbaits. Most fish are caught in the boat harbors and near the Geneva Bubble-up. The Provo River Inlet is another good spot to try. Early morning hours are best. Biologists have netted some 15-pound walleyes in Utah Lake, so be prepared for a trophy!

Utah Lake is very popular with anglers pursuing big catfish. Most fish are caught in 4 to 5 feet of water. The boat harbors, Lincoln Beach, the west shoreline, and Bird Island are all good areas to try. Favorite baits are night crawlers and shrimp, with some anglers using stinkbaits and chicken livers. One good way to rig up is to use an egg sinker above a swivel with another 3 feet of leader to the bait. This allows the angler to give slack line when the bait is picked up, preventing the catfish from feeling resistance.

White bass are fast growing fish that travel in large schools. If you catch one, there are usually more around. Jigs tipped with bait are good. Fish can be found just off of rocky dikes and in the boat harbors. Late November and December often see a unique ice-fishing situation for Utah Lake's white bass. Anglers stand on the docks in the boat harbors to fish through the thin ice.

How to Get There

Anglers from the Salt Lake Valley will approach Utah Lake by taking I-15 south. The other option is to take Redwood Road south to reach the west side of the lake.

Accessibility

There are several boat harbors around the lake. Most are on the east side and can be reached from I-15.

To reach the American Fork Harbor, take Exit 219, and then take 6800 North Street to 6000 West Street and go south to the harbor.

For Utah Lake State Park, take Exit 268 and turn west on Center Street / SR 114. Turn north, staying on SR 114, and turn west into the state park after you cross the Provo River.

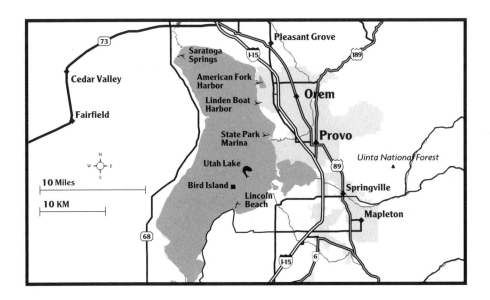

GPS Coordinates

American Fork Harbor	N 40° 20' 34" W 111° 47' 57"
Lindon Boat Harbor	N 40° 19' 39" W 111° 45' 52"
State Park Marina	N 40° 14' 20" W 111° 44' 16"
Lincoln Beach	N 40° 08' 42" W 111° 48' 35"
Bird Island	N 40° 10' 35" W 111° 48' 02"
Saratoga Springs	N 40° 20' 57" W 111° 54' 09"

Maps

USGS 1:24000   Lincoln Point, West Mountain, Goshen Valley
                             North, Soldiers Pass, Saratoga Springs,
                             Pelican Point, Orem, Provo

Utah Atlas and Gazetteer   Pages 45, 53

When to Go

Walleye and bass fishing are usually best in the spring. Look for catfish to be feeding through all the warm months of the year. White bass fishing can really pick up in late fall. ◆

Services

Utah Lake State Park   tel: (801) 375-0731   *(No gas)*
American Fork Boat Harbor   tel: (801) 763-3055   *(Camping, no gas)*

Willard Bay Reservoir

 illard Bay is a 9,900-acre reservoir located just 8 miles north of Ogden. It provides a range of recreational opportunities that are close and easily accessible to the major population centers of the state.

Willard Bay is a dynamic fishery with an unusual diversity of warmwater game species. The introduction of gizzard shad has improved the quantity and quality of the larger predatory fish in the reservoir. The seasonal fluctuation of this forage fish has a great impact on angling success.

Fish Species

Channel catfish, largemouth bass, smallmouth bass, bluegill, green sunfish, black crappie, yellow perch, walleye, and wipers (white bass/striped bass hybrid).

Special Regulations

Willard Bay Reservoir:

❑ Wiper (white bass/striped bass hybrid) limit, 2.

❑ Crappie limit, 10.

❑ Walleye limit, 6; but only 1 over 20 inches.

❑ Possession of gizzard shad, dead or alive, is unlawful.

❑ Dead yellow perch may be used as bait.

Willard Bay Reservoir Inlet Channel from the bouyed start of the channel near the South Marina boat ramp up the channel to the second set of baffles. This does not include the South Marina proper or the normal boating channel out of the South Marina into the reservoir:

❑ **Closed** March 1 through 6 a.m. on the last Saturday of April (April 24, 1999).

❑ Crappie limit, 10.

❑ Walleye limit, 6; but only 1 over 20 inches.

❑ Possession of gizzard shad, dead or alive, is unlawful.

Tactics

Early season (April and May) is a great time to chase pre-spawn walleyes. Trolling night crawler harnesses and crankbaits along the dikes in 10 feet of water is popular. Shore anglers have luck casting soft plastic-tailed jigs and crankbaits along the dikes for cruisers. Low-light periods (early morning, late evening, and after dark) are best for walleyes. Many of the larger female walleyes are caught by anglers casting or trolling large jigs and crankbaits in or near the mouth of the South Marina. Fish-finders can pinpoint locations where these fish stack up.

Gizzard shad begin spawning in June and the larger sport fish in the reservoir start to feed heavily on the shad. Wipers begin to "boil" on these juvenile shad in July. Look for activity along the east dike, north dike, north marina, and inlet channel. Some of the biggest fish are taken along the north dike. Small jigs, crankbaits, and flies 1 to 2 inches long are the key to success.

Black crappie are mostly found in the winter and spring, with April and May being the best months. Look for them at the North Marina. Small jigs work well.

Smallmouth bass are increasing in numbers, and good fishing can be had from May to August. Crayfish are a favorite food of smallmouths so look for them in areas with rip-rap. Try the east dike and near the South Marina. Cast flies or jigs that resemble crayfish into the rip-rap, or troll small crankbaits along these areas.

Bluegills and green sunfish share the same areas as the smallmouth bass. A worm and a bobber are the preferred tactic, but small jig flies also work well.

How to Get There

From Salt Lake City, take I-15 north past Ogden. Take Exit 354 to reach the South Marina. Exit 360 takes you to the North Marina.

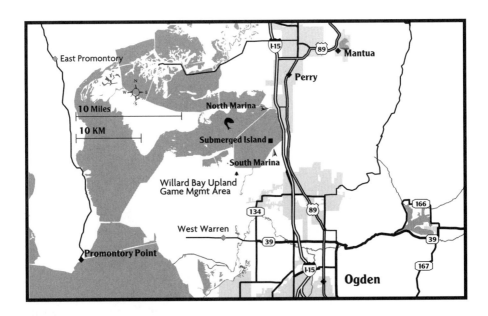

Willard Bay wiper.
(PHOTO: COURTESY UTAH OUTDOORS)

Accessibility

Both marinas are easily found by following signs from the interstate freeway. There is a $5.00 day-use fee. Both sites have wheelchair-accessible restrooms. Camping, boating, and swimming are available, in addition to fishing. The North Marina also has a picnic area and boat slip rentals.

GPS Coordinates

North Marina	N 41° 24′ 34″ W 112° 03′ 15″
South Marina	N 41° 21′ 17″ W 112° 04′ 30″
Submerged Island (near South Marina)	N 41° 22′ 01″ W 112° 05′ 25″

Maps

USGS 1:24000   Willard, Plain City, Plain City SW, Whistler Canal

Utah Atlas and Gazetteer   Page 60

When to Go

This a year round fishery, but the greatest success comes early, before the post-spawn explosion of the gizzard shad population. Anglers who adapt to this change in the reservoir will still find good fishing throughout the summer. ◆

Services

Camping:

Willard Bay State Park
tel: (435) 734-9494
Reservations: (800) 322-3770 (In Salt Lake City, call 322-3770)

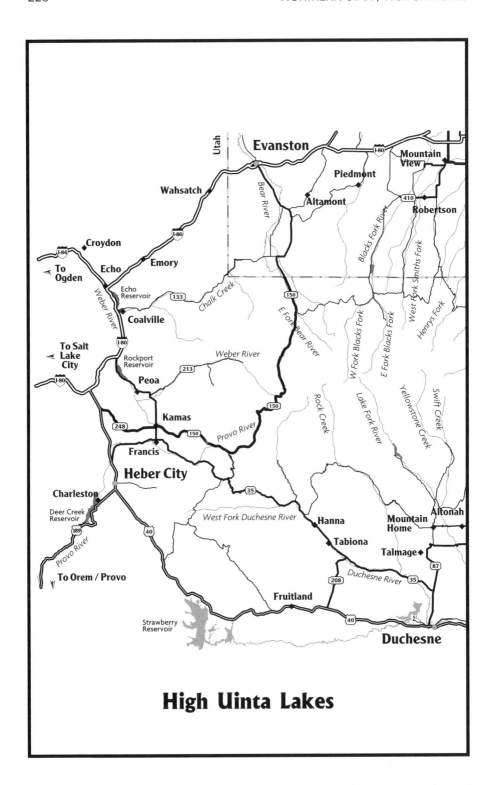

High Uinta Lakes

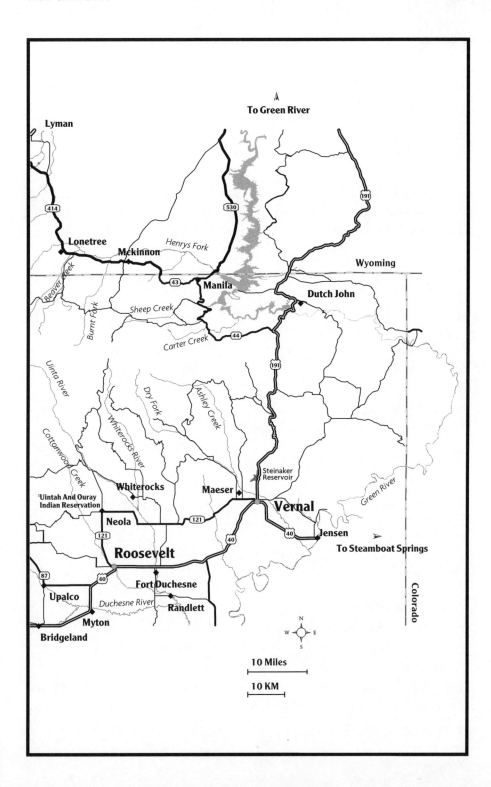

To Green River

Lyman

414

Lonetree

McKinnon

Henrys Fork

530

43

Manila

Dutch John

Wyoming

191

Beaver Creek

Burnt Fork

Sheep Creek

Carter Creek

44

191

Uinta River

Dry Fork

Whiterocks River

Ashley Creek

Cottonwood Creek

Steinaker Reservoir

Green River

Whiterocks

Maeser

Vernal

Uintah And Ouray Indian Reservation

Neola

121

121

40

40

Jensen

To Steamboat Springs

87

Roosevelt

Colorado

Upalco

Fort Duchesne

Duchesne River

Randlett

Myton

Bridgeland

N
W   E
S

10 Miles

10 KM

Uinta Mountain Lakes

T he Uintas comprise the highest mountain range in Utah. They have the distinction of being the only major range in the lower 48 states that runs from east to west. Kings Peak, the highest point in the state, rises to a height of 13,528 feet above sea level.

In 1984, the High Uintas Wilderness Area was established to protect more than 460,000 acres of this mountainous area. Alpine flora dominates above timberline, which generally occurs above 11,000 feet. The Uintas hold the largest alpine area in the Intermountain West, as well as its largest continuous forest.

This area has over 1,000 lakes and ponds, with more than 500 of them managed as fisheries by the DWR. In addition, there are 400 miles of streams.

Both lake and stream systems are very dynamic in this harsh high country. A particular body of water can fish well one year and produce nothing the next. Lakes that are shallow and/or have very low flows can be decimated by winterkill when oxygen levels fall too low, causing part or all of the fish in the lake to die. Low flows and formation of "anchor ice" can adversely affect streams.

As lakes are the primary fishing and camping destinations, they are listed in the following sections by drainage. Only lakes believed to sustain viable fisheries are listed. But don't overlook the streams here, even though they are too numerous to mention. They often hold good numbers of fish, particularly above and below lakes.

Enjoying a dinner of fresh trout on your Uinta Mountain trip can be a great experience. Keep in mind, though, that you will have less of an impact on the fishery if you harvest fish from lakes with large populations of smaller trout. Waters that hold only a few big fish generally have little or no natural reproduction. Therefore, trout kept in these places will not likely be replaced for future anglers.

Special Regulations

General season, bag, and possession limits apply in most of the Uintas. There are, however, provisions for specific waters ("special regulations") for 1999, as listed below:

Ashley Creek (Uintah County) — *Steinaker (Thornburg) diversion to the water treatment plant near the mouth of Ashley Gorge:*

❏ Artificial flies and lures only.

❑ Trout limit, 2.

Brown Duck Basin (Duchesne County) — Uinta Mountains, all streams in the Brown Duck Basin and the outlet of Clements Reservoir to its confluence with Lake Fork Creek):

❑ **Closed** January 1 through 6 a.m. on the second Saturday of July (July 10, 1999).

Grandaddy Lake Tributaries (Duchesne County) — Uinta Mountains, all tributaries to Grandaddy Lake:

❑ **Closed** January 1 through 6 a.m. on the second Saturday of July (July 10, 1999).

Moon Lake (Duchesne County):

❑ Trout limit, 8; only 2 splake may be taken.

Sheep Creek Lake (Daggett County):

❑ **Closed** to fishing.

*Fishing from a boat with a motor of any kind is **prohibited** on the following waters:*

❑ Bonnie Lake (Duchesne River drainage)

❑ Bud Lake (Duchesne River drainage)

❑ Butterfly Lake (Duchesne River drainage)

❑ Lilly Lake (Provo River drainage)

❑ Lost Lake (Provo River drainage)

❑ Mirror Lake (Duchesne River drainage)

❑ Moosehorn Lake (Duchesne River drainage)

❑ Pass Lake (Duchesne River drainage)

❑ Teapot Lake (Provo River drainage)

❑ Trial Lake Reservoir (Provo River drainage)

❑ Washington Lake (Provo River drainage)

Tactics

Conditions can vary a great deal from one lake to the next. You should adapt your methods accordingly. Take time to study each new body of water. Polarized glasses can help you find deep water and underwater structure. You will see more from a high vantage point. Lakes with the fewest fish often hold the largest individuals. Many lakes can appear dead at midday, only to come alive in the early morning or evening.

Some lakes have extensive shallows where fish cruise on their search for a meal. The best strategy in this situation is to find a vantage point where you can see fish approaching, then place a cast in their path, but well ahead of them. Let your fly or lure rest on the bottom until retrieval brings it across their line of sight and about 5 feet in front of them. Generally these fish have a route that they will follow time after time. If things don't work out on the first pass, be patient; your quarry will likely return if not spooked.

Fly tackle is the most effective way to quietly present an offering without disturbing wary trout. It is the method of choice when fishing shallow water or casting to fish close to the shoreline. Fish in some lakes are considerably more cautious than others, and a carefully presented fly is often the most effective way to coax a trout to eat. The last hour before dark often brings fish to the surface to take dry flies with abandon. Schedule your time so that you are ready to take advantage of this evening rise.

Many lakes in the Uintas have thick timber down to the shoreline, making fly casting difficult. A spinning outfit, with either a small spinner or a casting bubble and a fly works well in this circumstance. There are also times when the fish all seem to be rising in the middle of the lake. Good quality and well-maintained spinning tackle will give you the greatest casting range. The terminal tackle used with spinning gear is heavier and makes more disturbance when it hits the water. Try to cast past your target or off to the side so as not to spook fish.

Popular dry flies for the Uintas include mosquitoes, Adams, Goddard Caddis, stimulators, ants, grey hackle/peacocks, and royal Wulffs. Small wooly buggers, wooly worms, damselfly nymphs, pink and olive scuds, cased caddis nymphs, and most bead head nymphs will prove effective under the surface. Small sizes of Mepps, Panther Martin, and Vibrax spinners work well, especially in deeper waters that hold brook trout. Commercially prepared baits like Power Bait, flavored marshmallows, and cured salmon eggs are easier to deal with than worms in the backcountry, especially on longer trips. These fish are opportunistic feeders and should respond well to whatever bait you are most comfortable with.

How to Get to Trailheads

The table lists basic directions to each of the main trailheads. More details are given in each drainage section, where applicable.

Main Trailheads	Directions
Bald Mountain............	On SR 150 at Bald Mountain Pass.
Bullocks Park	From Lonetree, WY, go S 6 mi. on a dirt road, W 10 mi. on FR 058.
Browne Lake	From Lonetree, WY, go E 10 mi. on SR 414, S 11 mi. on FR 221, then E 2.5 mi. on FR 096. There are 3 separate trailheads here.
Burnt Fork.................	From Lonetree, WY, go S 6 mi. on a dirt road, then SE on FR 058 (past Hoop Lake) for 10 mi.
Cache	From SR 150, go E 18 mi. on the North Slope Road (FR 058), then S 5.5 mi. on FR 065.
Center Park...............	Go 7 mi. up Hells Canyon Road from the Yellowstone River Road. Very rough road.
Chepeta	From Whiterocks, go N 22 mi. on FR 117, then N 11 mi. on FR 110.
China Meadows..........	From Mountain View, WY, go S on SR 410 6 mi., then S 4 mi. on FR 072.
Christmas .... Meadows	From SR 150 just N of Stillwater Campground, go S 5 mi. on FR 057.
Crystal Lake	SR 150 to Trial Lake, then W 1 mile, N 1 mile.
Dry Gulch	From Yellowstone River Road, go E 7 mi. on FR 119, then 4 mi. N on FR 122. Rough.
East Fork .... Bear River	From SR 150, go E 1.5 mi. on the North Slope Road (FR 058), then go S 4 mi. on FR 059.
East Fork .... Blacks Fork	From SR 150, go E 18 mi. on the North Slope Road (FR 058), then S 7 mi. on FR 065.
Georges Park	From Lonetree, WY, go S 6 mi. on a dirt road, SW 1.5 mi. on FR 058, then S 3 mi. on FR 164.
Grandview	Go 10 mi. NW of Hanna, on FR 144, then 6 mi. NE on FR 315.
Henrys Fork	From Mountain View, WY, go S on SR 410 for 6 mi., then S 5 mi. on FR 077.
High Line	On SR 150, just 0.1 mile past Butterfly Lake.
Holiday Park /............ Gardners Fork	From Oakley, go E 21 mi. on SR 183 (SR 213). There are 3 different trailheads here.

Main Trailheads	Directions
Hoop Lake	From Lonetree, WY, go S 6 mi. on a dirt road, then S on FR 058 for 5 mi.
Jackson Park	From Yellowstone River Road, go E 5 mi. on FR 119 then 3 mi. NW on FR 120. Rough.
Lake Fork	On Moon Lake Road (FR 131) next to Moon Lake.
Ledgefork	From Oakley, go E 12 mi. on SR 183 (SR 213), then S 3 mi. on FR 033.
Middle Beaver	From Lonetree, WY, go S 6 mi. on a dirt road, SW 1.5 mi. on FR 058, then S 3 mi. on FR 164.
Mill Flat	Go 12 mi. NW of Hanna on FR 144.
Mirror Lake	On SR 150 0.5 mi. W of Mirror Lake.
Pass Lake	On SR 150 0.7 mi. N of Mirror Lake.
Rock Creek	From Mountain Home, WY, go 22 mi. NW on FR 134.
Spirit Lake	From Lonetree, WY, go E 10 mi. on SR 414, S 11 mi. on FR 221, then W on FR 001 another 6 mi.
Swift Creek	Go to the end of the Yellowstone Canyon Road.
Uinta	Go 17 mi. N from Neola on FR 118.
Upper Setting	On SR 150, go 9.3 mi. E of Kamas, Utah, then 7 mi. N on rough Upper Setting Road (FR 034).
West Fork (Beaver River)	From Lonetree, WY, go S 6 mi. on a dirt road, W 6 mi. on FR 058, then N on FR 125.
West Fork Blacks Fork	From SR 150, go E 15 mi. on the North Slope Road (FR 058), then FR 063 SW for 6 mi. You will need a good 4-wheel-drive vehicle.
West Fork Whiterocks	From Whiterocks, go N 22 mi. on FR 117, then N 4 mi. on FR 110, then NW 1 mile.
Wolverine	From SR 150, just N of Stillwater Campground, go S 2 mi. on FR 057.
Yellow Pine	On SR 150, 7 mi. E of Kamas.

Accessibility

Much of this area is remote and at high elevations. One should not venture into the backcountry without being well prepared for the unexpected. Carry extra clothing and rain gear, use good reliable footwear and be sure to let someone know where you intend to go and when you will be back.

Navigation in these rugged mountains is interesting and challenging. Backcountry travelers should always be equipped with a good compass and topographic maps (1:24000 scale are best). We have included a large number of posi-

GPS Trailhead Coordinates

Bullocks Park......	N 40° 55' 36" W 110° 15' 37"	Pass Lake	N 40° 42' 45" W 110° 53' 37"
Burnt Fork	N 40° 54' 13" W 110° 05' 10"	Rock Creek	N 40° 33' 39" W 110° 42' 05"
Center Park	N 40° 36' 10" W 110° 26' 34"	Spirit Lake..........	N 40° 50' 15" W 110° 00' 08"
China .... Meadows	N 40° 55' 22" W 110° 24' 17"	Swift Creek	N 40° 36' 05" W 110° 20' 49"
Crystal Lake........	N 40° 40' 59" W 110° 57' 57"	Uinta	N 40° 37' 54" W 110° 09' 08"
East Fork............. Bear River	N 40° 51' 32" W 110° 45' 14"	Upper Setting	N 40° 40' 08" W 111° 05' 48"
Georges Park......	N 40° 55' 21" W 110° 11' 06"	West Fork .... (Beaver)	N 40° 56' 15" W 110° 14' 04"
Henrys Fork........	N 40° 54' 32" W 110° 19' 52"	West Fork .... Blacks Fork	N 40° 53' 05" W 110° 40' 11"
Holiday Park / ..... Gardner Fork	N 40° 46' 50" W 110° 59' 33"	West Fork .... Whiterocks	N 40° 43' 38" W 110° 03' 38"
Jackson Park	N 40° 35' 02" W 110° 17' 14"	Wolverine...........	N 40° 50' 50" W 110° 48' 52"
Ledgefork	N 40° 44' 22" W 111° 05' 34"	Yellow Pine.........	N 40° 37' 47" W 111° 10' 27"
Mill Flat	N 40° 33' 33" W 110° 53' 17"		

tions that can be entered into GPS receivers to ease navigation, but this equipment is no substitute for maps, good navigational skills, and common sense. Most GPS units will only tell you the direction and distance to a destination. They do not warn of obstacles in your path, or display nearby trails that will ease your journey. The best equipment is of no use without the skills to use it properly in the field. Take the time to practice before you are a day's hike away from the road.

Maps

Trails Illustrated   High Uintas Wilderness (#711)

When to Go

In normal years, most areas are not accessible until mid-June, and many of the high passes do not open until mid-July. Since this is dependent on snow pack and weather, it can vary quite a bit from year to year.

Mosquitoes and biting flies can be annoying in the early part of the season, but are mostly gone by mid-August. The first two weeks of September are a favorite time, as weather is still good and few people are in the backcountry at this time. Snowstorms are possible any time after mid-September, so be prepared. ◆

In the tables for each drainage, the following abbreviations were used:

AT	= albino trout	NW	= northwest
BK	= brook trout	RA	= road access
CG	= campground	RT	= rainbow trout
CT	= cutthroat trout	S	= south
E	= east	SE	= southeast
ESE	= east southeast	SP	= splake
FK	= fork	SR	= state route
FR	= forest road	SW	= southwest
GR	= arctic grayling	TR	= trail
Lw	= lower	Trhd	= trailhead
Mdws	= meadows	Up	= upper
N	= north	W	= west
NE	= northeast	WSW	= west southwest

Searching for a rainbow as an afternoon storm rolls past. (PHOTO: COURTESY UTAH OUTDOORS)

Ashley Creek Drainage

Uintah County

This large drainage is divided into three main basins: Dry Fork Creek, South Fork of Ashley Creek, and North Fork of Ashley Creek. Paradise Park Reservoir, Long Park Reservoir, Hacking Lake, and Ashley Twins are all accessible by road.

There are three main trailheads. Paradise Park is the most important. Blanchett Park lies 3 miles farther up a very rough road. If you don't have a good 4-wheel-drive vehicle, consider starting at Paradise Park to reach destinations that list Blanchett Park as the closest trailhead. Both Paradise Park and Blanchett Park make good base camps for day-hikers. The trailheads at Ashley Twins and Hacking Lake are at either ends of the same trail and are separated by about 6 miles.

Lake Descriptions

Name	Fish	Trailhead	Mi.	GPS Coordinates
Ashley Twins	BK	FR 027	RA	N 40° 43' 27" W 109° 48' 11"
Red Cloud Loop Road to FR 027. Heavy use.				
Blue	BK	Blanchett Park	6.5	N 40° 45' 21" W 109° 53' 31"
1.5 mi. SE of Deadman Lake.				
Deadman	BK	Blanchett Park	5.0	N 40° 46' 19" W 109° 54' 36"
Heavy pressure. Used by Scout groups.				
DF-4	CT	Blanchett Park	4.5	N 40° 44' 44" W 109° 56' 27"
1 mi. W of confluence of Reynolds Creek and Dry Fork. Rugged solitude.				
DF-11 (East Kibah)	BK	Blanchett Park	1.2	N 40° 43' 03" W 109° 55' 59"
1 mi. NW from Blanchett Park. No trail. Easternmost Kibah Lake.				
DF-12 (Finger Kibah)	BK	Blanchett Park	1.3	N 40° 43' 03" W 109° 56' 14"
Long, narrow southern lake in basin. Moderate pressure from day-hikers.				
DF-14 (West Kibah)	BK	Blanchett Park	1.7	N 40° 43' 02" W 109° 56' 40"
W corner of Kibah Basin. No trail.				
DF-15 (North Kibah)	*	Blanchett Park	1.8	N 40° 43' 28" W 109° 56' 30"
*May not hold fish. Northern edge of Kibah Basin. May winterkill.				
DF-16 (Island Kibah)	BK	Blanchett Park	1.5	N 40° 43' 11" W 109° 56' 17"
Center of basin with island. Moderate pressure from day-hikers.				
Fish	CT	Paradise Park	8.3	N 40° 43' 16" W 109° 51' 01"
2.3 mi. NE from N Twin on faint trail up E inlet. Mosquitoes. Heavy use.				
Goose 2	CT	Ashley Twins	0.8	N 40° 43' 57" W 109° 48' 10"
N on trail from Ashley Twins.				

Name	Fish	Trailhead	Mi.	GPS Coordinates
Goose 1	CT	Ashley Twins	0.5	N 40° 43' 51" W 109° 47' 52"
0.5 mi. NE from Ashley Twins.				
GR-52	BK	Paradise Park	7.4	N 40° 43' 41" W 109° 52' 27"
0.4 mi. ESE of Red Belly Lake.				
Hacking	BK	FR 043	RA	N 40° 46' 27" W 109° 48' 40"
From Red Cloud Loop Road, go W 7.8 mi. on FR 043, past Long Park.				
Hooper (Hopper)	CT	Ashley Twins	1.2	N 40° 44' 18" W 109° 48' 43"
Good fly-fishing and easy access on good trail.				
Lakeshore	BK	Hacking Lake	4.5	N 40° 45' 13" W 109° 51' 45"
Good fishing. Heavy sheep grazing.				
Long Park Reservoir	BK	FR 043	RA	N 40° 46' 24" W 109° 46' 05"
From Red Cloud Loop Road, go W 5 mi. on FR 043.				
Marsh	BK	Ashley Twins	1.0	N 40° 43' 05" W 109° 49' 14"
WSW cross country from Ashley Twins.				
Mud	CT	Ashley Twins	0.5	N 40° 42' 52" W 109° 48' 26"
0.5 mi. SSW from Ashley Twins.				
North Twin	BK	Paradise Park	6.0	N 40° 43' 00" W 109° 53' 17"
Good fishing but pressure is fairly heavy.				
Paradise Park Res	RT	Paradise Park	RA	N 40° 40' 19" W 109° 55' 13"
Campground below dam. Heavy use.				
Paul	BK	Paradise Park	2.2	N 40° 41' 50" W 109° 55' 57"
Follow trail 0.3 mi. N of Elk Lake.				
Red Belly	CT	Paradise Park	7.0	N 40° 43' 50" W 109° 52' 58"
1 mi. N of North Twin Lake.				
Sandy	CT	Ashley Twins	1.3	N 40° 43' 56" W 109° 49' 05"
0.5 mi. W of Goose 2.				
Shaw	CT	Paradise Park	7.8	N 40° 43' 31" W 109° 51' 33"
0.4 mi. NW of Fish Lake. Good fly-fishing. Light use.				
South Twin	BK/CT	Paradise Park	5.5	N 40° 42' 47" W 109° 53' 20"
Good for pan-sized trout. Heavy usage and litter.				

Maps

USGS 1:2 00 — Paradise Park, Whiterocks Lake, Leidy Peak, Marsh Peak

Utah Atlas and Gazetteer — Page 56

240

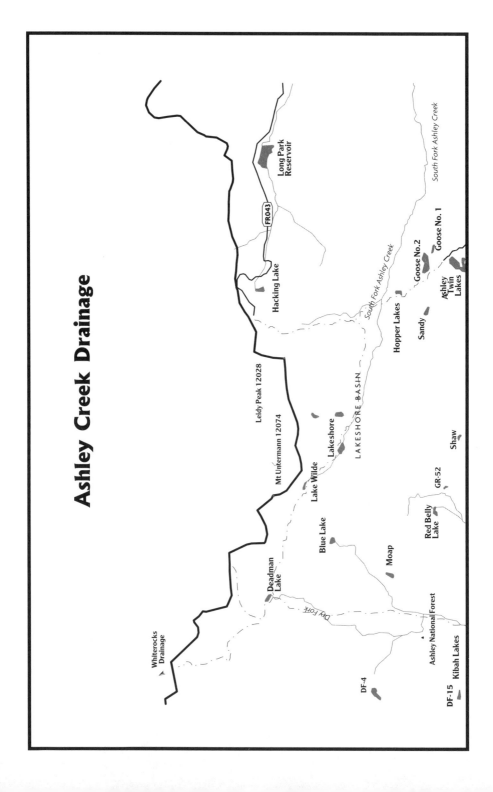

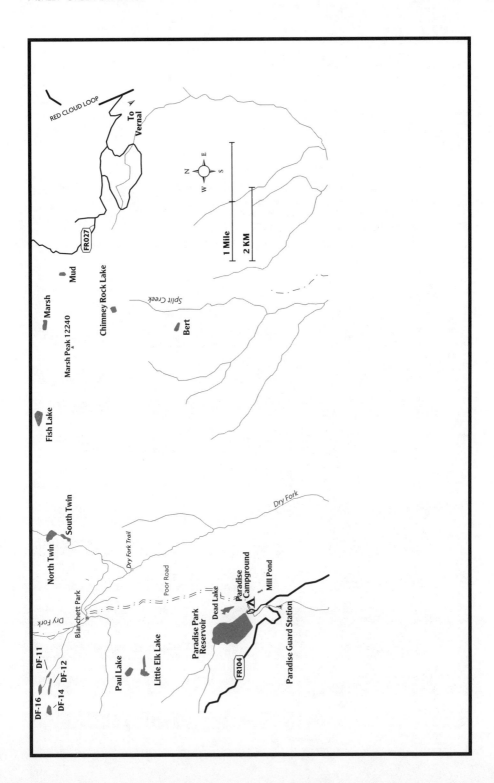

Bear River Drainage

SUMMIT COUNTY

T his is a rugged and scenic drainage that covers more land area than any other drainage in the Uinta Mountains. The Mirror Lake Highway (SR 150) is an excellent paved road that follows the Hayden Fork of the Bear River and greatly eases vehicular access into the mountainous area. There are six campgrounds spaced along SR 150 in this drainage to serve as base camps for anglers.

The two main trailheads are the East Fork Bear River Trailhead and Christmas Meadows Trailhead. The short Ruth Lake Trail is a good starting point for several day hikes to lakes in that area.

Lake Descriptions

Name	Fish	Trailhead	Mi.	GPS Coordinates
Allsop	CT	East Fork Bear River	8.5	N 40° 45′ 32″ W 110° 41′ 54″
Beautiful cirque lake. Moderate fishing pressure and open shoreline.				
Amethyst	BK/CT	Christmas Meadows	6.2	N 40° 45′ 04″ W 110° 45′ 27″
Emerald green lake with moderate fishing pressure.				
Baker	BK	Bear Riv. Scout Camp	4.2	N 40° 44′ 57″ W 110° 46′ 20″
Open for fly-casters. Good campsites and open shoreline.				
Beaver	RT/BK/CT	Moffit Pass Road	RA	N 40° 49′ 39″ W 110° 56′ 30″
0.5 mi. W of S end of Whitney Reservoir. Boats and float tubes are good idea.				
Bourbon	BK	SR 150	1.0	N 40° 47′ 05″ W 110° 53′ 53″
Also known as Gold Hill. Cross country from Sulphur Campground.				
BR-2	BK	SR 150	1.0	N 40° 47′ 01″ W 110° 53′ 47″
Cross country from Sulphur Campground.				
BR-16	BK / CT	Christmas Meadows	8.3	N 40° 43′ 36″ W 110° 49′ 20″
Small narrow pond 0.1 mi. downstream from Ryder Lake.				
BR-17	BK	Christmas Meadows	8.8	N 40° 43′ 19″ W 110° 49′ 40″
Just S of Ryder Lake. Good campsites, light use. Open for fly-casters.				
BR-18	BK	Christmas Meadows	8.8	N 40° 43′ 18″ W 110° 49′ 26″
Just SE of Ryder Lake. Light fishing pressure and good campsites.				
BR-24	CT	Christmas Meadows	5.1	N 40° 45′ 31″ W 110° 46′ 17″
0.7 mi. NW of Amethyst Lake. Spotty fishing.				
Cutthroat	BK	Ruth Lake	2.0	N 40° 44′ 09″ W 110° 53′ 50″
1 mi. W of Ruth Lake. Rough going, no trail.				
Hayden	CT	Ruth Lake	1.1	N 40° 43′ 59″ W 110° 53′ 12″
Just W of Ruth Lake. Moderate pressure.				

Name	Fish	Trailhead	Mi.	GPS Coordinates
Hell Hole	CT	Main Fork	5.0	N 40° 46' 56" W 110° 50' 25"
Pan-size cutthroat trout. Poor trail, many mosquitoes.				
Jewel	CT	Ruth Lake	1.4	N 40° 44' 19" W 110° 53' 18"
Popular with day-hikers.				
Kermsuh	CT	Christmas Meadows	6.8	N 40° 44' 54" W 110° 49' 45"
Long narrow lake in West Basin. Good chance of solitude. Poor campsites.				
Lily	RT	FR 120	RA	N 40° 52' 36" W 110° 48' 36"
Best fishing early in the season.				
Lorena	BK	East Fork Bear River	3.5	N 40° 49' 10" W 110° 44' 25"
Access is difficult. No trail last 1.5 mi. This is a good place for solitude.				
Lym	BK	Lym Lake Jeep Trail	RA	N 40° 53' 24" W 110° 43' 08"
Up Mill Creek Road from Mill Creek Guard Station.				
McPheters	CT	Christmas Meadows	9.0	N 40° 43' 54" W 110° 49' 52"
0.5 mi. NW of Ryder Lake. This is a beautiful lake near timberline.				
Meadow	BK	Christmas Meadows	8.6	N 40° 43' 15" W 110° 48' 52"
0.4 mi. E of BR-18. Light pressure and solitude.				
Mt. Elizabeth	CT	Elizabeth Mtn. Road	RA	N 40° 58' 21" W 110° 43' 20"
Take FR 058. Moderate fishing pressure.				
Norice	CT	East Fork Bear River	8.3	N 40° 45' 34" W 110° 43' 40"
Many cutthroat trout. A shallow lake with fairly open shoreline. Many biting insects.				
Ostler	BK/CT	Christmas Meadows	5.2	N 40° 45' 44" W 110° 46' 40"
1 mi. NW of Amethyst Lake. Popular with Boy Scouts.				
Priord	CT	East Fork Bear River	9.0	N 40° 45' 08" W 110° 44' 17"
0.8 mi. S of Norice. A beautiful emerald green lake in a treeline cirque.				
Ruth	BK	Ruth Lake	0.8	N 40° 44' 00" W 110° 52' 51"
Popular lake with easy access from SR 150.				
Ryder	BK	Christmas Meadows	8.5	N 40° 43' 30" W 110° 49' 39"
Many brook trout. Beautiful lake with good fishing and campsites. Many other lakes close.				
Salamander	BK	Christmas Meadows	3.5	N 40° 46' 41" W 110° 46' 50"
SW up the ridge from first meadow in Amethyst Basin.				
Scow	BK	East Fork Bear River	3.3	N 40° 49' 16" W 110° 46' 52"
Heavy timber. Shallow lake subject to winterkill. Many biting insects.				
Seidner	BK	Christmas Meadows	4.3	N 40° 46' 49" W 110° 49' 34"
Many brook trout. 2.2 mi. S on Stillwater Trail. Then 2 mi. W up outlet from Seidner Lake.				
Teal	CT	Ruth Lake	2.0	N 40° 44' 33" W 110° 53' 58"
1.2 mi. NW of Ruth Lake. Rough, no trail.				
Toomset	BK	Christmas Meadows	4.8	N 40° 46' 05" W 110° 46' 37"
An Amethyst Basin Lake that is often overlooked. Poor campsites.				

Name	Fish	Trailhead	Mi.	GPS Coordinates
Whiskey Is.	GR	FR 636	0.9	N 40° 45' 42" W 110° 54' 23"
Also known as Guy's. 1.5 mi. W of SR 150. No direct trail access. Subject to winterkill.				
Whitney	RT/CT/BK	FR 069	RA	N 40° 50' 04" W 110° 55' 45"
Whitney Road to FR 069. There is a campground.				

Maps

USGS 1:24000   Whitney Reservoir, Mirror Lake, Hayden Peak,
                         Christmas Meadows, Red Knob, Elizabeth
                         Mountain, Deadman Mountain.

Utah Atlas and Gazetteer   Pages 54, 55

Bear River in the Uinta Mountains. (PHOTO: EMMETT HEATH / WESTERN RIVERS FLYFISHER)

Summer in the Uintas. (PHOTO: COURTESY UTAH OUTDOORS) ▶

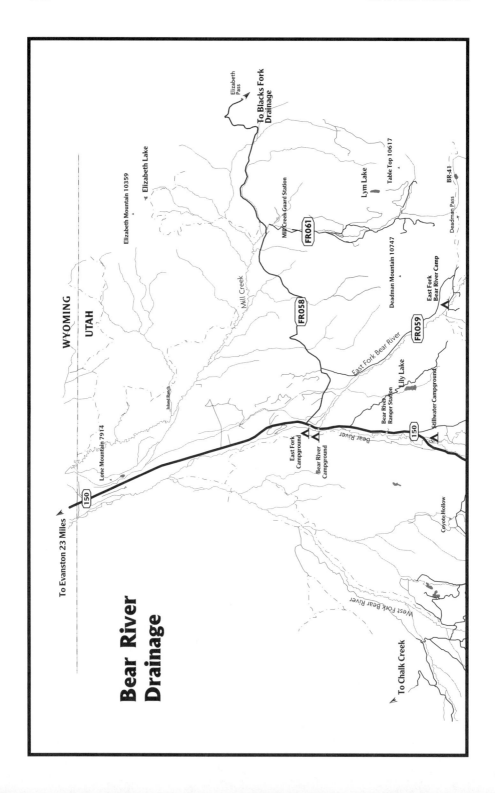

Bear River Drainage

To Evanston 23 Miles

WYOMING

UTAH

Lone Mountain 7914

Island Ranch

Elizabeth Mountain 10359

◄ Elizabeth Lake

Elizabeth Pass ◄

To Blacks Fork Drainage

Mill Creek

Mill Creek Guard Station

FR061

Table Top 10617

Lym Lake

BR-41

Deadman Pass

FR058

East Fork Bear River

Deadman Mountain 10747

FR059

East Fork Bear River Camp

Bear River Ranger Station

Lily Lake

150

Stillwater Campground

East Fork Campground

Bear River Campground

Bear River

150

Coyote Hollow

West Fork Bear River

To Chalk Creek

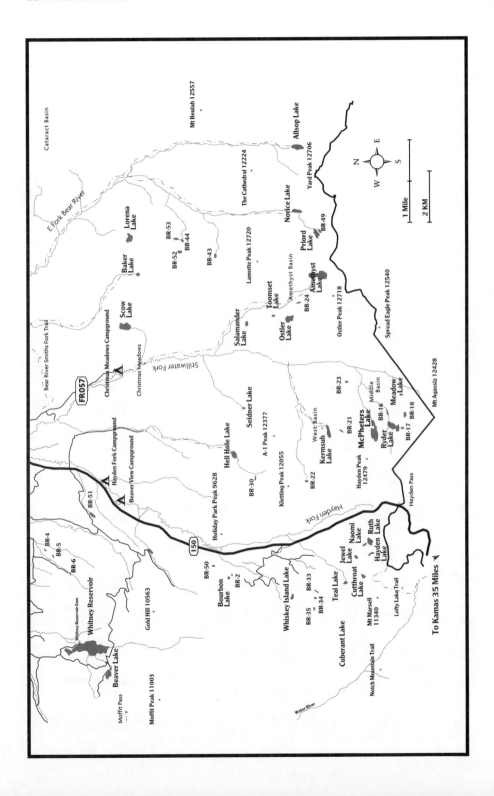

Beaver Creek Drainage

T his is a remote drainage that receives few visitors. It is a good choice for anglers seeking solitude and unsophisticated fish. Gilbert Lake deserves special mention as a lake that fishes very well for those willing to make the journey.

The main trailhead here is Middle Beaver at Georges Park, but both the trail and the road in are rough, so many anglers opt to start from Hoop Lake, adding about 2 miles to the hike.

Lake Descriptions

Name	Fish	Trailhead	Mi.	GPS Coordinates
Beaver	BK	Middle Beaver	7.0	N 40° 51′ 07″ W 110° 13′ 44″
Popular lake with good camping, moderate use.				
Coffin	CT	Middle Beaver	8.0	N 40° 50′ 29″ W 110° 14′ 15″
Marginal for camping. Light use, no trail.				
Dine	BK	Middle Beaver	6.0	N 40° 51′ 57″ W 110° 14′ 20″
May winterkill. Marginal camping. Solitude.				
Gilbert	BK/CT	W. Fork Beaver Creek	9.3	N 40° 50′ 36″ W 110° 19′ 17″
Trail hard to follow. Very good fly-fishing for small fish. Good camping.				
GR-145	CT	Middle Beaver	8.7	N 40° 50′ 03″ W 110° 14′ 15″
Experimental fishery. Just S of Coffin.				
GR-151	BK	W. Fork Beaver Creek	9.7	N 40° 50′ 15″ W 110° 19′ 26″
Good fishing in stream above and below.				
GR-152	BK	W. Fork Beaver Creek	10.3	N 40° 49′ 55″ W 110° 19′ 24″
Frozen to mid-July. No campsites. Seldom visited.				
GR-153	BK / CT	W. Fork Beaver Creek	9.9	N 40° 50′ 12″ W 110° 19′ 44″
Old beaver dam. Fluctuating water level. Good fly-fishing.				
GR-155	BK	W. Fork Beaver Creek	9.0	N 40° 50′ 54″ W 110° 19′ 05″
Camping to W. Light fishing pressure. Water cloudy from glacial flour.				
GR-160	BK	Middle Beaver	0.5	N 40° 55′ 42″ W 110° 11′ 33″
Experimental for brook trout. Pothole lake 0.3 mi. N of GR-162. Poor campsites.				
GR-161	BK	Middle Beaver	0.6	N 40° 55′ 35″ W 110° 11′ 48″
Experimental for brook trout. Steep-sided pothole lake just E of GR-162.				
GR-162	BK	Middle Beaver	0.8	N 40° 55′ 36″ W 110° 12′ 02″
Experimental for brook trout. Many lakes in area. Use topographical map. Snags in lake.				
GR-163	BK	Middle Beaver	0.9	N 40° 55′ 23″ W 110° 12′ 15″
Experimental for brook trout. 0.3 mi. S of GR-162. Marginal campsites.				

Name	Fish	Trailhead	Mi.	GPS Coordinates
GR-172	BK	FR 058 at Willow Park	0.5	N 40° 55' 16" W 110° 13' 07"
Experimental for brook trout. Marginal campsites. May be subject to winterkill.				
GR-173	BK	FR 058 at Willow Park	0.6	N 40° 55' 12" W 110° 13' 14"
Experimental for brook trout. Marginal camping. Snags and deadfall in lake.				
GR-177	CT	Middle Beaver	8.6	N 40° 50' 06" W 110° 12' 39"
Shallow with glacial flour. 1 mi. SE of Beaver Lake.				
Hidden	BK	Middle Beaver	5.5	N 40° 52' 45" W 110° 13' 40"
0.5 mi. N of trail junction. Seldom visited.				

Maps

USGS 1:24000	Kings Peak, Fox Lake, Hole in the Rock, Hoop Lake, Gilbert Peak NE
Utah Atlas and Gazetteer	Page 55

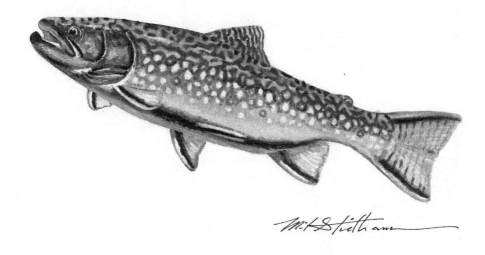

Brook trout. (ARTIST: MIKE STIDHAM)

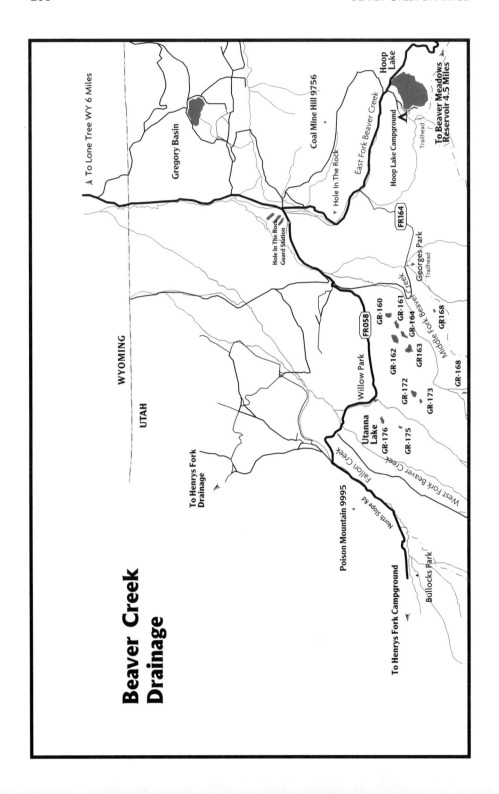

Beaver Creek Drainage

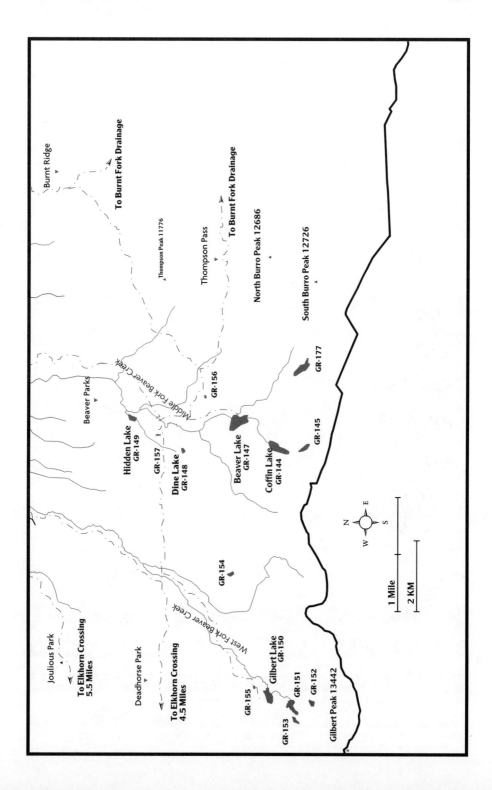

Burnt Ridge

To Burnt Fork Drainage

Thompson Peak 11776

Thompson Pass

To Burnt Fork Drainage

North Burro Peak 12686

South Burro Peak 12726

Beaver Parks

Middle Fork Beaver Creek

GR-156

GR-177

Hidden Lake
GR-149

GR-157

Dine Lake
GR-148

Beaver Lake
GR-147

Coffin Lake
GR-144

GR-145

GR-154

Joulious Park

To Elkhorn Crossing
5.5 Miles

Deadhorse Park

To Elkhorn Crossing
4.5 Miles

West Fork Beaver Creek

Gilbert Lake
GR-150

GR-151

GR-152

GR-155

GR-153

Gilbert Peak 13442

N E S W

1 Mile

2 KM

Blacks Fork Drainage

M ost of the lakes in this drainage are small, widely scattered, and at high elevations. Nearly half are above timberline. These factors contribute to light use in this drainage and create opportunities for anglers seeking a large measure of solitude. The small lakes up the Little East Fork of Blacks Fork (G-65 to G-71) see very few visitors.

The main trailheads are the West Fork of Blacks Fork, the East Fork of Blacks Fork, and Cache.

Lake Descriptions

Name	Fish	Trailhead	Mi.	GPS Coordinates
Bob's	CT	Cache	10.5	N 40° 49′ 38″ W 110° 37′ 48″
Headwaters of Middle Fk Blacks Fk. Above timberline. Poor campsites.				
Dead Horse	CT	W. Fork Blacks Fork	11.5	N 40° 44′ 41″ W 110° 40′ 24″
Emerald green lake at foot of Dead Horse Pass. Moderate use.				
Ejod	CT	W. Fork Blacks Fork	12.0	N 40° 45′ 02″ W 110° 40′ 30″
0.4 mi. NW of Dead Horse Lake. Often overlooked.				
G-65	BK	E. Fork Blacks Fork	7.2	N 40° 48′ 46″ W 110° 32′ 13″
0.8 mi. W of trail. Follow its outlet stream from N end of large meadow.				
G-66	BK	E. Fork Blacks Fork	6.0	N 40° 49′ 09″ W 110° 31′ 59″
Follow indistinct side trail W 0.7 mi. from trail. This is a good base camp.				
G-67	BK	E. Fork Blacks Fork	8.0	N 40° 48′ 11″ W 110° 32′ 39″
In a rugged cirque 1 mi. NW of G-69. High and open; poor campsites.				
G-69	CT	E. Fork Blacks Fork	8.8	N 40° 47′ 34″ W 110° 32′ 07″
Above timberline; no good campsites near the lake.				
G-71	BK	E. Fork Blacks Fork	9.0	N 40° 46′ 09″ W 110° 31′ 33″
Rough access. Milky glacial lake with fluctuating water level.				
G-74	BK	Cache	10.5	N 40° 49′ 39″ W 110° 37′ 02″
Faint trail. Good campsites. May winterkill.				
G-80	BK	W. Fork Blacks Fork	7.3	N 40° 48′ 22″ W 110° 40′ 19″
Difficult access and marginal campsites.				
G-81	CT	W. Fork Blacks Fork	5.1	N 40° 50′ 00″ W 110° 40′ 44″
Rough access to this turquoise-colored lake. Good camping.				
Little Lyman	RT/BK	Lyman Lake Road	RA	N 40° 56′ 06″ W 110° 36′ 51″
Take FR O58. There is a campground here. Annual stocking.				
Lyman	RT/BK	Lyman Lake Road	RA	N 40° 56′ 21″ W 110° 36′ 41″
Take FR O58. A large and scenic lake that sustains heavy fishing pressure.				

Maps

USGS 1:24000   Explorer Peak, Red Knob, Mount Lovenia, Lyman Lakes, Elizabeth Mountain

Utah Atlas and Gazetteer   Page 55

Rugged solitude of the High Uinta Lakes. (PHOTO: COURTESY UTAH OUTDOORS)

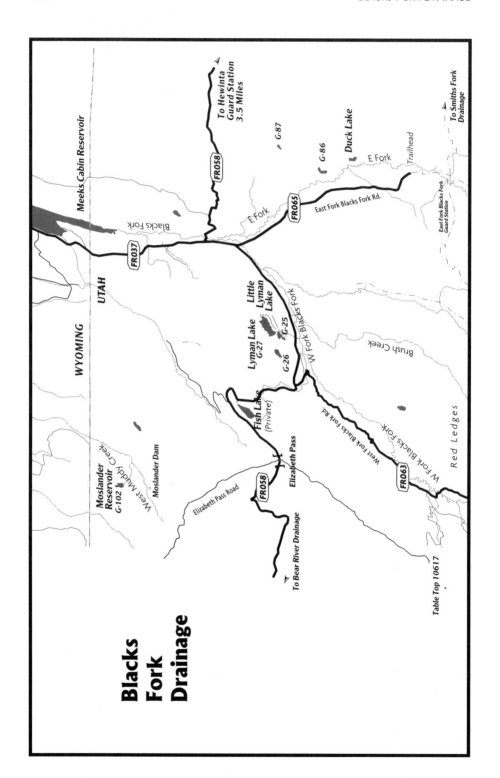

Blacks
Fork
Drainage

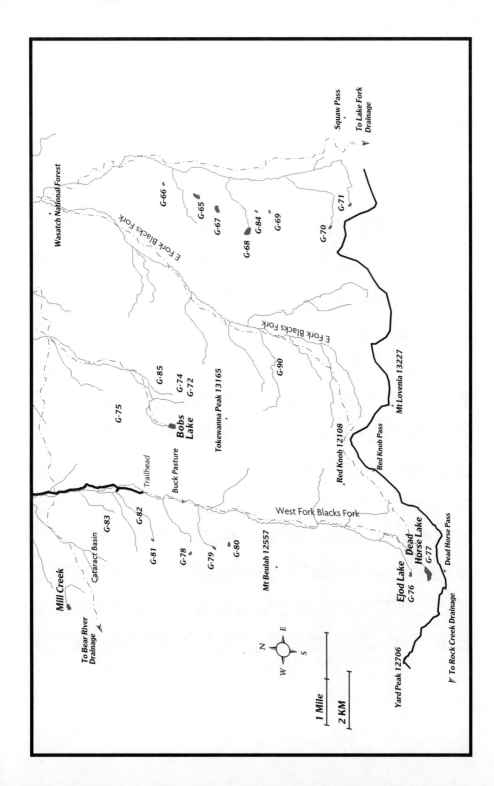

Burnt Fork Drainage

his is a small drainage between Sheep Creek and Beaver Creek on the Uinta's North Slope. Cutthroat trout are the predominant fish. Access is by the trailhead at Hoop Lake or Spirit Lake.

Lake Descriptions

Name	Fish	Trailhead	Mi.	GPS Coordinates
Beaver Meadow	RT/CT/BK	FR 058	RA	N 40° 54' 13" W 110° 03' 29"
5.5 mi. E from Hoop Lake. A good-sized reservoir at 9,376 feet.				
Bennion, Lower	CT/BK	Hoop Lake	10.1	N 40° 50' 04" W 110° 09' 35"
0.8 mi. W of Island Lake. Light fishing pressure.				
Bennion, Upper	CT/BK	Hoop Lake	10.1	N 40° 49' 58" W 110° 09' 46"
Not a stocked lake, but fish move in from downstream.				
Boxer	CT	Spirit Lake	6.5	N 40° 49' 27" W 110° 04' 38"
0.3 mi. SE of Burnt Fork Lake.				
Burnt Fork	CT	Spirit Lake	6.1	N 40° 49' 42" W 110° 04' 56"
1 mi. S on faint trail from W end of Fish Lake.				
Crystal	CT/BK	Spirit Lake	6.7	N 40° 49' 30" W 110° 05' 36"
0.6 mi. SW of Burnt Fork Lake. Follow outlet stream.				
Fish	BK/CT	Spirit Lake	5.1	N 40° 50' 12" W 110° 04' 05"
Large lake with good trail access. Moderate use.				
Hoop	RT/CT	Hoop Lake	RA	N 40° 55' 22" W 110° 07' 04"
FR 058 from Lonetree, WY. Past Hole in The Rock Guard Station.				
Island	CT/BK	Hoop Lake	8.9	N 40° 49' 44" W 110° 08' 43"
Great campsites. Popular with Boy Scouts.				
Kabell	CT	Hoop Lake	5.2	N 40° 51' 49" W 110° 07' 32"
Popular with large groups. Moderate use.				
Round	CT	Hoop Lake	9.3	N 40° 49' 55" W 110° 07' 49"
0.4 mi. SE of Island Lake. Moderate use.				
Snow (Andrea)	CT	Hoop Lake	9.9	N 40° 49' 47" W 110° 07' 08"
0.3 mi. E of Round Lake. No trail.				
Whitwall	CT/BK	Hoop Lake	9.8	N 40° 49' 56" W 110° 09' 19"
Between Bennion and Island. Light fishing use.				

Maps

USGS 1:24000   Hoop Lake, Hole in the Rock, Fox Lake,
                        Chepeta Lake

Utah Atlas and Gazetteer   Pages 55, 56

Quiet morning in upper Burnt Fork drainage. (PHOTO: COURTESY UTAH OUTDOORS)

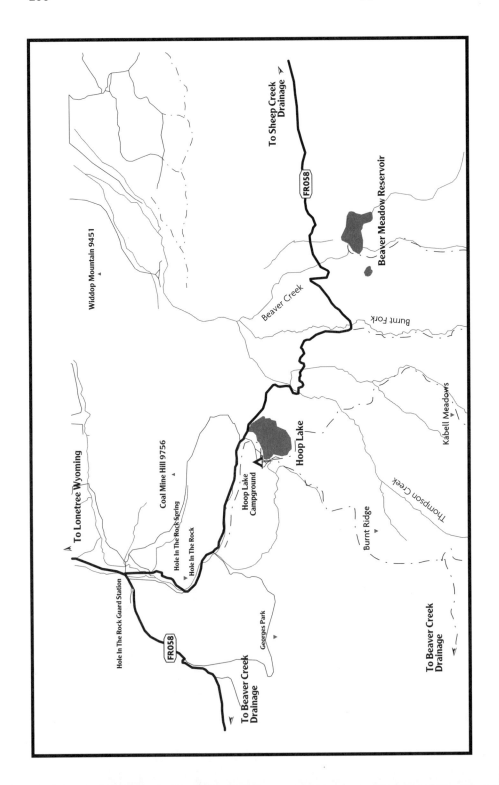

To Sheep Creek Drainage

FR058

Beaver Meadow Reservoir

Beaver Creek

Burnt Fork

Widdop Mountain 9451

Kabell Meadows

Hoop Lake

Thompson Creek

Coal Mine Hill 9756

To Lonetree Wyoming

Hole In The Rock Spring

Hole In The Rock

Hoop Lake Campground

Burnt Ridge

Hole In The Rock Guard Station

Georges Park

FR058

To Beaver Creek Drainage

To Beaver Creek Drainage

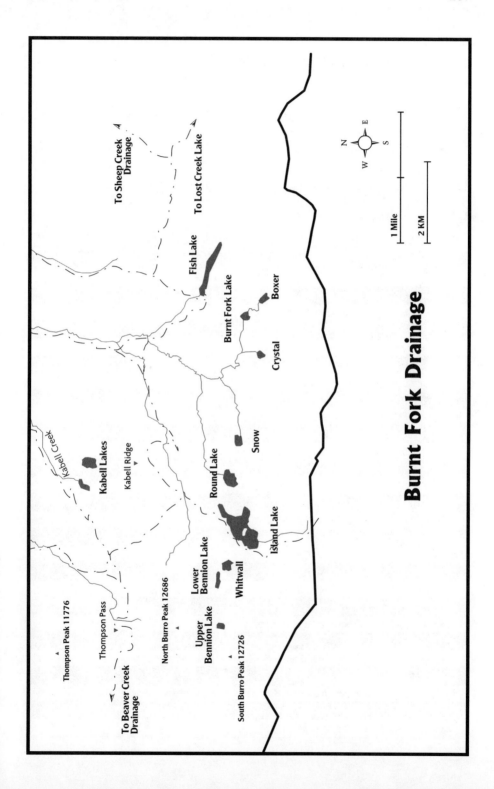

Burnt Fork Drainage

Dry Gulch Drainage

Dry Gulch is the smallest drainage on the Uinta's South Slope and is composed of Heller and Crow Basins. Access is by way of Dry Gulch Road (FR 122), which is closed to vehicles 2 miles before Heller Lake at the Dry Gulch Trailhead. Other access is by way of the Timothy Creek Jeep Trail (FR 120), which is closed to vehicles 3 miles before Jackson Park.

Lake Descriptions

Name	Fish	Trailhead	Mi.	GPS Coordinates
Crow	CT	Jackson Park	4.3	N 40° 38' 11" W 110° 17' 23"
From Jackson Park descend to DG-6, then S 0.8 mi. to Crow Lake.				
DG-6	CT	Jackson Park	3.5	N 40° 38' 47" W 110° 17' 50"
Westernmost of 3 lakes in series. Light pressure.				
DG-7	CT	Jackson Park	3.6	N 40° 38' 50" W 110° 17' 42"
Middle of 3 lakes in series. May winterkill.				
DG-8	CT	Jackson Park	3.8	N 40° 38' 52" W 110° 17' 31"
Easternmost of 3 lakes in series. May winterkill.				
DG-9	CT	Jackson Park	4.3	N 40° 39' 10" W 110° 18' 02"
0.5 mi. N of DG-6. Follow inlet stream. Light use.				
DG-10	CT	Jackson Park	4.6	N 40° 39' 22" W 110° 17' 42"
Healthy cutthroat trout. 1 mi. N of DG-9. Follow inlet stream.				
DG-14	CT	Jackson Park	6.0	N 40° 39' 55" W 110° 18' 10"
2 mi. N of Crow Lake at head of canyon. No trail.				
DG-15	CT	Jackson Park	6.2	N 40° 39' 43" W 110° 18' 44"
A few cutthroat trout. 0.8 mi. NW of DG-9.				
DG-16	CT	Jackson Park	6.2	N 40° 39' 38" W 110° 18' 45"
A few cutthroat trout. 0.8 mi. NW of DG-9.				
DG-17	CT	Jackson Park	6.2	N 40° 39' 38" W 110° 18' 38"
Many cutthroat trout. 0.8 mi. NW of DG-9.				
Heller	BK	Dry Gulch Road	2.0	N 40° 36' 34" W 110° 13' 50"
Pan-sized brook trout. Heavily used area. Litter is a problem.				
Hidden	BK	Dry Gulch Road	4.0	N 40° 37' 49" W 110° 14' 46"
Some large brook trout. NE 2 mi. from Heller Lake on poor trail. Light use.				
Lower Lily Pad	BK	Dry Gulch Road	3.9	N 40° 37' 35" W 110° 15' 43"
1.9 mi. NE from Heller Lake. No trail. 0.8 mi. W of Hidden Lake. 7.5 mi. over Flat Top Mtn.				
Upper Lily Pad	BK/CT	Dry Gulch Road	4.1	N 40° 37' 39" W 110° 15' 56"
Just W of Lower Lily Pad. Some larger fish.				

Maps

USGS 1:24000   Mount Emmons, Bollie Lake, Heller Lake,
                      Burnt Mill Spring

Utah Atlas and Gazetteer   Page 55

Come live with me,

and be my love,

And we shall some

new pleasure prove

Of golden sands,

and crystal brooks,

With silken lines,

and silver hooks.

John Donne (1571-1631)
from the poem "The Bait"

PHOTO: BYRON GUNDERSON / FISH TECH OUTFITTERS

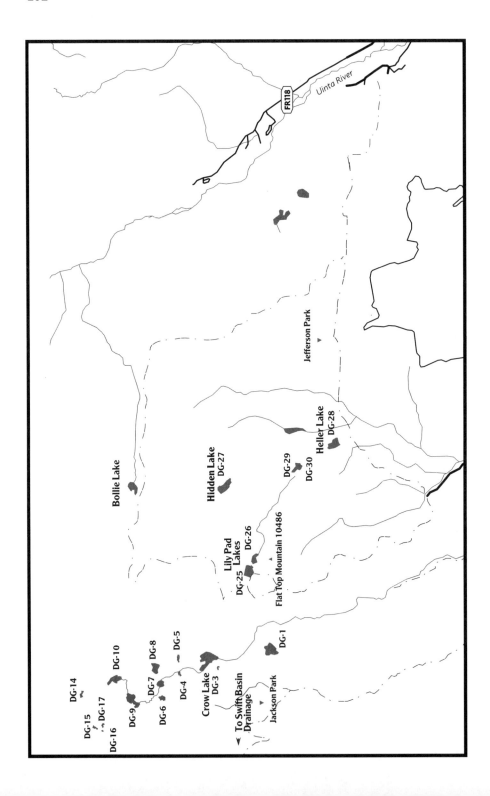

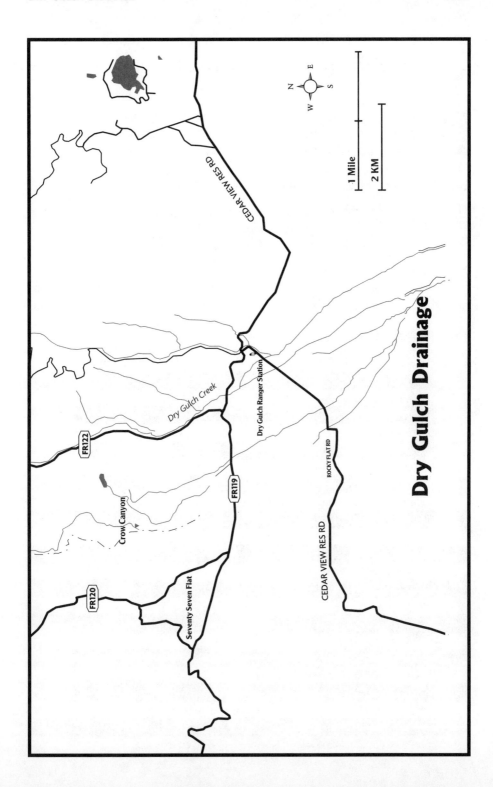

Dry Gulch Drainage

Duchesne River Drainage   DUCHESNE COUNTY

T he Duchesne River Drainage contains some of the most popular lakes in the Uinta Mountains. Much of this area is easily accessible from the Mirror Lake Highway, SR 150. Anglers can travel from the heart of Salt Lake City to Mirror Lake in 1 1/2 hours. From here it is just a short hike into the High Uintas Primitive Area with its many lakes and streams.

Highline and Mirror Lake are the two main trailheads here. Both start above 10,000 feet elevation in spectacular mountains. Be prepared to give yourself time to adjust to the altitude, particularly if you normally live near sea level.

Many of the lakes in this drainage can be reached by road or by a very short hike. The Murdock Basin Road gives access to this beautiful high country, giving anglers a chance to get off the main Mirror Lake Highway without having to hike.

Lake Descriptions

Name	Fish	Trailhead	Mi.	GPS Coordinates
Blue	BK	Highline	5.8	N 40° 42' 20" W 110° 48' 48"
Small brook trout. In Naturalist Basin. Moderate pressure.				
Blythe	BK	Mirror Lake	0.5	N 40° 42' 16" W 110° 52' 27"
No trail, 0.5 mi. N of Mirror Lake Trailhead.				
Bonnie	BK/C T	Mirror Lake	1.0	N 40° 42' 38" W 110° 52' 34"
Only 150 yards S of SR 150 near Scout Lake turnoff.				
Broadhead	BK	Little Deer Cr. Dam	0.8	N 40° 37' 07" W 110° 55' 36"
Take Duchesne Tunnel Road to the dam. No trail.				
Bud	BK	Butterfly Campground	0.2	N 40° 43' 04" W 110° 52' 11"
Small brook trout. Just S of SR 150. Subject to winterkill.				
Butterfly	RT/AT/BK	Butterfly Campground	RA	N 40° 43' 20" W 110° 51' 58"
Adjacent to SR 150. Very heavy use.				
Carolyn	GR/BK/CT	Highline	6.1	N 40° 40' 47" W 110° 47' 06"
Moderate fishing pressure.				
Castle	CT	Butterfly Campground	0.3	N 40° 43' 20" W 110° 52' 30"
No trail. Moderate pressure.				
D-19	BK/CT	Mirror Lake	1.0	N 40° 42' 34" W 110° 52' 31"
S of Bonnie Lake. Often overlooked. Many fish.				
D-26	BK	Echo Lake	0.5	N 40° 40' 09" W 110° 53' 34"
Marginal for brook trout. 0.3 mi. N of Echo Lake, E of Gem Lake. No trail.				
Echo	BK	Murdock Basin Road	RA	N 40° 39' 51" W 110° 53' 39"
Lots of brook trout. 5.2 mi. on Murdock Basin Road to Echo Lake turnoff.				

Name	Fish	Trailhead	Mi.	GPS Coordinates
Emerald	BK	Mirror Lake	0.2	N 40° 42' 17" W 110° 53' 43"
Experimental for brook trout. W of SR 150 across from Mirror Lake.				
Everman	BK	Highline	5.2	N 40° 41' 57" W 110° 47' 36"
No trail last 0.1 mi. Subject to winterkill.				
Farney	GR	Grandview	5.5	N 40° 37' 35" W 110° 49' 47"
No trail. Approach from Fish Hatchery Lake.				
Fehr	BK	Fehr Lake Trail	0.3	N 40° 41' 23" W 110 53' 10"
Many small brook trout. Start near Moosehorn Lake. Heavy pressure.				
Gem	BK	Echo Lake	0.5	N 40° 40' 07" W 110° 53' 53"
NW of Echo Lake 0.3 mi., W of D-26.				
Hades	RT/BK	Grandview	0.7	N 40° 34' 19" W 110° 50' 07"
No trail. NW of trailhead at foot of steep ridge.				
Hoover	BK/CT/GR	Murdock Basin Road	RA	N 40° 40' 46" W 110° 52' 12"
8 mi. on Murdock Basin Road to Hoover Lake turnoff. Excessive fishing pressure.				
Joan	BK	Echo Lake	0.4	N 40° 39' 51" W 110° 54' 04"
W of Echo Lake. No trail. Rough. Moderate use.				
Jordan	BK	Highline	5.7	N 40° 42' 18" W 110° 47' 43"
Good fly-fishing in stream below. Heavy use.				
Le Conte	CT/GR	Highline	6.2	N 40° 42' 33" W 110° 48' 13"
May be some arctic grayling. Moderate use. Easier approach from Shaler Lake. May winterkill.				
Maba	BK	Murdock Basin Road	0.1	N 40° 40' 58" W 110° 52' 13"
N of Hoover Lake on Murdock Basin Road.				
Marsell	CT	Grandview	5.0	N 40° 36' 58" W 110° 50' 06"
Leave trail 0.5 mi. N of Betsy Lake; go W 0.8 mi.				
Marshall	BK/CT	Murdock Basin Road	0.4	N 40° 40' 32" W 110° 52' 26"
SW 0.3 mi. from Hoover Lake.				
Mirror	RT/AT/BK	Mirror Lake Campgrd	RA	N 40° 42' 16" W 110° 53' 15"
On SR 150. Most popular lake in the Uintas. Campground, boat ramp, no motors.				
Moosehorn	RT/AT	Moosehorn Campgrd	RA	N 40° 41' 43" W 110° 53' 34"
Full service campground. Heavy angling pressure.				
Morat 1	CT	Highline	5.5	N 40° 42' 06" W 110° 48' 50"
Westernmost of Morat Lakes. Use is moderate.				
Morat 2	CT	Highline	5.5	N 40° 42' 04" W 110° 48' 37"
East of Morat 1. Naturalist Basin.				
Packard	BK	Highline	3.5	N 40° 40' 55" W 110° 50' 09"
Scenic, overlooking E Fork Duchesne. Heavy use.				
Pass	RT/AT/BK	SR 150	RA	N 40° 42' 41" W 110° 53' 29"
N of Mirror Lake 0.5 mi. Good fishing. Sites for primitive camping.				
Pyramid	BK	Murdock Basin Road	RA	N 40° 39' 10" W 110° 54' 00"
Murdock Basin Road to Echo Lake turnoff. First left, then W 0.3 mile. Heavy use.				

Name	Fish	Trailhead	Mi.	GPS Coordinates
Scout	RT	Camp Steiner Turnoff	0.5	N 40° 43' 00" W 110° 53' 00"
Boy Scout summer camp. No camping. Heavy use.				
Shaler	CT/BK	Highline	6.5	N 40° 42' 40" W 110° 47' 00"
Open tundra. Good late season fly-fishing.				
Shepard	CT/RT	Murdock Basin Road	0.4	N 40° 40' 52" W 110° 52' 29"
Murdock Basin Road to Hoover Lake turnoff; W 0.3 mi.				
Sonny	BK	Grandview	5.3	N 40° 37' 09" W 110° 50' 20"
Leave trail 0.5 mi. N of Betsy Lake; go W 0.8 mi. to Marsell. NW to Sonny. May winterkill.				
Wilder	BK	Highline	2.8	N 40° 41' 27" W 110° 50' 35"
Highline Trail to Packard Trail, then S 0.3 mi. Heavy use.				
Wyman	BK	Highline	3.3	N 40° 41' 25" W 110° 51' 00"
Subject to winterkill. Use is moderate.				

Maps

USGS 1:24000   Hayden Peak, Mirror Lake, Iron Mine Mountain, Grandaddy Lake

Utah Atlas and Gazetteer   Pages 54, 55

Golden-colored albino trout may be found in several lakes of the Duchesne drainage.
(PHOTO: STEVE COOK)

Anglers can drive into Murdock Basin. (PHOTO: EMMETT HEATH / WESTERN RIVERS FLYFISHER)

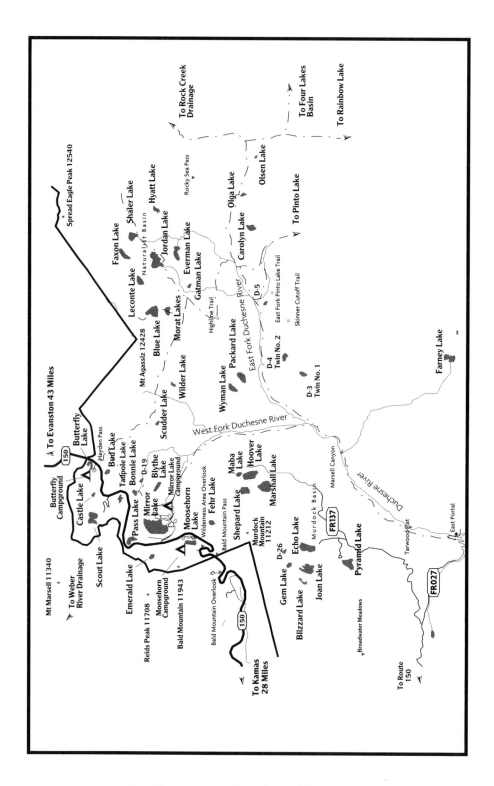

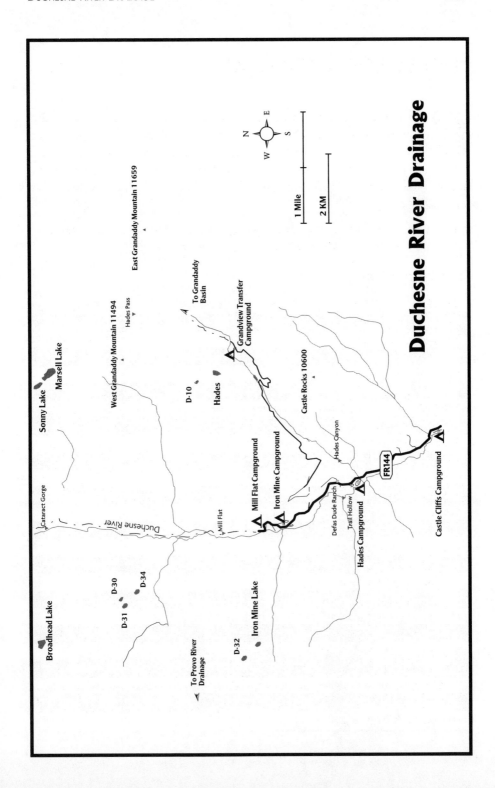

Duchesne River Drainage

Henrys Fork Drainage

T his is a small North Slope drainage with most of its lakes located in high country at the top of the watershed. The highest lakes are in rugged basins above timberline. The main concentration of lakes, from Bear Lake to Blanchard Lake, gets a fair amount of use. If solitude is your goal, you might consider a lesser-used drainage or look for lakes here that are smaller or more remote.

The main access point is the Henrys Fork Trailhead, about 25 miles north of Mountain View, Wyoming. There is a campground at the trailhead.

Lake Descriptions

Name	Fish	Trailhead	Mi.	GPS Coordinates
Alligator	BK/CT	Henrys Fork	3.0	N 40° 53' 07" W 110° 22' 04"
Heavy fishing pressure. Easy access.				
Bear	BK/CT	Henrys Fork	6.5	N 40° 50' 46" W 110° 23' 54"
Popular lake. Fairly heavy use. Help keep it clean.				
Blanchard	CT	Henrys Fork	10.4	N 40° 48' 25" W 110° 24' 16"
Pan-sized cutthroat trout. Good fly-fishing. Moderate pressure.				
Castle	BK	Henrys Fork	10.0	N 40° 48' 53" W 110° 24' 46"
1 steep mi. SW from Island Lake. Poor camps.				
Cliff	CT	Henrys Fork	11.8	N 40° 47' 28" W 110° 24' 25"
Tundra and talus. Remote and unpressured.				
Dollar	BK/CT	Henrys Fork	7.2	N 40° 49' 37" W 110° 22' 32"
Good camping and moderate use.				
G-10	BK	Henrys Fork	7.6	N 40° 50' 09" W 110° 23' 46"
May winterkill. Light fishing pressure.				
G-39	BK	Henrys Fork	8.3	N 40° 49' 37" W 110° 23' 47"
Light use. Marginal camping.				
G-44	CT	Henrys Fork	9.5	N 40° 48' 57" W 110° 24' 01"
Marginal for cutthroat trout. 0.5 mi. SW of Henrys Fork Lake. Light use.				
G-62	BK	Henrys Fork	5.5	N 40° 51' 53" W 110° 23' 33"
Maybe brook trout. 4.5 mi. from trailhead, W up inlet stream 0.7 mi. Marginal camping.				
Grass*	BK/CT	Henrys Fork	8.6	N 40° 49' 35" W 110° 23' 36"
**USGS map mislabeled. Pan-sized trout. Great fly-fishing. Receives moderate use. Good camping.*				
Henrys Fork	CT	Henrys Fork	9.0	N 40° 49' 13" W 110° 23' 23"
Heavy-use area; minimize your impact.				

Name	Fish	Trailhead	Mi.	GPS Coordinates
Island	BK/CT	Henrys Fork	8.8	N 40° 49' 23" W 110° 23' 56"
Beautiful, shallow lake. Marginal campsites.				
Little Blanchard	CT	Henrys Fork	10.5	N 40° 48' 25" W 110° 23' 58"
Many cutthroat trout. No campsite. Good fly-fishing. Light use.				
Sawmill	BK/CT	Henrys Fork	6.5	N 40° 50' 47" W 110° 23' 33"
Just below Bear Lake. Heavily used.				

Maps

USGS 1:24000   Mount Powell, Kings Peak, Gilbert Peak NE,
                        Bridger Lake

Utah Atlas and Gazetteer   Page 55

What happened? (PHOTO: COURTESY UTAH OUTDOORS)

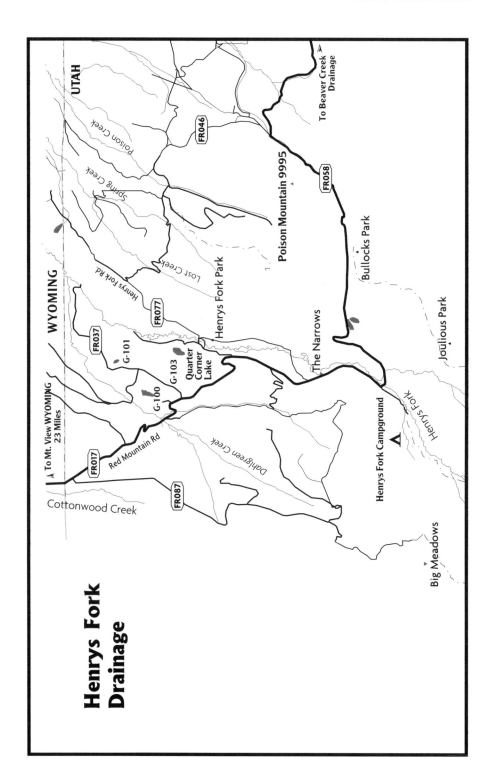

Henrys Fork Drainage

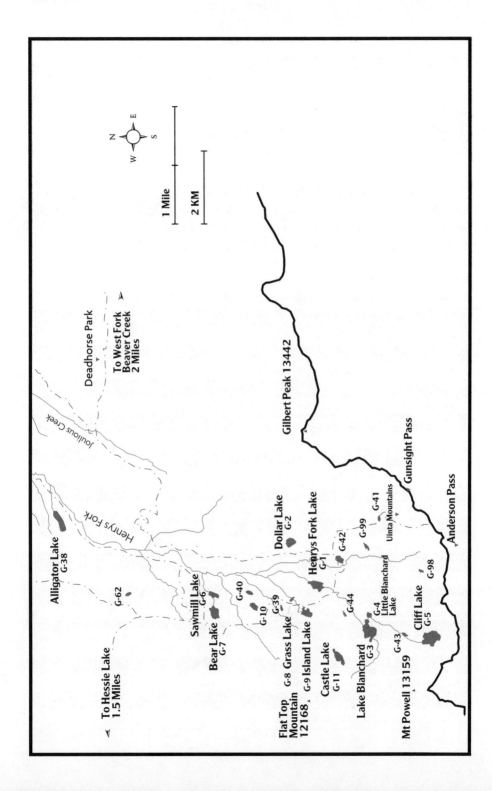

Henrys Fork Drainage

Deadhorse Park

To West Fork
Beaver Creek
2 Miles

Joutlous Creek

Gilbert Peak 13442

Gunsight Pass

Anderson Pass

1 Mile
2 KM

N E S W

Alligator Lake
G-38

Henrys Fork

G-62

Sawmill Lake
G-6

Dollar Lake
G-2

G-41

Uinta Mountains

G-99

Henrys Fork Lake
G-1

G-42

Bear Lake
G-7

G-40

G-39

G-10

Grass Lake
G-8

Island Lake
G-9

G-44

Little Blanchard
Lake
G-4

Cliff Lake
G-5

G-98

To Hessie Lake
1.5 Miles

Flat Top
Mountain
12168

Castle Lake
G-11

Lake Blanchard
G-3

G-43

Mt Powell 13159

Lake Fork Drainage

T he three main tributaries to the Lake Fork Drainage are Lake Fork itself, Brown Duck Creek, and Fish Creek. This is a very scenic drainage, particularly around Mt. Lovenia, Squaw Peak, Explorer Peak, and East Basin.

The Lake Fork Trailhead at Moon Lake is the main entry point for trips into this beautiful corner of the Uinta Mountains. The Brown Duck Trail accesses the majority of the lakes here, while the Lake Fork Trail follows the creek and is a shorter route to the upper end of the drainage.

Lake Descriptions

Name	Fish	Trailhead	Mi.	GPS Coordinates
Aspen	BK	Lake Fork	9.0	N 40° 36' 38" W 110° 35' 18"
Fed by undergound flows. Exceptionally clear water.				
Atwine	BK	Lake Fork	9.0	N 40° 36' 50" W 110° 34' 32"
Many brook trout. Near trail. Moderate fishing pressure.				
Big Dog	GR	Lake Fork	8.0	N 40° 35' 09" W 110° 35' 32"
No trail for last mile. Subject to winterkill.				
Brown Duck	CT	Lake Fork	7.0	N 40° 35' 36" W 110° 35' 42"
Camping areas are overused. Much pressure.				
Clements	CT	Lake Fork	11.0	N 40° 37' 35" W 110° 35' 35"
Natural lake increased with dam. Moderate use.				
Crater	BK	Lake Fork	17.0	N 40° 43' 27" W 110° 38' 19"
Good for brook trout. Deepest lake in Uintas, 147-feet deep.				
East Slide	BK	Lake Fork	9.8	N 40° 40' 17" W 110° 32' 31"
No trail. Very rough 1 mi. ENE of confluence of Oweep Creek/Lake Fork.				
Hook	BK	Lake Fork	18.0	N 40° 38' 49" W 110° 37' 15"
1 mi. S of Picture Lake. Rough terrain. Light use.				
Island	CT	Lake Fork	8.0	N 40° 36' 00" W 110° 36' 00"
Between Brown Duck and Kidney. Heavy use.				
Kidney	CT	Lake Fork	9.0	N 40° 36' 01" W 110° 36' 58"
Large 190-acre lake with moderate pressure.				
Lambert	BK	Lake Fork	17.0	N 40° 43' 49" W 110° 34' 21"
Nearly 11,000 feet. Light angling pressure.				
LF-16	BK	Lake Fork	17.5	N 40° 38' 46" W 110° 36' 36"
Shallow, productive lake with light pressure.				

Name	Fish	Trailhead	Mi.	GPS Coordinates
LF-43	BK	Lake Fork	15.7	N 40° 43' 09" W 110° 37' 01"
Marginal for brook trout. 1.3 mi. ESE of Crater Lake. Shallow.				
Lily Pad	BK/CT	Lake Fork	9.8	N 40° 35' 59" W 110° 37' 29"
Between Kidney and Tworoose. Moderate use.				
Little Dog	BK	Lake Fork	7.7	N 40° 35' 27" W 110° 36' 12"
0.5 mi. SW from Brown Duck. Light pressure.				
Moon	RT/CT/BK/SP	FR 131	RA	N 40° 34' 29" W 110° 30' 19"
At end of Moon Lake Road. A large reservoir with a campground and Moon Lake Lodge.				
Mud	BK	Lake Fork	9.5	N 40 37' 03" W 110 35' 05"
Marginal for brook trout. A meadow lake surrounded by springs and ponds.				
Oweep	BK	Lake Fork	21.0	N 40° 43' 53" W 110° 31' 25"
From Lambert Lake, E 3.6 mi. on trail, then S 1 mi. Use a map.				
Ottoson, Lower	CT	Lake Fork	14.7	N 40° 42' 19" W 110° 37' 41"
No trail the last 1.7 mi. Angling pressure is light.				
Ottoson, Upper	CT	Lake Fork	15.0	N 40° 42' 22" W 110° 38' 08"
No trail the last 2 mi. Pressure is light.				
Picture	RT	Lake Fork	17.0	N 40° 39' 27" W 110° 37' 07"
Cross East Basin Pass. Faint trail last mile.				
Porcupine	BK	Lake Fork	16.0	N 40° 45' 35" W 110° 30' 20"
7 mi. E of Lambert Meadows on Highline Trail.				
Stewart	BK	Lake Fork	11.3	N 40° 37' 57" W 110° 35' 27"
0.3 mi. N of Clements Lake. Light pressure.				
Toquer	BK/CT	Center Park	3.0	N 40° 37' 44" W 110° 28' 38"
From Center Park W of Hells Canyon Trailhead.				
Twin	BK	Lake Fork	13.5	N 40° 37' 37" W 110° 36' 38"
W from Clements Lake up inlet stream. May winterkill.				
Tworoose	CT	Lake Fork	11.0	N 40° 36' 17" W 110° 37' 54"
At the base of Tworoose Pass. Light pressure.				
X-61	CT	Lake Fork	8.0	N 40° 36' 12" W 110° 35' 43"
Maybe cutthroat trout. Second in series of 3 ponds just NE of Island Lake. May winterkill.				
X-62	CT	Lake Fork	8.0	N 40° 36' 26" W 110° 35' 45"
Maybe cutthroat trout. Third in series of 3 ponds 0.3 mi. NE Island Lake. May winterkill.				
X-75	CT	Lake Fork	11.7	N 40° 37' 41" W 110° 35' 49"
0.8 mi. W of Clements Lake. Light use.				
X-78	CT	Lake Fork	11.8	N 40° 38' 14" W 110° 35' 50"
Maybe cutthroat trout. NW of Clements, past Stewart Lake.				
X-80	BK/CT	Lake Fork	16.0	N 40° 39' 42" W 110° 36' 40"
Second pond on stream below Picture Lake.				

Name	Fish	Trailhead	Mi.	GPS Coordinates
X-84	BK	Lake Fork	16.2	N 40° 40' 27" W 110° 36' 05"
Easternmost of Three Lakes in East Basin.				
X-85	BK	Lake Fork	16.0	N 40° 40' 32" W 110° 36' 23"
Northernmost of Three Lakes. Light Pressure.				
X-86	BK	Lake Fork	15.9	N 40° 40' 17" W 110° 36' 25"
Largest of Three Lakes. Pressure is light.				

Maps

USGS 1:24000   Oweep Creek, Mount Lovenia, Explorer Peak, Kidney Lake, Tworoose Pass, Lake Fork Mountain, Garfield Basin.

Utah Atlas and Gazetteer   Page 55

Fresh grayling are delicious by the lake. (PHOTO: COURTESY UTAH OUTDOORS)

Kevin Schieffer

This poem is dedicated to C.B. so often my inspiration.

TYIN' FLIES

She asked, whatcha doin?
Tyin' flies, was my reply.
Why, what ever did they do?
Just shook my head in disbelief
I went on with the task at hand.

As I set there late that eve
My mind ran yonder still
'Bout such a question one could have.
Could anyone be so naive
to wonder such a simple thing.

I so very often am amazed
Of the wonder in my kids.
The perspective of their thought
The colored glass they must look through.
To come with a query as that
What ever did they do, indeed.
It makes me chuckle still.

Tyin' flies means one sweet thing
Some time of peace near or far
Perhaps a fish or two.
But most certainly solitude
Along a lake or stream.

My flies I do not care their past
Nor if they've committed crime.
No, my flies whether innocent or guilt
Will all reach the end of my line.

I will cast my bread upon the water,
And there in, the flies fate.
To be judged by the highest court of all

WILL THAT TROUT TAKE MY BAIT!!!!!!!!

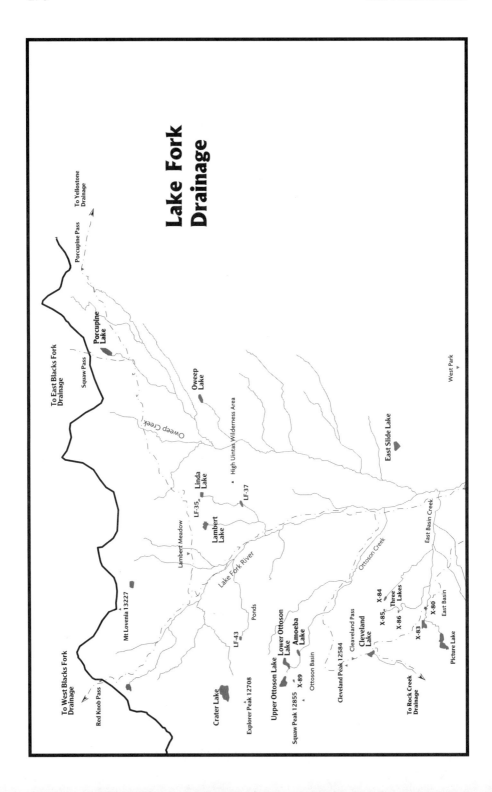

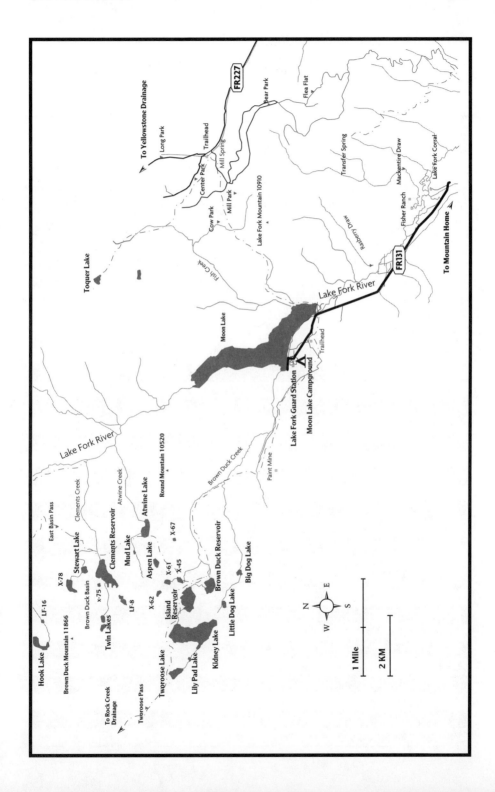

Provo River Drainage   SUMMIT AND WASATCH COUNTIES

T he combination of the Mirror Lake Highway, the Spring Canyon Road, 13 different campgrounds, and an extensive trail system make this the most accessible drainage in the Uintas. None of its lakes are more than 5 miles from a road or trailhead. The Trial Lake area is only 60 miles from the Salt Lake Valley. This portion of the Uintas is perfect for anglers seeking a quiet place to fish and to escape the valley for a day.

Crystal Lake is the main trailhead for this drainage, with some of the lakes being accessed from Bald Mountain. Spring Canyon Road (FR 041) is a good choice for anglers who prefer a fishing hole with easy road access. The Upper Setting Road takes you up to 9,800 feet, but it is rough and slow-going. Passenger cars can reach the trailhead so long as the road is dry.

Lake Descriptions

Name	Fish	Trailhead	Mi.	GPS Coordinates
Alexander	BK	FR 041	0.3	N 40° 36′ 34″ W 110° 58′ 36″
3 mi. N of SR 150 on FR 041. Good camping, heavy use.				
Azure	CT	FR 041	1.0	N 40° 39′ 26″ W 110° 58′ 44″
2 mi. S of Trial Lake on FR 041, then 0.5 mi. W of Haystack. Rockslides make for rough hiking.				
Beaver	BK	Crystal Lake Trhd	4.0	N 40° 40′ 04″ W 111° 01′ 28″
0.5 mi. SW of Duck Lake. Subject to winterkill.				
Beth	BK	FR 041	0.2	N 40° 39′ 07″ W 110° 58′ 04″
2.2 mi. S of Trial Lake, then 0.2 mi. W of FR 041. Heavily used.				
Big Elk	BK/CT	FR 068	1.0	N 40° 40′ 35″ W 111° 03′ 10″
From SR 150, go N on FR 068 (Norway Flats Rd) 7.5 mi. Last mile rough; 4x4 recommended.				
Blue	BK/GR	FR 041	1.8	N 40° 38′ 47″ W 110° 58′ 46″
On good trail from Buckeye Lake. Campsites and moderate use.				
Booker	BK	Crystal Lake	1.7	N 40° 42′ 13″ W 110° 58′ 16″
Just NW of Clyde Lake. May winterkill.				
Brook	BK	Crystal Lake	4.2	N 40° 39′ 52″ W 110° 01′ 10″
0.6 mi. S of Duck Lake. May winterkill.				
Buckeye	BK	FR 041	RA	N 40° 38′ 17″ W 110° 58′ 25″
Good campsites. Please keep vehicles off fragile meadow around lake.				
Clegg	BK	Bald Mountain	1.5	N 40° 41′ 54″ W 110° 55′ 32″
May winterkill. Heavy day-use. Mostly shallows.				
Cliff	CT	Crystal Lake	0.5	N 40° 41′ 20″ W 110° 57′ 59″
Pan-sized cutthroat trout. Heavy use. Good campsites.				

Name	Fish	Trailhead	Mi.	GPS Coordinates
Clyde	BK	Crystal Lake	1.5	N 40° 42′ 09″ W 110° 58′ 12″
Small brook trout. Limited camping and heavy use.				
Crystal	BK	Crystal Lake	0.1	N 40° 40′ 55″ W 110° 58′ 00″
Heavy use. Campground nearby at Trial Lake.				
Cutthroat	BK	Crystal Lake	3.0	N 40° 40′ 53″ W 111° 00′ 33″
Small brook trout. N of trail 1 mi. W of Long Lake Dam. Good camps.				
Diamond	BK	Trial Lake Campground	0.3	N 40° 41′ 08″ W 110° 56′ 38″
NE of Trial Lake. Angler use is moderate.				
Divide 1	BK	Crystal Lake	1.8	N 40° 42′ 15″ W 110° 58′ 23″
Just W of Booker Lake. Good campsites.				
Duck	BK/CT	Crystal Lake	3.3	N 40° 40′ 29″ W 111° 01′ 02″
Good campsites. Use is moderate. Trees to shore.				
Fire	CT	Crystal Lake	3.8	N 40° 40′ 38″ W 111° 01′ 20″
0.3 mi. S of Island Lake. Steep and rocky.				
Haystack	BK/CT	FR 041	0.5	N 40° 39′ 22″ W 110° 58′ 16″
2 mi. S of Trial on FR 041, then W on trail. Heavy use. Good camps.				
Hidden	BK	Crystal Lake	5.0	N 40° 39′ 17″ W 111° 01′ 19″
1.8 mi. S of Weir Lake. Small, remote basin.				
Hourglass	BK/CT	Norway Flats Road	0.4	N 40° 39′ 38″ W 111° 04′ 09″
0.4 mi. W of Little Elk Lake. No trail, but heavy angler use.				
Island	BK/CT	Crystal Lake	3.5	N 40° 41′ 02″ W 111° 01′ 02″
Popular camping and fishing lake. Picturesque.				
Jacks	BK	Crystal Lake	2.6	N 40° 40′ 31″ W 110° 59′ 57″
To Weir Lake, then E. Light use. May winterkill.				
James	BK	Crystal Lake	1.9	N 40° 42′ 25″ W 110° 58′ 18″
0.2 mi. N of Booker Lake. May winterkill.				
John	BK	Crystal Lake	1.5	N 40° 42′ 21″ W 110° 58′ 01″
Small brook trout. Just N of Clyde Lake. Campsites. Rocky.				
Junior	CT	Crystal Lake	3.7	N 40° 40′ 46″ W 111° 01′ 23″
0.2 mi. SW from Island Lake. Fast fishing for cutthroat trout. May winterkill.				
Lambert	BK	FR 041 to FR 107	0.2	N 40° 37′ 40″ W 110° 59′ 29″
From SR 150, 2 mi. N on FR 041 (Spring Canyon Road), then 2 mi. N on FR 107.				
Lillian	BK	Crystal Lake	2.0	N 40° 40′ 48″ W 110° 59′ 30″
Just 0.2 mi. S of Long Lake. Light pressure.				
Lilly	RT/BK	SR 150	RA	N 40° 40′ 55″ W 110° 56′ 13″
1.2 mi. E of Trial Lake turnoff. Campground.				
Lily, Lower	BK	Crystal Lake	0.1	N 40° 41′ 03″ W 110° 57′ 43″
Angling pressure is moderate to heavy.				
Lily, Upper	*	Crystal Lake	0.1	N 40° 41′ 02″ W 110° 57′ 49″
*Not stocked. Botanical study sight.				

Name	Fish	Trailhead	Mi.	GPS Coordinates
Little Elk	BK	Norway Flats Road	0.1	N 40° 39' 38" W 111° 03' 41"
7 mi. N of SR 150 on FR 068 (Norway Flats Road). Has winterkilled in past. Heavy use.				
Long Pond	BK/CT	Crystal Lake	2.1	N 40° 40' 46" W 110° 59' 53"
Small pond below Dam of Long Lake.				
Long	BK/CT	Crystal Lake	2.0	N 40° 41' 03" W 110° 59' 35"
Water level fluctuates. Good camps. Heavy use.				
Lost	RT	SR 150	RA	N 40° 40' 32" W 110° 56' 14"
Popular lake. Has a campground. Heavy use.				
Marjorie	GR	Crystal Lake	2.5	N 40° 40' 22" W 110° 59' 52"
Many small arctic grayling. Water level fluctuates. Easy hike to good fishing.				
Petit	BK	Crystal Lake	0.7	N 40° 41' 29" W 110° 58' 01"
Light fishing pressure and good campsites.				
Pot	BK	Crystal Lake	2.7	N 40° 40' 25" W 111° 00' 26"
0.3 mi. SW of Weir Lake. Camping. Light use.				
Ramona	BK	Crystal Lake	3.8	N 40° 41' 13" W 111° 00'35"
0.3 mi. NE of Island Lake. No trail.				
Rock	BK	FR 041	1.2	N 40° 39' 35" W 110° 58' 49"
0.4 mi. NW from Haystack Lake. No trail. Rough terrain.				
Shadow	BK	FR 041	1.3	N 40° 39' 50" W 110° 58' 33"
0.5 mi. NNW from Haystack Lake or 0.5 S of Washington.				
Shingle Cr - E	BK	Upper Setting Trhd	1.5	N 40° 40' 48" W 111° 05' 07"
Good campsites. Heavy use due to easy access.				
Shingle Cr - Lwr	BK	Upper Setting Trhd	1.3	N 40° 39' 51" W 111° 04' 28"
Cross country all the way. Steep terrain. This lake is seldom visited.				
Shingle Cr - W	BK	Upper Setting Trhd	1.6	N 40° 40' 52" W 111° 05' 48"
Marginal for brook. Shallow lake; fluctuating water level. Receives little use.				
Spectacle	BK	FR 041	0.2	N 40° 37' 57" W 110° 58' 49"
Also known as Hourglass. From Trial Lake, go S 5 mi. on FR 041 to small pond, then W 0.2 mi.				
Star	BK/CT	Trial Lake CG	0.8	N 40° 41' 29" W 110° 56' 45"
Follow Trial Lake inlet stream NE 0.6 mi.				
Tail	RT/BK	FR 041	0.8	N 40° 40' 10" W 110° 58' 20"
On inlet stream at S end of Washington Lake. Heavy angling pressure.				
Teapot	RT/AT	SR 150	RA	N 40° 40' 50" W 110° 56' 30"
1.2 mi. E of Trial Lake at Lilly Lake Campground.				
Trial	RT/AT	SR 150	RA	N 40° 41' 00" W 110° 57' 14"
Very heavy pressure due to large campground.				
Trident	BK	FR 041	RA	N 40° 38' 56" W 110° 57' 44"
2.5 mi. S of Trial Lake. Heavy angling pressure.				
Twin, Lower	BK/CT	Crystal Lake	2.3	N 40° 42' 14" W 110° 57' 40"
Just S of "The Notch." There are campsites.				

Name	Fish	Trailhead	Mi.	GPS Coordinates
Twin, Upper	BK	Crystal Lake	2.3	N 40° 42' 17" W 110° 57' 42"
Good campsites. Moderate pressure.				
Wall	CT	Crystal Lake	1.0	N 40° 41' 54" W 110° 57' 37"
Extreme water level fluctuations. Heavy use.				
Washington	RT/BK/CT	FR 041	0.1	N 40° 40' 32" W 110° 58' 03"
I mi. E of SR 150 by Trial Lake. Extreme water level fluctuations. Heavy use.				
Watson	BK	Crystal Lake	1.0	N 40° 41' 41" W 110° 58' 10"
0.3 mi. W from S end of Wall Lake.				
Weir	CT	Crystal Lake	2.5	N 40° 40' 29" W 111° 00' 10"
Water level fluctuates. Good campsites.				

Maps

USGS 1:24000	Mirror Lake, Erickson Basin, Soapstone Basin, Iron Mine Mountain
Utah Atlas and Gazetteer	Page 54

Provo River. (PHOTO: EMMETT HEATH / WESTERN RIVERS FLYFISHER)

Provo River Drainage

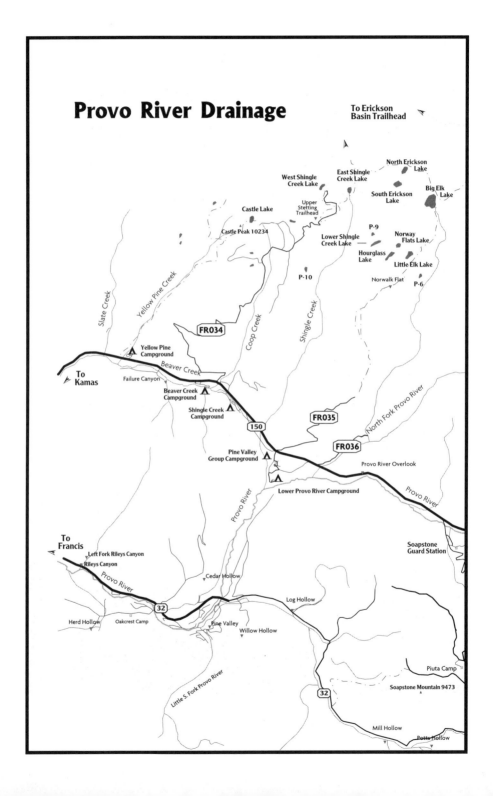

To Erickson
Basin Trailhead

North Erickson
Lake

West Shingle
Creek Lake

East Shingle
Creek Lake

South Erickson
Lake

Big Elk
Lake

Upper
Stetting
Trailhead

Castle Lake

Castle Peak 10234

Lower Shingle
Creek Lake

P-9

Norway
Flats Lake

Hourglass
Lake

Little Elk Lake

P-10

Norwalk Flat

P-6

Slate Creek

Yellow Pine Creek

FR034

Coop Creek

Shingle Creek

North Fork Provo River

Yellow Pine
Campground

Beaver Creek

To
Kamas

Failure Canyon

Beaver Creek
Campground

Shingle Creek
Campground

150

FR035

FR036

Pine Valley
Group Campground

Provo River Overlook

Lower Provo River Campground

Provo River

Provo River

To
Francis

Soapstone
Guard Station

Left Fork Rileys Canyon

Rileys Canyon

Provo River

Cedar Hollow

Log Hollow

32

Herd Hollow

Oakcrest Camp

Pine Valley

Willow Hollow

Piuta Camp

Little S. Fork Provo River

32

Soapstone Mountain 9473

Mill Hollow

Potts Hollow

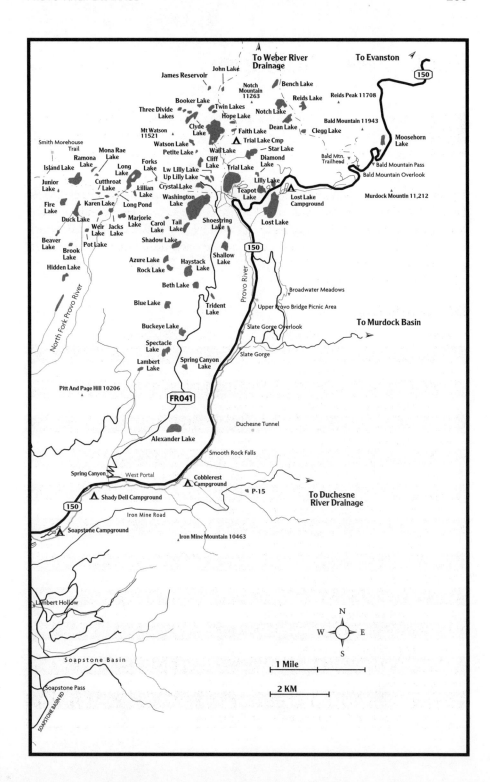

Rock Creek Drainage

R ock Creek is the largest drainage of the Uinta's south slope. It is formed by Squaw Basin Creek, the East Fork of Rock Creek, the Main Rock Creek, and Fall Creek. This is very scenic country, particularly at the head of Rock Creek.

Upper Stillwater is the main trailhead for this drainage and follows Rock Creek. Grandaddy Basin is most easily reached from the Grandview Trailhead. The Mirror Lake Trailhead gives access to this area by way of Rocky Sea Pass, which is above 11,200 feet and, therefore, may not be open until late summer. Hikers can also use the Moon Lake Trailhead and cross Tworoose Pass (also above 11,200 feet) to enter the drainage.

Lake Descriptions

Name	Fish	Trailhead	Mi.	GPS Coordinates
Allen	GR/BK	Grandview	9.0	N 40° 39' 28" W 110° 45' 40"
No trail to lake. Light fishing pressure.				
Amlen	BK	Upper Stillwater	9.0	N 40° 39' 16" W 110° 40' 05"
Good for brook trout. 300 yards W of Shamrock Lake.				
Anderson	BK/CT	Upper Stillwater	15.6	N 40° 42' 47" W 110° 39' 56"
Moderate to heavy fishing pressure.				
Arta	CT	FR 143	0.5	N 40° 34' 59" W 110° 47' 26"
At end of FR 143. Hike W 0.6 mi. Water level fluctuates. Light fishing pressure.				
Audry	BK	Miners Gulch	2.5	N 40° 34' 12" W 110° 39' 34"
This is a jeep trail. Light fishing pressure. Hard to reach.				
Bedground	BK	Grandview	8.9	N 40° 39' 37" W 110° 46' 33"
Large brook trout. Off trail. Moderate fishing pressure.				
Betsey	CT	Grandview	3.4	N 40° 36' 34" W 110° 48' 43"
W of Grandaddy. Heavy fishing pressure.				
Black	BK/CT	Mirror Lake	10.6	N 40° 43' 04" W 110° 44' 50"
Moderate pressure. Area subject to overuse.				
Boot	CT	Mirror Lake	14.3	N 40° 44' 16" W 110° 41' 59"
Light fishing pressure. High elevation.				
Brinkley	BK	Mirror Lake	9.7	N 40° 42' 25" W 110° 44' 56"
Heavy angler use.				
Cabin	BK	Moon Lake	10.7	N 40° 36' 20" W 110° 40' 14"
Some large brook trout. Rugged approach from Rudolph Lake.				

Name	Fish	Trailhead	Mi.	GPS Coordinates
Continent	CT/BK	Stillwater	15.4	N 40° 44′ 09″ W 110° 41′ 02″
High elevation. Light fishing pressure.				
Dale	BK	Mirror Lake	8.7	N 40° 40′ 20″ W 110° 45′ 45″
In Four Lakes Basin. Heavy fishing pressure.				
Daynes	BK/GR	Mirror Lake	8.7	N 40° 40′ 05″ W 110° 45′ 46″
In Four Lakes Basin. Fairly heavy pressure.				
Dean	BK	Mirror Lake	8.7	N 40° 40′ 43″ W 110° 45′ 37″
In Four Lakes Basin. Moderate pressure.				
Diamond	BK	Stillwater	9.0	N 40° 37′ 25″ W 110° 39′ 22″
Hard to find. Take Mid Lake outlet NW 0.5 mi.				
Docs	BK	Stillwater	6.0	N 40° 35′ 47″ W 110° 44′ 46″
Above reservoir, go W 2.3 mi. NW on TR 073. Hard climb SW 0.8 mi.				
Doug	CT	Mirror Lake	14.6	N 40° 44′ 02″ W 110° 42′ 12″
Lots of cutthroat trout. Small pond S of Boot Lake.				
Fern	BK	Grandview	5.7	N 40° 36′ 23″ W 110° 46′ 18″
Follow faint trail S of LaMarla Lake.				
Fish Hatchery	CT/BK	Grandview	5.3	N 40° 37′ 30″ W 110° 49′ 14″
Popular with hikers. Heavy fishing pressure.				
Gibby	BK	Grandview	3.2	N 40° 36′ 22″ W 110° 48′ 25″
Pothole lake by Grandaddy				
Gladys	BK	Mirror Lake	12.4	N 40° 43′ 41″ W 110° 45′ 43″
Fishing pressure is light to moderate.				
Governor Dern	BK/CT	Grandview	7.7	N 40° 39′ 15″ W 110° 47′ 50″
Grandaddy Basin. Heavy fishing pressure.				
Grandaddy	CT/BK	Grandview	3.2	N 40° 36′ 02″ W 110° 48′ 11″
Most popular lake w/o vehicle access. No fishing in tributaries until mid-July.				
Heart	CT	Grandview	2.6	N 40° 35′ 38″ W 110° 48′ 37″
Grandaddy Basin. Heavy fishing pressure.				
Helen	BK	Mirror Lake	12.3	N 40° 44′ 22″ W 110° 44′ 55″
Fishing pressure is moderate.				
Horseshoe	BK	Upper Stillwater	9.5	N 40° 37′ 20″ W 110° 40′ 10″
Hard to find. Seldom visited.				
Huntley	BK	Mirror Lake	9.6	N 40° 42′ 18″ W 110° 44′ 60″
Three interconnecting ponds.				
Jack	CT / BK	Mirror Lake	12.1	N 40° 43′ 30″ W 110° 43′ 59″
By Jill and Ouray Lakes. Moderate pressure.				
Jean	BK/CT	Mirror Lake	8.4	N 40° 40′ 32″ W 110° 45′ 59″
Four Lakes Basin. Use decreases in late summer.				
Jill	BK	Mirror Lake	12.1	N 40° 43′ 34″ W 110° 44′ 06″
By Jack Lake of course. Moderate pressure.				

Name	Fish	Trailhead	Mi.	GPS Coordinates
Ledge	BK	Upper Stillwater	14.4	N 40° 43' 31" W 110° 40' 33"
Lake subject to winterkill in some years.				
Lightning	BK/CT	Mirror Lake	12.1	N 40° 44' 10" W 110° 45' 00"
Fishing pressure is light to moderate.				
Lily Pad	BK	Grandview	6.1	N 40° 35' 59" W 110° 37' 29"
In a boggy meadow. Moderate pressure.				
Lodgepole	BK/CT	Grandview	4.1	N 40° 36' 27" W 110° 47' 43"
NE of Grandaddy Lake. Moderate pressure.				
Lost	BK	Grandview	5.8	N 40° 38' 03" W 110° 47' 44"
Marginal for fish. Subject to winterkills.				
Margie	BK	Mirror Lake	11.9	N 40° 43' 03" W 110° 46' 05"
SW of Rosalie Lake. Light fishing pressure.				
Margo	CT	Grandview	9.5	N 40° 39' 16" W 110° 49' 26"
Trail from west inlet of Pinto Lake.				
Mid	BK	Upper Stillwater	10.2	N 40° 37' 05" W 110° 38' 57"
In heavy timber north of Rudolph Lake.				
Mohawk	BK/CT	Grandview	4.1	N 40° 36' 27" W 110° 49' 23"
Very popular with Boy Scout groups.				
Ouray	CT/BK	Mirror Lake	11.6	N 40° 43' 37" W 110° 44' 28"
Many fish. Open around the lake.				
Palisade	BK/CT	Grandview	5.3	N 40° 38' 00" W 110° 48' 18"
Grandaddy Basin. Heavy fishing pressure.				
Phinney	BK/CT	Upper Stillwater	13.6	N 40° 43' 05" W 110° 39' 48"
Popular with hikers. Moderate pressure.				
Pine Island	BK	Grandview	5.9	N 40° 38' 26" W 110° 49' 17"
Popular with Boy Scouts. Heavy pressure.				
Pinto	BK	Grandview	8.2	N 40° 39' 38" W 110° 48' 26"
NW of Governor Dern Lake. Heavy pressure.				
Powell	CT	Grandview	6.3	N 40° 37' 50" W 110° 47' 05"
Trail from Lost Lake in Grandaddy Basin.				
Rainbow	BK	Grandview	7.0	N 40° 38' 47" W 110° 47' 38"
At trail junction. Popular with hikers				
Reconnaissance	BK/CT	Mirror Lake	14.9	N 40° 44' 33" W 110° 42' 38"
Picturesque. No trail the last mile.				
Rock (1)	BK	Upper Stillwater	10.7	N 40° 40' 15" W 110° 40' 10"
Lots of brook trout. Approach from Rock Lake 2.				
Rock (2)	BK	Upper Stillwater	10.8	N 40° 40' 06" W 110° 40' 02"
Follow E Fork Rock Creek 0.5 mi. from trail junction. 1 mi. N of Shamrock Lake.				
Rosalie	BK	Mirror Lake	11.5	N 40° 43' 10" W 110° 45' 52"
West of Black Lake. Light fishing pressure.				

Name	Fish	Trailhead	Mi.	GPS Coordinates
Rudolph Lake (1)	BK	Moon Lake	9.8	N 40° 36' 47" W 110° 39' 00"
Largest of three Rudolph Lakes.				
Rudolph Lake (2)	BK	Moon Lake	9.8	N 40° 36' 41" W 110° 38' 50"
Middle Lake. Fishing pressure is moderate.				
Rudolph (3)	BK	Moon Lake	9.8	N 40° 36' 40" W 110° 38' 43"
Few brook trout. Subject to winterkill. No longer stocked.				
Sea Lion	CT	Mirror Lake	10.7	N 40° 39' 22" W 110° 43' 56"
Hard to reach. 1 mi. SE of Cyclone Pass.				
Shadow	BK/CT	Grandview	5.3	N 40° 37' 12" W 110° 48' 00"
Lies 0.5 mi. SE of Brinton Meadows Guard Station				
Shamrock	BK	Upper Stillwater	9.0	N 40° 39' 19" W 110° 39' 48"
Approach from Amlen Lake.				
Squaw	BK	Upper Stillwater	9.8	N 40° 39' 29" W 110° 39' 18"
Popular with hiking groups. Heavy pressure.				
Survey	BK	FR 143	0.5	N 40° 35' 12" W 110° 47' 38"
At the end of FR 143. Hike W 0.8 mi. Light pressure. Can winterkill in severe winters.				
Thompson	BK	Mirror Lake	10.5	N 40° 40' 40" W 110° 44' 31"
Some large brook trout. Hard to reach. 0.8 mi. N of Cyclone Pass.				
Uintah	BK	Mirror Lake	12.0	N 40° 42' 37" W 110° 45' 49"
No trail to lake. Fishing pressure is light.				
Up. Stillwater	RT/CT/BK	FR134	RA	N 40° 34' 03" W 110° 41' 59"
At the end of Rock Creek Road. There is a campground and boat ramp here.				
Young	CT	Upper Stillwater	10.5	N 40° 40' 40" W 110° 41' 25"
Small pond 0.3 mi. W of Ledge Trail. Rough.				

Maps

USGS 1:24000	Tworoose Pass, Explorer Peak, Hayden Peak, Grandaddy Lake
Utah Atlas and Gazetteer	Pages 54, 55

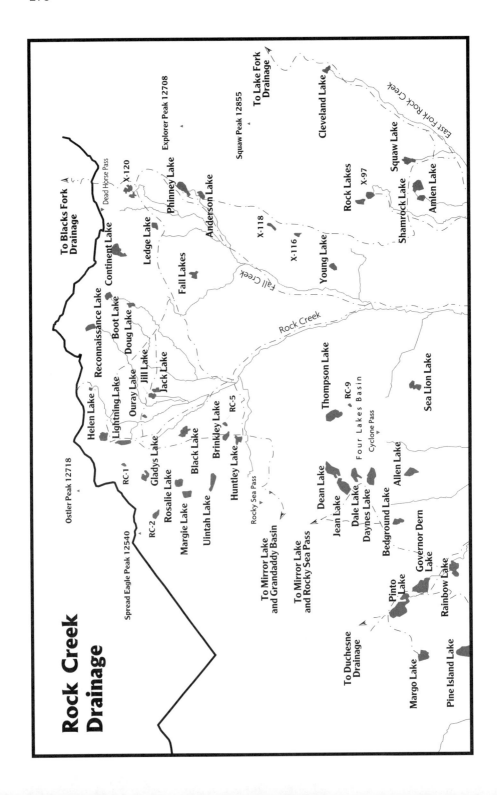

Rock Creek Drainage

To Blacks Fork Drainage

Dead Horse Pass

Ostler Peak 12718

Spread Eagle Peak 12540

Explorer Peak 12708

Squaw Peak 12855

To Lake Fork Drainage

East Fork Rock Creek

Cleveland Lake

Rock Lakes

X-97

Squaw Lake

Shamrock Lake

Amlen Lake

X-120

Phinney Lake

Anderson Lake

Continent Lake

Ledge Lake

Fall Lakes

X-118

X-116

Young Lake

Reconnaissance Lake

Boot Lake

Doug Lake

Jill Lake

Jack Lake

Fall Creek

Rock Creek

Thompson Lake

RC-9

Four Lakes Basin

Sea Lion Lake

Helen Lake

Lightning Lake

Ouray Lake

Gladys Lake

Brinkley Lake

RC-5

Huntley Lake

Cyclone Pass

Allen Lake

RC-1

Rosalie Lake

Black Lake

Dean Lake

RC-2

Margie Lake

Uintah Lake

Rocky Sea Pass

Jean Lake

Dale Lake

Daynes Lake

Bedground Lake

Governor Dern Lake

To Mirror Lake and Grandaddy Basin

To Mirror Lake and Rocky Sea Pass

Pinto Lake

Rainbow Lake

To Duchesne Drainage

Margo Lake

Pine Island Lake

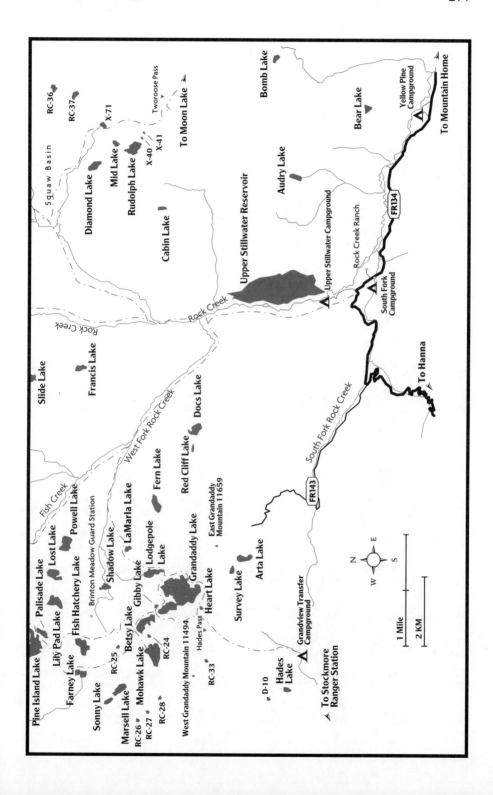

Sheep and
Carter Creek Drainages

T hese two drainages are at the eastern end of the Uinta's North Slope. They are combined here, as there is no major geographical feature separating them. There are a large number of very small ponds, particularly in the Teepee Lakes area. Many of these contain fish if they have a direct connection to a sizeable stream.

There are two main trailheads: the Spirit Lake Trailhead and the Browne Lake Trailhead. Both have adjacent campgrounds. Several lakes are within easy range of day-hikers, making this area ideal for anglers who don't wish to camp in the backcountry.

Lake Descriptions

Name	Fish	Trailhead	Mi.	GPS Coordinates
Anson, Lower	BK/CT	Spirit Lake	6.2	N 40° 48' 44" W 109° 56' 15"
Weyman Lakes Basin. Moderate pressure.				
Anson, Upper	BK	Spirit Lake	6.9	N 40° 48' 18" W 109° 56' 23"
Faint trail from Lower Anson. Moderate use.				
Browne	RT/CT/BK	Browne Lake	RA	N 40° 51' 54" W 109° 48' 47"
Spirit Lake Road to FR 096.				
Bummer	BK	Browne Lake	6.5	N 40° 48' 05" W 109° 53' 45"
From junction of TR 018-TR 017, SW 1.7 mi. Follow ridge on E side.				
Candy	BK/CT	Spirit Lake	6.9	N 40° 49' 33" W 109° 56' 55"
0.3 mi. from Hidden Lake. 1 mi. NNW from Anson. Winterkills.				
Clear	CT	Spirit Lake	6.6	N 40° 48' 32" W 109° 56' 47"
0.4 mi. W from Anson Lake.				
Columbine	BK	Spirit Lake	1.3	N 40° 49' 15" W 110° 00' 38"
Few brook trout. Follow Middle Fork of Sheep Creek. Light use.				
Daggett	RT/CT	Spirit Lake	2.6	N 40° 49' 45" W 109° 58' 17"
Good trail. Mosquitoes. Heavy fishing pressure.				
Ewe	BK/CT	Browne Lake	7.5	N 40° 48' 01" W 109° 55' 19"
From junction of TR 018-TR 017, SW 2.7 mi. Follow ridge on W side. Winterkills.				
Gail	CT/BK	Spirit Lake	1.1	N 40° 49' 31" W 110° 00' 58"
0.3 mi. S of Jessen Lake. Fishing pressure is light.				
GR-11	BK	Spirit Lake	7.1	N 40° 48' 11" W 109° 56' 17"
0.1 mi. SE from Upper Anson. Marginal for brook trout.				

Name	Fish	Trailhead	Mi.	GPS Coordinates
GR-13	BK	Spirit Lake	7.8	N 40° 48' 24" W 109° 57' 18"
0.8 mi. W from Upper Anson. Rough going.				
GR-20	BK	Browne Lake	6.6	N 40° 48' 02" W 109° 53' 55"
Just SW of Bummer. From junction of TR 018-TR 017, SW 1.7 mi. Marginal for brook trout.				
GR-21	BK	Browne Lake	6.5	N 40° 48' 09" W 109° 53' 50"
NW of Bummer Lake. May winterkill. Marginal for brook trout.				
GR-31	BK	Browne Lake	4.1	N 40° 49' 41" W 109° 51' 21"
Follow Sheep Creek Canal 1.2 mi. from TR 021.				
Hidden (GR-7)	BK/CT	Spirit Lake	6.8	N 40° 49' 17" W 109° 56' 48"
0.3 mi. NW of Lower Anson. Rough.				
Hidden (GR-112)	BK/CT	Spirit Lake	0.8	N 40° 50' 36" W 110° 00' 49"
0.8 mi. NW of Spirit Lake Campground.				
Jesson	BK/CT	Spirit Lake	1.0	N 40° 49' 51" W 110° 01' 04"
Rocky trail from Spirit Lake. Heavy use.				
Judy	BK	Spirit Lake	1.8	N 40° 49' 38" W 110° 01' 49"
0.4 mi. S from Tamarack up steep slope to bench.				
Lost	CT	Spirit Lake	1.1	N 40° 50' 23" W 110° 00' 52"
0.3 mi. N of trail to Tamarack past Lily Pad.				
Mutton	BK	Browne Lake	7.0	N 40° 47' 34" W 109° 54' 06"
0.6 mi. S from Bummer following inlet stream.				
One Fish	BK	Browne Lake	3.0	N 40° 49' 15" W 109° 50' 19"
Dense timber makes fly-fishing difficult.				
Penguin	BK	Spirit Lake	7.1	N 40° 48' 15" W 109° 56' 32"
Pan-sized brook trout. Just W of Upper Anson. Light fishing pressure.				
Potter, Lower	BK	Browne Lake	6.8	N 40° 48' 16" W 109° 52' 36"
NE of Upper Potter.				
Potter, Upper	BK	Browne Lake	6.5	N 40° 48' 05" W 109° 52' 42"
Trail to Lamb Lake Basin. Use topo map.				
Ram	CT	Browne Lake	6.9	N 40° 47' 59" W 109° 54' 32"
0.6 mi. WSW from Bummer Lake.				
Red	BK	Browne Lake	4.4	N 40° 47' 41" W 109° 50' 02"
1.2 mi. S of Teepee Lake. Light pressure.				
Sesame	BK	Spirit Lake	7.4	N 40° 48' 18" W 109° 56' 57"
W 0.4 mi. from Upper Anson. May winterkill.				
Sheep Creek	BK/CT	Spirit Lake Rd	RA	N 40° 53' 21" W 109° 50' 60"
Closed to fishing in 1999. Spirit Lake Road from SR 44.				
Spirit	RT	Spirit Lake Rd	RA	N 40° 50' 29" W 109° 59' 53"
Spirit Lake Road from SR 44.				
Summit	GR	Spirit Lake	1.0	N 40° 49' 25" W 110° 00' 18"
Arctic grayling may be stocked. Winterkill in past. Check with Vernal DWR. N of Spirit Lake 1 mi.				

Name	Fish	Trailhead	Mi.	GPS Coordinates
Tamarack	BK/CT	Spirit Lake	1.4	N 40° 50' 09" W 110° 01' 38"
Good for day hike & Boy Scout groups. Heavy use.				
Teepee, Lower	BK	Browne Lake	2.9	N 40° 48' 56" W 109° 49' 54"
Follow Sheep Creek Canal 0.3 mi. from trail crossing.				
Teepee, Upper	CT	Browne Lake	3.1	N 40° 48' 52" W 109° 49' 47"
Spotty for cutthroat trout. SE of Lower Teepee.				

Maps

USGS 1:24000   Leidy Peak, Whiterocks Lake, Chepeta Lake

Utah Atlas and Gazetteer   Page 56

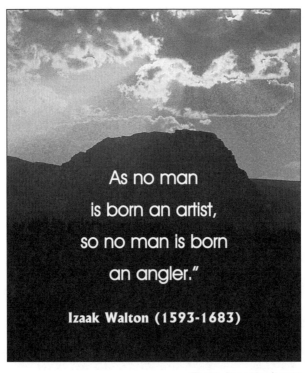

As no man
is born an artist,
so no man is born
an angler."

Izaak Walton (1593-1683)

(PHOTO: BRAD NICHOLSON)

Somewhere over the rainbow. (PHOTO: DENNIS BREER / TROUT CREEK FLIES)

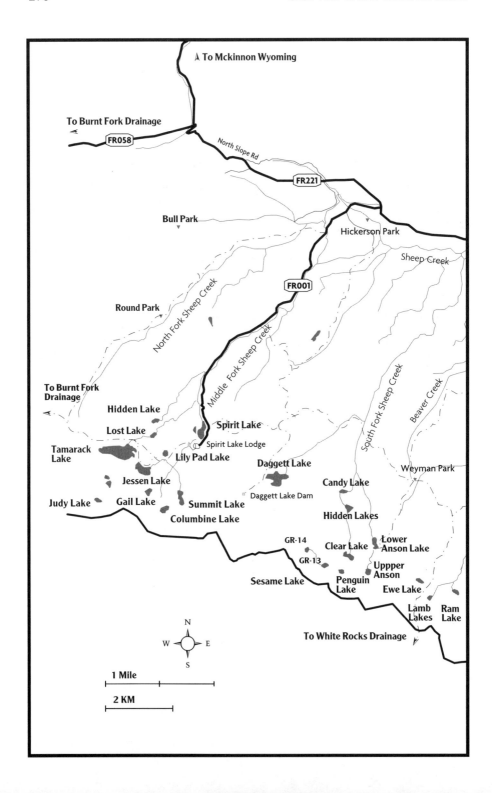

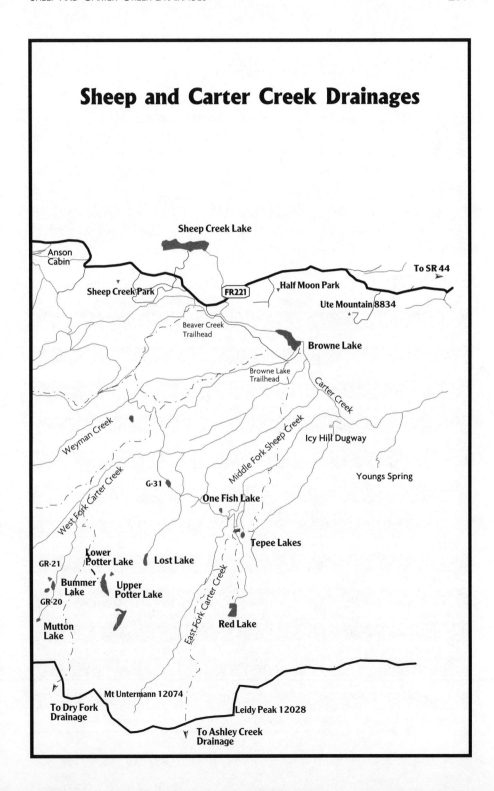

Sheep and Carter Creek Drainages

Sheep Creek Lake

Anson Cabin

To SR 44

Sheep Creek Park

FR221

Half Moon Park

Ute Mountain 8834

Beaver Creek Trailhead

Browne Lake

Browne Lake Trailhead

Carter Creek

Weyman Creek

Middle Fork Sheep Creek

Icy Hill Dugway

Youngs Spring

West Fork Carter Creek

G-31

One Fish Lake

Tepee Lakes

Lower Potter Lake

Lost Lake

GR-21

Bummer Lake

Upper Potter Lake

East Fork Carter Creek

GR-20

Mutton Lake

Red Lake

Mt Untermann 12074

To Dry Fork Drainage

Leidy Peak 12028

To Ashley Creek Drainage

Smiths Fork Drainage

T he Smiths Fork Drainage is composed of the East and West Forks. Many of the lakes here are at or above timberline. This includes the popular Red Castle area, which can experience high winds and severe weather with little notice. Make sure you are prepared for emergencies before you enter this high country.

The main trailhead to this basin is from China Meadows near China Lake on FR 072. Most of the lakes here are beyond the range of day-hikers, so plan an overnight trip when you can find the time.

Lake Descriptions

Name	Fish	Trailhead	Mi.	GPS Coordinates
Bald	BK	Mansfield Mdws Rd	4.0	N 40° 52' 03" W 110° 29' 29"
Many brook trout. W Fork Trail 2.5 mi. S to the junction. Follow stream 1.5 mi. SW.				
Bridger	RT/BK	FR 072	RA	N 40° 57' 45" W 110° 23' 10"
Popular lake with campground. Heavy use.				
China	BK/CT	FR 072	0.1	N 40° 56' 25" W 110° 24' 18"
Short hike. Heavy use. Campground at nearby China Meadows.				
G-13	BK	China Mdws	9.4	N 40° 48' 40" W 110° 27' 21"
Just E of Lower Red Castle. May winterkill. Good campsites.				
G-34	RT/BK	FR 072	RA	N 40° 55' 55" W 110° 24' 12"
Campground at nearby China Meadows.				
G-45	BK	China Mdws	10.6	N 40° 47' 42" W 110° 27' 04"
Rugged windswept terrain with poor campsites. May winterkill.				
G-49	BK/CT/RT	China Mdws	9.8	N 40° 48' 10" W 110° 28' 07"
Often overlooked by anglers. Water level fluctuates.				
G-50	BK	China Mdws	6.2	N 40° 51' 07" W 110° 28' 10"
0.7 mi. W of trail in Broadbent Meadow. Good campsites.				
G-51	BK	China Mdws	8.2	N 40° 50' 06" W 110° 26' 48"
1.6 mi. SE of G-50. Faint trail to lake. Moderate to light use. Good camping.				
G-52	CT	China Mdws	10.2	N 40° 50' 01" W 110° 29' 17"
Marginal for cutthroat trout. NW of G-53. Shallow lake is subject to winterkill. No campsites.				
G-53	CT/BK	China Mdws	10.0	N 40° 49' 53" W 110° 29' 05"
East Fork Trail to Bald Mountain Trail, then cross country. Use topo maps.				
G-56	BK	China Mdws	10.9	N 40° 48' 13" W 110° 29' 14"
Open and windswept. Poor camping. Seldom visited.. 1 mi. WSW of Lower Red Castle Lake..				

Name	Fish	Trailhead	Mi.	GPS Coordinates
G-58	CT	China Mdws	6.3	N 40° 52' 02" W 110° 25' 37"
Small lake on outlet stream from Hessie. Good campsites. Heavy use.				
G-59	BK	China Mdws	6.8	N 40° 51' 41" W 110° 25' 41"
0.5 mi. S of Hessie. Water level fluctuates and may winterkill.				
G-60	BK	China Mdws	6.3	N 40° 51' 49" W 110° 25' 05"
Small remnant of old beaver pond. Light fishing pressure.				
G-61	BK	China Mdws	6.6	N 40° 51' 40" W 110° 25' 07"
May winterkill. Good camping and light pressure.				
G-64	CT	Cache	4.5	N 40° 52' 19" W 110° 26' 09"
0.5 mi. S of Jct. of Highline and W Fk. Trails. May winterkill. Good camping.				
Hessie	CT	China Mdws	6.2	N 40° 52' 06" W 110° 25' 45"
Popular lake with good camping. Please pack out trash.				
Marsh	RT/AB	FR 072	RA	N 40° 57' 27" W 110° 23' 42"
Two campgrounds. Heavily used area.				
Red Castle	CT	China Mdws	11.0	N 40° 47' 22" W 110° 28' 22"
Popular area. Raft or float tube is helpful on this large lake. High elevation.				
Red Castle, East	CT	China Mdws	11.0	N 40° 47' 50" W 110° 27' 19"
Large and wary cutthroat trout. Moderate fishing pressure. Open with poor campsites.				
Red Castle, Lw	RT/CT/BK	China Mdws	9.0	N 40° 48' 44" W 110° 27' 44"
Popular with good, but overused, campsites. Minimize your impact.				
Red Castle, Up	CT	China Mdws	12.1	N 40° 46' 46" W 110° 28' 29"
Slow for large cutthroat. Rough access to this high and rocky lake. No good campsites.				
Smiths Fork Pass	CT	China Mdws	11.2	N 40° 47' 30" W 110° 26' 47"
Open shoreline good for fly-fishing. Good camps in trees 0.3 mi. N.				

Maps

USGS 1:24000	Mount Lovenia, Mount Powell, Bridger Lake, Lyman Lake
Utah Atlas and Gazetteer	Page 55

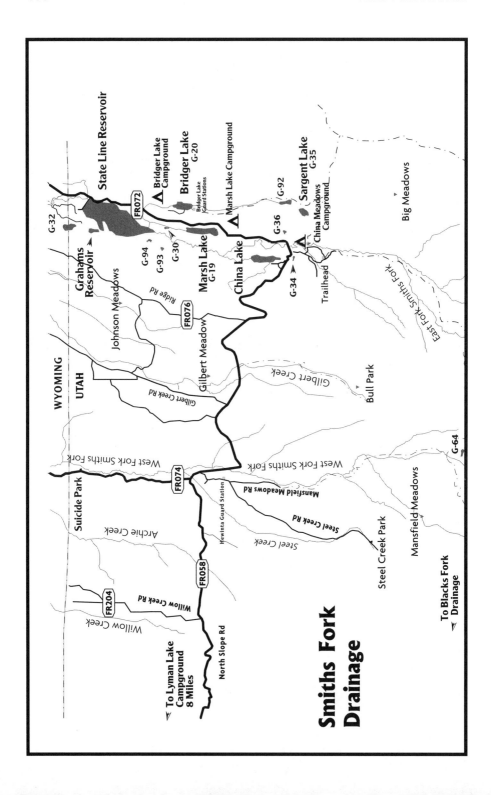

Smiths Fork Drainage

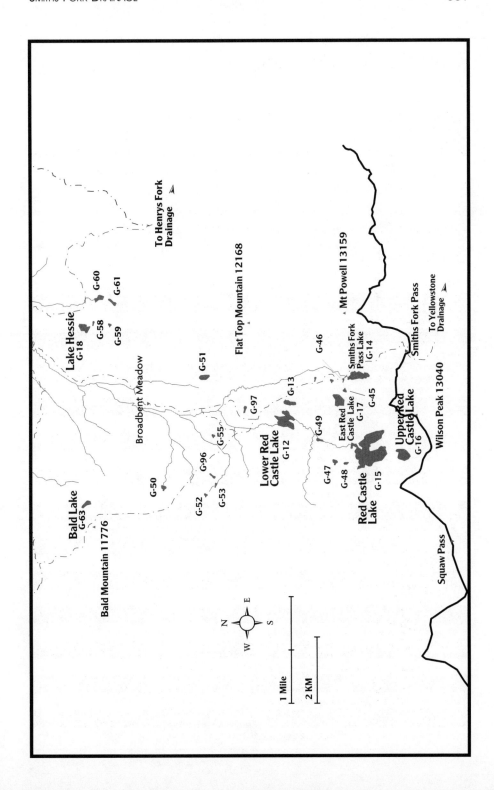

Swift Creek Drainage

DUCHESNE COUNTY

T his is a smaller steep-sided drainage with 17 large lakes. Some are natural lakes whose size has been increased by man-made dams, and they are subject to water level fluctuations. They are commonly low in late summer and fall. Most of the lakes are clustered in the Farmers Lake area or in the Timothy Lake Basin.

The entrance to this drainage is from the trailhead at the Swift Creek Campground. The trail is steep and rocky, but well marked and maintained.

Lake Descriptions

Name	Fish	Trailhead	Mi.	GPS Coordinates
Carrol, East	CT	Swift Creek	10.0	N 40° 43' 08" W 110° 20' 40"
NE 0.5 mi. from East Timothy Lake.				
Carrol, Lower	BK	Swift Creek	9.5	N 40° 42' 57" W 110° 21' 03"
Many brook trout. N 0.5 mi. from East Timothy Lake.				
Carrol, Upper	BK	Swift Creek	9.8	N 40° 43' 20" W 110° 21' 15"
Many small brook trout. Natural reproduction. Moderate use.				
Deer	BK/CT	Swift Creek	6.0	N 40° 40' 19" W 110° 21' 45"
Heavy use. Low water in late summer.				
Farmers	BK	Swift Creek	8.0	N 40° 41' 53" W 110° 22' 30"
Few campsites. Angling pressure is moderate.				
Grayling	BK	Swift Creek	5.7	N 40° 39' 40" W 110° 21' 20"
Swift Creek to outlet stream from Grayling.				
Lily	BK	Grant Springs	1.0	N 40° 36' 40" W 110° 20' 00"
Water Lily on USGS map. From Grant Springs by Swift Creek Campground. Steep trail NE.				
Timothy, Center	BK	Swift Creek	9.7	N 40° 42' 34" W 110° 21' 37"
W of East Timothy Lake. Heavy use.				
Timothy, East	BK/CT	Swift Creek	9.5	N 40° 42' 36" W 110° 21' 13"
Good fly-fishing below dam. Heavy use.				
Timothy, West	BK	Swift Creek	10.0	N 40° 42' 56" W 110° 21' 50"
Moderate pressure. NW 0.3 mi. from East Timothy Lake.				
Twin (X-50)	CT	Swift Creek	8.0	N 40° 41' 22" W 110° 23' 02"
Productive for cutthroat trout. W 0.7 mi. from White Miller Lake. Light use.				
White Miller	BK	Swift Creek	7.3	N 40° 41' 12" W 110° 22' 16"
Many mosquitoes and horseflies in summer.				
X-22	BK/CT	Swift Creek	10.3	N 40° 42' 37" W 110° 20' 10"
Angling pressure light. E of East Timothy Lake 0.8 mi.				

Name	Fish	Trailhead	Mi.	GPS Coordinates
X-24	CT	Swift Creek	8.8	N 40° 41′ 50″ W 110° 23′ 06″
W 0.8 mi. on trail from Farmers Lake.				
X-25	CT	Swift Creek	9.0	N 40° 42′ 06″ W 110° 23′ 09″
NW 1 mi. on trail from Farmers Lake.				
X-26	BK	Swift Creek	9.2	N 40° 42′ 11″ W 110° 22′ 46″
NW of Farmers Lake 0.3 mi. and E from X-25.				
X-51	CT	Swift Creek	7.0	N 40° 40′ 43″ W 110° 22′ 46″
Halfway between White Miller and Deer Lakes. 0.5 mi. W of connecting stream. Use map.				

Maps

USGS 1:24000   Garfield Basin, Mount Emmons,
Burnt Mill Spring

Utah Atlas and Gazetteer   Page 55

"There is nothing so clean as a fish."

Welsh proverb

(PHOTO: JAMES R. HENDERSON)

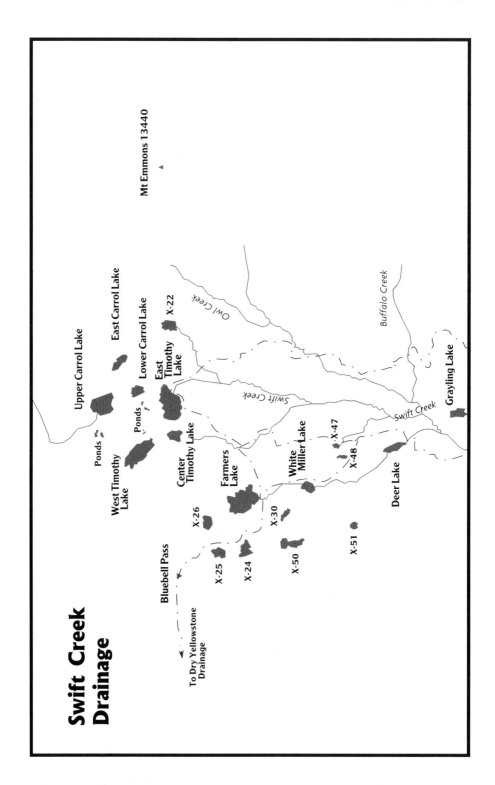

Swift Creek Drainage

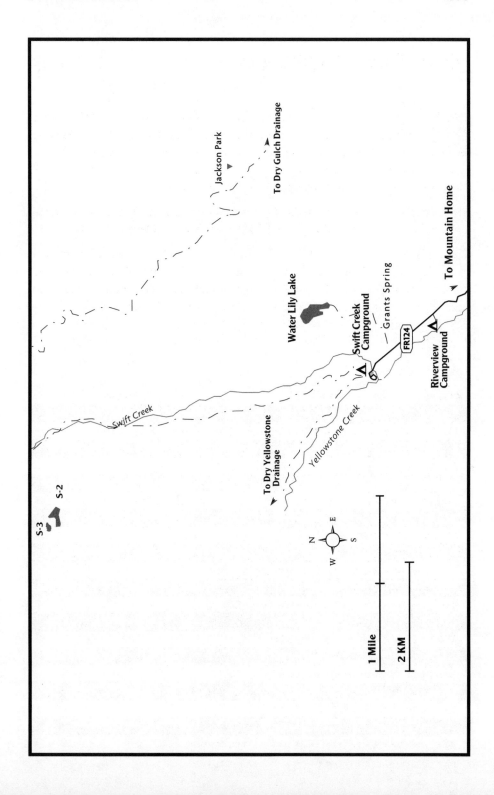

Uinta River Drainage

DUCHESNE COUNTY

T
his is one of the largest and most diverse of the Uinta Mountains' drainages. It is made up of seven different basins: Krebs, Atwood, Painter, Painter Lakes, Gilbert, Kidney Lakes, and Fox. Almost all of the lakes in this drainage are past the range of day-hikers, so count on spending the night and consider horse-packing to cover greater distances.

Kings Peak is located at the head of Painter Basin and is the highest point in the state of Utah. It reaches a height of 13,528 feet above sea level.

There are two main trailheads into this drainage. The Uinta Canyon Trailhead is by the U-Bar Ranch and 21 miles north of Neola. This trail begins at 8,000 feet and rises gradually as it follows the Uinta River into the high country. The West Fork of the Whiterocks Trailhead is 25 miles north of the town of Whiterocks. This trail starts at 10,000 feet, but hikers must cross the Fox-Queant Pass at 11,400 feet or North Pole Pass at 12,200 feet to reach the Uinta drainage.

Lake Descriptions

Name	Fish	Trailhead	Mi.	GPS Coordinates
Albert	CT	Jefferson Park	7.0	N 40° 40' 15" W 110° 16' 31"
Many cutthroat trout. Rough. NW from Bollie Lake 2 mi. up ridge and descend talus.				
Allred	BK	Uinta Canyon	18.0	N 40° 44' 26" W 110° 17' 57"
Fast fly-fishing for brook trout. Trail is rocky and steep. Seems farther than it is.				
Atwood	BK/GT	Uinta Canyon	18.0	N 40° 44' 42" W 110° 17' 54"
May still hold golden trout. Moderate use. Has many brooks and a chance to catch Golden Trout.				
B-29	BK	Uinta Canyon	17.5	N 40° 43' 52" W 110° 16' 41"
Many brook trout. 0.3 mi. E of Carrot Lake. Bring insect repellent.				
Beard	BK	Uinta Canyon	22.2	N 40° 45' 03" W 110° 20' 48"
Cross Trail Riders Pass. Open tundra. Light use.				
Bollie	CT	Jefferson Park	5.0	N 40° 39' 08" W 110° 14' 32"
Old logging road past Jefferson Park; take trail W for 2 mi.				
Bowden	BK	Uinta Canyon	18.5	N 40° 47' 28" W 110° 13' 24"
SE 0.5 mi. from Kidney. No trail. May winterkill.				
Brook	BK	W. Fork Whiterocks	7.3	N 40° 47' 27" W 110° 08' 05"
Cross North Pole Pass. Fishing pressure is light.				
Carrot	BK	Uinta Canyon	17.5	N 40° 43' 44" W 110° 17' 40"
The fishing is good and the pressure is light.				
Chain 1, Lwr	BK	Uinta Canyon	11.5	N 40° 42' 08" W 110° 14' 40"
Many small brook trout. Heavy use in early summer; decreases later.				

Name	Fish	Trailhead	Mi.	GPS Coordinates
Chain 2, Mid	BK	Uinta Canyon	12.0	N 40° 42' 24" W 110° 15' 07"
Abundant brook trout. Above Lower Chain 0.5 mi. Moderate use.				
Chain 3, Upper	BK	Uinta Canyon	12.5	N 40° 42' 41" W 110° 15' 22"
Many small brook trout. Fast fishing on flies or spinners.				
Chain 4	CT	Uinta Canyon	13.5	N 40° 43' 03" W 110° 15' 40"
Fishes better in late season. Light pressure.				
Craig	CT/BK	Uinta Canyon	16.0	N 40° 45' 32" W 110° 14' 47"
S 2 mi. from North Fork Park. No trail.				
Crescent	CT/BK	W. Fork Whiterocks	8.0	N 40° 47' 04" W 110° 09' 34"
Over Fox-Queant Pass. Popular with Boy Scout groups.				
Davis, North	BK	W. Fork Whiterocks	14.5	N 40° 48' 55" W 110° 13' 10"
Pan-sized brook trout. Over Fox-Queant Pass. These fish are hard to catch.				
Davis, South	BK	W. Fork Whiterocks	14.5	N 40 48' 46" W 110° 13' 18"
Pan-sized brook trout. Over Fox-Queant Pass. 1 mi. N of Kidney Lake. Good fly-fishing.				
Divide	CT	W. Fork Whiterocks	10.5	N 40° 48' 39" W 110° 09' 03"
N of Fox Lake. No campsites.				
Dollar (Dime)	BK	W. Fork Whiterocks	9.5	N 40° 47' 49" W 110° 09' 50"
Small brook trout. Sometimes used by large groups. Excellent camping sites.				
Fox	BK/CT	W. Fork Whiterocks	8.5	N 40° 47' 30" W 110° 09' 01"
Pressure is moderate, but can be used by large groups.				
George Beard	BK	Uinta Canyon	20.0	N 40° 45' 05" W 110° 20' 07"
Abundant brook trout. 1.6 mi. up trail to Trail Riders Pass from Atwood Lake.				
Gilbert	BK	Uinta Canyon	20.5	N 40° 50' 37" W 110° 19' 19"
Sheep graze here in late summer. Light pressure.				
Kidney, East	BK	W. Fork Whiterocks	15.0	N 40° 47' 54" W 110° 13' 31"
Heavy use from large groups. 18 mi. from Uinta Canyon Trailhead.				
Kidney, West	BK	W. Fork Whiterocks	15.0	N 40° 47' 58" W 110° 13' 42"
Campsites between the lakes are overused.				
Lily	BK	W. Fork Whiterocks	15.5	N 40° 48' 00" W 110° 13' 07"
Go 0.3 mi. NE of Kidney Lakes. No trail, much less pressure. Not labeled on USGS map.				
Lily Pad	BK/RT	Uinta Canyon	8.0	N 40° 41' 55" W 110° 13' 16"
First lake on Chain Lakes Trail. Many fish. Lily Pad appears as Lily Lake on USGS map.				
Milk	BK/CT	Uinta Canyon	19.0	N 40° 47' 38" W 110° 18' 14"
In cirque on N edge of Painter Basin. 5 mi. W of North Fork Park.				
Mt. Emmons	BK/GT	Uinta Canyon	18.5	N 40° 44' 10" W 110° 18' 12"
Also known as Allen. May be some golden trout remaining. 0.3 mi. SW of Allred Lake.				
Oke Doke	CT	Uinta Canyon	15.0	N 40° 43' 02" W 110° 16' 56"
1 mi. W of Roberts Pass. Ideal for small groups.				
Penny Nickell	CT	W. Fork Whiterocks	10.7	N 40° 45' 02" W 110° 09' 24"
S 2 mi. from S end of Crescent Lake. No trail. Use maps. Light use.				

Name	Fish	Trailhead	Mi.	GPS Coordinates
Pippen (Is.)	BK	Uinta Canyon	10.0	N 40° 41' 37" W 110° 14' 52"
0.5 mi. S of Chain 1 (Lower). Good fly-fishing.				
Rainbow	BK/RT/CT	W. Fork Whiterocks	16.0	N 40° 48' 31" W 110° 14' 22"
Heavy day use by large groups staying at Kidney Lakes. No campsites.				
Roberts	CT/BK	Uinta Canyon	19.4	N 40° 44' 03" W 110° 19' 19"
1 mi. SW of Atwood Lake. Faint trail from Mt. Emmons Lake.				
Samuals	BK	W. Fork Whiterocks	12.8	N 40° 48' 25" W 110° 11' 25"
Abundant brook trout. W 3.5 mi. on trail from Fox. N 0.8 mi. Away from crowds at Kidney.				
U-19	BK	Uinta Canyon	20.4	N 40° 44' 43" W 110° 19' 58"
0.5 mi. S of George Beard Lake. Open tundra.				
U-35	BK/CT	Uinta Canyon	16.0	N 40° 48' 34" W 110° 14' 03"
Few brook and cutthroat trout. First pond below Rainbow Lake on outlet stream.				
U-36	BK	Uinta Canyon	15.8	N 40° 48' 28" W 110° 13' 56"
Below U-35. 1 mi. NW of Kidney Lakes.				
U-37	BK	Uinta Canyon	16.5	N 40° 48' 48" W 110° 14' 07"
0.5 mi. NE of Rainbow Lake. Pressure is light.				
U-38	CT	Uinta Canyon	16.7	N 40° 48' 56" W 110° 14' 25"
0.5 mi. N of Rainbow Lake past U-39.				
U-39	BK	Uinta Canyon	16.5	N 40° 48' 46" W 110° 14' 25"
May still hold brook trout. 0.3 mi. N of Rainbow Lake.				
U-42	CT	Uinta Canyon	16.7	N 40° 48' 57" W 110° 14' 58"
Marginal for cutthroat trout. 0.5 mi. NW from Rainbow Lake.				
U-50	BK	W. Fork Whiterocks	9.5	N 40° 47' 58" W 110° 10' 12"
0.3 mi. NW of Dollar Lake. Light pressure.				
U-75	BK	Uinta Canyon	22.0	N 40° 45' 39" W 110° 21' 02"
1 mi. NW of Trail Riders Pass. Cold and windy.				
U-76	BK/CT	Uinta Canyon	22.8	N 40° 46' 14" W 110° 21' 21"
True wilderness experience. 11,475 feet.				
U-88	BK	Uinta Canyon	17.0	N 40° 45' 46" W 110° 15' 43"
Nice brook trout. Largest lake in Painter Basin. 1 mi. W of Craig.				
U-89	BK	Uinta Canyon	17.0	N 40° 45' 39" W 110° 15' 56"
Few brook trout. In Painter Basin 100 yds. SW of U-88.				
U-93	CT	Uinta Canyon	17.5	N 40° 45' 52" W 110° 16' 37"
W end of Painter Basin. Very remote. Lightest use.				
Verlie	BK/CT	Uinta Canyon	15.7	N 40° 47' 54" W 110° 14' 30"
0.5 mi. W of Kidney Lakes. Moderate use.				

Maps

USGS 1:24000	Kings Peak, Mount Emmons, Bollie Lake, Fox Lake, Chepeta Lake, Rassmussen Lake.
Utah Atlas and Gazetteer	Pages 55, 56

Services

Pack Trips and Cabins:

U-Bar Ranch on the Uinta River
tel: (435) 645-7256 / (800) 303-7256

Golden trout. (ARTIST: MIKE STIDHAM)

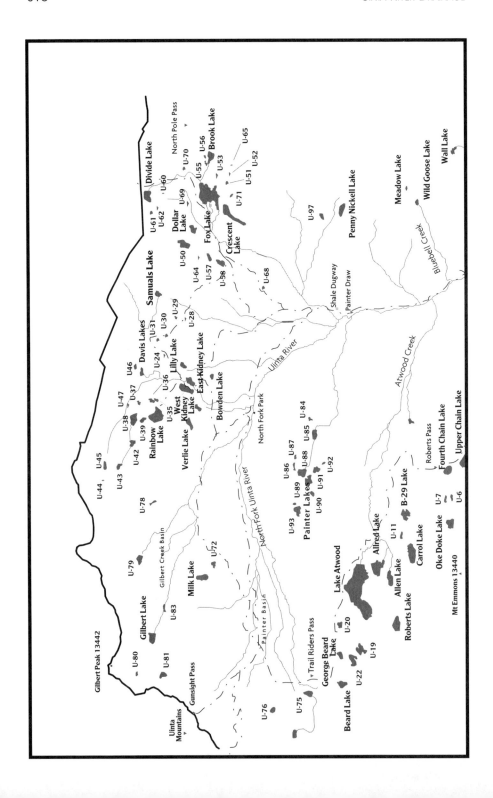

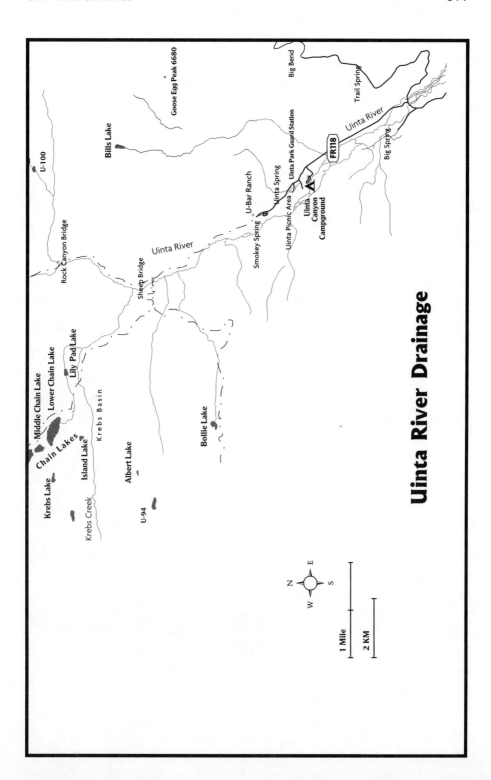

Uinta River Drainage

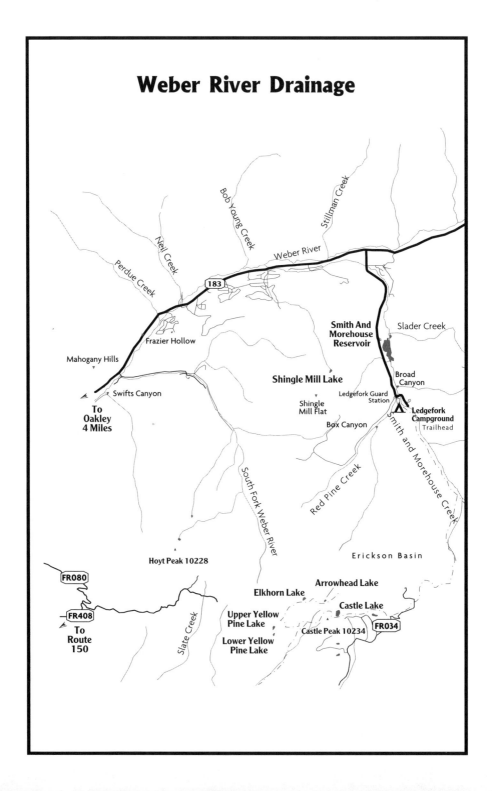

Weber River Drainage

Bob Young Creek

Stillman Creek

Neil Creek

Perdue Creek

Weber River

183

Frazier Hollow

Mahogany Hills

Swifts Canyon

**To
Oakley
4 Miles**

Smith And
Morehouse
Reservoir

Slader Creek

Broad
Canyon

Shingle Mill Lake

Shingle
Mill Flat

Ledgefork Guard
Station

Box Canyon

**Ledgefork
Campground**
Trailhead

Smith and Morehouse Creek

Red Pine Creek

South Fork Weber River

Hoyt Peak 10228

Erickson Basin

FR080

FR408

**To
Route
150**

Slate Creek

Arrowhead Lake

Elkhorn Lake

**Upper Yellow
Pine Lake**

Castle Lake

Castle Peak 10234

FR034

**Lower Yellow
Pine Lake**

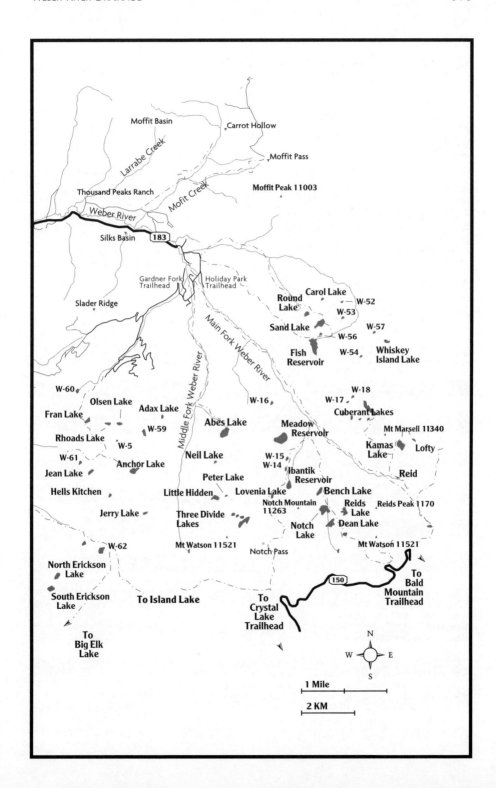

Weber River Drainage

T his large drainage is on the west end of the Uinta Mountains and one of the closest to the Salt Lake Valley. It lies outside of the High Uintas Wilderness so road access is generally better here. The majority of these lakes are less than 5 miles from a trailhead and make good destinations for day trips.

There are 7 different trailheads anglers can use to enter this area. Bald Mountain Trailhead, Pass Lake Trailhead, Crystal Lake Trailhead, and Yellowpine Trailhead are all easily accessible from SR 150. Upper Setting is 9 miles north of SR 150 on a rough road. Ledgefork and Holiday Park/Gardeners Fork can be reached on SR 183 east of Oakley.

Lake Descriptions

Name	Fish	Trailhead	Mi.	GPS Coordinates
Abes	CT	Holiday Park	3.5	N 40° 43' 53" W 110° 58' 41"
Middle Fork Trail 2.5 mi. S, then 1 mi. E.				
Adax	CT	Holiday Park	3.5	N 40° 44' 13" W 111° 00' 25"
Middle Fork Trail 2.5 mi. S, then 1 mi. W.				
Anchor	BK	Gardners Fork	7.0	N 40° 43' 09" W 111° 01' 11"
Many small brook trout. The Gardners Fork jeep road. Driveable first 2 mi. with 4-wd.				
Arrowhead	BK	Upper Setting Rd	3.8	N 40° 40' 34" W 111° 08' 23"
6 mi. N of SR 150 on Upper Setting Rd. N 1 mi. on logging road. Trail to Up. Yellowpine, then N.				
Bench	BK	Bald Mountain	2.8	N 40° 42' 43" W 110° 56' 09"
May winterkill. Moderate use. Good campsites.				
Carol	BK	Holiday Park	4.0	N 40° 46' 37" W 110° 56' 07"
NE 0.5 mi. (no trail) from Round Lake.				
Castle	BK	Upper Setting Rd	0.3	N 40° 40' 17" W 111° 07' 29"
6 mi. N of SR 150 on Upper Setting Road. N 1 mi. on logging road. Trail 0.3 mi. to lake.				
Cuberant 1	BK	Pass Lake	2.8	N 40° 44' 08" W 110° 54' 54"
Fast fishing for brook trout. Trail is steep. Moderate use. Poor campsites.				
Cuberant 2	BK	Pass Lake	2.8	N 40° 44' 06" W 110° 55' 10"
Excellent campsites. Moderate pressure.				
Cuberant 3	BK	Pass Lake	3.0	N 40° 44' 11" W 110° 55' 22"
Pan-sized brook trout. Just NW of Cuberant 2. Good camping at S end.				
Cuberant 4	CT	Pass Lake	3.0	N 40° 44' 21" W 110° 54' 49"
Largest of Cuberants. Good camping.				

Name	Fish	Trailhead	Mi.	GPS Coordinates
Dean	BK/CT	Bald Mountain	2.0	N 40° 42′ 06″ W 110° 55′ 51″
May winterkill. Heavy angling pressure.				
Erickson, South	BK	Upper Setting	2.5	N 40° 40′ 54″ W 111° 03′ 57″
Easy hike. Campsites. Moderate use.				
Erickson, North	BK	Upper Setting	2.7	N 40° 41′ 09″ W 111° 03′ 47″
Shallow and subject to winterkill.				
Fish	GR/BK	Holiday Park	4.0	N 40° 45′ 39″ W 110° 56′ 17″
Steep, rocky trail. Many small grayling.				
Fran	BK	Gardners Fork	5.0	N 40° 44′ 08″ W 111° 02′ 26″
The Gardners Fork jeep road. Driveable first 2 mi. with 4-wd.				
Ibantik	BK	Crystal Lake	3.0	N 40° 42′ 50″ W 110° 56′ 59″
Cross "The Notch." Water level fluctuates.				
Jean	CT	Ledgefork	4.0	N 40° 43′ 08″ W 111° 02′ 20″
1 steep mi. W of Anchor Lake.				
Kamas	CT	Pass Lake	1.5	N 40° 43′ 38″ W 110° 53′ 58″
Moderate to heavy use. Good campsites.				
Little Hidden	BK	Crystal Lake	2.5	N 40° 42′ 36″ W 110° 58′ 55″
Larger brook trout. W 1.2 mi. from S side of "The Notch." No trail.				
Lofty	CT	Pass Lake	2.3	N 40° 43′ 43″ W 110° 53′ 38″
Heavy use by Boy Scouts. 1 mi. NW of Camp Steiner.				
Lovenia	BK	Crystal Lake	2.8	N 40° 42′ 38″ W 110° 57′ 28″
Top of Notch Pass. Campsites. Heavy use.				
Meadow	CT	Crystal Lake	4.0	N 40° 43′ 47″ W 110° 57′ 09″
Water level fluctuates. Good camping.				
Neil	BK	Crystal Lake	4.3	N 40° 43′ 21″ W 110° 58′ 46″
1.5 mi. NW of Lovenia. Rough, no trail.				
Notch	BK	Bald Mtn.	2.3	N 40° 42′ 22″ W 110° 56′ 02″
Water level fluctuation. May winterkill.				
Olsen	BK	Gardners Fork	6.0	N 40° 44′ 04″ W 111° 01′ 34″
0.5 mi. E of Fran Lake. May winterkill.				
Rhoads	BK	Gardners Fork	5.7	N 40° 44′ 05″ W 111° 01′ 52″
Good for brook trout. 0.3 mi. E of Fran Lake. Campsites.				
Round	GR	Holiday Park	3.5	N 40° 46′ 14″ W 110° 56′ 30″
Heavily used campsites. Rough, rocky trail.				
Sand	GR	Holiday Park	4.4	N 40° 46′ 03″ W 110° 56′ 08″
Many arctic grayling. Trees to water's edge. Good camping.				
W-17	BK	Pass Lake	3.6	N 40° 44′ 28″ W 110° 55′ 20″
0.3 mi. W from N end of Cuberant 4.				
W-52	BK	Holiday Park	4.5	N 40° 46′ 38″ W 110° 55′ 35″
0.4 mi. E of Carol Lake. Rough, no trail.				

Name	Fish	Trailhead	Mi.	GPS Coordinates
W-53	BK	Holiday Park	4.8	N 40° 46' 06" W 110° 55' 39"
0.3 mi. E of Sand Lake. Rocky, no trail.				
W-57	BK	Holiday Park	5.5	N 40° 45' 38" W 110° 55' 19"
0.5 mi. E from Fish Lake.				
W-59	BK	Holiday Park	4.0	N 40° 43' 54" W 111° 00' 54"
0.5 mi. SW from Adax. Rough, marginal camps.				
W-62	BK	Crystal Lake	4.0	N 40° 41' 17" W 111° 01' 27"
Seldom visited. Good campsites.				
Yellowpine, Lower	BK	Yellowpine	3.6	N 40° 39' 51" W 111° 09' 10"
Heavily used area. Pack out trash.				
Yellowpine, Upper	BK	Yellowpine	3.7	N 40° 39' 59" W 111° 09' 12"
Heavily used area. Pack out trash.				

Maps

USGS 1:24000   Whitney Reservoir, Slader Basin, Hidden Lake, Mirror Lake, Erickson Basin, Hoyt Peak

Utah Atlas and Gazetteer   Page 54

Tree-shrouded Sand Lake above Holiday Park. (PHOTO: COURTESY UTAH OUTDOORS)

Whiterocks River Drainage

T his drainage has very good vehicular access. Almost all the lakes with viable fisheries are accessible enough to be considered for day-hikers. The road to Chepeta Lake is spectacular and stops just 2 miles short of the divide between the North and South Slopes.

The two main trailheads are the West Fork of the Whiterocks and Chepeta Lake. There are good facilities at the West Fork and new facilities are being built at Chepeta Lake. The Rock Lakes are most easily reached from the Pole Creek Campgrounds.

There are three high-clearance roads open to the public in this drainage. One goes from Paradise Park to Cliff Lake. It is extremely rough past Johnson Creek and not recommended. The other two go most of the way to Rasmussen Lakes or R.C. No. 1. These are very rough and don't save much distance over using the main West Fork Whiterocks Trailhead. It's better to use your legs and not abuse your vehicle. Don't consider any of these roads unless you have a very competent 4-wheel-drive and the skills to operate it in severe conditions.

Lake Descriptions

Name	Fish	Trailhead	Mi.	GPS Coordinates
Angel	CT	West Fork	0.7	N 40° 42' 51" W 110° 03' 48"
May winterkill. Rocky. Pressure is light.				
Ann	CT	West Fork	4.0	N 40° 44' 40" W 110° 07' 33"
Subject to winterkill. Very light pressure.				
Becky	BK	West Fork	4.2	N 40° 43' 45" W 110° 07' 05"
Very little pressure. 1.5 mi. W of Rasmussen.				
Chepeta	BK/CT	FR 110	RA	N 40° 47' 32" W 110° 01' 05"
Fishing pressure is heavy due to easy access.				
Cirque	GR	West Fork	2.1	N 40° 43' 34" W 110° 05' 53"
Experimental arctic grayling. 0.3 mi. SW of Rasmussen Lakes.				
Cleveland	BK/CT	West Fork	4.0	N 40° 45' 46" W 110° 06' 39"
Open for fly-fishing. Moderate pressure.				
Cliff	BK/CT	Chepeta Lake	5.6	N 40° 43' 31" W 109° 58' 59"
There is road access here on FR 459, but it is not recommended. Rough.				
Denise	BK	West Fork	5.9	N 40° 46' 55" W 110° 05' 08"
1.9 mi. NNE of Queant. 0.3 mi. S of Taylor.				
Dollar	BK/CT	Chepeta Lake	4.0	N 40° 46' 26" W 109° 57' 17"
0.5 mi. S of Whiterocks Lake. Moderate use.				

Name	Fish	Trailhead	Mi.	GPS Coordinates
Elbow	BK	Chepeta Lake	1.9	N 40° 47' 45" W 110° 02' 25"
Follow inlet stream W from NW corner Chepeta Lake. Rough terrain.				
Eric	BK/CT	West Fork	3.7	N 40° 44' 20" W 110° 06' 58"
Follow the W Fk. Whiterocks. Light use.				
Figure Eight	CT	Chepeta Lake	0.7	N 40° 47' 51" W 110° 01' 31"
Many small cutthroat trout. 0.3 mi. from NW corner of Chepeta Lake.				
Hidden	BK	FR 110	0.2	N 40° 44' 40" W 110° 01' 56"
W of road to Chepeta Lake in heavy timber.				
Horseshoe	CT/BK	Reader Creek	2.6	N 40° 47' 27" W 110° 03' 31"
Last 0.5 mi. cross country. Moderate use.				
Katy	CT	West Fork	4.8	N 40° 45' 12" W 110° 07' 31"
1 mi. NW of Point Lake. Windy, rough. Solitude.				
Larvae	BK	Jct FR117 and FR110	0.3	N 40° 40' 31" W 110° 02' 16"
Subject to winterkill some years. Moderate use.				
Lower Rock	BK	Pole Creek CG	1.4	N 40° 41' 09" W 110° 04' 37"
From Campground, N 0.5 mi. to meadow. Take stream W to Lower Rock.				
Middle Rock	BK	Pole Creek CG	1.7	N 40° 41' 25" W 110° 04' 44"
Timber and rocks to shoreline. 200 yds. N of Lower Rock.				
Moccasin	BK/CT	Chepeta Lake	0.7	N 40° 47' 35" W 110° 00' 29"
Easy access from Chepeta. Heavily used.				
Nellie	CT	West Fork	3.7	N 40° 44' 27" W 110° 07' 28"
0.4 mi. W of Eric Lake. No trails. Light use.				
Ogden	CT	West Fork	5.2	N 40° 46' 37" W 110° 06' 39"
May winterkill. More solitude than Queant.				
Papoose	BK/CT	Chepeta Lake	1.0	N 40° 48' 01" W 110° 00' 32"
Open for easy fly-fishing. Moderate pressure.				
Pearl	CT/BK	Chepeta Lake	4.5	N 40° 47' 21" W 109° 57' 23"
0.7 mi. N of Whiterocks Lake. Very light use.				
Point	BK	West Fork	3.2	N 40° 44' 42" W 110° 06' 07"
West Fork Trail, then up outlet stream from Point.				
Pole Creek	RT	FR 117	RA	N 40° 40' 34" W 110° 03' 32"
Used heavily. Has campground.				
Queant	BK	West Fork	4.0	N 40° 44' 55" W 110° 05' 58"
Most traffic on this trail is headed to Queant Lake.				
Rasmussen 1	BK	West Fork	1.8	N 40° 43' 53" W 110° 05' 31"
Easy access and good campsites.				
Rasmussen 2	BK	West Fork	1.6	N 40° 43' 43" W 110° 05' 19"
Easy access and generally good fishing.				
R.C. No 1	CT	West Fork	2.6	N 40° 44' 59" W 110° 04' 55"
1 mi. ENE from Point Lake. Light use.				

Name	Fish	Trailhead	Mi.	GPS Coordinates
R.C. No 2	CT	West Fork	2.5	N 40° 44' 58" W 110° 05' 04"
0.9 mi. ENE from Point Lake. Light use.				
Robb	BK	West Fork	5.7	N 40° 46' 26" W 110° 07' 34"
May winterkill some years. Light pressure.				
Sand	BK/CT	Chepeta Lake	4.9	N 40° 46' 09" W 109° 57' 33"
Many brook and cutthroat trout. Open for fly-fishing. Fast fishing. Light use.				
Saucer	BK	West Fork	4.8	N 40° 45' 46" W 109° 57' 43"
0.4 mi. east of Ted's in heavy timber.				
Sharlee	BK/CT	Chepeta Lake	1.9	N 40° 47' 05" W 110° 02' 40"
Easy access W from Chepeta. Moderate use.				
Tamara	CT	West Fork	4.2	N 40° 44' 40" W 110° 07' 55"
No trail. Light use. Very picturesque and remote.				
Taylor	BK	Chepeta Lake	4.0	N 40° 47' 14" W 110° 05' 27"
Open for fly-fishing. Rocky and brushy shore.				
Ted's	BK/CT	Chepeta Lake	4.2	N 40° 45' 50" W 109° 58' 21"
Spooky fish in near shore shallows. Evenings best.				
Upper Rock	CT	Pole Creek CG	2.3	N 40° 41' 51" W 110° 04' 56"
N of Middle Rock. Very rough and rocky. Subject to winterkill.				
Walk-Up	BK	Chepeta Lake	2.7	N 40° 48' 41" W 110° 02' 16"
Beautiful deep cirque. Light use due to difficult access from Papoose.				
Watkins	BK	Chepeta Lake	6.2	N 40° 43' 13" W 109° 58' 33"
Just SE of Cliff Lake. Light fishing pressure.				
Whiterocks	BK/CT	Chepeta Lake	3.5	N 40° 46' 42" W 109° 56' 56"
Few brook and cutthroat. Few fish. Lake level fluctuates. Light use.				
Wigwam	BK/CT	Chepeta Lake	0.9	N 40° 47' 60" W 110° 00' 51"
Easy access. Moderate use.				
Wooley	BK	Chepeta Lake	6.4	N 40° 45' 05" W 109° 57' 24"
0.7 mi. S of Ted's Lake. Light fishing pressure.				
Workman	BK/CT	Chepeta Lake	5.2	N 40° 45' 08" W 109° 58' 42"
1 mi. E of Wooley Lake. Light to moderate use.				

Maps

USGS 1:24000   Chepeta Lake, Fox Lake, Bollie Lake,
                        Rasmussen Lakes, Paradise Park,
                        Whiterocks Lake

Utah Atlas and Gazetteer   Pages 55, 56

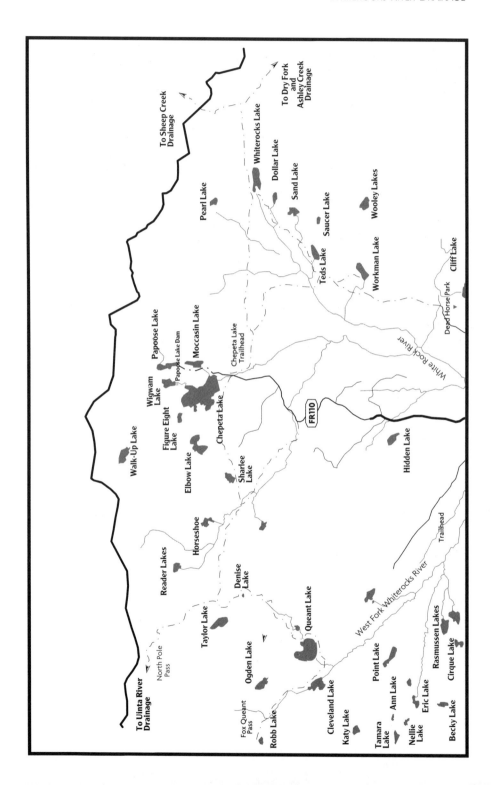

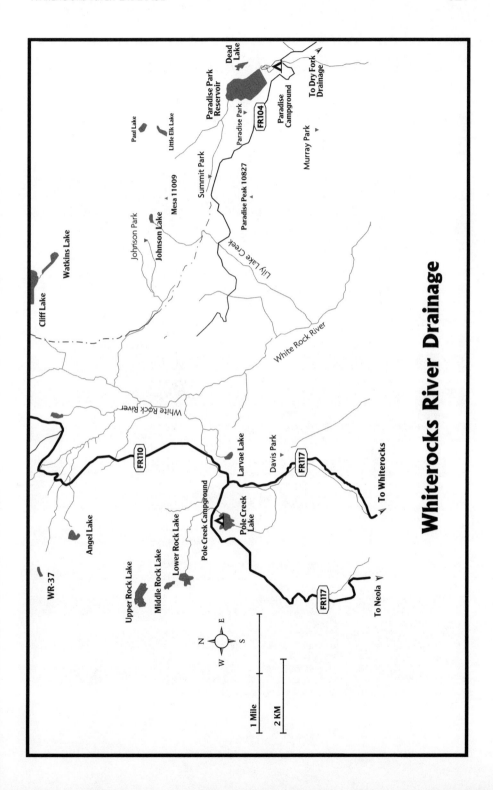

Whiterocks River Drainage

Yellowstone Creek Drainage   DUCHESNE COUNTY

 he Yellowstone Creek Drainage is made up of three basins: Swasey Hole, Garfield Basin, and the Tungsten Lake area. All the lakes here are of glacial origin.

There are two main trailheads to the drainage, the Swift Creek Campground on Yellowstone Creek and the Center Park Trailhead on Hells Canyon Road. Distances to many lakes in the Yellowstone Creek Drainage are roughly the same from either trailhead, but the Center Park Trailhead is about 2,000 feet higher, so hikers can conserve energy by beginning here.

Excellent fishing can be had in some of the streams. Anglers may want to opt for the Swift Creek Campground Trailhead, so they can fish Yellowstone Creek.

Lake Descriptions

Name	Fish	Trailhead	Mi.	GPS Coordinates
Bluebell	BK/CT	Center Park	11.5	N 40° 41' 46" W 110° 29' 04"
From Spider Lake SW along inlet stream.				
Doll	BK	Swift Creek CG	13.0	N 40° 43' 25" W 110° 29' 28"
Many small brook trout. 0.8 mi. WNW up ridge from Five Point Lake.				
Drift	BK	Center Park	11.5	N 40° 42' 06" W 110° 29' 12"
From N end of Spider Lake W 0.5 mile.				
Five Point Res.	BK/CT	Swift Creek CG	12.0	N 40° 43' 07" W 110° 28' 32"
Moderate pressure, many fish. Care for fragile area.				
Gem	BK/CT	Swift Creek CG	12.2	N 40° 42' 35" W 110° 28' 18"
0.5 mi. SE from Five Point outlet stream.				
Kings	CT	Center Park	21.0	N 40° 45' 07" W 110° 23' 20"
Marginal for cutthroat. From Tungsten Pass NE 3 mi., S 2 mi. following ridge into cirque. Rough.				
Little Superior	BK	Swift Creek CG	13.5	N 40° 44' 00" W 110° 28' 21"
From Superior, follow inlet stream 0.3 mi. NW.				
Milk	BK	Swift Creek CG	11.0	N 40° 43' 15" W 110° 23' 24"
Light pressure. Sits in a deep cirque.				
North Star	BK	Center Park	16.5	N 40° 45' 13" W 110° 27' 03"
Open tundra. Moderate fishing pressure.				
Spider	BK/CT	Center Park	11.0	N 40° 42' 01" W 110 28' 41"
Few brook and cutthroat trout. Heavy pressure and litter. Please pack out trash.				

Name	Fish	Trailhead	Mi.	GPS Coordinates
Superior	BK	Swift Creek CG	13.0	N 40° 43' 43" W 110° 28' 19"
Many brook trout. Moderate pressure. Between Five Point and Little Superior.				
Swasey	BK/CT	Center Park	7.0	N 40° 40' 01" W 110° 28' 05"
A large, popular lake with heavy pressure.				
Tungsten	BK/CT	Swift Creek CG	16.0	N 40° 44' 57" W 110° 26' 32"
Open tundra. Moderate pressure.				
X-57	BK	Center Park	8.0	N 40° 39' 59" W 110° 29' 05"
No trail. Approach from Swasey Lake. W 1 mile.				
X-59	BK/CT	Center Park	6.8	N 40° 39' 51" W 110° 27' 53"
SE of Swasey Lake. Use is moderate.				
X-60	CT/BK	Center Park	7.5	N 40° 40' 13" W 110° 28' 30"
NW 0.3 mi. from Swasey Lake.				
X-105	CT	Swift Creek CG	14.0	N 40° 44' 33" W 110° 28' 42"
NNW 0.7 mi. from Little Superior along inlet stream.				
Y-2	BK	Center Park	17.0	N 40° 45' 45" W 110° 27' 14"
N 0.5 mi. along inlet stream of North Star Lake.				
Y-4	BK	Center Park	17.1	N 40° 45' 50" W 110° 27' 20"
Many small brook trout. Second lake from S in chain of lakes.				
Y-5	BK	Center Park	17.3	N 40° 45' 54" W 110° 27' 33"
Many small brook trout. Third Y lake from S. Light pressure.				
Y-19	BK	Swift Creek CG	16.6	N 40° 44' 48" W 110° 25' 58"
E of Tungsten Pass 0.5 mile. Light use.				
Y-20	GR	Swift Creek CG	16.5	N 40° 44' 26" W 110° 26' 01"
SE 0.3 mi. from Tungsten Pass. Light use.				
Y-31	BK	Swift Creek CG	12.5	N 40° 42' 58" W 110° 29' 12"
Many small brook trout. W 0.5 mi. from Five Point Lake. No trail, but easy.				
Y-36	BK	Center Park	11.3	N 40° 41' 35" W 110° 28' 29"
S 0.3 mi. from Spider Lake in timber.				
Y-37	BK	Center Park	11.8	N 40° 41' 28" W 110° 28' 54"
S 0.3 mi. from Bluebell Lake. Light pressure.				

Maps

USGS 1:24000	Garfield Basin, Lake Fork Mountain, Burnt Mill Spring, Mount Emmons, Mount Powell.
Utah Atlas and Gazetteer	Page 55

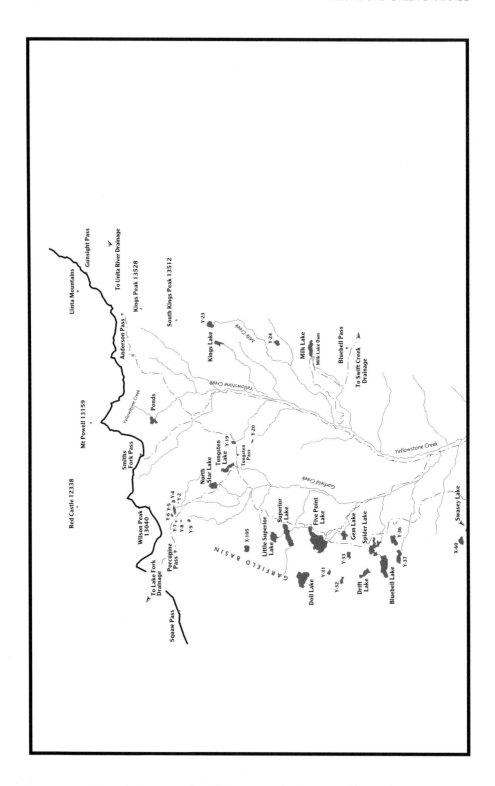

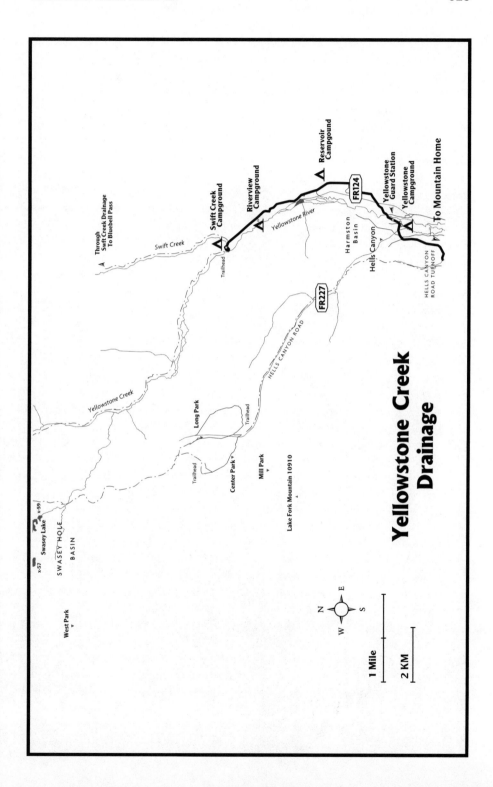

Yellowstone Creek Drainage

PHOTO: EMMETT HEATH / WESTERN RIVERS FLYFISHER

Southern Utah

This is desert country. It is surprising how many fisheries can be found scattered through this dry land. Southern Utah's redrock ledges and dry hills form a stunning backdrop for many of these waters. The rivers and streams here are small. Some are small enough to step across.

Anglers can find good fishing through the colder months. A weekend spent chasing fish in southern Utah can be the perfect cure for cabin fever.

The following four chapters describe fishing destinations in the southern half of Utah. They are divided as follows:

- Rivers and Streams
- Coldwater Lakes and Reservoirs
- Warmwater Lakes and Reservoirs
- Boulder Mountain Area Lakes

Coldwater Lakes and Reservoirs include waters where cold-water species (trout and kokanee salmon) are the primary target. In *Warmwater Lakes and Reservoirs*, anglers are more apt to pursue bass, walleye, pike, perch and bluegills. ♦

Antimony Creek

 his small stream is mostly above 7,000 feet and runs down out of the Dixie National Forest. You can often find good water conditions here when other streams nearby are muddy.

The views here are stunning, with needles and towers of pink and white sandstone.

Fish Species

Primarily wild rainbow trout, although the lower section contains some brown trout.

Special Regulations

General season, bag, and possession limits apply.

Catch and release is recommended.

Tactics

This stream has mayflies, caddisflies, and stoneflies. Nymph imitations of these insects should be effective underneath. Hare's ears are a particular favorite. During the warm months, try stimulators, yellow sally's, Adams, and renegades.

Spin-fishers can try the deeper pools with small spinners. Salmon eggs and worms with a small split-shot will also work well.

How to Get There

From I-70 at Sevier Junction take Exit 23. Get on US 89 south and go through Marysvale and Junction, then turn left onto SR 62. At Otter Creek Reservoir take SR 22 south to Antimony. Turn east onto FR 138 just north of the creek.

Accessibility

This clear, cold-water stream is located southeast of Otter Creek Reservoir and 2.2 miles south of the town of Antimony. The fishable portion is located on the Dixie National Forest. It is accessible by dirt road from the mouth of the canyon for several miles and then becomes accessible by foot trail along most of its length.

There is an old and rundown campground near the end of the road. Anglers will want 4-wheel-drive above the campground.

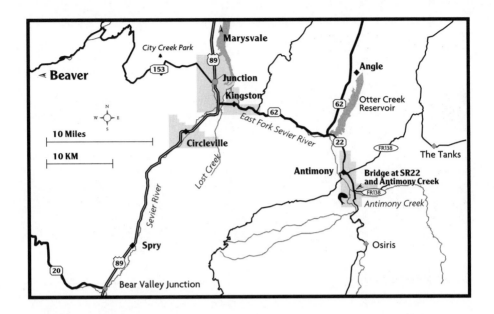

GPS Coordinates

Bridge at 22 and Antimony Creek	N 38° 05′ 27″ W 111° 58′ 51″

Maps

USGS 1:24000   Antimony, Pollywog Lake, Barker Reservoir

Utah Atlas and Gazetteer   Page 27

When to Go

The best times will be June through October, but in fine weather, you can have good fishing through the winter. Runoff will usually be March, April, and May. ◆

Beaver Creek

ne of more than a dozen "Beaver Creeks" in the state, this small stream just outside of Marysvale, makes a nice side trip for anglers visiting the Fishlake National Forest.

Bullion Creek is just to the south; Otter Creek and Piute Reservoirs are also nearby if you are planning a longer trip.

Fish Species

Contains rainbow trout and a few cutthroat trout. Some hatchery rainbows are stocked in the more accessible and heavily used areas.

Special Regulations

General season, bag, and possession limits apply.

Tactics

Try terrestrial and attractor patterns on top and standard nymphs underneath. The cutthroat in the upper stretches should take trudes and renegades.

Spin-fishers should try small spinners and one-half of a night crawler in the deeper holes.

How to Get There

From Marysvale, go west out of town on FR 113. The mouth of Beaver Creek Canyon is about 1 mile west of Marysvale.

Accessibility

The road follows this stream for about 4 miles before they part ways. If you begin fishing upstream from this point you will be in a rough canyon that sees little pressure.

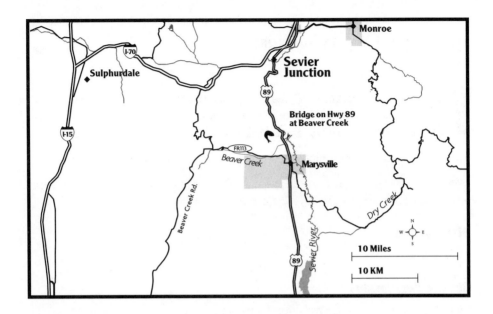

GPS Coordinates

Bridge on US 89 at Beaver Creek	N 38° 28′ 17″ W 112° 14′ 8″

Maps

USGS 1:24000   Marysvale, Mount Brigham

Utah Atlas and Gazetteer   Page 26

When to Go

Expect best fishing June through October. Warm weather in November and December can also be good. ◆

Beaver Dam Wash   WASHINGTON COUNTY

his remote stream is located in the extreme southwest corner of the state. Its headwaters begin on the Dixie National Forest then flow into Nevada through Beaver Dam State Park before coming back into Utah.

Anglers vacationing at Gunlock Reservoir may want to explore here as a side trip.

While the stream and fish are very small, the main attraction is catching trout while surrounded by the Mojave Desert ecosystem.

Fish Species

Wild rainbow trout.

Special Regulations

General season, bag, and possession limits apply.

Tactics

Not much is known about the fishing here. Preferred methods should take into account the small size of the stream and low flows.

How to Get There

From St. George, go west on SR 8 and continue through the Shivwits Indian Reservation. Roads are not clearly labeled from here, but head northwest along Pahcoon Spring Wash all the way to Motoqua.

From Caliente, Nevada, go north on US 93, then east 28 miles on a gravel road. This will bring you to Beaver Dam State Park. You will need a valid Nevada fishing license to fish here. It is only 1.5 miles from the park to the Utah State line.

Accessibility

Make sure you bring maps and other navigational aids such as a compass or GPS.

You can follow a poor road north up to Beaver Dam Wash from Motoqua for several miles, and then hike in from there. There is private land for the first few miles above Motoqua. Access by the road is limited and much of the stream is accessible only by hiking.

If you come from Nevada, you will have to hike up the creek about 2 miles before it crosses into Utah.

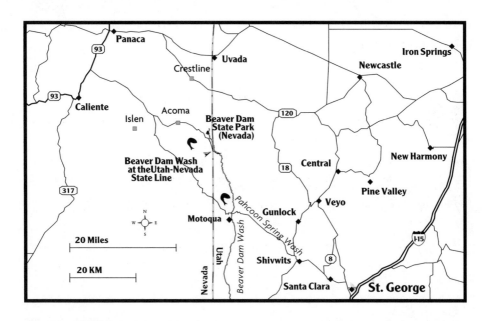

GPS Coordinates

Motoqua	N 37° 18' 13" W 113° 59' 54"
Beaver Dam Wash at UT-NV State Line	N 37° 28' 19" W 114° 03' 06"
Beaver Dam State Park (Nevada)	N 37° 29' 53" W 114° 03' 50"

Maps

USGS 1:24000   Motoqua, Dodge Spring, Docs Pass,

Utah Atlas and Gazetteer   Page 16

When to Go

Summers are hot in this area and not the best time to fish. The cooler waters of winter and spring will probably produce the best fishing. You can expect this stream to get very muddy after a substantial rain. Expect very low flows from June through September. ◆

Beaver River

This beautiful river is very easy to access from SR 153. Anglers who want to hike away from the road have opportunities to do so. This river does not seem to receive a lot of pressure.

Rainbow trout are stocked in the water that flows through the campground and picnic areas, although wild brown trout are also plentiful.

There is a lot of good fishing available to anglers staying in Beaver. Try Minersville Reservoir and North Creek.

This river is known to harbor whirling disease. Please see the whirling disease section in the guide for precautions to ensure that you don't help to spread this disease.

Fish Species

Rainbow and brown trout. Cutthroat and brook trout can be found, but are more abundant in the headwaters.

The water below Minersville Reservoir is managed as a brown trout fishery.

Special Regulations

From Minersville Reservoir upstream to bridge at Greenville:

❏ **Closed** January 1 through May 21.

Tactics

There is good dry fly-fishing here. On the upper water, try terrestrial patterns like ants; mosquito and caddisfly imitations work well when cast upstream.

On the stretch below Minersville Reservoir, the browns will take grasshoppers in late summer and early fall. When fish become serious about spawning in October and November, streamers and spinners will attract aggressive trout.

Look for big rainbows to move up from Minersville Reservoir during the spawn.

How to Get There

From Beaver, go east on SR 153. You will follow along the Beaver River as it enters into the Fishlake National Forest boundary, which begins about 3.5 miles from the center of town.

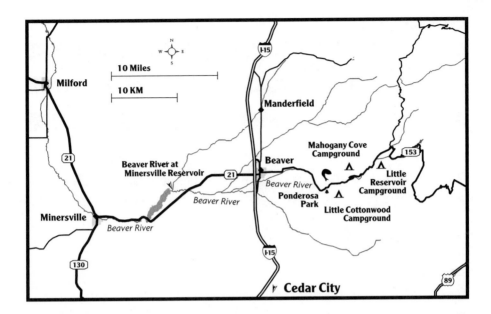

To reach the river below Minersville Reservoir, take SR 21 southwest 18 miles from Beaver. You will cross the Beaver River below the dam.

Accessibility

The main fishable portion is located east of Beaver on the Fishlake National Forest. The paved road (SR 153) runs parallel to much of the Beaver River in the national forest so access is very good. The river is diverted to a canal near Mile Marker 4, so don't try to fish until you are east (above) here. There are several campgrounds in the canyon.

Fishable tributaries include the South Fork, Lake Stream, and Merchant Creek, as well as other smaller streams.

The South Fork enters the Beaver River near Little Reservoir Campground; the upper stretch can be reached on FR 137 above Kents Lake.

There are brown trout in the Beaver River from Minersville Reservoir down to the town of Minersville. There is both state and private land below the dam, so be sure to ask permission before crossing private lands. The first stretch of river below the SR 21 bridge is posted.

GPS Coordinates

Beaver River at Minersville Reservoir	N 38° 15' 09" W 112° 47' 35"
Little Cottonwood Campground	N 38° 15' 25" W 112° 32' 35"
Ponderosa Park	N 38° 15' 42" W 112° 30' 19"
Mahogany Cove Campground	N 38° 16' 10" W 112° 29' 06"
Little Reservoir Campground	N 38° 15' 40" W 112° 29' 19"

Maps

USGS 1:24000   Beaver, Greenville Bench, Adamsville, Black
                                Ridge, Shelly Baldy Peak, Delano Peak,
                                Circleville Mountain

Utah Atlas and Gazetteer   Page 26

When to Go

Good water conditions can be expected by July and may occur earlier in some
years. Fishing will remain productive into October and warm weather in
November can keep fish active. ◆

Services

Camping:

Beaver Canyon Campground
1419 E Canyon Road
Beaver, UT 84713
tel: (435) 438-5654

Minersville State Park
Beaver
tel: (435) 438-5472
Reservations: (800) 322-3770
(In Salt Lake City, call 322-3770)

Boulder Creek

GARFIELD COUNTY

T his is another scenic fishery located in the Boulder Mountain area of the Dixie National Forest. It has more access options than some of the other canyons in the area. It is a worthy destination by itself, or it can be combined with other waters in the vicinity.

One intriguing possibility is to make a loop with Deer Creek. Anglers could fish down one creek and back up the other, with one night spent in the canyons.

Fish Species

Brown trout are found in the lower end of the stream, rainbows at mid-elevation areas, and brook and cutthroat trout inhabit the upper elevations. One can even find some good-sized catfish just above the confluence with the Escalante River.

Special Regulations

❑ Trout limit, 6; only 2 trout over 13 inches.

Because a lot of people use this canyon, fish numbers can quickly be reduced from pressure and overuse. It is recommended that you fish with artificial flies and lures, and release everything you catch.

Tactics

Attractor flies like royal Wulffs and trudes should serve you well higher up the creek.

Wooly buggers and small spinners are good if you are fishing downstream from SR 12.

Deep in the canyon, hare's ears and cased caddis are good nymphs. Stimulators, small hoppers and yellow humpies work well on the surface in the warmer months. If you venture here in the winter months and action is slow, try a Kastmaster or other heavy spoons.

How to Get There

From Boulder, you can reach the upper waters on the West Fork and the East Fork of Boulder Creek by driving north on SR 12 about 5.5 miles. Turn northwest on to FR 165. Take the first right onto FR 508 to reach the East Fork or take the second left onto FR 165 for the West Fork.

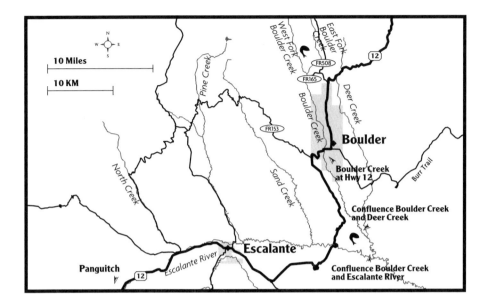

You can get on the stream as it crosses SR 12 about 1.3 miles southwest of Boulder. The north side of the road is private, but you can hike down into the canyon from here.

Sam Webb of *Utah Outdoors* Magazine, has pioneered another route into the canyon. Be cautious if you attempt this hike. Park 0.6 miles south of Mile Marker 78 and head down the drainage going east. You should be just south of where the powerline leaves the road. You will have to descend several dry falls in the slickrock. The creek will be 50 feet straight below you. Follow the ledge 0.2 miles upstream and you will be able to get down to the stream. Leave this pristine area as you found it. Practicing catch and release will maintain the quality of fishing here.

The other option is to take SR 12 south to the Escalante River. Park at the trailhead and hike downstream 6.5 miles to the confluence of Boulder Creek.

Accessibility

The upper waters are in the Dixie National Forest and the lower reaches below SR 12 are located on BLM lands. The water is surrounded by private land as it runs through the town of Boulder.

Make sure you are well prepared before descending into the canyon. You will need plenty of water in hot weather and good footwear is essential. If you have doubts about your abilities to negotiate the slickrock and canyons, try something easier first like Calf Creek.

Due to the risk of flash flooding, check weather and flows before entering the canyon.

GPS Coordinates

Confluence Boulder Cr. and Escalante River	N 37° 45' 26" W 111° 20' 57"
Confluence Boulder Creek and Deer Creek	N 37° 47' 03" W 111° 21' 42"
Boulder Creek at SR 12	N 37° 54' 04" W 111° 26' 10"

Maps

USGS 1:24000   King Bench, Calf Creek, Boulder Town

Utah Atlas and Gazetteer   Pages 20, 28

When to Go

Best times will be April and early May, then again in September and October. November can be great if the weather is good and any warm spell in winter can provide good fishing.

Watch out for the vicious biting flies along the Escalante in summertime. Fish early and late during the summer as fishing slows during the heat of the day.

Check weather forecasts before entering the canyon, particularly in summer, as thunderstorms higher up in the mountains can result in flash flooding down in the desert canyons. ◆

Services

Guides & Outfitters:

Escalante Canyon Outfitters
840 W SR 12
Boulder, UT 84716
tel: (435) 335-7311 / (888) 326-4453
fax: (435) 335-7499
www.ecohike.com
e-mail: ecohike@color-country.net

Lodging:

Boulder Mountain Lodge
Junction of Burr Trail and SR 12
P.O. Box 1397
Boulder, UT 84716
tel: (435) 335-7460 / (800) 556-3446
fax: (435) 335-7461
www.boulder-utah.com
e-mail: bmlut@color-country.net

Boulder Mountain Guest Ranch
Salt Gulch
Boulder, UT 84716
tel: (435) 335-7480

Box Creek

T his remote destination allows for peaceful introspection and a few fish. The stream is also very steep, as it drops from nearly 9,000 feet at the reservoirs to less than 7,000 feet at the town of Greenwich, while traveling a distance of only 6 miles.

Once on top, you are close to Manning Meadow Reservoir and Manning Creek—ample water to occupy any angler for a few days.

Fish Species

Rainbow and brook trout are found in this Monroe Mountain stream and reservoirs.

Special Regulations

General season, bag, and possession limits apply.

Tactics

Since this is small, steep water, short accurate casts are called for.

Try fishing the deeper water with a weighted nymph, flipping it to the tops of pools and keeping a tight line as it sinks and drifts back toward you.

This technique works with fly or spin tackle, and small wooly buggers, spinners and even worms can replace the nymph.

How to Get There

From Richfield, take SR 119 east to the junction with SR 24. Take SR 24 south until you pass Koosharem Reservoir, then take SR 62 south to the town of Greenwich. Box Creek crosses SR 62 just south of town. From Greenwich, take FR 069 west, which will take you to Upper and Lower Box Creek Reservoirs.

Accessibility

There is good access on FR 195, which follows the stream up the canyon for about 5 miles.

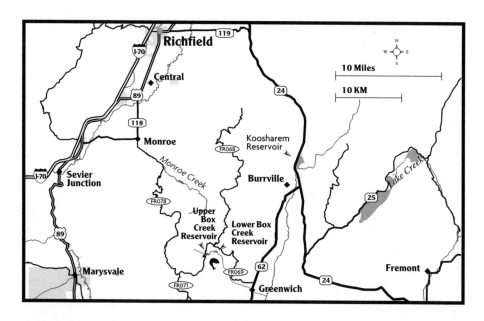

GPS Coordinates

Greenwich	N 38° 25' 50" W 111° 55' 19"
Lower Box Creek Reservoir	N 38° 28' 52" W 111° 58' 56"
Upper Box Creek Reservoir	N 38° 28' 41" W 111° 59' 40"

Maps

USGS 1:24000   Marysvale Peak, Greenwich

Utah Atlas and Gazetteer   Page 27

When to Go

June through October will usually be the best time. Both Upper and Lower Box Creek Reservoirs are used to store water for irrigation. Flows in Box Creek will vary depending on water demands. ◆

Bullion Creek (Pine Creek)   PIUTE COUNTY

imilar to Beaver Creek, this small Tushar Mountain stream flows into the town of Marysvale from the southwest. 60 foot Bullion Falls is worth a look.

Some hatchery rainbow trout are stocked near a popular picnic area that was once a historic gold mining town. This stocking usually takes place at the end of May and consists of 10-inch trout.

Note: USGS Maps label this as Pine Creek running out of Bullion Canyon.

Fish Species

Rainbow and cutthroat trout.

Special Regulations

General season, bag, and possession limits apply.

Tactics

Try attractor patterns like renegades and royal Wulffs on top and standard nymphs underneath.

This steep stream drops nearly 2,000 feet in 6 miles. Make short accurate casts and keep your line tight so you can set the hook quickly.

Spin-fishers should try small spinners and one-half of a night crawler in the deeper holes.

How to Get There

From Marysvale, go west out of town and bear southwest to reach FR 1110, which follows Bullion Creek up the canyon.

Accessibility

A dirt road follows the lower end of the stream. The upper reaches of the stream are accessible only by hiking.

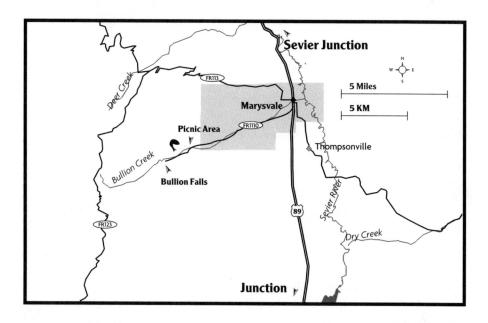

GPS Coordinates

Picnic Area	N 38° 25' 35" W 112° 17' 05"
Bullion Falls	N 38° 24' 36" W 112° 20' 17"

Maps

USGS 1:24000   Marysvale, Mount Brigham

Utah Atlas and Gazetteer   Page 26

When to Go

Expect best fishing June through October. Warm weather in November and December can also be good. ♦

Calf Creek

T his is a great destination for outdoor families. The canyon offers a variety of landscapes and recreational opportunities. There are tall sandstone cliffs, Anasazi ruins and rock art, a beautiful clear stream with beaver ponds and wild brown trout. To top it off, there is a gorgeous waterfall dropping 126 feet into the pool at its base.

Spring arrives here a few weeks earlier than along the Wasatch Front, making it a good early-season trip when you're longing for some warm weather and sunshine.

There are a lot of other fishing attractions in the area: Boulder Creek, Pine Creek, and Sand Creek; or, in the heat of summer, it is a short drive up to the cooler elevations of the Boulder Mountain lakes.

Fish Species

Wild brown trout.

Special Regulations

❏ Trout limit, 6; only 2 trout over 13 inches.

There are many visitors and fishing can be easily damaged by overuse. It is recommended that you fish with artificial flies and lures, and release everything you catch.

Tactics

This is a very small stream with a lot of foot traffic. These wild brown trout are very spooky. Approach the water quietly and stay hidden if possible. Fly-fishing will allow anglers to offer a more quiet presentation.

Best success will be in the numerous beaver ponds. Do not stand on the dams as this will scare fish and damage the beaver's work. Yellow humpies and elk hair caddis are both good choices on top here. Try stripping olive damselfly nymphs in the ponds.

Hikers going to and from the falls can spook fish next to the trail. Try fishing at sunup before others are out; fish away from the trail where possible.

How to Get There

From Boulder, go south on SR 12 for 13.5 miles to the Calf Creek Recreation Area. Or take SR 12 east from Escalante and go 12 miles.

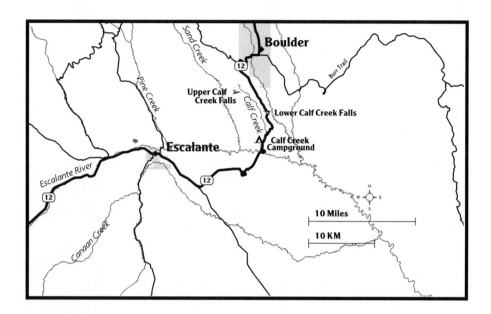

Accessibility

There is a very good trail from the campground to the Lower Falls. There are trail markers that will lead you to historical and archeological sites as well as vegetation and wildlife.

The trail to the Lower Falls is 5.5 miles round trip and is well maintained with few steep sections. Bring plenty of water to drink as it can be very hot here in summer.

It is a difficult hike over sandstone to the Upper Falls. Hikers start from the highway on SR 12 at a point 5.5 miles north of the Calf Creek Campground. We are not aware of any fishing opportunities on this upper section of Calf Creek.

GPS Coordinates

Calf Creek Campground	N 37° 47′ 38″ W 111° 24′ 50″
Lower Calf Creek Falls	N 37° 49′ 45″ W 111° 25′ 09″
Upper Calf Creek Falls	N 37° 51′ 19″ W 111° 27′ 05″

Maps

USGS 1:24000   Calf Creek

Utah Atlas and Gazetteer   Pages 19, 20, 28

When to Go

This can be a pleasant destination from mid-March through the end of October. There is a chance of high water in May and June. July and August can be very hot and fishing will be slow then, particularly during midday.

This is a popular recreation and tourist destination, so if fishing is your goal, try to schedule your trip during the week and away from holidays. ♦

Services

Guides & Outfitters:

Escalante Canyon Outfitters
840 W SR 12
Boulder, UT 84716
tel: (435) 335-7311 / (888) 326-4453
fax: (435) 335-7499
www.ecohike.com
e-mail: ecohike@color-country.net

Lodging:

Boulder Mountain Lodge
Junction of Burr Trail and SR 12
P.O. Box 1397
Boulder, UT 84716
tel: (435) 335-7460 / (800) 556-3446
fax: (435) 335-7461
www.boulder-utah.com
e-mail: bmlut@color-country.net

Boulder Mountain Guest Ranch
Salt Gulch
Boulder, UT 84716
tel: (435) 335-7480

Calf Creek Falls. (PHOTO: COURTESY UTAH OUTDOORS)

Chalk Creek MILLARD COUNTY

he majority of this stream is located on the Fishlake National Forest, directly east of Fillmore. A hiking trail provides the only access to the upper end of the North Fork.

This creek was damaged by floods in the early 80s, but has since recovered.

Fish Species

The South Fork contains mostly rainbow trout. Some cutthroat trout are found in the higher elevations, and a few brown trout are found in the lower end of the stream. The North Fork has wild cutthroat and rainbow/cutthroat hybrids.

Catchable-size rainbows are stocked near the picnic areas, about 5 miles up the canyon. In 1998, there were 3,500 fish released on the last day of May.

Special Regulations

General season, bag, and possession limits apply.

Tactics

Try terrestrial flies and attractor patterns on top and standard nymphs underneath. The cutthroat in the upper stretches should take trudes and renegades.

Spin-fishers should try small spinners and one-half of a night crawler in the deeper holes.

How to Get There

From Fillmore, take 200 South Canyon Road east, following signs for USFS picnic areas. This road will lead you to FR 100, which heads up Chalk Creek.

Accessibility

The North and South Forks split approximately 1.5 miles from the start of the canyon.

The South Fork is easily accessible from FR 100, which runs next to the creek for about 7 miles. There are four nice picnic areas with toilets and tables beginning 5 miles up the canyon. You will need 4-wheel-drive to access the road above the picnic areas.

The North Fork is accessible only by hiking. A Forest Service trail (TR 109) provides access from FR 100 or you can hike down from FR 096 (also known as the Paiute ATV Trail).

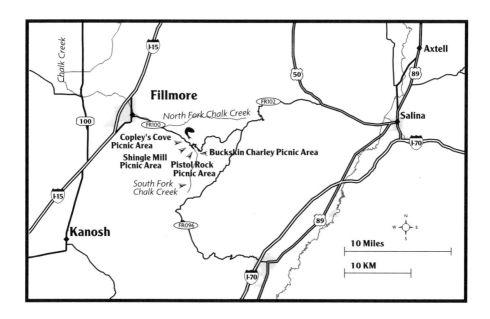

GPS Coordinates

Copley's Cove Picnic Area	N 38° 56' 01" W 112° 13' 48"
Shingle Mill Picnic Area	N 38° 55' 33" W 112° 13' 07"
Buckskin Charley Picnic Area	N 38° 55' 24" W 112° 13' 01"
Pistol Rock Picnic Area	N 38° 55' 20" W 112° 12' 54"

Maps

USGS 1:24000   Fillmore, Mount Catherine

Utah Atlas and Gazetteer   Pages 36, 37

When to Go

Best times will be late June through October. In general, high water starts in April and begins to drop in June. ◆

Clear Creek   SEVIER COUNTY

C lear Creek Canyon is home to the largest Fremont Indian site ever discovered in Utah. This glimpse into the lifestyle and culture of the Ancients is protected and preserved for the public in Fremont Indian State Park.

Fremont Indians occupied the village in Clear Creek Canyon from 1000 A.D. to 1250 A.D. There may have been 150-250 people living together at a time. It is known that they raised corn, beans, and squash. They hunted deer, sheep, elk, and bison and also depended on wild plants.

The tour guides will not only take you to see some of the rock art left by these inhabitants, but will also share some of the legends and stories of the people who called Clear Creek their home.

There is also some fine fishing in Clear Creek on state park lands, providing an opportunity for a family trip that combines educational activities and piscatorial pursuit.

Fish Creek and Shingle Creek are both tributaries that hold trout.

Fish Species

Wild rainbow trout and brown trout are plentiful in this stream.

Special Regulations

General season, bag, and possession limits apply.

Tactics

This is small water, and anglers will be rewarded for approaching with caution.

The open creek bottom is home to large numbers of grasshoppers in late summer. Fly-fishers will do well with a Dave's hopper or parachute hopper. Mosquito and ant patterns also work well.

Anglers can fish with baits like salmon eggs or one-half of a night crawler drifted through the deeper holes.

How to Get There

From I-70 take Exit 17 to reach Fremont Indian State Park.

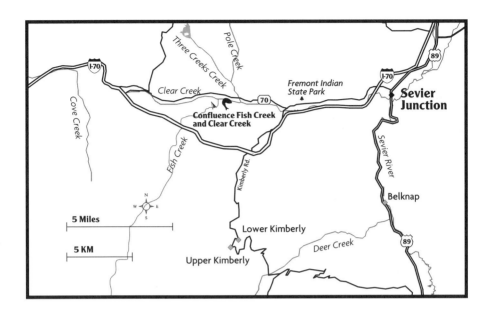

Accessibility

There are about 8 miles of accessible water, some on private land, but much of the lower reach (4 miles) is within the Fremont Indian State Park (tel: 435-527-4631). The stream follows I-70 for a distance, although the stream can be fished while hardly noticing the interstate. A fair portion of Clear Creek received mitigation efforts and habitat improvement work during the interstate construction. The upper reaches of Clear Creek are located on the Fishlake National Forest.

GPS Coordinates

Fremont Indian State Park	N 38° 35' 00" W 112° 20' 00"
Confluence of Fish and Clear Creeks	N 38° 35' 00" W 112° 24' 29"

Maps

USGS 1:24000   Marysvale Canyon, Antelope Range, Trail Mountain

Utah Atlas and Gazetteer   Page 26

When to Go

June through November. Expect best fishing in August and September when grasshoppers are plentiful. ◆

Corn Creek   MILLARD COUNTY

T his pretty central Utah stream is close to Chalk Creek. These two waters could be combined for a nice weekend trip. There are several springs feeding into Corn Creek. There are smooth lime deposits on much of the stream bottom below Big Spring, making it easy to observe trout holding and feeding in the clear water.

Fish Species

Predominantly brown trout. A few rainbow trout are stocked near the campground, about 4 miles up the canyon.

Special Regulations

General season, bag, and possession limits apply.

Tactics

Try casting hoppers and other terrestrials in the lower portion of the creek. Humpies, trudes, and elk hair caddis are effective farther up.

A cautious approach and delicate presentation are important on this clear water.

Brown trout in Corn Creek will be spawning in October and November. Try wooly buggers and spruce flies. Spinners will also excite territorial fish that become more aggressive during the spawn.

This creek is occasionally overrun with a large insect called a Mormon cricket. Try fishing large black crickets in the weeks after their arrival.

How to Get There

From Kanosh, travel southeast out of town onto FR 106. The pavement will end after a mile, then you will enter the Fishlake National Forest in about 2 more miles. The road follows Corn Creek up Kanosh Canyon for about 4.5 miles before they part ways.

Accessibility

This stream is easily accessible from FR 106.

The upper 3 miles of stream are reached by a foot trail which leaves the road about 0.5 miles east of the Adelaide Campground. Look for the Corn Creek Canyon Trail Marker by the bridge.

Most of the stream is located on the Fishlake National Forest.

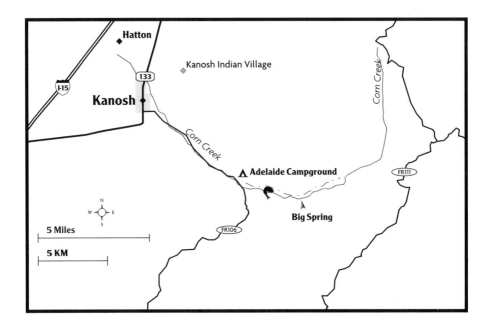

GPS Coordinates

Adelaide Campground	N 38° 45' 13" W 112° 21' 49"
Big Spring	N 38° 44' 29" W 112° 18' 44"

Maps

USGS 1:24000   Kanosh, Sunset Peak, Joseph Peak,
                                White Pine Creek

Utah Atlas and Gazetteer   Page 36

When to Go

June through November. High water generally runs through April and May. The
water is usually fishable by June. ♦

Cottonwood Creek

EMERY COUNTY

ater flows out of Joe's Valley Reservoir into Straight Canyon before it joins Cottonwood Creek on its descent towards Orangeville. This stream has many deep holes and large boulders in the upper section (Straight Canyon) that hide some respectable trout.

Very low flows occur some winters and can greatly reduce fish numbers.

Fish Species

Mostly brown trout with a few rainbows.

Special Regulations

General season, bag, and possession limits apply.

Tactics

Try drifting weighted or bead head nymphs through the deeper holes. Small wooly buggers are also effective when fished slow and deep. There is some dry fly-fishing in this stream, but most of the action is underneath.

Casting spinners and small spoons can be effective. Give them time to sink near the bottom of deep water sections.

How to Get There

From Orangeville, go west on SR 29.

Accessibility

The upper end of the canyon is public and there is easy access from SR 29. The road is normally open all year. The best fishing will be found in Straight Canyon rather than Cottonwood Creek itself.

GPS Coordinates

Joe's Valley Reservoir Dam	N 39° 17' 19" W 111° 16' 10"
Confl. Sraight Canyon and Cottonwood Cr.	N 39° 16' 31" W 111° 10' 24"

Maps

USGS 1:24000	Joe's Valley Reservoir, Mahogany Point
Utah Atlas and Gazetteer	Page 38

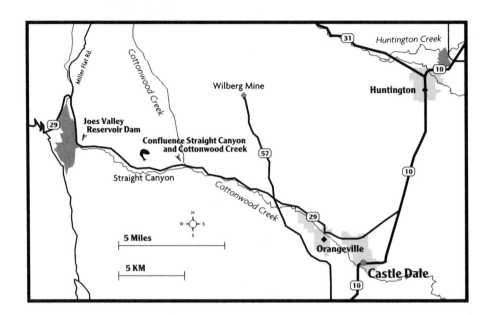

When to Go

Good fishing can be found here most of the year. Best time is from June to October. Late April and early May, depending on weather, will be the peak of runoff with the worst water conditions. ◆

One of the big pools in Straight Canyon above Cottonwood Creek.
(PHOTO: EMMETT HEATH / WESTERN RIVERS FLYFISHER)

Deer Creek

T his is another beautiful and remote stream in the Escalante Drainage. Don't travel into the lower canyon without being prepared for the weather and climate of desert country. Fishing in a wild landscape of this quality is rare; make sure you leave it as you found it.

Fish Species

There are rainbow, cutthroat and brook trout in the upper waters. The lower sections hold some nice wild browns.

Special Regulations

❐ Trout limit, 6; only 2 trout over 13 inches.

Tactics

Fish in the headwaters will take renegades and other attractor flies readily in summertime.

Small wooly buggers work well if fishing downstream from the Burr Trail, as will small spinners. This is small water — quiet and cautious anglers will be rewarded. The stream banks are thickly covered with willows, so walking down the stream is often the only option.

Ambitious anglers coming up from the Escalante have a chance at some nice fish. Yellow humpies and grasshoppers work well in warm weather, especially early and late in the day. Wooly buggers, cased caddis and bead head nymphs are all good choices underneath the surface. Larger spinners and spoons can attract spawning browns in December and January.

How to Get There

From Boulder, go east on the Burr Trail about 7 miles and you will reach Deer Creek.

The other option is to take SR 12 to where the highway crosses the Escalante River. From the trailhead, hike downstream 6.5 miles to the confluence of Boulder Creek. Go up Boulder Creek 4.5 miles to its confluence with Deer Creek.

You can also reach the West Deer Creek and Frisky Creek, from SR 12 or TR 113, which cross these headwaters just north of Boulder on the Dixie National Forest.

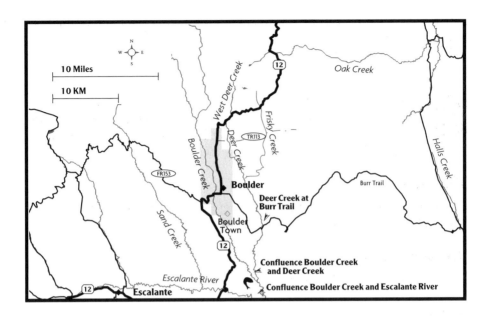

Accessibility

Once you reach the stream at the Burr Trail, you can fish up or down. There is some private land upstream.

If you make the effort to reach Deer Creek from the Escalante River, you are in for a treat. This rugged, beautiful canyon that sees few visitors. You may be rewarded with some nice trout as well. Make sure you are fully prepared for this trip and wear good, protective footwear.

GPS Coordinates

Confluence Boulder Cr. and Escalante River	N 37° 45' 26" W 111° 20' 57"
Confluence Boulder Creek and Deer Creek	N 37° 47' 03" W 111° 21' 42"
Deer Creek at Burr Trail	N 37° 51' 14" W 111° 21' 16"

Maps

USGS 1:24000   King Bench, Steep Creek Bench, Boulder Town

Utah Atlas and Gazetteer   Pages 20, 28

When to Go

Best times will be April and early May, then again in September and October.

Watch out for the vicious biting flies along the Escalante in summertime. Fish early and late during the summer as fishing slows during the heat of the day. ♦

East Fork Sevier River

T here are three sections on this river to consider fishing. The headwaters are on the Dixie National Forest near Bryce Canyon. The river section that runs through Black Canyon, just south of the town of Antimony, is rough and beautiful with some nice fish. The flow through Kingston Canyon is of a different character — deep and canal-like in places, but known to produce some extremely big fish.

There are good camping facilities at Otter Creek Reservoir, a good starting point for the many fishing opportunities in this area. Check the descriptions in this guide for Antimony Creek, Otter Creek, Box Creek, and Piute Reservoir.

The headwaters of the East Fork are adjacent to Bryce Canyon National Park. There is good camping, hiking, and sightseeing in the area.

Fish Species

Upstream from Tropic Reservoir, the East Fork contains primarily brook and cut-throat trout. The stream below Tropic Reservoir does not have enough water dur-ing summer to sustain a fishery.

The Black Canyon area water is home to brown trout, with some rainbow and cutthroat trout.

Kingston Canyon has browns, rainbows, and a few cutthroats.

Special Regulations

Feeder canal from diversion near Antimony to Otter Creek Reservoir:

❏ **Closed** January 1 through May 21.

❏ May 22 through December 31, trout limit, 6.

Kingston Canyon, including all portions of the river and spillway ponds between Otter Creek and Piute Reservoirs:

❏ Trout limit, 6.

Tactics

Kingston Canyon fishes well with terrestrials in the warmer months. A variety of nymphs also work well here, especially size 14 scuds in olive and orange. Streamers can move larger trout. Spinning rod enthusiasts should try swimming small green and rootbeer colored jigs through the holes. Roostertail spinners are another good choice. Big browns will take Rapalas in the fall. Bait-fishing with worms is also effective.

In Black Canyon, try weighted nymphs and wooly buggers in the deep pools. Spinners and small spoons will also work well when allowed to sink to the bottom of deeper water. Night crawlers are the most effective bait in these deep pools This section used to produce very large fish and there is hope that with the current restoration efforts, it will do so again.

The brook and cutthroat trout above Tropic Reservoir eagerly take terrestrial and attractor patterns, as well as small spinners and night crawlers.

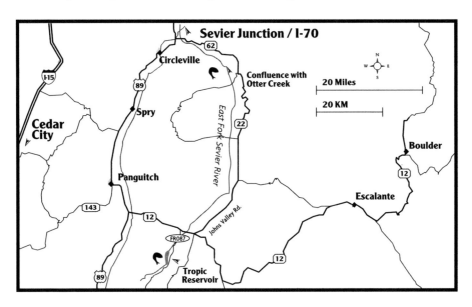

How to Get There

Take I-70 to Sevier Junction, then take Exit 23 to US 89 and continue south through Marysvale and Junction until you come to the junction with SR 62. Take SR 62 east, which runs up Kingston Canyon alongside the East Fork of the Sevier.

To reach Black Canyon, turn south on SR 22 near Otter Creek Reservoir and go past the town of Antimony. You will reach the bottom of Black Canyon in about 5 miles. Habitat Authorization funds have been used to rehabilitate the stream and make parking areas for fishers.

You can reach the headwaters by continuing south along SR 22, which becomes the Johns Valley Road (FH 16). At the junction with SR 12, head west on SR 12 until you reach the East Fork of the Sevier Road (FR 087). Another route is to head south from the town of Panguitch on US 89 until you come to the junction with SR 12. Turn east on SR 12 and travel 11.5 miles to FR 087 (East Fork of the Sevier River Road). Head south 8.2 miles to reach Tropic Reservoir.

Accessibility

Much of Kingston Canyon is on private land, but public access is available on BLM and DWR property. There is good access below Otter Creek Reservoir, a section of river that occasionally produces some very large fish.

Black Canyon is accessible via the county road (Johns Valley Road) between Antimony and Bryce Canyon. There is good access on DWR lands just below the canyon. This section of river is undergoing restoration. In the canyon itself, there are steep banks, loose rocks, and large boulders. Getting around in here is difficult. Near Antimony, the river runs through private land.

The headwaters upstream from Tropic Reservoir are accessible by a gravel road (FR 087).

GPS Coordinates

Tropic Reservoir	N 37° 36' 48" W 112° 15' 00"
Confluence with Otter Creek	N 38° 09' 56" W 112° 01' 37"

Maps

USGS 1:24000	Podunk Creek, Tropic Reservoir, Bryce Point, Grass Lakes, Antimony, Deep Creek, Phonolite Hill, Junction
Utah Atlas and Gazetteer	Pages 18, 19, 26, 27

When to Go

Good fishing below Otter Creek Reservoir in April, as well as November and early December. The remainder of the East Fork will fish well in June (once the water has come down) and July. September to November is also good. Black Canyon and Kingston Canyon can be slow during the dog days of summer. ◆

Ferron Creek

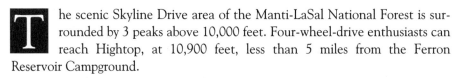

he scenic Skyline Drive area of the Manti-LaSal National Forest is surrounded by 3 peaks above 10,000 feet. Four-wheel-drive enthusiasts can reach Hightop, at 10,900 feet, less than 5 miles from the Ferron Reservoir Campground.

Ferron Canyon is also rugged and a spectacular place to fish, its sheer sandstone walls rising 1,000 feet above the trail-less creek in places.

Fish Species

Rainbow and cutthroat trout.

Special Regulations

Ferron Reservoir Tributaries:

❑ **Closed** January 1 through 6 a.m. on the second Saturday of July (July 10, 1999)

Tactics

The more remote sections of Ferron Creek fish well with a variety of patterns. Humpies are a good choice as they float well and are easy to see.

Small lead-head jigs with green tube bodies work in the water around Ferron Canyon Campground. Swim them through the deeper holes. Gold and silver spinners are also effective.

How to Get There

From Ferron, go west on Ferron Canyon Road. This road becomes FR 022, which leads to Ferron Reservoir.

Accessibility

Ferron Canyon Road runs past the state park at Millsite Reservoir and follows the creek to the bottom of Ferron Canyon.

There is access to Indian Creek, a headwater for Ferron Reservoir. You can reach Ferron Creek above the Canyon by going north on FR 109 or FR 049.

The upper portion of Ferron Canyon above its confluence with Big Bear Creek is very good fishing, but keep in mind that this is an extremely rugged and remote area. There is a large active slide area on Big Bear Creek which brings a lot of sediment into the creek and also affects Ferron Creek below the confluence.

The creek below Millsite Reservoir runs through private lands and is extensively used for irrigation.

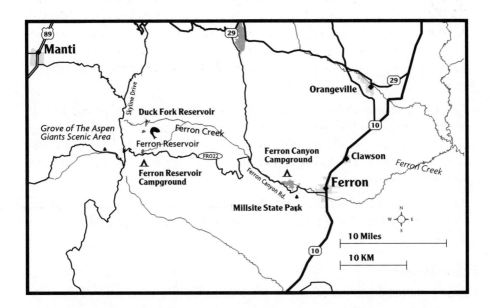

GPS Coordinates

Millsite State Park	N 39° 05' 30" W 111° 11' 31"
Ferron Canyon Campground	N 39° 07' 27" W 111° 15' 38"
Ferron Reservoir Campground	N 39° 08' 17" W 111° 27' 08"
Duck Fork Reservoir	N 39° 10' 10" W 111° 26' 58"

Maps

USGS 1:24000   Ferron Reservoir, Ferron Canyon, Flagstaff Peak, Ferron, Molen

Utah Atlas and Gazetteer   Page 38

When to Go

High water persists until the first of July in most years. Best fishing will be from July to October. November can be very good if the weather is warm.

Avoid the water below Big Bear Creek after heavy rains, as the slide will continue to release a lot of sediment into the creek for years to come. ◆

Fremont River

T his river begins below Johnson Valley Reservoir on the Fishlake National Forest not far from Fish Lake. Reduced winter flows limit the fishery in the stretch immediately below Johnson Reservoir. After it reaches Mamoit Springs, good perennial flows persist downstream to Mill Meadow Reservoir. This section supports a good population of browns and some rainbow trout.

Below Mill Meadow Reservoir, the stream is again de-watered for irrigation use until it reaches the Bicknell Bottoms area. There are a large number of springs here. Before the river was treated with rotenone to control whirling disease, this water supported some very large brown trout. These big fish have had time to re-establish residence.

This river is known to harbor whirling disease. Please see the whirling disease section in the guide for precautions to ensure that you don't help to spread this disease.

Fish Species

Brown trout and rainbow trout are the predominant fish; above Mill Meadow one can find tiger trout, brownbows and splake.

Special Regulations

General season, bag, and possession limits apply.

Tactics

Above Mill Meadow Reservoir there is good fly-fishing, but it is tight and brushy in places. A shorter fly rod (7 to 8 feet) will make casting easier. Expect fast fishing above the reservoir on wooly buggers and nymphs underneath the surface. Terrestrials such as large ants and hoppers are good on top in August and September.

 Below Bicknell, wooly buggers and prince nymphs will work well. Terrestrials can be also be effective. Fall is spawning time for the big browns, so streamers can be very good once the weather turns cool. Try light and dark spruce flies.

How to Get There

To fish the upper section, take SR 72 northeast from the town of Loa to the Gooseberry/Fremont Road (FR 36), which runs between Mill Meadow Reservoir

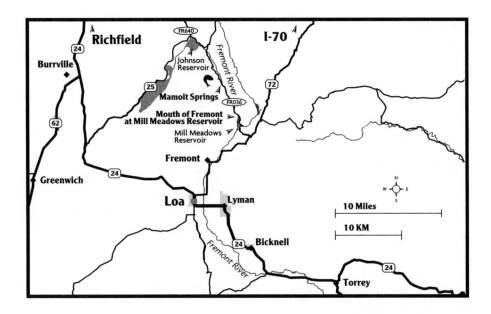

and Johnson Reservoir. To reach the Fremont below Bicknell, take SR 24 south from Loa.

Accessibility

The upper section of the river runs parallel to FR 036. There is also camping.

Access is available in the Bicknell Bottoms on DWR property near the town of Bicknell. There is a lot of private land on this lower portion of the river. Respect private property by asking permission before you enter.

GPS Coordinates

Mamoit Springs	N 38° 33′ 33″ W 111° 35′ 30″
Mouth of Fremont at Mill Meadows Res.	N 38° 31′ 19″ W 111° 34′ 14″

Maps

USGS 1:24000   Fish Lake, Forsyth Reservoir, Loa, Lyman, Bicknell, Torrey, Twin Rocks

Utah Atlas and Gazetteer   Pages 27, 28, 37

When to Go

The stretch above Mill Meadow Reservoir will be good from June to October. The consistency and volume of the springs at Bicknell Bottoms means fishing can be good throughout the year. ◆

Services

Food:

Cafe Diablo
599 W Main Street
Torrey, UT 84775
tel: (435) 425-3070
(Exceptionally good food)

Guides & Outfitters:

Outdoor Source
HC 61, P.O. Box 230
Fremont, UT 84747
tel: (435) 836-2372
cell: (801) 558-7952
winter: (702) 795-1552
www.outdoorsource.net
info@outdoorsource.net

Lodging:

The Lodge at Red River Ranch
2900 W SR 24
P.O. Box 69
Teasdale, UT 84773
tel: (435) 425-3322
fax: (435) 425-3329
(800) 20-LODGE or 205-6343
www.redriverranch.com
e-mail:thelodge@redriverranch.com

Boulder View Inn
385 W Main Street
Torrey, UT 84775
tel: (435) 425-3800 / (800) 444-3980

Fremont rewards: Striking redrock cliffs and big trout. (PHOTOS: JOHN CAMPBELL / WWW.OUTDOORSOURCE.NET)

Gooseberry Creek

T his stream flows south from Salina Canyon off the Fishlake National Forest. A number of small trout lakes are also available in the area: Abes, Twin, Cold Springs, Farnsworth, Salina, Gates, and Hamilton, as well as Harves River Reservoir. These are fairly easy to reach on Forest Service roads above the Gooseberry Campgrounds.

Fish Species

Rainbow trout are stocked near the campground.

Special Regulations

General season, bag, and possession limits apply.

Tactics

Heaviest fishing pressure is near the campground. You will be more successful if you seek out stretches of the stream away from the road and campground.

Fly-fishers will do well with attractor dry flies and terrestrial patterns.

Spin-fishers can try salmon eggs, Power Bait, and night crawlers.

How to Get There

Take I-70 to Exit 61. Go south on FR 31.

Accessibility

FR 31 and FR 640 follow the stream south from I-70 to the headwaters near Gooseberry Campground.

GPS Coordinates

Gooseberry Campground	N 38° 48′ 09″ W 111° 41′ 05″

Maps

USGS 1:24000	Gooseberry Creek, Steves Mountain
Utah Atlas and Gazetteer	Page 37

When to Go

Good fishing from June to October. The headwaters are at nearly 8,000 feet, so weather can change quickly and dramatically. ♦

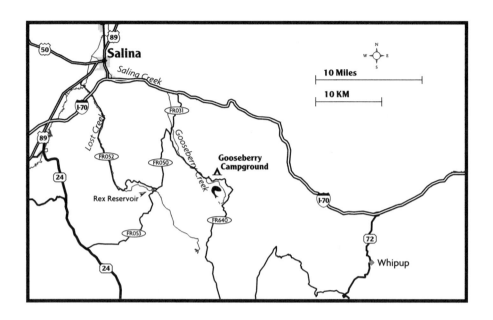

Leeds Creek   Washington County

 The headwaters of Leeds Creek begin in the Pine Valley Wilderness and flow off the southeast side of Pine Valley Mountain. This is a very steep stream, dropping 2,000 feet over 5 miles.

Fish Species

This creek contains a transplanted population of native Bonneville cutthroat trout, which were obtained from the west side of Pine Valley Mountain.

Even though cutthroat trout numbers are expanding, particularly in the lower sections, catch-and-release fishing is strongly recommended.

This is a nice side trip for anglers staying at Quail Creek Reservoir.

Special Regulations

General season, bag, and possession limits apply.

Tactics

The Bonneville cutthroat are good-sized and fairly willing to take a fly or lure. The biggest challenge is getting to them as the riparian area is overgrown with wild grapes. Wading and casting upstream is your best option in most places.

Bait-fishing is not recommended, as it is difficult to release fish in good condition.

How to Get There

From I-15 north of St. George, take Exit 23 at the town of Leeds. Go northwest on FR 032.

Accessibility

Access is difficult here, even though Forest Road 032 follows the stream up to the headwaters near Oak Grove Campground. Wild grapes have turned much of this canyon into a thick jungle.

The tributary streams of Pig Creek, Horse Creek, and Spirit Creek are accessible by hiking.

If water is low you will usually find better fishing conditions downstream from Ash Grove Spring.

Red Cliffs Campground is on Quail Creek, about 0.5 miles up from its confluence with Leeds Creek.

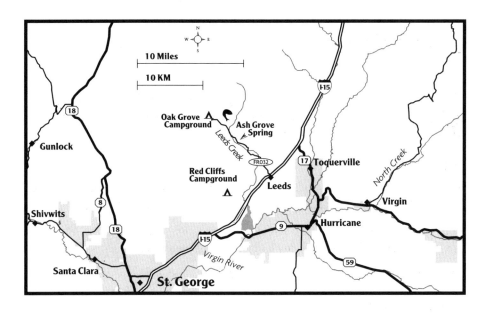

GPS Coordinates

Oak Grove Campground	N 37° 19' 02" W 113° 27' 09"
Ash Grove Spring	N 37° 17' 47" W 113° 24' 47"
Red Cliffs Campground	N 37° 13' 31" W 113° 24' 15"

Maps

USGS 1:24000   Harrisburg Junction, Signal Peak, Pintura

Utah Atlas and Gazetteer   Page 17

When to Go

Fishing here should be consistent during April and May. Activity will slow down during the heat of summer. Low water in fall and winter will make fish spooky. ◆

Mamie Creek

 his is a very small stream in a spectacular canyon. Only strong hikers should attempt this arduous trip, and you must be willing to get in the creek many times through the course of the hike.

Make hiking and enjoying the scenery your priority. The fish are spooky and if there are other hikers in the canyon you may have a hard time finding fish.

Fish Species

Wild brown trout.

Special Regulations

❑ Trout limit, 6; only 2 trout over 13 inches.

Since fish are limited in numbers here, catch and release is recommended. Every wild trout taken is one less for the next angler to experience and enjoy.

If you really want to keep your catch, explore a tiny creek crossing the trail about midway between Mamie Creek and Sand Creek. It enters the Escalante from the north. Follow this stream up to where it ends in a pool at the head of a box canyon. There are many small, bright, and stunted blugills here. Still, keep only a few so that others can share in the thrill of catching fish in the desert canyons.

Tactics

The clear water will give your presence up to these wary browns. The more delicate cast of a fly rod is the preferred method of choice for soft presentations. Adams, yellow humpies, and stimulators, size 14 to 18, are all good dry-fly choices.

Early-season fishing is best with small, brass head or weighted nymphs, like a size 14 or 16 CK nymph (trimmed palmered grizzly hackle over gray dubbing). These weighted nymphs will reach fish without the additional "plunk" of split shot.

There is a large and unusual insect here called the "Child of the Earth." It looks like an overgrown ant, with a light tan body and dark-brown stripes around its abdomen. Large yellow humpies size 8 or 10 are an approximate imitation. You can tie your own pattern, or modify a pattern like the Green River cicada, but use tan-colored foam and skip the wing.

How to Get There

From Boulder, go south on SR 12 and park at the trailhead on the Escalante River. You will hike upriver about 7 miles; watch for Mamie Creek to enter from the north.

As you hike in, watch along the south canyon wall for Escalante Natural Bridge and an Ansazi ruin.

Another alternative is to come down the Escalante River from the town of Escalante, a distance of 8 miles. Be prepared to spend much of your time hiking in the river.

Accessibility

This is an arduous hike through rugged terrain, so be prepared. Like all adventures in the desert country, plenty of water is essential. Bring maps, compass and/or GPS. Footwear is of prime consideration, since you will be in and out of the water many times. There are cacti and thorns as well. A solid wading boot is recommended as it will protect your feet, stand up to miles of walking when wet, and let water drain out.

Once you are in Death Hollow, it is difficult to lose your way. You can go up and down the canyon, but getting out the sides is another story. There are places where the canyon is very narrow — at one point you must choose between climbing up a small waterfall or crawling on your hands and knees under a ledge. This is further complicated if you are carrying a backpack.

Where Mamie Creek and Death Hollow Creek meet in the canyon you will probably want to go to the right up Death Hollow Creek. You can continue all the way up to the Old Mail Trail, which runs from Boulder to Escalante.

Best fishing begins about 0.5 miles above the Escalante and continues to the confluence with Death Hollow Creek

GPS Coordinates

Confluence Mamie Cr. and Escalante River	N 37° 46' 52" W 111° 30' 17"
Confl. Mamie Cr. and Death Hollow Cr.	N 37° 48' 45" W 111° 31' 12"

Maps

USGS 1:24000   Escalante, Roger Peak, Calf Creek

Utah Atlas and Gazetteer   Pages 19, 27

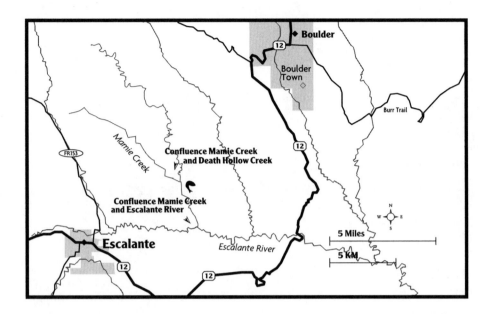

When to Go

Check weather forecasts before entering the canyon and be on the lookout for thunderstorms and potential flash flooding. One can find good conditions hiking in this area from mid-March to mid-May. It can be pleasant weather in the canyon while it snows up on Boulder Mountain. Expect it to be hot in summer. September and October are beautiful here.

Other hikers will spook fish in this narrow canyon, so go during the week if possible. I have come here to fish only to find others racing each other down the stream. Respect the quiet and solitude of this wonderful place. If there are other anglers, work with each other so everyone can fish some undisturbed water. ◆

Mammoth Creek   GARFIELD COUNTY

ammoth Creek gets most of its water from Mammoth Springs. In summer time, it transitions from a dry stream bed to a full blown stream in about 20 feet.

Fish Species

Rainbow and brown trout, with some brook trout in the uppermost waters.

Special Regulations

General season, bag, and possession limits apply.

Tactics

There are reports that the largest trout here are about 2 lbs., but there are rumors of larger browns.

Fly-fishers will want to try standard nymphs and dry flies here. Spinners, salmon eggs, and worms will also be effective.

How to Get There

From Panguitch, there are two different routes. You can take SR 143 south past Panguitch Lake to FR 068. Turn east here to reach Mammoth Springs. The other route is to go south on US 89 past Hatch and then turn west onto FR 067, which will take you to the Mammoth Creek Fish Hatchery.

Accessibility

Most of the length of the stream is on private land. The extreme upper end is located on the Dixie National Forest. There is a short section of stream here from Mammoth Springs to private land.

There is posted land above and below the fish hatchery, but there are about 5 miles of accessible water if you drive a short distance above.

GPS Coordinates

Mammoth Springs Campground	N 37° 38′ 16″ W 112° 40′ 15″
Mammoth Creek Fish Hatchery	N 37° 37′ 21″ W 112° 28′ 19″
US 89 Bridge at Mammoth Creek	N 37° 37′ 42″ W 112° 27′ 19″

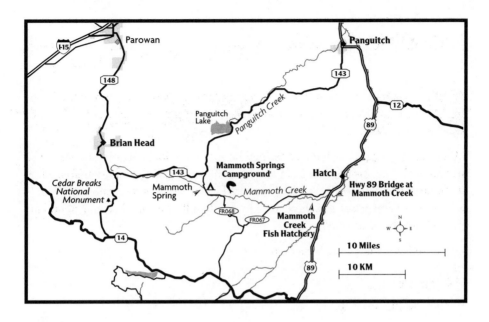

Maps

USGS 1:24000   Hatch, George Mountain, Asay Bench, Haycock
                                 Mountain, Panguitch Lake, Henrie Knolls

Utah Atlas and Gazetteer   Page 18

When to Go

Best time should be July through October. The elevation is fairly high, with
Mammoth Springs at 8,000 feet. ♦

Manning Creek

his stream flows off the west side of Monroe Mountain through a beautiful canyon away from any roads, just a few miles south of the town of Marysvale.

Manning Meadow Reservoir and Barney Reservoir are located on branches of the stream at the headwaters. Both of the reservoirs and the stream are managed by stocking native Bonneville cutthroat trout. The stream was renovated in 1996. It will take several years for these fish to reach full size and become abundant throughout the stream.

Catch-and-release fishing is recommended.

Fish Species

Bonneville cutthroat trout.

Special Regulations

Manning Meadows Reservoir, Spillway and Tributaries:

❐ Artificial flies and lures only.

❐ **Closed** to fishing January 1 through 6 a.m. on the second Saturday of July (July 10, 1999).

❐ Catch and release only. All trout caught must be immediately released.

No special regulations in the stream below the reservoir, but catch and release is recommended.

Tactics

Use heavily hackled dry flies or weighted nymphs. The stream corridor is very small with pine trees along the banks. Extending your arm and fly rod, then "dapping" the fly on the surface is often the most productive approach.

How to Get There

From 300 South in Marysvale, go east on Old US 89. Turn south on Thompsonville Road, go through Thompsonville, and continue to Monroe Mountain Road. Go east to Dry Creek Road and continue east from there.

Accessibility

Dry Creek Road will cross Manning Creek and then continue on up to Manning

Meadow Reservoir. The lower section of the Creek can be reached by turning north on to The Manning Creek Road (FR 153) from the Dry Creek Road near Elbow Ranch.

There is a USFS trail (TR 092) that runs from the Manning Creek Road along Manning Creek for several miles. This trail comes out on the Dry Creek Road 1.7 miles southeast from where the road crosses Manning Creek.

The entire fishable portion of the stream is located on public lands, including the Fishlake National Forest, BLM, and DWR property.

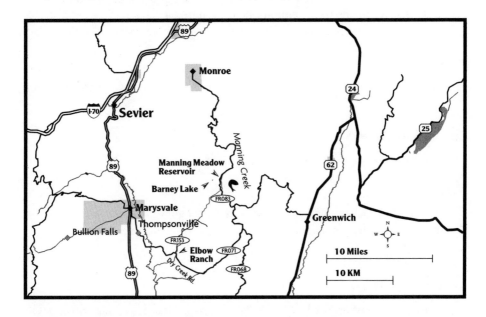

GPS Coordinates

Manning Meadow Reservoir	N 38° 29' 17" W 112° 04' 15"
Barney Lake	N 38° 29' 06" W 112° 05' 15"
Elbow Ranch	N 38° 23' 28" W 112° 09' 07"

Maps

USGS 1:24000	Monroe Peak, Marysvale Peak, Marysvale, Piute Reservoir
Utah Atlas and Gazetteer	Pages 26, 27

When to Go

July to October. ◆

North Creek

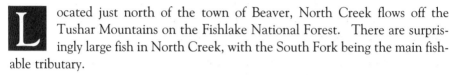 ocated just north of the town of Beaver, North Creek flows off the Tushar Mountains on the Fishlake National Forest. There are surprisingly large fish in North Creek, with the South Fork being the main fishable tributary.

There is a chance of finding a rattlesnake along any stream in southern Utah, although many streams have reputations that are exaggerated. However, if you hike North Creek, there is a good chance that you will encounter a rattlesnake.

Fish Species

An abundant population of wild rainbow trout and rainbow/cutthroat trout hybrids.

Special Regulations

General season, bag, and possession limits apply.

Tactics

The lack of road access here keeps pressure very light. Take the time to hike a distance up the canyon and you may be rewarded by a good-sized trout.

Try an elk hair caddis, or an attractor pattern like a stimulator.

How to Get There

From Beaver, go east on SR 153 to the North Creek Road (1200 East Street). Go north about 5.9 miles. After the first 90-degree turn to the right, stay to the right for the South Fork, or turn left for the North Fork.

Accessibility

The South Fork has vehicle access to the mouth of the canyon at the lower end.

About 12 miles of stream extends between the two access points connected by Forest Trails TR 062 and TR 172.

The extreme upper end can be reached by hiking from the Paiute ATV Trail (FR 123) that goes over the Tushar Mountains. The Mud Lake Trailhead is 3.5 miles north of Big John Flats. You can pick up the well defined trail on the north side of the lake. There is a junction 0.5 miles in from where you head north to Blue Lake and the top of the South Fork of North Creek.

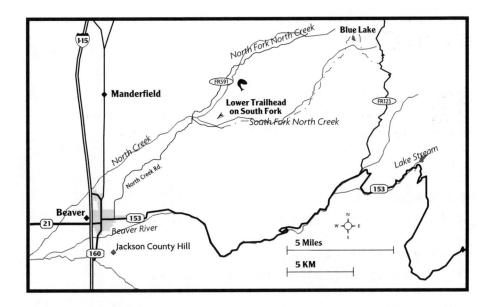

GPS Coordinates

Lower Trailhead on South Fork	N 38° 20′ 18″ W 112° 32′ 33″
Blue Lake	N 38° 23′ 53″ W 112° 25′ 06″

Maps

USGS 1:24000   Beaver, Black Ridge, Shelly Baldy Peak, Mount Belknap

Utah Atlas and Gazetteer   Page 26

When to Go

Late June to October. ◆

North Creek

L ocated just northwest of the town of Escalante, this stream joins up with Birch Creek and Upper Valley Creek to form the Escalante River. Anglers traveling to Pine Creek should think about spending a day fishing North Creek as well. The easily accessible stream supports a variety of trout species.

Fish Species

Wild populations of brook, rainbow, and cutthroat trout.

Special Regulations

❑ Trout limit, 6; only 2 trout over 13 inches.

Tactics

A stealthy approach will avoid spooking the fish along the small water.

Fly-fishers will want to try standard nymphs and dry flies here. Spinners, salmon eggs, and worms will also be effective.

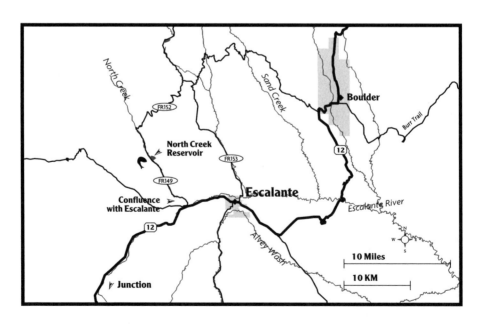

How to Get There

From Escalante, go west on SR 12 about 5.5 miles. Turn north on North Creek Road (FR 149).

Accessibility

The gravel road to Barker Reservoir and the North Creek Lakes runs along North Creek for much of its length. Most of the stream is on the Dixie National Forest.

GPS Coordinates

Confluence with Escalante	N 37° 45' 55" W 111° 40' 56"
North Creek Reservoir	N 37° 50' 35" W 111° 45' 27"

Maps

USGS 1:24000   Wide Hollow Reservoir, Griffin Point

Utah Atlas and Gazetteer   Pages 19, 27

When to Go

One can find good water conditions from mid-March to mid-May. You will want to avoid high water runoff, which normally occurs in June. Summer weather can be quite hot and fishing can slow down. September and October have beautiful weather and good fishing. ◆

Oak Creek   MILLARD COUNTY

T his stream flows out of the canyon just east of Oak City. This is very small stream. Don't choose this destination unless you are looking for a stream you can step across. Plan on adapting your tactics and expectations to the size of the water.

Fish Species

Smaller-sized wild brown trout.

Special Regulations

General season, bag, and possession limits apply.

Tactics

A cautious approach and short accurate casts with dry flies should work well here. Stimulators and other caddisfly imitations are recommended.

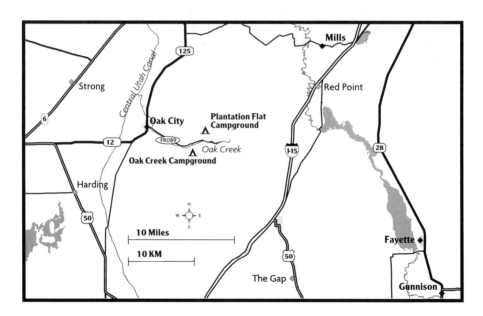

How to Get There

From Oak City, go east on Canyon Road (FR 089) which follows Oak Creek.

Accessibility

Good access on the gravel road that extends up the canyon to a public camp-ground on the Fishlake National Forest.

GPS Coordinates

Oak Creek Campground	N 39° 20' 58" W 112° 15' 58"
Plantation Flat Campground	N 39° 21' 20" W 112° 13' 38"

Maps

USGS 1:24000   Oak City South, Williams Peak

Utah Atlas and Gazetteer   Page 36

When to Go

Late June through October. ♦

PHOTO: EMMETT HEATH / WESTERN RIVERS FLYFISHER

Otter Creek

 his small, beautiful stream runs out of Koosharem Reservoir and into Otter Creek Reservoir. Flows are consistent due to consistent release from Koosharem. There are good numbers of fish here.

This stream is known to harbor whirling disease. Please see the whirling disease section in the guide for precautions to ensure that you don't help to spread this disease.

Fish Species

Rainbows and brown trout.

Special Regulations

☐ Trout limit, 6.

From Otter Creek upstream to the Angle Diversion:

☐ **Closed** January 1 through May 21.

Tactics

Look for fish to be hiding beneath undercut banks. Try red or black wooly buggers. Spinners are also effective.

The most productive method is to drift worms through deeper holes and undercut banks.

How to Get There

From I-70 north of Richfield, take SR 24 south (or from Richfield, take SR 119 east to SR 24), until you pass Koosharem Reservoir and reach SR 62. Take SR 62 south, which will run along to the west of Otter Creek for its length. You can also take US 89 at Sevier Junction (I-70) south past Piute Reservoir to SR 62, and then head east on 62 to the southern end of Otter Creek Reservoir.

Accessibility

There are BLM lands about 6 miles above Otter Creek Reservoir, but most of this creek runs over private land. Be sure to obtain permission before crossing private lands.

There are over 25 miles of creek between the two reservoirs.

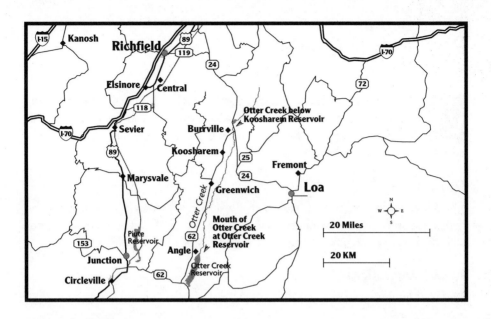

GPS Coordinates

Mouth of Otter Cr. at Otter Cr. Reservoir	N 38° 14′ 57″ W 111° 57′ 55″
Otter Creek below Koosharem Reservoir	N 38° 35′ 26″ W 111° 50′ 47″

Maps

USGS 1:24000   Burrville, Abes Knoll, Greenwich, Parker Knoll, Angle

Utah Atlas and Gazetteer   Pages 27, 37

When to Go

You can find good conditions here from May to November. This stream will discolor quite a bit after heavy rains. ◆

Panguitch Creek   GARFIELD COUNTY

 riginating as the outflow from Panguitch Lake, this creek extends downstream to the town of Panguitch, where it enters the Sevier River. This is fairly good-sized water as southern Utah streams go. It normally maintains good flows through September.

Fish Species

The lower reach supports a population of wild brown trout. The area along the highway is stocked with hatchery rainbow trout. The DWR stocked 8,000 catchable rainbows in Panguitch Creek on the last day of May in 1998.

Special Regulations

❏ Trout limit, 6.

Tactics

The meadow section above the canyon has a great cranefly hatch in September. Try surface imitations of this long-legged insect. Drifting cranefly larvae along the undercut banks can be productive throughout the summer for big rainbows.

Wooly buggers in black, olive, and red sparkle work well in the meadows and also down into the canyon.

How to Get There

From Panguitch, take SR 143 (FR 036), which runs south alongside the upper portion of Panguitch Creek.

Accessibility

The stream parallels FR 036 for several miles below Panguitch Lake, and flows through private land and portions of the Dixie National Forest. There is good access through most of this stretch.

Further downstream, it leaves the highway and flows through a roadless canyon for about 5 miles. Be prepared for a rugged hike. Begin where the road leaves the creek.

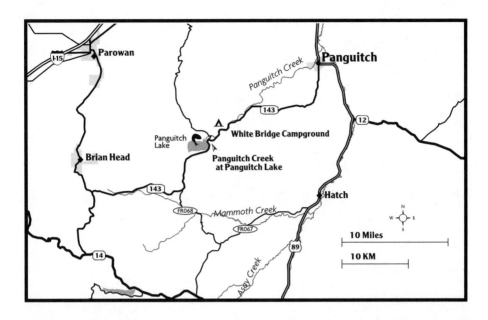

GPS Coordinates

Panguitch Creek at Panguitch Lake	N 37° 43′ 29″ W 112° 37′ 38″
White Bridge Campground	N 37° 44′ 44″ W 112° 35′ 11″

Maps

USGS 1:24000   Panguitch Lake, Haycock Mountain,
                      Fivemile Ridge, Panguitch

Utah Atlas and Gazetteer   Pages 18, 26

When to Go

Best times to fish Panguitch Creek are July through October. High water normally occurs in May or June. Flows can stay moderately high through September some years. ◆

Pine Creek   GARFIELD COUNTY

T here are more than a dozen "Pine Creeks" in Utah, but the panoramic location of this water is perhaps the most striking. From the Hell's Backbone Road it drops down into The Box — a narrow sandstone canyon with walls rising more than 800 feet above the stream. It is an incredible hike, with good fishing as an added bonus.

Pine Creek begins on the Boulder Mountain and flows toward the town of Escalante where it enters the Escalante River.

Fish Species

Wild brown trout.

Special Regulations

❏ Trout limit, 6; only 2 trout over 13 inches.

❏ Catch and release is recommended.

Tactics

This stream is small, shallow, and usually clear. Fly-fishing with a stealthy approach is essential to success.

One effective tactic is "dapping" dry flies. This is accomplished by sneaking into a position where one can hold the rod tip over a pool or other good water. The fly is suspended over the water then lowered to the surface. Let the fly dance around and float down a ways, then lift the fly up and drop it back again. Bushy dry flies with a lot of hackle are particularly good for this tactic.

Fish will respond to nymphs in the early season. Small bead head nymphs are especially good, as you don't need to add weight, resulting in a more quiet presentation. Yellow humpies and royal trudes are good patterns here.

How to Get There

From Escalante, go north on Hell's Backbone Road or FR 153 (some maps list it as the Posy Lake Road or Pine Creek Road). This road follows Pine Creek for a while then crosses it again near Blue Spruce Campground. Another route is to follow the Hell's Backbone Road over from the town of Boulder.

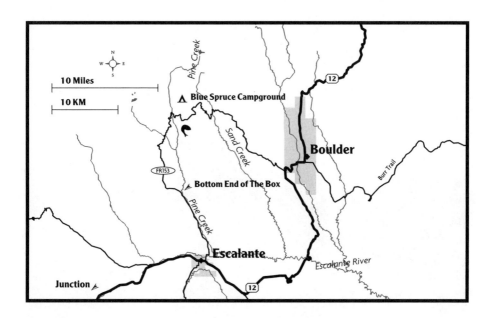

Accessibility

Access is good from the Hell's Backbone Road near the Blue Spruce Campground on the Dixie National Forest. Downstream from here the creek enters the Box-Death Hollow Wilderness. Hikers can come up from the bottom of "The Box," beginning where Pine Creek leaves FR 153 and heading north. If you are primarily interested in fishing, starting at the bottom and fishing upstream into areas that get less pressure is recommended.

Anglers that don't have the time or energy to hike into The Box will find good fishing near and above Blue Spruce Campground.

GPS Coordinates

Bottom End of The Box	N 37° 51' 44" W 111° 38' 18"
Blue Spruce Campground	N 37° 58' 23" W 111° 39' 04"

Maps

USGS 1:24000   Escalante, Wide Hollow Reservoir, Posy Lake

Utah Atlas and Gazetteer   Pages 19, 27

When to Go

Check weather forecasts before entering the canyon, and avoid thunderstorm activity. Even if it isn't raining down in the canyon, runoff from higher up can result in powerful and dangerous flash flooding. Best time for hiking is from mid-

March to mid-May. It can be pleasant spring weather in the canyon while it snows up on the Aquarius Plateau. Expect it to be hot in summer. September and October are beautiful. High water will usually occur in May and June.

Other hikers will spook fish in this narrow canyon, so go during the week if possible. ◆

A beautiful rainbow returns to freedom. (PHOTO: EMMETT HEATH / WESTERN RIVERS FLYFISHER)

Pine Creek

T his stream originates on the northwest side of Boulder Mountain near the Aquarius Guard Station. Pine Creek Reservoir is located near the headwaters. The stream flows towards Bicknell, where it joins the Fremont River.

Fish Species

Wild brook and rainbow trout.

Special Regulations

General season, bag, and possession limits apply.

Tactics

At the higher elevations, try stimulators and renegades. Terrestrials are effective on the lower stretches.

Small spinners and worms will take fish the length of the creek.

There are some beaver ponds below the Aquarius Guard Station that hold some very nice brook trout. These fish are spooky and difficult to catch.

How to Get There

From Bicknell, go south 2.8 miles on SR 24, then turn southwest on Bicknell Circle which follows Pine Creek for about 4 miles. You can continue on to FR 178 and go south to reach Pine Creek upstream on national forest lands. FR 178 goes past the Aquarius Guard Station.

Accessibility

Pine Creek crosses the Dixie National Forest, BLM, state, and private lands. The gravel road to the guard station provides access to a small section of stream. Much of the rest of the stream can be reached by hiking.

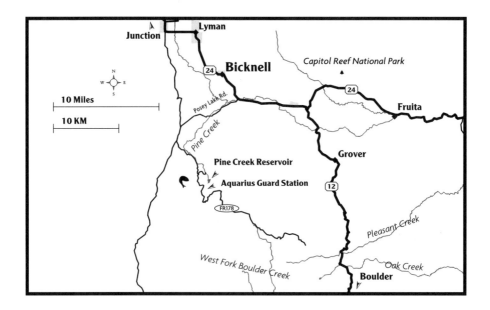

GPS Coordinates

Pine Creek Reservoir	N 38° 12′ 04″, W 111° 34′ 01″
Aquarius Guard Station	N 38° 11′ 44″, W 111° 34′ 31″

Maps

USGS 1:24000   Government Point, Bicknell

Utah Atlas and Gazetteer   Page 27

When to Go

Late June through October. Review of historic stream flow data indicates that
normal high water is in late May or early June, and of a fairly short duration in
most years. ◆

Pleasant Creek

GARFIELD COUNTY

his is another Boulder Mountain stream that flows off the east side towards Capitol Reef National Park. Hatchery rainbow trout are stocked near the campground but most of the stream supports wild trout.

This is slightly larger water than the neighboring Oak Creek.

Fish Species

The upper reach contains brook trout. The lower stream contains rainbow trout.

Special Regulations

❏ Trout limit, 6; only 2 trout over 13 inches.

Tactics

Fish are not generally fussy here. Try attractor flies like renegades and royal Wulffs. Small spinners and worms should also prove effective.

How to Get There

From Boulder, go north 22 miles on SR 12 to the Pleasant Creek Campground.

Accessibility

Most of its length is on the Dixie National Forest. From the campground, the upper reach is accessible by hiking. The lower stream, extending towards Capitol Reef, can be reached on FR 181 and FR 168.

GPS Coordinates

Pleasant Creek Campground	N 38° 06′ 03″ W 111° 20′ 14″
Lower Bowns Reservoir	N 38° 06′ 24″ W 111° 16′ 18″

Maps

USGS 1:24000   Lower Bowns Reservoir, Grover, Golden Throne

Utah Atlas and Gazetteer   Page 28

When to Go

July through October. The lower portion of the stream may begin to fish sooner. The Pleasant Creek Campground is at 8,600 feet, so prepare for weather that changes dramatically. ♦

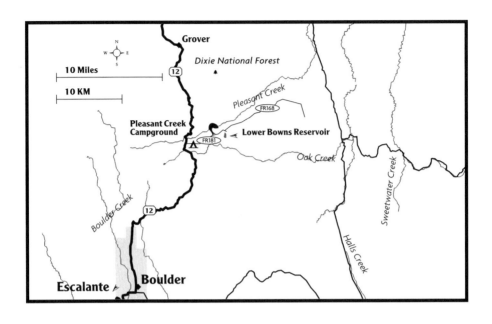

Brown trout. (ARTIST: MIKE STIDHAM)

Salina Creek

T here is a chance to catch some larger browns on this good-sized stream. There is easy access yet little fishing pressure, perhaps because the aesthetics are impacted by the nearness of I-70.

Fish Species

Hatchery rainbow trout are stocked in the vicinity of the interstate, while wild rainbow trout and cutthroat trout are found further upstream. There are some nice brown trout here as well.

Special Regulations

General season, bag, and possession limits apply.

Tactics

Fly-fishers will enjoy throwing grasshopper and beetle imitations from July to September. Wooly buggers fished slow and deep in the larger holes can produce the bigger browns.

Anglers using spinning gear may want to try swimming small green and root beer jigs along the bottom.

How to Get There

From I-70, either Exits 61 or 71 will put you right on the creek.

Accessibility

The I-70 frontage road follows the creek and crosses it several times, providing easy access.

A gravel road follows the stream after it leaves the freeway near Exit 71. Much of the upper stream is on the Fishlake National Forest, but there is some private land as well.

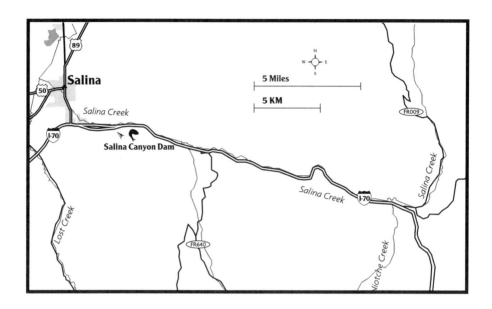

GPS Coordinates

Salina Canyon Dam	N 38° 55' 50" W 111° 48' 43"

Maps

USGS 1:24000   Salina, Steves Mountain, Water Hollow Ridge

Utah Atlas and Gazetteer   Page 37

When to Go

Late June through October. This creek will get very muddy in the spring or after heavy rains. ◆

Sand Creek

GARFIELD COUNTY

 arger than other Escalante drainage streams, Sand Creek has more than 15 miles of fishable water. The lower end of Sand Creek is probably your best chance for a large fish in these desert canyons.

Fish Species

The headwaters contain rainbow and cutthroat trout while the lower end is populated with brown trout.

Special Regulations

❐ Trout limit, 6; only 2 trout over 13 inches.

Tactics

There are some larger pools and runs in the lower stretches. Nymphing in this deeper water can produce some larger fish. Try large cased caddis nymphs or bead head hare's ears. There are many grasshoppers on this lower stretch in summer, and larger browns will chase wooly buggers in the fall.

If you hike in on the Old Mail Trail, best fishing is away from the trail where fish have not been harvested. There are good numbers of brown trout about one mile above the trail. Small wooly buggers and spinners work well here.

Try casting renegades and trudes to the rainbow and cutthroat on the upper water along Hell's Backbone Road.

How to Get There

From Boulder, go south on SR 12 and park at the trailhead on the Escalante River. Hike upriver about 3.3 miles, watching for Sand Creek to enter from the north. Escalante Natural Bridge will appear on the south canyon wall just before you reach Sand Creek. When you get close, either walk in the river or on the north bank or you can miss Sand Creek. Be prepared for strenuous hiking and many water crossings.

An alternative route is to take the Hell's Backbone Road from Boulder, going towards Escalante and cross Sand Creek at its headwaters. This is the only road access to Sand Creek.

Another option is a rugged hike down the Old Mail Trail to Sand Creek. Reach this trail from the Boulder Landing Strip, located 4.5 miles southwest of Boulder on SR 12. Go about 0.5 miles past the landing strip to the trailhead.

Accessibility

This is rough canyon country. Make sure you are prepared before entering the canyon. Good footwear that will protect your feet and hold up to repeated soaking in the creek is essential.

The farther you are willing to go away from access, the better the fishing. Especially between the Escalante River and the Old Mail Trail.

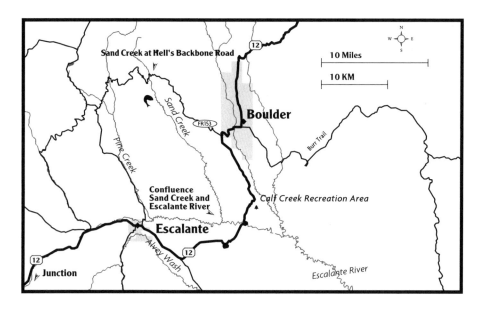

GPS Coordinates

Confluence of Sand Creek and Escalante River	N 37° 46′ 30″ W 111° 27′ 25″
Sand Creek at Hell's Backbone Road	N 37° 58′ 15″ W 111° 34′ 57″

Maps

USGS 1:24000   Roger Peak, Escalante, Calf Creek, Boulder Town

Utah Atlas and Gazetteer   Pages 20, 27, 28

When to Go

Best times will be April and early May, and September through October.

Watch out for the vicious biting flies at the lower end of Sand Creek and along the Escalante in summertime. Fish early and late during the summer as activity slows during the heat of the day. Check weather forecasts before entering the canyon to avoid flash flood conditions. Fish mid-week to avoid pressure from other anglers or hikers if possible. ◆

Santa Clara River WASHINGTON COUNTY

T his stream originates from the west side of the Pine Valley Mountain Wilderness area. There are some nice browns in the gorge between the towns of Pine Valley and Central. Low flows make the section below Baker Reservoir marginal for fishing.

Fish Species

Hatchery rainbow trout and wild brown trout below Pine Valley Reservoir.

Special Regulations

From the Pine Valley Reservoir downstream to the confluence of the Virgin River:

❐ Trout limit, 4.

Tactics

Wooly buggers and weighted nymphs work well in the gorge above Central.

Spinners are effective here in the winter.

How to Get There

From St. George, go north on SR 18 to Central. Take FR 035 and continue east up to Pine Valley.

Accessibility

Pine Valley Reservoir, and a short distance of stream below the reservoir, are located within the Dixie National Forest. Most of the stream in Pine Valley, however, is on private land.

Just downstream from Pine Valley the stream re-enters the national forest. The stream flows through a remote lava gorge for about 8 miles between Pine Valley and the small community of Central. This canyon is extremely rugged, with sharp rocks, cacti, and rattlesnakes, with access limited to hiking.

GPS Coordinates

Pine Valley Reservoir	N 37° 22′ 43″ W 113° 28′ 25″
Baker Reservoir Recreation Area Campground	N 37° 22′ 34″ W 113° 38′ 15″
Gunlock State Park	N 37° 15′ 13″ W 113° 47′ 01″

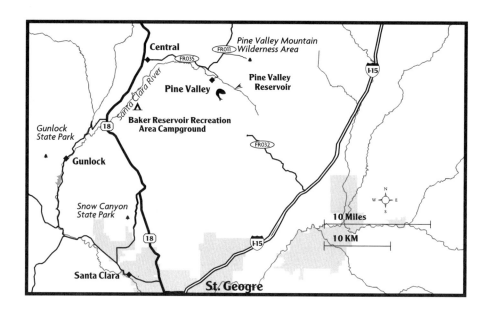

Maps

USGS 1:24000   Signal Peak, Grass Valley, Central East,
                                Central West, Veyo, Gunlock

Utah Atlas and Gazetteer   Pages 16, 17

When to Go

Hiking in this area in mid-summer is not recommended. The best fishing here is
during the winter. Think of the Santa Clara when you have cabin fever and want
to catch a trout while fishing in shirt sleeves. Expect higher flows from late April
to early June. ◆

Services

Lodging:

Dixie Deer Lodge   Pine Valley Lodge
148 E Center Road   960 E Main
Central, UT 84722   Pine Valley, UT 84781s
tel: (435) 574-2650   tel: (435) 574-2544

Sevenmile Creek

T his stream begins near the Mt. Terrill Ranger Station at about 9,000 foot elevation on the Fishlake National Forest. It is the major tributary to Johnson Valley Reservoir in the Fremont River drainage. It is just up the road from Fish Lake and can be a nice side trip for anglers who need a break from chasing the lake's bigger trout.

Fish Species

Wild brook trout, and some cutthroat trout.

Special Regulations

General season, bag, and possession limits apply.

Catch and release is recommended.

Tactics

These are simple uncomplicated trout that have a few months in the summer to eat enough to get through the winter. As long as you walk softly and stand back from the creek so as not to spook fish, you will have fast action.

Anglers can do very well with an ultralight spinning outfit and ½ night crawler with no weight.

The key to small streams like this is to fish a spot and then keep moving.

How to Get There

Take SR 24 west of Loa to SR 25. Follow SR 25 up past Fish Lake (on FR 640) and you will reach the lower section of Sevenmile Creek by the Piute Parking Area near Johnson Valley Reservoir.

Accessibility

Much of the stream is located adjacent to FR 640 (also known as the Gooseberry Fremont Road), which winds up the canyon below Mt. Terrill, majestic at its 11,531-foot elevation.

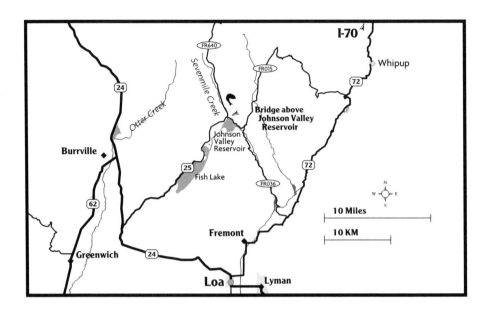

GPS Coordinates

Bridge above Johnson Valley Reservoir	N 38° 37′ 16″ W 111° 38′ 48″

Maps

USGS 1:24000   Fish Lake, Mount Terrill

Utah Atlas and Gazetteer   Pages 27, 37

When to Go

Sevenmile Creek will fish well as soon as the high water recedes in June. The brook trout will be even more colorful and aggressive in September and October as they prepare to spawn. ◆

Sevier River (Main Stem)   PIUTE COUNTY

T he health of this stretch of river is tied directly to Piute Reservoir. Extreme drawdowns of the reservoir in low water years have had an adverse effect on the river below.

It seems that many of the fish in this section come from the reservoir above. You can find very few fish on one visit, and large numbers another time. If you come to fish here, be prepared with a backup plan, like Kingston Canyon, Otter Creek, or one of the reservoirs.

Fish Species

Rainbow and brown trout.

Special Regulations

Downstream from Piute Reservoir for 5 miles to the Dry Creek Road Bridge:

❏ Trout limit, 6.

Tactics

When fish are present, fly-fishers can do well with hoppers, wooly buggers, and large scuds in olive and orange.

Spinners are also effective, as are worms and Power Bait.

How to Get There

From Marysvale, go south on US 89, 8.5 miles to the turnoff to Piute State Park (6.5 miles north of Junction). Go east 0.5 miles from US 89, then turn north for another 0.6 miles. Turn east again and it is 1.3 miles to the river.

Accessibility

There is good access at the base of the dam below Piute Reservoir.

GPS Coordinates

Sevier River below Piute	N 38° 19′ 38″ W 112° 11′ 16″

Maps

USGS 1:24000   Piute Reservoir, Marysvale

Utah Atlas and Gazetteer   Pages 26, 27

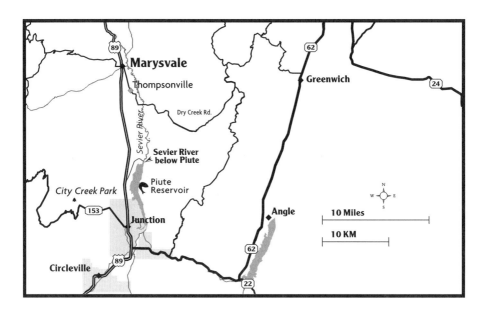

When to Go

Should fish well in June and July, and then again in October and November. ♦

Kingston Canyon of the Sevier River. (PHOTO: COURTESY UTAH OUTDOORS)

South Ash Creek   WASHINGTON COUNTY

S outh Ash Creek offers spectacular views of the badlands that extend towards the Hurricane and Vermillion Cliffs. The stream flows from the east side of the Pine Valley Mountain Wilderness, and includes Harmony Creek and Mill Creek as tributaries.

Don't be concerned if there is no water in the stream at the junction with the interstate.

Fish Species

Similar to Leeds Creek, these streams contain native Bonneville cutthroat trout that were introduced from the west side of Pine Valley Mountain. These fish have grown to good size.

Special Regulations

General season, bag, and possession limits apply.

Catch-and-release fishing is strongly recommended.

Tactics

These fish are not particularly educated and your favorite dry flies will probably serve you well. Wooly buggers and spinners will also catch fish.

Bait is not recommended as it is difficult to release fish in good condition.

How to Get There

From north of St. George, on I-15 at the Browse Exit (Exit 30), take FR 037 to the northwest and follow it up the canyon.

Accessibility

Most of the length of these streams are restricted to the road-less canyons that border the Pine Valley Mountain Wilderness on the Dixie National Forest.

A rough, 4-wheel-drive road (FR 037) extends northwest from the Browse Exit to the Browse Guard Station. The road crosses these streams near the confluence of Harmony Creek and Mill Creek, and again comes into contact with Mill Creek near its headwaters at the guard station.

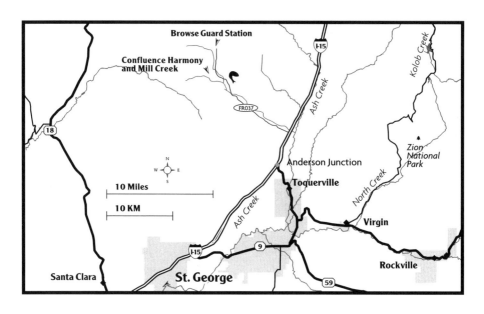

GPS Coordinates

Browse Guard Station	N 37° 23' 08" W 113° 21' 10"
Confluence Harmony and Mill Creek	N 37° 21' 51" W 113° 20' 02"

Maps

USGS 1:24000   New Harmony, Pintura

Utah Atlas and Gazetteer   Page 17

When to Go

June, and then again in September and October. High water normally occurs in May. ◆

UM Creek

U M Creek is a tributary to the Fremont River and is the main inflow to Forsyth Reservoir, located on the Fishlake National Forest. The trout population was removed as part of a whirling disease control program during 1992-95. The current fishing proclamation should be checked for special fishing regulations.

Fish Species

Native Colorado River cutthroat trout were reintroduced into UM Creek in 1996. There are also sterile hybrid tiger trout in the stream. Brown trout are found in the section between Forsyth Reservoir and Mill Meadow Reservoir. Mill Meadow has also been stocked with tiger trout, splake, brownbows and rainbows, giving anglers a chance to pursue a variety of fish on the same body of water.

Special Regulations

❏ Artificial flies and lures only.

❏ Trout limit, 4.

Upstream from Forsyth Reservoir:

❏ **Closed** to the possession of cutthroat trout or trout with cutthroat markings.

Tactics

The tiger trout here are very aggressive. They will often attack your fly with reckless abandon. Black and purple wooly buggers in small sizes work well as do terrestrial patterns on top. These active fish should respond well to small spinners also.

How to Get There

From Loa, take SR 72 northeast to FR 36 to get to the Mill Meadow area; or take FR 509 to reach above and below both Forsyth Reservoir and UM Creek. To reach the upper section at Water Flat, take FR 36 past Mill Meadow and up along the Fremont River, turning right (northeast) onto FR 15.

Accessibility

Most of the stream is in roadless canyons on the Fishlake National Forest. It does cross some private land. It can be accessed at Forsyth Reservoir from SR 72 and at Water Flat by FR 15 near Johnson Reservoir. There are some private lands above Forsyth Reservoir.

One can also go up from Mill Meadow Reservoir on FR 36. This bottom section is quite brushy.

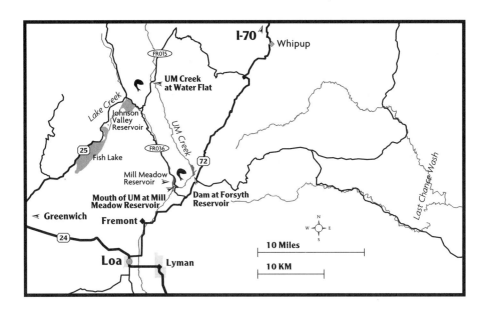

GPS Coordinates

Dam at Forsyth Reservoir	N 38° 30' 59" W 111° 31' 57"
UM Creek at Water Flat	N 38° 38' 30" W 111° 36' 04"
Mouth of UM at Mill Meadow Reservoir	N 38° 30' 08" W 111° 33' 22"

Maps

USGS 1:24000   Forsyth Reservoir, Hilgard Mountain

Utah Atlas and Gazetteer   Pages 27, 37

When to Go

At 8,000 feet, this is a good place to beat the heat in July and August. Should fish well until the weather gets cold in October or November. ◆

West Fork of the Sevier   KANE AND GARFIELD COUNTIES

T he West Fork of the Sevier, below the confluence with Mammoth and Asay Creeks, has recovered nicely after undergoing restoration work. It is now a beautiful stretch of river with deep pools, long runs, and undercut banks. This area does seem to receive heavy fishing pressure.

The river has little water after it works its way north of SR 12, and fishing beyond here is marginal.

Fish Species

Rainbows and brown trout.

Special Regulations

General season, bag, and possession limits apply.

Tactics

From July to September you will find good fishing with grasshopper and beetle patterns. In some years, the black beetles are everywhere and imitations will produce fish long after the beetles have disappeared.

Gold-colored wooly buggers with sparkle can be effective in the fall. Try your own favorite streamers on the large brown trout.

Jigs and spinners are good offerings in the pools.

How to Get There

From Panguitch, head south along US 89. The road runs just west of the river for its length.

Accessibility

There is good access from where Asay Creek crosses US 89, to well below Mammoth Creek. There is private land as you approach the town of Hatch.

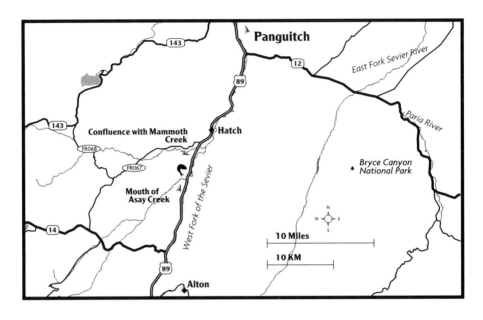

GPS Coordinates

Confluence with Mammoth Creek	N 37° 37' 34" W 112° 26' 41"
Mouth of Asay Creek	N 37° 35' 02" W 112° 28' 29"

Maps

USGS 1:24000   George Mountain, Hatch, Wilson Peak,
                        Casto Canyon, Panguitch

Utah Atlas and Gazetteer   Pages 18, 26

When to Go

Water will generally be down by June and fishing should hold through November.
Expect slow periods during the heat of summer. ◆

Baker Dam Reservoir   WASHINGTON COUNTY

T his reservoir holds water for irrigation and there is no mandated conservation pool; consequently, it can be completely drained in dry years. When water conditions are favorable, Baker can produce some large brown trout.

Fish Species

Rainbow and brown trout.

Special Regulations

General season, bag, and possession limits apply.

Tactics

The reservoir is stocked with catchable size rainbow early in the season (13,000 in February, March, and May in 1998). Bait-fishing with worms and Power Bait is a common and effective method.

The larger browns are mostly caught in the winter months. Try crankbaits and streamer flies that resemble small rainbow trout and bait fish.

How to Get There

From St. George, go north 21 miles on SR 18, then go east 1 mile to the reservoir.

Accessibility

Good access at Baker Reservoir Recreation Area. There is a campground here. There is no boat ramp, so float tubes and other small watercraft are recommended.

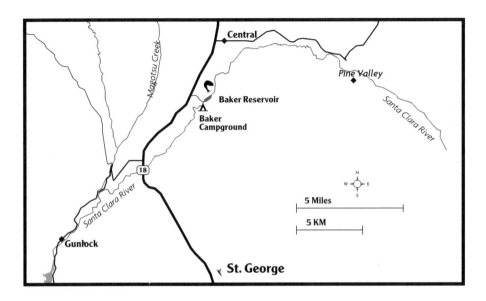

GPS Coordinates

Baker Res. Recreation Area Campground	N 37° 22' 34" W 113° 38' 15"

Maps

USGS 1:24000   Central West

Utah Atlas and Gazetteer   Page 16

When to Go

This reservoir usually remains ice free through the winter. Best fishing success is from late fall through February, especially for larger fish. April, May, and June is when the most stocked rainbows are available. ♦

Barney Lake

T his beautiful lake contains native Bonneville cutthroat trout at its head-waters in Manning Creek. It is only 1.5 miles from Manning Meadows Reservoir, so these waters can be easily combined for a weekend trip. You are allowed to keep two fish here if you want fresh trout for dinner.

This lake is above 10,000 feet. Make sure you bring warm gear if spending the night as it can get quite cold at this elevation any time of year.

Fish Species

Bonneville cutthroat trout.

Special Regulations

❏ Artificial flies and lures only.

❏ Trout limit, 2

❏ Fishing from a boat with a motor of any kind is **prohibited.**

Tactics

This lake will fish much like Manning Meadows Reservoir. Wooly buggers are the fly of choice underneath. There is good dry-fly fishing with mosquito or renegade patterns if you can spot cruisers and cast in front of them.

There are trees around part of the lake, so you may find it easier to use a spinning rod and a full bubble to cast your wooly buggers or a half full bubble for your dry flies. You can get more distance with this setup, but you are more likely to spook fish if you cast near them.

How to Get There

From Marysvale, go east on 300 South to Old US 89. Go south to Thompsonville Road. Go through Thompsonville and continue to Monroe Mountain Road. Go east to Dry Creek Road and continue east into the Fishlake National Forest.

Accessibility

About 0.5 miles before Manning Meadows Reservoir, FR 157 splits off to the northwest and it is a rough road for 0.7 miles to the lake.

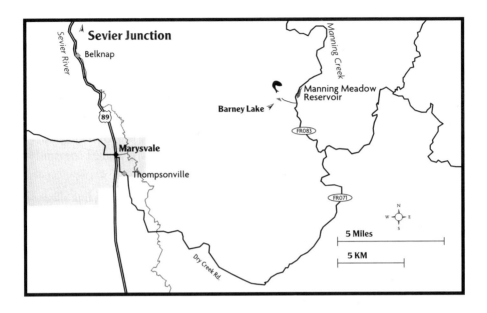

GPS Coordinates

Barney Lake	N 38° 29' 07" W 112° 05' 16"

Maps

USGS 1:24000   Marysvale Peak

Utah Atlas and Gazetteer   Page 27

When to Go

Expect good fishing from ice-off until it freezes. The road should be accessible by the first of July. ◆

Duck Fork Reservoir   Sanpete County

his is a fairly remote reservoir at 9,300 feet in the Manti-La Sal National Forest. It is only 5.5 miles away from the more accessible Ferron Reservoir.

The trophy regulations are fairly new, but expect the possibility of some large trout in the years to come.

Fish Species

Rainbow and cutthroat trout.

This lake may be used in the future as a brood stock lake for the Colorado River strain of cutthroat trout.

Special Regulations

❏ Artificial flies and lures only.

❏ Trout limit, 8.

❏ All trout 12 to 20 inches must be immediately released.

❏ Only 1 trout over 20 inches.

Tactics

Float tubes are an effective way to fish this small reservoir. Strip wooly buggers and damselfly nymphs under the surface. Surface action can be good here as well. Try adult damselflies, double renegades, and terrestrial imitations like ants.

How to Get There

From Ferron, go west 15 miles on the Ferron Canyon Road, then continue west on FR 022 for another 14 miles to Ferron Reservoir. Turn north on FR 049 and go 5.6 miles to Duck Creek Reservoir.

Accessibility

No facilities, but there are two campgrounds at Ferron Reservoir just 5.5 miles away. The road is unimproved and gets very slick when wet. Consider leaving if it starts to rain and avoid the road if it is saturated.

There is no boat ramp, but anglers do launch watercraft that are small enough to be carried to the water.

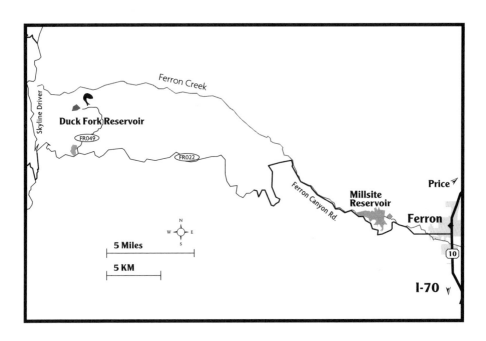

GPS Coordinates

Duck Fork Reservoir	N 39° 10' 10" W 111° 27' 00"

Maps

USGS 1:24000   Ferron Reservoir

Utah Atlas and Gazetteer   Page 38

When to Go

July through October. ◆

Enterprise Reservoirs

T hese scenic reservoirs are about 12 miles southwest of the small town of Enterprise in southern Utah. The Upper Reservoir is a good fishery. There is no mandated conservation pool in the Lower Reservoir, so fluctuating water levels have an adverse effect on the quality of fishing.

Fish Species

Rainbow trout.

Special Regulations

Enterprise Reservoirs Tributaries (Washington County) — tributaries to Upper and Lower Reservoirs:

☐ **Closed** January 1 through May 21.

Tactics

Still-fishing with baits like night crawlers and Power Bait is the most common approach for anglers seeking trout at Enterprise.

Casting and trolling spinners can be effective, especially when tipped with a worm.

How to Get There

From St. George, go north 39 miles on SR 18. Go 7.1 miles west on SR 120. Turn south on Veyo Shoal Creek Road just past the town of Hebron. Go south 5 miles and you will reach Lower Enterprise Reservoir and Reservoir Road. This will take you to Upper Enterprise Reservoir and Honeycomb Rock Campground.

Accessibility

The Veyo Shoal Creek Road gives access to the east side of the lower reservoir and Reservoir Road goes to the Forest Service campground and boat ramp.

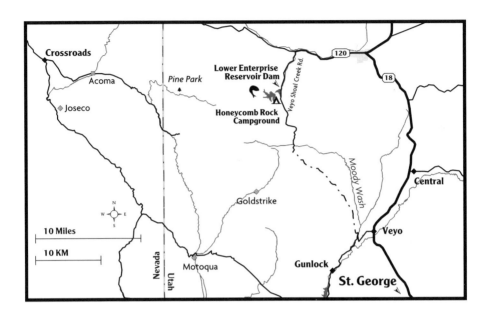

GPS Coordinates

| Lower Enterprise Reservoir Dam | N 37° 31′ 34″ W 113° 50′ 58″ |
| Honeycomb Rock Campground | N 37° 31′ 02″ W 113° 51′ 18″ |

Maps

USGS 1:24000   Hebron, Water Canyon Peak

Utah Atlas and Gazetteer   Page 16

When to Go

As with many southern Utah trout fisheries, the heat of summer makes for tough fishing. Best times are spring and fall. Conditions usually permit ice-fishing in January and February, but be sure to check the ice for safety. ◆

Ferron Reservoir

SANPETE COUNTY

F erron Reservoir sits majestic at an elevation of nearly 9, 500 feet and is surrounded by 3 peaks above 10,000 feet. It is only a few miles off Skyline Drive, a popular route through this area used by 4-wheel-drive enthusiasts.

Duck Fork Reservoir is just a few miles away and scenic Ferron Canyon provides good fishing for the hardiest anglers.

Fish Species

Rainbow and cutthroat trout.

Special Regulations

Ferron Reservoir Tributaries (Sanpete County) — Ferron Creek drainage above Ferron Reservoir:

☐ **Closed** January 1 through 6 a.m. on the second Saturday of July (July 10, 1999).

Tactics

Most anglers fish from shore here. Favorite baits include worms and Power Bait.

How to Get There

From Ferron, go west 15 miles on the Ferron Canyon Road, then continue west on FR 022 for another 14 miles to Ferron Reservoir.

Accessibility

There is road access to all but the north side of the lake. There are Forest Service campgrounds, and boat rentals.

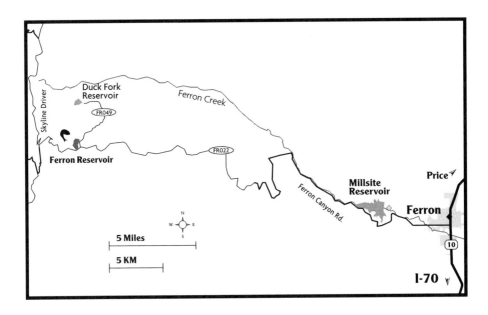

GPS Coordinates

Ferron Reservoir	N 39° 08' 32" W 111° 27' 06"

Maps

USGS 1:24000   Ferron Reservoir

Utah Atlas and Gazetteer   Page 38

When to Go

July to October. ♦

Fish Lake

his beautiful high alpine lake has been attracting fishers for many years. The deep blue waters and clear starry nights at 8,800 feet keep visitors coming back for more than the fishing.

While Flaming Gorge has taken the spotlight for record-sized lake trout, there are also huge fish here. The persistent angler has a good chance at lake trout over 20 lb., and fish over 30 lb. are a possibility. Large splake are found in Fish Lake. Joel Davenport set the state record here in 1992 with a 10 lb. 12 oz. trophy.

In the past, perch were illegally introduced here, severely reducing the Utah chub population that had been the main forage for lake trout. The DWR believes that numbers of lake trout are stable and balanced at present levels. Harvest of perch can help to maintain the current balance.

This lake contains Eurasian Watermilfoil. Carefully clean all vegetation from boats, trailers and other fishing equipment.

Fish Species

Rainbows, browns, lake trout, splake, and yellow perch.

Special Regulations

❏ Trout limit, 4, January 1 through May 21. No more than 2 may be lake trout/mackinaw and only 1 may be a lake trout/mackinaw larger than 20 inches.

❏ Trout limit, 8, May 22 through December 31. No more than 2 may be lake trout/mackinaw and only 1 may be a lake trout/mackinaw larger than 20 inches.

❏ The size of the hole when ice-fishing may not exceed 18 inches.

❏ Possession of a gaff while fishing is unlawful.

❏ Dead yellow perch may be used as bait.

Tactics

Perch and rainbows inhabit the upper layer of water. Fishing along the edge of the prevalent millfoil beds should produce perch all day long with the odd surprise from one of the trout species. Best fly-fishing for rainbows is often in the moss beds in the northeast corner of the lake.

Splake are a cross between brook and lake trout. They prefer deep water, but generally not as deep as lakers. The majority of them cruise at about 40 feet for much of the year, although you can often find them on the edge of the weeds. The DWR has caught splake as large as 16 pounds in a sample net. The best method for catching splake is jigs tipped with sucker meat or dead minnows.

There are still a few oversized brown trout in the lake. They are most often caught in the Twin Creek area by Fish Lake Lodge.

Many anglers come to Fish Lake hoping for one of the big lake trout. Look for the big fish to be spread out and active after "ice out." Casting lures that resemble small perch and rainbows will move fish. Trolling with downriggers picks up in July when mackinaws are concentrated in the deep water, most commonly around 90 feet down.

Late fall finds lakers moving into shallow water again as the spawning urge takes charge. Trollers like red-headed Davis plugs and large Flatfish. Jigging with large jigs tipped with sucker or chub meat is effective. The north end of the lake is a good place to hunt big mackinaws. As this lake is fairly long and narrow with few visual cues to help anglers return to good locations, effective use of GPS units and fish locators can be very beneficial.

This is a good ice-fishing location. Drill a hole on the edge of weed beds in 4 to 12 feet of water and you should catch a bunch of perch. The splake are also a very willing fish under the ice. You will sometimes catch big trout in these shallow

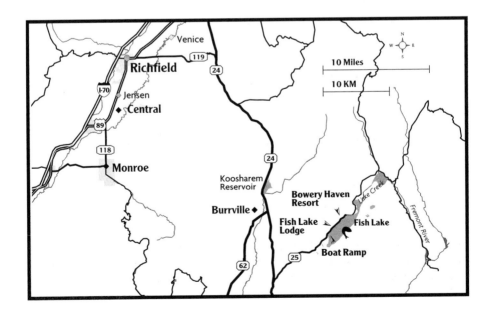

water holes, but if you are really after a big mackinaw, bring your fish locator and jig in deeper water.

How to Get There

From Richfield, take SR 119 east 9 miles to SR 24. Turn south on SR 24 and go 23 miles, then turn northeast onto SR 25. Another 8 miles brings you to Fish Lake.

Accessibility

This is a popular fishing destination. There are several private lodges on the lake and three different campgrounds. Route 25 is kept clear through the winter months for ice-fishers and snowmobilers.

GPS Coordinates

Boat Ramp	N 38° 32' 05" W 111° 44' 08"
Bowery Haven Resort	N 38° 33' 46" W 111° 42' 18"
Fish Lake Lodge	N 38° 32' 52" W 111° 43' 24"

Maps

USGS 1:24000   Fish Lake

Utah Atlas and Gazetteer   Page 27

When to Go

Fish Lake can provide good fishing throughout the year. Your favorite tactics will determine the best time to plan a trip.

Fly-fishers and trollers not using downriggers will find best success in early spring and fall when the larger lake trout and splake venture into shallow waters in search of food.

Anglers adept with fish locators and downriggers often prefer July and August when lake trout are concentrated in the deep water near the southeast shoreline.

Hardwater anglers usually find good ice conditions after the first of the year. Perch and splake fishing through the ice can be very fast. ◆

Services

National Forest Campgrounds:

tel: (877) 444-6777 or (800) 280-2267
Doctor Creek
Bowery
Mackinaw *(has showers)*

Lodging:

Lakeside Resort and Fish Lake Resort
tel: (435) 638-1000
Bowery Haven Resort
tel: (435) 638-1040

Joe's Valley Reservoir

T his pretty reservoir in the Manti-LaSal National Forest sits at about 7,000 feet elevation. Chub populations have increased in recent years. This prompted the DWR to change the size restriction on splake in hopes that these predators will be able to reduce chub numbers. There are some large splake living in the reservoir. A 15 lb. fish was caught and released in good condition from a sampling net.

Anglers looking for a change of pace from the reservoir will find some good stream fishing in Straight Canyon below the reservoir.

Fish Species

Rainbow, cutthroat, and splake trout.

Special Regulations

❏ Trout limit, 8.

❏ No more than 2 trout may be splake, all splake 15 to 20 inches must be immediately released.

Tactics

Anglers after splake will find good fishing in 20 to 30 feet of water just off the boat ramp. Other good areas for splake are at the south end of the reservoir and the point just south of the dam. Jigs and lures tipped with sucker meat or dead minnows are most productive. Kastmasters are a favorite lure of some Joe's Valley anglers.

The ice-fishing season is often the most productive time of year to catch splake.

How to Get There

From Orangeville, go west 18 miles on SR 29.

Accessibility

There is a Forest Service campground here, and a boat ramp.

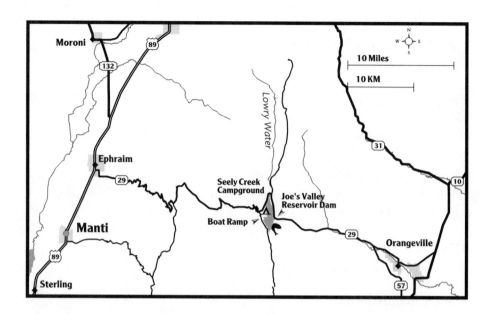

GPS Coordinates

Joe's Valley Reservoir Dam	N 39° 17′ 19″ W 111° 16′ 10″
Seely Creek Campground	N 39° 17′ 41″ W 111° 17′ 23″
Boat Ramp	N 39° 17′ 28″ W 111° 17′ 06″

Maps

USGS 1:24000   Joe's Valley Reservoir

Utah Atlas and Gazetteer   Page 38

When to Go

Ice-fishing season is normally from January through March, but this can vary a great deal (there was no safe ice in 1999). The road to the reservoir is open all year. ♦

Services

National Forest Campgrounds:
tel: (877) 444-6777 or (800) 280-2267
Indian Creek
Joe's Valley

Johnson Valley Reservoir   SEVIER COUNTY

 his attractive reservoir is in the Fish Lake National Forest. Sevenmile Creek, UM Creek, and the Fremont River are all close by and offer good stream fishing.

This reservoir suffers from large populations of non-game fish. Rotenone treatments to control rough fish are only effective here for a fairly short cycle of about 5 years before game fish decline again. Johnson Valley has not been treated for some time and it is being evaluated for future management options.

Fish Species

Rainbow, cutthroat, and brook trout; also yellow perch.

Special Regulations

General season, bag, and possession limits apply.

Tactics

Not a quality fishery at present. It is currently receiving some stocking of small rainbows.

How to Get There

From Richfield, go east 8.7 miles on SR 119, then south 23 miles on SR 24. Turn northeast onto SR 25 and go 14 miles to reach the reservoir.

Accessibility

There are several Forest Service campgrounds and a boat ramp. Fish Lake is just 3 miles to the southwest and there are lodgings, restaurants, and other facilities available there.

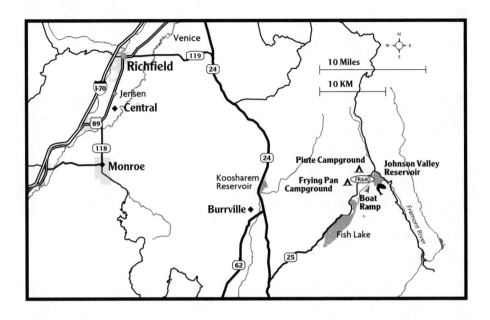

GPS Coordinates

Piute Campground	N 38° 37′ 17″ W 111° 38′ 53″
Frying Pan Campground	N 38° 36′ 33″ W 111° 40′ 45″
Boat Ramp	N 38° 36′ 39″ W 111° 37′ 55″

Maps

USGS 1:24000   Fish Lake

Utah Atlas and Gazetteer   Pages 27, 37

When to Go

Ice-fishing access is difficult and probably not worth the effort at present. Expect some fishing success in June after stocking takes place. ◆

Kolob Reservoir   WASHINGTON COUNTY

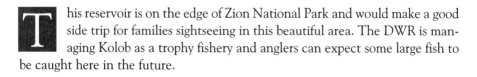

his reservoir is on the edge of Zion National Park and would make a good side trip for families sightseeing in this beautiful area. The DWR is managing Kolob as a trophy fishery and anglers can expect some large fish to be caught here in the future.

Fish Species

Rainbow, cutthroat, and brook trout. Rainbows are far more common.

Special Regulations

Kolob Reservoir (Washington County):

❑ Artificial flies and lures only.

❑ Only 2 trout over 18 inches.

❑ All trout less than 18 inches must be immediately released

Kolob Creek (Washington County) — Upstream from Kolob Reservoir:

❑ **Closed** January 1 through 6 a.m. on the second Saturday of July (July 10, 1999).

Tactics

Fly-fishers generally use float tubes and strip wooly buggers and damselfly nymphs for the sizeable trout.

Trolling small crankbaits and spinners is effective for anglers using small car-top boats.

Note: The artificial only regulation excludes lures with scented plastic bodies, and scents cannot be applied to lures.

How to Get There

From St. George, go 19 miles northeast on I-15 to exit 27. Take SR 17 south 6 miles, then SR 9 east for 6.3 miles. Turn onto Kolob Reservoir Road and travel north 25 miles to the reservoir.

Accessibility

There are no facilities, but there are roads around most of the reservoir. Small car-top boats, canoes, or float tubes provide the best access.

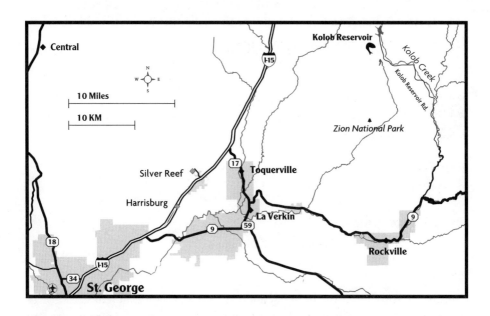

GPS Coordinates

Kolob Reservoir	N 37° 26′ 18″ W 113° 02′ 51″

Maps

USGS 1:24000   Kolob Reservoir

Utah Atlas and Gazetteer   Page 17

When to Go

Fall season is considered best, particularly the month of November. There is usually enough ice for ice-fishing, but the artificial only regulation still applies. ♦

Koosharem Reservoir   SEVIER COUNTY

his is another reservoir that suffers from a large population of rough fish. It has not been treated recently. Expect marginal fishing until treatment and restocking occur.

Fish Species

Rainbow trout.

Special Regulations

General season, bag, and possession limits apply.

Tactics

Still-fishing with bait is the most common approach. Power Bait and salmon eggs are popular. The combination of a worm and marshmallow is an effective way to present a bait just above the weeds on the bottom.

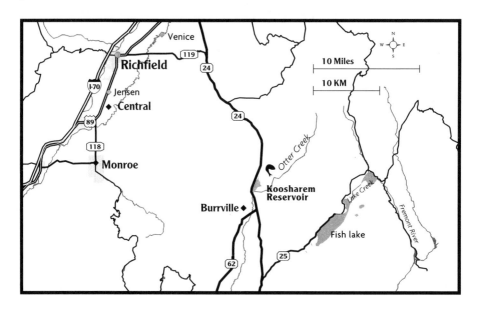

How to Get There

From Richfield, go east 8.7 miles on SR 119, then south on SR 24 for 14 miles.

Accessibility
There is access from SR 24. No facilities.

GPS Coordinates

Koosharem Reservoir	N 38° 35′ 59″ W 111° 50′ 31″

Maps

USGS 1:24000   Burrville

Utah Atlas and Gazetteer   Pages 27, 37

When to Go
Ice-off fishing can be good; otherwise the season is late May to October. Expect increased activity after stocking, which usually occurs at the end of May. ♦

A fish tale. (PHOTO: EMMETT HEATH / WESTERN RIVERS FLYFISHER)

Manning Meadows Reservoir   PIUTE COUNTY

his beautiful lake is managed to sustain Bonneville cutthroat trout. You can expect to catch some nice fish here — as long as you are willing to put them back.

Camping above the 9,700 foot level can be primitive. Be prepared for cold nights and quickly changing weather.

Fish Species

Bonneville cutthroat trout.

Special Regulations

Manning Meadows Reservoir, Spillway (cement structure on top of the dam and extending to the downstream toe of the dam) and Tributaries:

❏ Artificial flies and lures only.

❏ **Closed** January 1 through 6 a.m. on the second Saturday of July (July 10, 1999).

❏ Catch and release only. All trout caught must be immediately released.

Tactics

Wooly buggers in black and olive should produce good action. Dry flies also work well, especially when you cast in front of a cruising fish.

Spinners and small spoons also work, but since this is a catch-and-release fishery, consider replacing treble hooks with barbless single hooks.

How to Get There

From 300 South in Marysvale, go east to Old US 89. Turn south onto Thompsonville Road, go through Thompsonville, and continue to Monroe Mountain Road. Go east to Dry Creek Road and continue east from there.

Accessibility

The road eventually folllows around the west side of the reservoir.

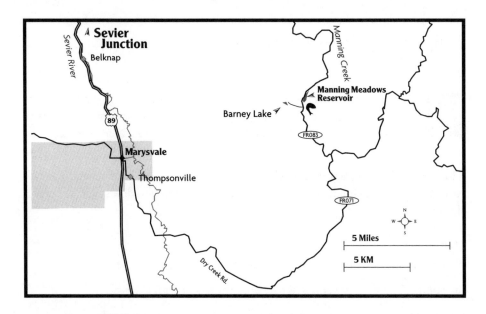

GPS Coordinates

Manning Meadows Reservoir	N 38° 29′ 19″ W 112° 04′ 13″

Maps

USGS 1:24000   Marysvale Peak

Utah Atlas and Gazetteer   Page 27

When to Go

Expect good fishing from ice-off until it freezes. The road should be accessible by
the first of July. ◆

Mill Meadow Reservoir   Sevier and Wayne County

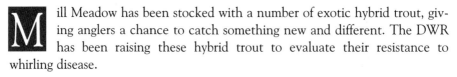 ill Meadow has been stocked with a number of exotic hybrid trout, giving anglers a chance to catch something new and different. The DWR has been raising these hybrid trout to evaluate their resistance to whirling disease.

This reservoir is known to harbor whirling disease. Please see the whirling disease chapter in this guide for precautions to ensure that you don't help to spread this disease.

Fish Species

This reservoir contains rainbows and the following hybrid trout:

☐ **Splake.** A cross between a female lake trout and a male brook trout.

☐ **Tiger.** A cross between a male brown trout and a female brook trout.

☐ **Brownbow.** A cross between a male brown and a female rainbow.

☐ **Brake.** A cross between a female lake trout and a male brown (these will no longer be stocked, but some may remain).

Special Regulations

General season, bag, and possession limits apply.

Tactics

Splake respond best to jigs and lures tipped with dead minnows or sucker meat. Tiger trout are aggressive and should respond well to spinners and streamer flies. Brownbows have some vision problems so are best pursued with bait.

How to Get There

From Loa, go northeast 11 miles on SR 72, then 3 miles northwest on the Gooseberry / Fremont Road to the reservoir.

Accessibility

There is road access to the east side of the reservoir, but no facilities. There is normally good access for ice-fishers.

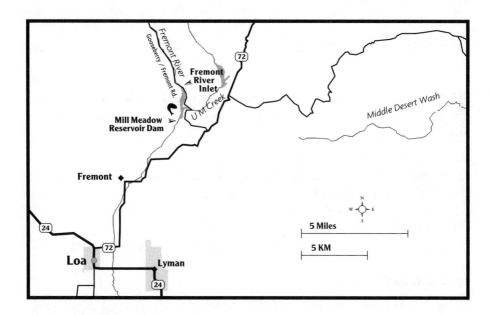

GPS Coordinates

Mill Meadow Reservoir Dam	N 38° 29' 41" W 111° 34' 07"
Fremont River Inlet	N 38° 31' 17" W 111° 34' 14"

Maps

USGS 1:24000   Lyman, Forsyth Reservoir

Utah Atlas and Gazetteer   Page 27

When to Go

Good ice-fishing from mid-January to February. Be sure to check ice. April though October should be consistent fishing. ◆

Millsite Reservoir

his scenic location is great for vacationing families. There is a beach and a nearby golf course. Areas are set aside for off-road vehicle and mountain bike use.

The reservoir is just a few miles below rugged and spectacular Ferron Canyon, where sheer sandstone walls rise 1,000 feet above the creek in places. There is good fishing for the adventurous in Ferron Creek.

Fish Species

Rainbows and cutthroat trout. Splake were added to the reservoir in 1998.

Special Regulations

General season, bag, and possession limits apply.

Tactics

Anglers pursue Millsite trout by trolling and bait-fishing. There is a lot of water-skiing and boating activity, so success is often better in the early mornings and late evenings.

How to Get There

From Ferron, go west on Ferron Canyon Road 4.7 miles.

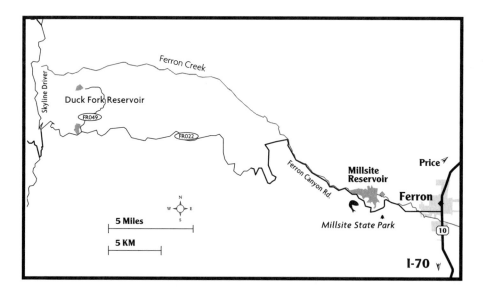

Accessibility

Millsite State Park has a boat ramp, camping, modern restrooms, and showers.

GPS Coordinates

Millsite State Park	N 39° 05′ 30″ W 111° 11′ 31″
Millsite Reservoir Dam	N 39° 05′ 60″ W 111° 11′ 19″

Maps

USGS 1:24000   Ferron

Utah Atlas and Gazetteer   Page 38

When to Go

May to October. ◆

Services

Camping:

Millsite State Park
Ferron
tel: (435) 384-2552
off-season: (435) 687-2491
Reservations: (800) 322-3770
(In Salt Lake City, call 322-3770)

Minersville Reservoir

T his reservoir sits in the middle of a treeless sage plain at 5,500 feet. It has rich water and excellent conditions for growing large trout. The DWR hopes that the trophy regulations will help this fishery produce the oversized rainbows and cutthroat it is capable of. This is probably one of the best places in the state for trout over 20 inches.

This reservoir is close to the Fishlake National Forest, so a trip to this area can include fishing at Piute Reservoir, Otter Creek, Koosharem Reservoir, and Fish Lake. Don't forget to check out the Beaver River below the dam as well.

This reservoir is known to harbor whirling disease. Please see the whirling disease section in the guide for precautions to ensure that you don't help to spread this disease.

Fish Species

Rainbow and cutthroat trout, also smallmouth bass.

Special Regulations

❐ Trout limit, 1 for all anglers; minimum size 20 inches.

❐ Artificial flies and lures only.

❐ Cement outlet channel between dam and spillway pond, approximately 55-feet long is **closed.**

Tactics

Float tubes and kick boats work very well here, allowing anglers to quietly cruise just off shore and fish back toward the edge where big trout like to cruise. Shore anglers and waders can also find success here by fishing parallel to the shoreline. Trollers will want to let out a lot of line so fish are not still spooked when the fly or lure comes by.

Wooly buggers are the most effective offering at Minersville Reservoir. Best colors are olive, brown, and black. Fish them on a sink tip fly line with short strips for best success. Floating lines with weighted flies or split shot can be good as well.

The many crayfish in this lake form the forage base for both trout and smallmouth bass. Flies and lures that imitate small crayfish are good choices. Fish these imitations right down on the bottom.

Using a spinning rod with a bubble and fly can be effective here. Fill the bubble with water and add shot to get it to sink. Make sure you cast past the water you want to fish. Full bubbles make quite a splash when they touch down.

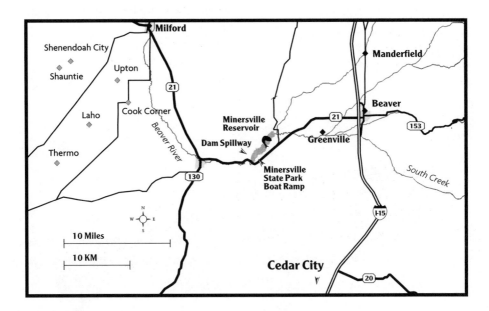

How to Get There
From Beaver, take SR 21 southwest 17 miles. Turn right for Minersville State Park.

Accessibility
The only facilities are at Minersville State Park, but there are dirt roads all around the lake where anglers can park.

GPS Coordinates

Minersville State Park Boat Ramp	N 38° 13' 07" W 112° 49' 44"
Dam Spillway	N 38° 13' 01" W 112° 50' 10"

Maps
USGS 1:24000   Minersville Reservoir, Adamsville

Utah Atlas and Gazetteer   Page 26

When to Go
This reservoir is a good choice from "ice out" until June. Fish move to deeper water in the dog days of summer. Activity picks up again in September and continues through November. ◆

Services

Camping:

Beaver Canyon Campground
1419 E Canyon Road
Beaver, UT 84713
tel: (435) 438-5654

Minersville State Park
Beaver
tel: (435) 438-5472
Reservations: (800) 322-3770
(In Salt Lake City, call 322-3770)

Rainbow trout. (ARTIST: MIKE STIDHAM)

Navajo Lake

 his high elevation (over 9,000 feet) reservoir is fairly shallow, so winterkill has been a problem. The DWR has worked to pipe spring water out into the lake to improve trout survival rates in wintertime.

The lake was also treated to remove rough fish in the fall of 1997, and so far no chubs have been discovered. It is hoped that they will not be reestablished, thus eliminating future competition with sport fish.

These improvements should mean that trout will be able to live longer and grow larger, improving sport and reducing stocking expense.

Fish Species

Rainbow and brook trout.

Special Regulations

General season, bag, and possession limits apply at Navajo Lake.

Note: Fishing from boats and float tubes is prohibited on Aspen-Mirror Lake and Duck Creek Springs Lake.

Tactics

This has been primarily a put-and-take fishery in the past and bait-fishing has been the most popular way to harvest fish.

How to Get There

From Cedar City, go southeast 26 miles on SR 14, then west 4 miles on Navajo Lake Road.

Accessibility

There are three campgrounds around Navajo Lake as well as a lodge, cabin rentals and a boat ramp. Aspen-Mirror Lake and Duck Creek Springs Lake are just east of Navajo Lake.

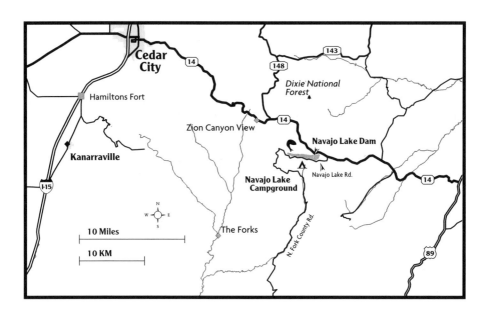

GPS Coordinates

Navajo Lake Campground	N 37° 31′ 15″ W 112° 47′ 21″
Navajo Lake Dam	N 37° 31′ 19″ W 112° 45′ 44″

Maps

USGS 1:24000   Navajo Lake

Utah Atlas and Gazetteer   Page 18

When to Go

Winter access is by snowmobile only, so not much ice-fishing is done here. The season starts late due to the high elevation, so plan trips from June to September. ◆

Newcastle Reservoir

his is a small, scenic lake near the town of Newcastle. There are lots of smallmouth bass. What they lack in size they make up for in numbers and fast action. Rainbows at Newcastle can grow to good size.

Golden shiners have been illegally introduced to this lake. Future productivity at Newcastle is threatened by this exotic species. As golden shiners grow in numbers, they will increasingly compete with game fish for food. Please observe regulations.

Fish Species

Rainbow trout and smallmouth bass.

Special Regulations

❏ Trout limit, 4.

Tactics

This is a great lake for float tubing. Fly-fishers can catch both bass and trout with wooly buggers and damselfly nymphs fished on sinking or sink tip lines. Jigs with plastic bodies are also effective.

Bait-fishing with Power Bait and worms is popular for the rainbows and will also produce some bass.

How to Get There

From St. George, go north 42 miles on SR 18, then turn east on Bench Road. Go 8.6 miles to the town of Newcastle. Turn southeast on West Pinto Road and go about 2.5 miles, then turn east to the reservoir.

Accessibility

A boat ramp and restrooms are available at Newcastle Reservoir.

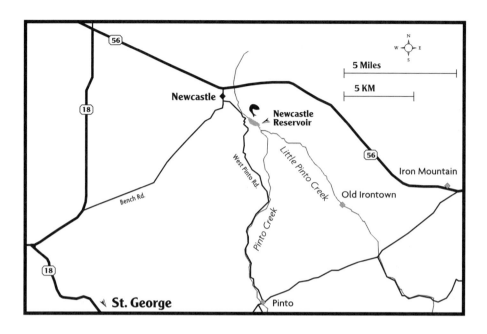

GPS Coordinates

Newcastle Reservoir	N 37° 39' 02" W 113° 31' 29"

Maps

USGS 1:24000   Newcastle

Utah Atlas and Gazetteer   Page 17

When to Go

The best fishing for rainbows is during fall and spring. There is enough ice for ice-fishing most winters, but the season is usually quite short. Spring and summer provide the best action for smallmouths. Recommended months are April through May. ◆

Ninemile Reservoir

SANPETE COUNTY

N inemile Reservoir was treated in the fall of 1998 to control rough fish populations. Fish will be stocked and available in 1999. Fish overwinter fairly well here. That fact combined with the recent rough fish removal, suggests that Ninemile should provide good fishing for the next several years, as long as there is no water shortage.

This reservoir has no facilities, but is only 4 miles from Palisade State Park at Palisade Reservoir.

Fish Species

Rainbow trout.

Special Regulations

General season, bag, and possession limits apply.

Tactics

Bait-fishing is the most common method of angling at this small reservoir. Fly-fishers casting wooly buggers from float tubes can expect good results.

How to Get There

From Gunnison, go west 8 miles on US 89.

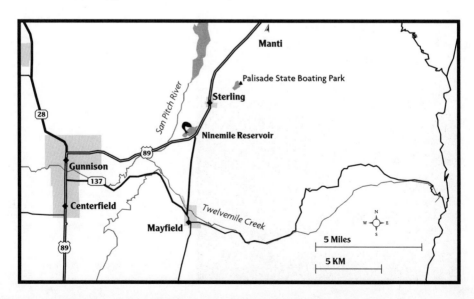

Accessibility

There are no facilities here, but there is an unimproved area where anglers launch boats.

The DWR is working with the water users in hopes of installing an improved boat launching area in the near future.

GPS Coordinates

Ninemile Reservoir	N 39° 10' 27" W 111° 42' 32"

Maps

USGS 1:24000   Sterling

Utah Atlas and Gazetteer   Page 37

When to Go

May to October. ◆

Services

Camping: tel: (435) 835-7275

Palisade State Park   Reservations: (800) 322-3770
Sterling   (In Salt Lake City, call 322-3770)

The best
time
to go
fishing
is
whenever
you can.

Common Sense

PHOTO: STEVE SCHMIDT / WESTERN
RIVERS FLYFISHER

Otter Creek Reservoir

PIUTE COUNTY

T his 3,000-acre reservoir is located at 6,300 feet. It has a constant water supply and does not suffer from extreme drawdowns like Piute Reservoir downstream. Its shallow waters grow moss beds that support much of the aquatic life that trout feed upon and then grow large. This lake has produced its share of double-digit rainbows in the past.

Otter Creek currently has an overlarge population of Utah Chubs and trout fishing has suffered as a result. The DWR plans to treat this reservoir with rotenone as soon as water levels are low enough, perhaps the fall of 1999.

Campers here are well based to fish the Sevier River and its tributaries, as well as Koosharem Reservoir, Fish Lake, and Panguitch Lake.

This reservoir is known to harbor whirling disease. Please see the whirling disease section in the guide for precautions to ensure that you don't help to spread this disease.

This lake contains Eurasian Watermilfoil. Carefully clean all vegetation from boats, trailers and other fishing equipment.

Fish Species
Rainbow, cutthroat, and brown trout.

Special Regulations
Otter Creek Reservoir (and spillway ponds immediately downstream from the dam):

☐ Trout limit, 6.

Otter Creek stream (from Otter Creek Reservoir upstream to the Angle Diversion):

☐ Trout limit, 6.

☐ **Closed** January 1 through May 21.

Tactics
Fly-fishers commonly fish from float tubes or wade. Olive wooly buggers are the pattern of choice. Muddlers, damselfly nymphs, and other favorite still-water flies have their place as well. The pond below the spillway and the pool just below the first bridge can be very kind to fly-fishers. Try large olive and orange scuds. Some surprisingly big rainbows live here.

Trollers do very well in this reservoir. Needlefish, triple teasers, and Flatfish are favorite lures. July and August will find trout in the deeper water and fishing can be very good as long as water temperatures stay in the mid-60s.

Bait-fishers like night crawlers and Power Bait. Larger fish can often be caught on dead minnows. Baits with garlic flavoring can be especially effective at times. The technique of using a marshmallow to float a worm just off the bottom and above the moss is especially effective here.

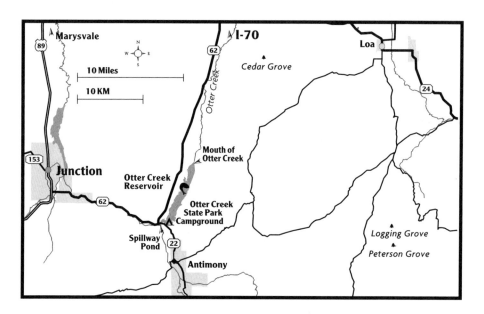

How to Get There

From the Salt Lake area, take I-15 south to I-70. Go east on I-70 to Sevier Junction and take Exit 23. Get on US 89 south through Marysvale and Junction, then turn left onto SR 62. Another 14 miles brings you to the state park at Otter Creek Reservoir.

Accessibility

There is good access to the shoreline here, as the lake is mostly bordered by BLM lands. The north end of the lake by the inlet is private. Get permission before crossing private property. The state park at the south end of the lake has good facilities, including a boat ramp and dock. There is good public access along the west side of the reservoir.

GPS Coordinates

Otter Creek State Park Campground	N 38° 09' 58" W 112° 00' 54"
Spillway Pond	N 38° 10' 09" W 112° 01' 21"
Mouth of Otter Creek	N 38° 14' 57" W 111° 57' 55"

Maps

USGS 1:24000   Angle, Phonolite Hill

Utah Atlas and Gazetteer   Page 27

When to Go

This reservoir can be good at "ice out" especially for fly-fishers who are float tubing near the inlet. Slow strips will help while the water remains cold.

Note: The DWR stocked 200,000 rainbows about 7 inches long at the end of September 1998. This should make for some fast spring fishing in 1999, both for these smaller fish and the larger trout, who have to compete with them for food.

Trollers have more success after the water warms up somewhat in May and fish become more active. July and August can be good here as the cool waters from Koosharem Reservoir and the high elevation keep this lake fishing while other bodies of water are suffering from summer doldrums.

Bait-fishing is good throughout the year, and is especially effective when runoff clouds the water, hindering success of other fishing methods. ◆

Services

Camping:

Otter Creek State Park
Antimony
tel: (435) 624-3268
Reservations: (800) 322-3770
(In Salt Lake City, call 322-3770)

Palisade Reservoir   SANPETE COUNTY

T his 70-acre reservoir and recreational facility is only two hours south of Provo and makes for a good family getaway. Gunnison and Ninemile Reservoirs are close by and offer some variety for anglers who spend several days here.

Fish Species

Rainbow and cutthroat trout.

Special Regulations

Fishing from a boat with a motor of any kind is prohibited on Palisade Reservoir.

In fact, no motors of any type are allowed on this reservoir.

Tactics

The regulation prohibiting motors makes this a particularly peaceful reservoir, especially in the early mornings and late evenings.

Float tubes are effective on this small water. Fly-fishers find success with wooly buggers and damselfly nymphs under the surface.

How to Get There

From Gunnison, go northeast 9 miles on US 89, then east 1.5 miles on Palisade Road. Turn north and go 1 mile to Palisade State Park.

Accessibility

Palisade State Park has a beach area, camping, and modern restrooms with showers. Canoe and paddle boat rentals are available and there is a small boat launch area. It is adjacent to an 18-hole golf course with practice range and pro shop.

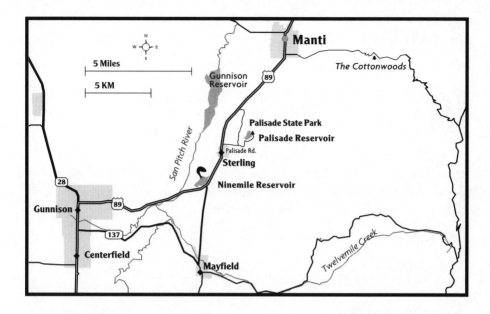

GPS Coordinates

Palisade State Park	N 39° 12′ 24″ W 111° 39′ 53″

Maps

USGS 1:24000   Sterling

Utah Atlas and Gazetteer   Page 37

When to Go

May to October. ♦

Services

Camping:

Palisade State Park
Sterling
tel: (435) 835-7275
Reservations: (800) 322-3770
(In Salt Lake City, call 322-3770)

Panguitch Lake
GARFIELD COUNTY

anguitch is a Piute word meaning "big fish." There are some big browns taken here from time to time. Most fish are medium-sized, fat, healthy rainbows.

Brian Head Ski Resort and Cedar Breaks National Monument offer a variety of recreational opportunities amidst stunning vistas. Nearby quality fishing waters include Panguitch Creek, the West Fork of the Sevier, and Mammoth Creek. Vacationing anglers can find plenty of water to occupy their time.

Fish Species

Rainbow, cutthroat, brown and brook trout are all found here. The DWR stocked 200,000 rainbow trout into the lake in 1998.

Special Regulations

Panguitch Lake:

❏ Trout limit, 6.

Panguitch Lake Tributaries (Garfield County) — excluding Blue Springs Creek upstream from Bunker Creek Road Bridge; bridge is approximately 1 mile upstream from Panguitch Lake; and excluding Clear Creek upstream from the Panguitch Lake North Shore Highway, located approximately 0.25 miles upstream from Panguitch Lake:

❏ Trout limit, 6.

❏ **Closed** January 1 through May 21.

Tactics

Anglers using float tubes do quite well at Panguitch Lake, although few people seem to try this approach. Casting wooly buggers and retrieving them slowly can produce large numbers of rainbows in the 12-14 inch range.

Trollers fishing the lake most often use pop gear and a worm, which is quite effective.

Most anglers use Power Bait, salmon eggs and worms. Try using a marshmallow to float a worm just off the bottom and above the moss.

Ice-fishers tempt these trout with cheese, Power Bait, and mealworms.

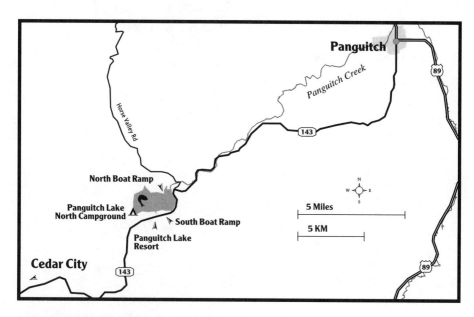

How to Get There

From Panguitch, go southwest 26.5 miles on SR 143.

Accessibility

There are two public boat ramps on the lake, with boat rentals available at Beaver Dam Lodge. Blue Springs Lodge will take ice-fishers out on the lake by snow-mobile and drill holes for them.

GPS Coordinates

Panguitch Lake North Campground	N 37° 42' 08" W 112° 39' 19"
Panguitch Lake Resort	N 37° 42' 29" W 112° 38' 27"
South Boat Ramp	N 37° 42' 34" W 112° 38' 09"
North Boat Ramp	N 37° 43' 17" W 112° 37' 56"

Maps

USGS 1:24000   Panguitch Lake, Haycock Mountain

Utah Atlas and Gazetteer   Page 18

When to Go

You can expect good fishing from ice-off until the lake freezes again in December. This is probably one of the best ice-fishing lakes in the state. Ice is usually stable by the end of December, and lasts until March and in some years April. ♦

Services

National Forest Campgrounds:

tel: (877) 444-6777
or (800) 280-2267
Panguitch Lake North
Panguitch Lake South

Lodging:

Beaver Dam Lodge
225 North Shore Road
P.O. Box 859
Panguitch, UT 84759
tel: (435) 676-8839 / (800) 262-9181
fax: (435) 676-8068
*(Lodging, food and fishing
gear on the lake)*

Blue Spring Lodge
120 W SR 143
P.O. Box 147
Panguitch, UT 84759
tel: (435) 676-2277
(800) 987-5634
www.bluespringslodge.com

Deer Trail Lodge & All Seasons Resort
Clear Creek Canyon
P.O. Box 647
Panguitch, UT 84759
tel and fax: (435) 676-2211

Panguitch Lake Resort
791 S Lake Shore Drive
P.O. Box 567
Panguitch, UT 84579
tel: (435) 676-2657

Early morning float tubing. (PHOTO: EMMETT HEATH / WESTERN RIVERS FLYFISHER)

Pine Lake

GARFIELD COUNTY

his pretty lake is located in the ponderosa pine stands of the Dixie National Forest about 25 mile northeast of Bryce Canyon National Park. It is a popular camping destination for local residents.

Pine Lake has suffered from winterkill in the past and the DWR installed pipes to carry spring water out into the lake to improve winter survival. The 1998 fishing season was good, and that will hopefully continue.

Fish Species

Rainbow, brook and cutthroat trout.

Special Regulations

Pine Lake Inflow (Garfield County) — Inflow including newly constructed spawning channel:

❑ Closed.

Tactics

Bait-fishing is effective here, particularly after mid-June when stocking occurs.

How to Get There

From Panguitch, go south 7 miles on US 89, then east 14 miles on SR 12. Turn northeast onto SR 22 and travel 11 miles. Turn east onto Pine Lake Road and go 4.7 miles, then turn south to the lake.

Accessibility

There is a Forest Service campground at Pine Lake and a boat ramp.

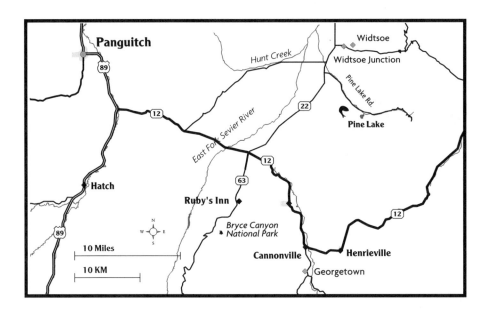

GPS Coordinates

Pine Lake	N 37° 44' 25" W 111° 57' 21"

Maps

USGS 1:24000   Pine Lake

Utah Atlas and Gazetteer   Page 19

When to Go

June to October. ♦

Piute Reservoir

T his 3,300-acre lake is subject to severe drawdowns for irrigation in dry years. At this time, there is no regulation providing for a conservation pool in this reservoir. Irrigation companies own all the water. The summer of 1996 saw extremely low water levels here.

Piute grows big rainbow and cutthroat trout so long as water levels are maintained. The cyclic nature of this fishery keeps it from getting much pressure. One can often fish in solitude. The main situation anglers will have to contend with here is the wind. Fishing seems to drop off when really big winds blow, and it does so fairly often.

Look for some good numbers of fish in the pool below the dam, particularly in late fall.

This is a good destination for anglers who don't like to be crowded. Just make sure that water levels have been sufficient to maintain fish stocks. Piute is close to Otter Creek, so the two waters can be combined in one trip and may include the Sevier River as well.

Fish Species

Rainbow, cutthroat, and brown trout; smallmouth bass.

Special Regulations

❏ Trout limit, 6.

Tactics

Float tubing works great here when the wind doesn't blow. Favorite fly patterns are wooly buggers, leeches, and cranefly larva. Springtime is preferred. You can look for fish in the coves along the southwest edge of the reservoir.

Spin-fishers find success with jigs on the bottom, especially soon after "ice out." Casting spinners and trolling needlefish or pop gear with a night crawler are effective.

Favorite baits will be the same as in Otter Creek Reservoir just upstream: night crawlers and Power Bait. Dead minnows and baits with garlic flavoring can also perform well.

How to Get There

From the Salt Lake area, take I-15 south to I-70. Go east on I-70 to Sevier Junction and take Exit 23. Take US 89 south through Marysvale. The left turn to the state park is 8.5 miles farther south of Marysvale and 6.5 miles north of Junction.

Accessibility

Piute Lake State Park (tel: 435-624-3268) has the only facilities on the lake and they are primitive. There is a concrete boat ramp. There is some access on dirt roads around the lake. You may also drive down to the pool below the dam.

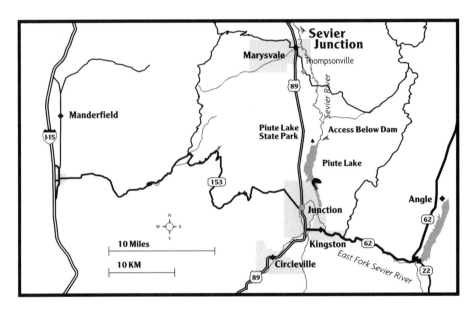

GPS Coordinates

Piute Lake State Park	N 38° 19′ 11″ W 112° 11′ 48″
Access Below Dam	N 38° 19′ 38″ W 112° 11′ 18″

Maps

USGS 1:24000   Piute Reservoir, Junction

Utah Atlas and Gazetteer   Page 26

When to Go

The best time of year here is ice-off, with good fishing as long as there is enough water and the wind isn't blowing. This is a popular area for deer hunting; consequently, the lake receives little pressure in the fall. ◆

Puffer Lake

 his small lake sits in the Tushar Mountains east of Beaver, at an elevation of 9,600 feet. Elk Meadows Ski Resort is close by. Over-winter survival is poor, so fishing is mainly for stocked trout.

There is good stream fishing in the Beaver River and its tributaries, Cottonwood Creek, and Bullion Creek.

Fish Species

Rainbow and brook trout.

Special Regulations

General season, bag, and possession limits apply.

Tactics

Most anglers at Puffer Lake use bait. Small spinners are also productive.

How to Get There

From Beaver, go east 22 miles on SR 153, then turn onto FR 129 to access the lake.

Accessibility

There are campgrounds, a café, and a lodge. Elk Meadows Ski Resort (tel: 888-881-7669) is about 7 miles away, and is open during the summer as well.

GPS Coordinates

Puffer Lake	N 38° 19' 01" W 112° 21' 45"
Elk Meadows Ski Resort	N 38° 19' 16" W 112° 22' 59"

Maps

USGS 1:24000   Delano Peak.

Utah Atlas and Gazetteer   Page 26

When to Go

Winter access is by snowmobile only. The open-water season is from May through October. ◆

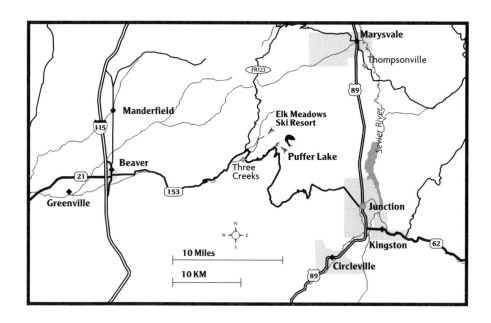

Bonneville cutthroat trout. (ARTIST: MIKE STIDHAM)

Tropic Reservoir

T ropic Reservoir is right at the edge of Bryce Canyon National Park. The erosion processes of wind and water have carved a variety of shapes called "hoodoos" from the vividly colored rocks. Iron oxides and manganese create reds, yellows, purples and lavender. The low-angled sunlight at dusk can create a visual spectacle you will not soon forget.

Water management in this reservoir is unusual in that it is often filled and drained several times during the winter. Consequently, few if any fish can survive. It is normally stocked by the end of May.

The East Fork of the Sevier feeds the reservoir and contains brook trout and cutthroat trout. A number of tributary streams in this area are also fishable.

Fish Species

Rainbow and cutthroat trout.

Special Regulations

General season, bag, and possession limits apply.

Tactics

Fishing is mainly for stocked rainbows. Bait-fishing with worms, salmon eggs or commercially prepared trout baits is the most common practice.

How to Get There

From Panguitch, go south on US 89 to SR 12. Turn east on SR 12 and travel 11 miles to East Fork Road (FR 087), turning south. You will reach Tropic Reservoir in about 8 miles.

Accessibility

There is a Forest Service campground here. It is only 12 miles from the reservoir to Best Western Ruby's Inn (435) 834-5341 (reservations: 800-528-1234), where anglers can find meals, lodgings, and a variety of recreational activities.

460

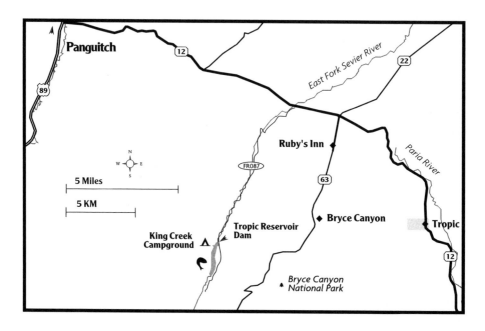

GPS Coordinates

Tropic Reservoir Dam	N 37° 36′ 48″ W 112° 15′ 00″
King Creek Campground	N 37° 36′ 34″ W 112° 15′ 35″

Maps

USGS 1:24000   Bryce Point, Tropic Reservoir

Utah Atlas and Gazetteer   Page 18

When to Go

May to October. ♦

Wide Hollow Reservoir GARFIELD COUNTY

 ust outside of the town of Escalante, the state park has interesting displays of petrified wood and dinosaurs which will interest young and old alike.

Pine Creek and North Creek offer nearby solitude for anglers seeking stream fishng in rugged canyons. The beautiful waterfalls of Calf Creek Recreation Area are a 25 minute drive to the east.

There is no mandated conservation pool here, so water levels can drop very low by late summer. There are currently some concerns about the safety of the dam at Wide Hollow Reservoir and it is possible that it may be drained in the near future.

Fish Species

Rainbow trout.

Special Regulations

General season, bag, and possession limits apply.

Tactics

This is primarily a put-and-take fishery for rainbows that are stocked here in February and March. Most fishers employ baits such as worms, salmon eggs, and Power Bait.

How to Get There

From Escalante, go west 1.5 miles on SR 12, then north to the reservoir.

Accessibility

Escalante State Park has camping, modern restrooms with showers, and natural history interpretive trails.

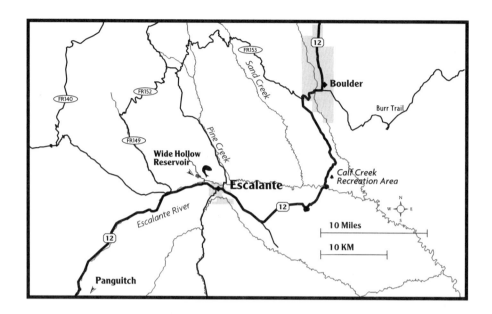

GPS Coordinates

Wide Hollow Reservoir	N 37° 47' 14" W 111° 38' 11"

Maps

USGS 1:24000   Wide Hollow Reservoir

Utah Atlas and Gazetteer   Page 19

When to Go

Best fishing is in March and April. Both water levels and trout numbers decline through the summer and conditions can be poor by the end of August. ♦

Services

Camping:

Escalante State Park
tel: (435) 826-4466
Reservations: (800) 322-3770
(In Salt Lake City, call 322-3770)

D.M.A.D. Reservoir

T his reservoir is a sport-fish smorgasbord with six different species. You never know what might decide to bite next. This reservoir is subject to large fluctuations in water level, which can have a profound effect on angling. Fishing success varies from year to year. If you experience poor angling here, Gunnison Bend Reservoir is only about 10 miles away. It has a similar mix of fish species, and usually provides faster fishing.

You might consider calling the DWR's Central Region office in Springville (tel: 801-489-5678) and check conditions before traveling here.

Fish Species

Channel catfish, white bass, bluegill, crappie, yellow perch, and walleye.

Special Regulations

General season, bag, and possession limits apply.

D.M.A.D. Reservoir is open to the use of two poles by anglers purchasing a second pole permit for $10.00 along with their regular fishing or combination license (see current proclamation).

Tactics

Bait-fishing with worms or dead minnows will likely produce the most success for the white bass, bluegill, crappie, and yellow perch.

Conventional bass tactics are recommended, and should prove effective when good numbers of bass are present in the reservoir.

The pool in the Sevier River below the spillway of D.M.A.D. Reservoir often provides the best fishing.

How to Get There

From Delta, go 5.3 miles northeast on US 6, then 2 miles east to the reservoir.

Accessibility

No facilities.

GPS Coordinates

D.M.A.D. Reservoir Dam	N 39° 23′ 45″ W 112° 29′ 01″
Mouth of Sevier River to D.M.A.D.	N 39° 25′ 36″ W 112° 26′ 46″

Maps

USGS 1:24000   Strong

Utah Atlas and Gazetteer   Pages 36, 44

When to Go

Best fishing is from March through September, but if the reservoir experiences a severe drawdown, fishing success can decline much earlier in the year. ♦

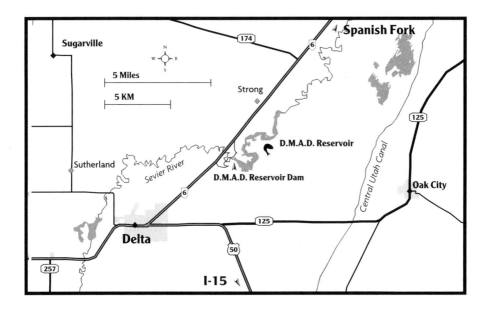

Gunlock Reservoir   WASHINGTON COUNTY

his 240-acre warmwater fishery is a popular spot for boating and water sports, located just 15 miles from St George. It is a good choice for early season bass fishing when northern Utah waters are still cold.

Fish Species

Largemouth bass, black crappie, bluegill, green sunfish, and channel catfish.

Special Regulations

❏ Bass limit, 6; 4 under 10 inches and 2 over 20 inches.

Gunlock Reservoir is open to the use of two poles by anglers that purchase a second pole permit for $10.00 along with their regular fishing or combination license (see regulations).

Tactics

Although this reservoir does occasionally produce some large bass, it has a reputation for tough fishing. Try your favorite bass techniques, particularly during the pre-spawn period in February and early March when fish are still deep. Bass will move into the shallows in March.

Channel catfish provide good action here. Try worms or dead minnows on a slip sinker rig.

How to Get There

From St. George, go north of town 1 mile on SR 18. Then west on Sunset Blvd 0.5 miles to Santa Clara Drive, then go west 4 miles to old US 191. When the road forks past the town of Shivwits, go to the north and about 12 miles to the reservoir.

Accessibility

There is a state park at Gunlock Reservoir with camping and a boat ramp.

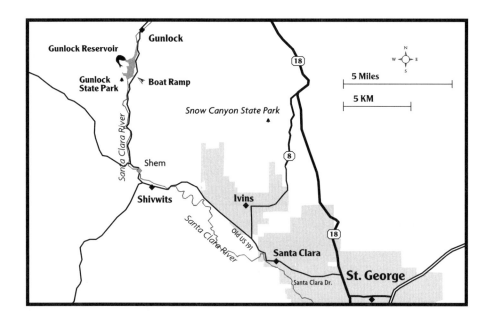

GPS Coordinates

Gunlock State Park	N 37° 15' 13" W 113° 47' 01"
Boat Ramp	N 37° 15' 21" W 113° 46' 20"

Maps

USGS 1:24000   Gunlock, Shivwits

Utah Atlas and Gazetteer   Page 16

When to Go

Best bass-fishing is usually from February through the end of March. Try to get on the water early or stay late to avoid water sports activity. ♦

Services

Camping:

Gunlock State Park
St. George
tel: (435) 628-2255
Reservations:(800) 322-3770
(In Salt Lake City, call 322-3770)

Gunnison Bend Reservoir   MILLARD COUNTY

A great number of people engage in water sports in this reservoir. If you're looking for solitude, this might not be a good choice. The water levels are more consistent here than at nearby D.M.A.D. Reservoir; consequently, Gunnison Bend is considered a better fishery. Still, angler success can vary a great deal from year to year.

Fish Species

Channel catfish, white bass, bluegill, crappie, yellow perch, and walleye.

Special Regulations

General season, bag, and possession limits apply.

Gunnison Bend Reservoir is open to the use of two poles by anglers purchasing a second pole permit for $10.00 along with their regular fishing or combination license (see current proclamation).

Tactics

Bait-fishing with worms or dead minnows will likely produce the most success for the white bass, bluegill, crappie, and yellow perch.

Conventional bass tactics are recommended, and should prove effective when good numbers of bass are present in the reservoir.

How to Get There

Gunnison Reservoir lies just west of the town of Delta. Go west 2 miles on US 6 to 1000 South Street. Go west 0.5 miles to 2000 West Street and follow it north to the reservoir.

Accessibility

There is a boat ramp.

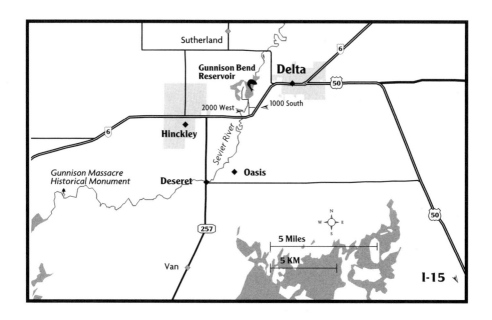

GPS Coordinates

Gunnison Bend Reservoir	N 39° 21' 02", W 112° 36' 59"

Maps

USGS 1:24000   Delta, Hinckley

Utah Atlas and Gazetteer   Page 36

When to Go

Best fishing is from March through September. Late season fishing can be adversely affected by low water. ♦

Gunnison Reservoir

his reservoir has no mandated conservation pool so it can be completely drained in dry years. There are no facilities, but it is only 3 miles from Palisade State Park at Palisade Reservoir.

Gunnison was very productive in the early 1990s, but was drained in 1992. It has been restocked and is making a comeback. Anglers should check water conditions before making a trip.

Fish Species

Largemouth bass, bluegill, yellow perch, and channel catfish.

Special Regulations

Dead yellow perch may be used as bait.

Tactics

Use your favorite bass tactics or try worms or dead minnows on a slip-sinker rig for channel catfish.

How to Get There

From Gunnison, go northeast 9 miles on US 89, then turn west and go 1 mile to the reservoir. It is just 3 miles west of Palisade Reservoir.

Accessibility

There is an unimproved area where anglers launch boats on the west side of the reservoir. There are no other facilities.

GPS Coordinates

Gunnison Reservoir Dam	N 39° 12' 21" W 111° 42' 34"

Maps

USGS 1:24000   Sterling, Manti

Utah Atlas and Gazetteer   Page 37

When to Go

April through October. ♦

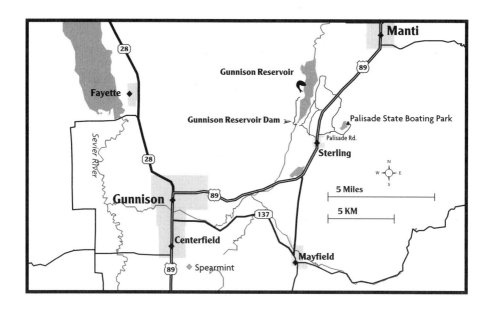

Bluegill. (ARTIST: MIKE STIDHAM)

Huntington North Reservoir   EMERY COUNTY

T his is a great recreation area just outside the town of Huntington, at 5,800 feet. Trout are fairly new to this reservoir, as they were first stocked in the fall of 1997. These coldwater fish have trouble surviving the warmer months, so the fishery is mainly for stocked rainbows of catchable size.

Fish Species

Rainbow and brown trout, largemouth bass, and bluegill.

Special Regulations

❏ Largemouth bass limit, 2.

❏ All bass over 12 inches must be immediately released.

Huntington North Reservoir is open to the use of two poles by anglers that purchase a second pole permit for $10.00 along with their regular fishing or combination license (see regulations).

Tactics

There are some large bass in Huntington North, but there is not much good bass habitat. Jigs, crankbaits, and spinnerbaits are all effective lures once you succeed in locating bass.

Trout anglers usually employ still-fishing techniques using bait.

How to Get There

From Huntington, go northeast on SR 10 about 2 miles.

Accessibility

Huntington State Park has camping, modern restrooms, showers, and a boat launching area.

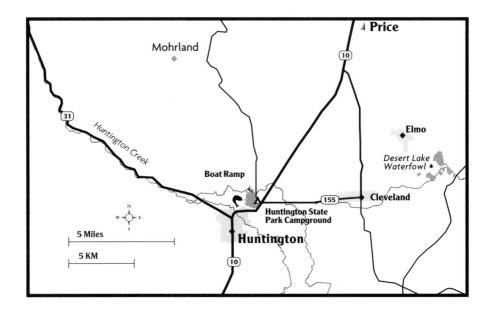

GPS Coordinates

Huntington State Park Campground	N 39° 20' 45" W 110° 56' 28"
Boat Ramp	N 39° 20' 47" W 110° 56' 37"

Maps

USGS 1:24000   Huntington

Utah Atlas and Gazetteer   Page 38

When to Go

This is primarily a warmwater lake, so trout fishing is only good during the colder months from September to May. Bass and bluegill fishing is best in the spring during the spawning period and continues fair until the fall. ◆

Services

Camping:

Huntington State Park
tel: (435) 687-2491
Reservations: (800) 322-3770
(In Salt Lake City 322-3770)

Lake Powell

KANE, SAN JUAN, AND GARFIELD COUNTIES

L ake Powell, named after Major John Wesley Powell, is the second largest man-made reservoir in the world, flooding the narrow canyons of the Colorado River and its tributaries. It is 186 miles long with over 1,800 miles of shoreline, and yet it has only four main access points for vehicles. It is a boater's paradise with miles and miles of flooded canyons to explore and in which to seek solitude. Lake Powell is also home to Rainbow Bridge, the largest natural bridge in the world.

It is a place of paradox and contrast. Water in the desert. It is a visual paradise with its unusual blending of orange, buff, and pink canyon walls rising out of the cool, clear lake. Fish are swimming where Anasazi carried water to their precious crops two centuries before.

Fish Species

Channel catfish, largemouth, smallmouth, and striped bass (stripers), bluegill, green sunfish, crappie, and walleye.

Special Regulations

The southwestern end of Lake Powell is in Arizona, and the following regulations regarding licensing should be noted: (Check the section on Interstate Waters in your Utah fishing proclamation.)

☐ The purchase of a reciprocal fishing stamp allows a person to fish across state boundaries of interstate waters.

☐ Any person qualifying as an Arizona resident having in their possession a valid resident Arizona fishing license and a Utah reciprocal fishing stamp for Lake Powell can fish within the Utah boundaries of Lake Powell.

☐ Anglers are subject to the laws and rules of the state in which they are fishing.

☐ Only one bag limit may be taken and held in possession even if licensed in both states.

For Utah waters of Lake Powell:

☐ Chumming with dead anchovies only is allowed for taking striped bass.

☐ Crappie limit, 20.

☐ Channel catfish limit, 25.

☐ Striped bass, no limit.

❏ Walleye limit, 10.

❏ Unlicensed anglers 13 years of age or younger may take a full bag and possession limit.

Lake Powell is open to the use of two poles by anglers that purchase a second pole
permit for $10.00 along with their regular fishing or combination license (see reg-
ulations).

Note: Use of live crayfish for bait is legal only on the water where the crayfish is
captured. It is unlawful to transport live crayfish away from the water where
captured.

Entrance Fees

Following is a list of fees to enter Glen Canyon National Recreation Area:

One or two vehicles registered to same owner:

1 to 7 days	$ 5.00
Annual Pass	$15.00

One pedestrian or cyclist:

1 to 7 days	$ 3.00
Annual Pass	$15.00

Golden Age or Access pass: 50% discount

Navajo Lands

Much of the south shore of Lake Powell forms the northern border of the Navajo
Indian Reservation. Navajo lands are mostly accessible without any permits or
problems. It is necessary to cross the reservation to get to the upper San Juan
Arm. Please remember that you are a visitor and respect their lands.

Once at the lake the land belongs to the National Park Service to an elevation
20 feet above the high water mark of 3700 feet (3720 feet).

Tactics

The most popular method for catching striped bass is bait-fishing with cut dead
anchovies. These are easy to find at bait and tackle stores in the area. Fishers who
prefer artificials use crankbaits and spoons. Threadfin shad are the main forage
fish in the lake, so lures that resemble them are most effective. Jigs are also popular, with white being the best color. Those who use fish-finders are able to max-
imize their catch by locating fish quickly. A variety of trolling methods can prove
effective.

Stripers will chase baitfish and create "boils" on the surface, especially in spring

*The glory days of
Lake Powell fishing.*
(PHOTO: COURTESY UTAH
OUTDOORS)

and fall. You can sometimes find these areas by observing birds and motoring within casting range. If you can get a plug or bait into the action, you are almost guaranteed a strike.

Chumming with anchovies is allowed to help anglers catch more striped bass. This is to control striped bass populations, which are in danger of overpopulating and destroying their forage base of threadfin shad. Chop or grind anchovies into small pieces and scatter them in the area where you are fishing. If there are striped bass around, you should get action in 15 to 20 minutes. If not, move on and try another location. Look for fish along prominent points, submerged islands, and steep canyon walls in deep water.

Shad reproduction in 1997 and 1998 was moderate and striped bass numbers are high. Consequently, stripers are running out of food and are in danger of a population collapse. You should keep and utilize any striped bass caught to help preserve this great fishery.

Favorite baits for largemouth and smallmouth bass are crayfish and water dogs, when available. Present them to fish at the edge of deep water around boulders and rock piles. Crankbaits, spinnerbaits, and jigs with soft plastic bodies or marabou are all effective on bass in Lake Powell. Lures that represent the threadfin shad that bass feed on are especially good. Bass spawn here from mid-April to mid-May. Look for fish in the deep water adjacent to spawning areas early in the month. Warm weather will trigger them to come up into shallows to spawn.

There is a wide array of technical gear available to the modern bass angler, such as fish-finders, depth sounders, electric trolling motors, temperature gauges, and pH meters. Fishers who become competent with this equipment will catch more fish.

Bluegills and sunfish are often ignored in favor of larger fish, but they can provide great sport, especially for the younger angler. These colorful and tasty fish are easily caught with live worms under a bobber. Small plastic baits can also work well. Fly-fishers can use poppers and dry flies as well as wooly buggers and damselfly nymphs under the surface. These fish have small mouths, so size offerings accordingly. Look for these fish in shallow bays with cover and moss. During spawning in the spring, one can find heavy concentrations of fish that can be caught on nearly every cast.

Crappie are difficult to find. Your best chance is in April. You can't fish live minnows here as in other crappie hotspots across the country. Small soft plastic minnow bodies on jigs are a good bet, as are the smallest sized crankbaits.

The best approaches for walleye are bottom bouncing or spinner rigs with live

GPS Coordinates

Bull Frog Marina	N 37° 30' 58" W 110° 43' 40"
Halls Crossing Marina	N 37° 27' 48" W 110° 42' 56"
Hite Marina	N 37° 51' 46" W 110° 23' 42"

Maps

USGS 1:24000	Bowdie Canyon West, Sewing Machine, Copper Point, Hite North, Hite South, Good Hope Bay, Ticaboo Mesa, Knowles Canyon, Bullfrog, Halls Crossing, Alcove Canyon, The Rincon, Deep Canyon North, Wilson Creek, Nasja Mesa, Davis Gulch, Stevens Canyon South, Rainbow Bridge, Cathedral Canyon, Gregory Butte, Mazuki Point, Sit Down Bench, Gunsight Butte, Warm Creek Bay, Lone Rock
Utah Atlas and Gazetteer	Pages 19, 20, 21,29

night crawlers or trolling crankbaits around main lake points and along the vertical walls. The large population of striped bass has really reduced the population of threadfin shad, and walleyes are hungry. The best walleye fishing is along the main channel in May and June and good fishing can start as early as April. Most walleyes will be 15 to 20 inches, although some are larger.

Don't forget catfish, especially after dark. They can usually be found on shallow sandy areas during summer. Use stinkbaits or anchovies.

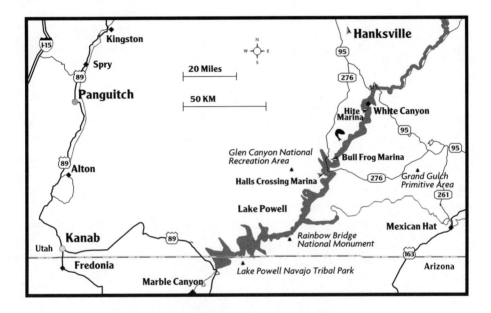

How to Get There

From Salt Lake City, take I-15 south 40 miles to US 6 at Spanish Fork and travel southeast 128 miles to I-70 near Green River. Go east on I-70 for 8.8 miles to SR 24, then go south 44 miles to Hanksville. From here take SR 95 south. Either go 47 miles southeast to Hite Marina (just across the lake on 95) or turn left onto SR 276 and proceed southwest to Bullfrog Marina. There is a ferry here that can take you to Halls Crossing on the other side of the lake.

Accessibility

Most of the shoreline is inaccessible with only four main access points, three of them in Utah. There are full-service marinas and launch ramps at these access sites: Bullfrog, Hall's Crossing, and Hite. Wahweap Marina can be found on the Arizona side of the lake. Dangling Rope Marina in the middle provides gas and services for boaters traveling the lake, but can only be reached by water. Dirt road access and primitive launching is available at Piute Farms on the San Juan Arm of Farley Canyon near Hite and at Blue Notch Canyon in Good Hope Bay.

When to Go

Spring and fall are the best time to visit Lake Powell. Weather is most comfortable in these seasons and fishing is prime. Bass and blue gill fishing are good in the early season due to spawn, and stripers can be found near the surface. Autumn brings stripers back to the surface to "boil" on baitfish. Threadfin shad can become depleted in the fall, leaving their predators hungry and more aggressive. Summer fishing can still be pleasant and most of the lake does not freeze in winter, giving anglers a chance to beat cabin fever. ♦

Services

Lake Powell Resorts & Marinas
P.O. Box 56909
Phoenix, AZ 85079-6909
tel: (602) 278-8888 / (800) 528-6154
fax: (602) 331-5258
website: www.visitlakepowell.com
(*Four full-service marinas, lodging and dining; reservations and information for Halls Crossing, Hite, Bullfrog and Wahweap.*)

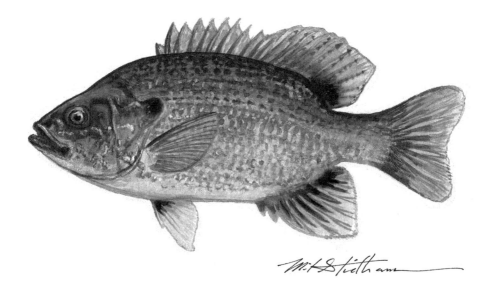

Green sunfish. (ARTIST: MIKE STIDHAM)

Quail Creek Reservoir WASHINGTON COUNTY

T his year-round state park (often called Quail Lake) does not freeze in winter, making it a great place to escape cabin fever. Twenty minutes from St. George, it is a popular place for people to cool off in summertime. Jet-skiing and waterskiing are very popular. If you want some peaceful fishing, try very early mornings and evenings.

This reservoir does produce some large bass. Dennis Miller caught and released a 27-inch largemouth in March of 1998, and currently holds the Utah catch-and-release record.

Drained, repaired, and refilled after a dike broke in 1989, this water is probably near the peak of its ability to produce large bass. If you would like a chance at a state record bass, make a trip to Quail Creek soon.

Fish Species
Rainbow trout, largemouth bass, bluegill, crappie, and bullheads.

Special Regulations
Quail Creek Reservoir has a maximum boat capacity of 70.

There is also a launch restriction in effect from May 1 to Labor Day. Only boats with odd bow registration numbers are allowed to launch on odd days, etc. Call Quail Creek State Park at (435) 789-4432 if you have questions.

❑ Trout limit, 6.

❑ Bass limit, 6; 4 under 10 inches and 2 over 20 inches.

Tactics
Bass-fishers do well with plastic worms and jigs fished deep and slow during the pre-season period in late February and early March. Fish will continue to hold in the shallow water through the spawn in March. Try poppers and surface plugs.

Crayfish and rainbow trout are the main forage for bass in Quail Creek Reservoir. Try crankbaits that imitate either of these.

How to Get There
From St. George, go northeast 7 miles on I-15 to Exit 16. Turn east on SR 9 for three miles, then turn north to the state park.

Accessibility

Quail Creek State Park (tel: 435-879-2378) has camping, modern restrooms, and a boat launch area. Red Cliffs Campground is just a few miles northwest of the reservoir — a good choice if the state park is full.

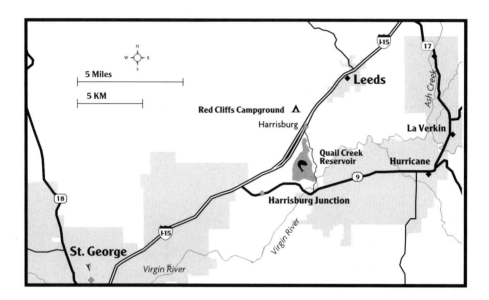

GPS Coordinates

Quail Creek Reservoir	N 37° 11′ 08″ W 113° 23′ 02″
Red Cliffs Campground	N 37° 13′ 31″ W 113° 24′ 15″

Maps

USGS 1:24000 — Harrisburg Junction, Hurricane (the reservoir does not appear on currently available USGS Maps)

Utah Atlas and Gazetteer — Page 17

When to Go

February through mid-May is the best time to find a trophy bass and avoid the congestion of summer pleasure boaters. ◆

Redmond Lake

ne of the few places in Utah where anglers can pursue northern pike (Yuba Reservoir, further down the Sevier River, is another). This lake is also a good side trip for anglers staying at Palisade State Park.

Fish Species

Northern pike, largemouth bass, channel catfish, and bullheads.

Special Regulations

General season, bag, and possession limits apply.

Tactics

Red and white Daredevils are a favorite pike lure. Fly-fishers can use red and white streamer patterns on sinking lines. Pike are very toothy, so wire leaders are a good idea.

Bait-fishing with anchovies underneath a bobber can be very effective.

This is a small lake and most anglers fish from shore.

How to Get There

From Gunnison, go south 8 miles on US 89, then southwest 3.7 miles on SR 256. In the town of Redmond, turn west on 300 South for 0.2 miles, then southwest on Redmond Lake Road and continue to the reservoir.

Accessibility

There are no facilities here.

GPS Coordinates

Redmond Lake	N 38° 59' 45" W 111° 52' 14"

Maps

USGS 1:24000	Aurora, Salina
Utah Atlas and Gazetteer	Page 37

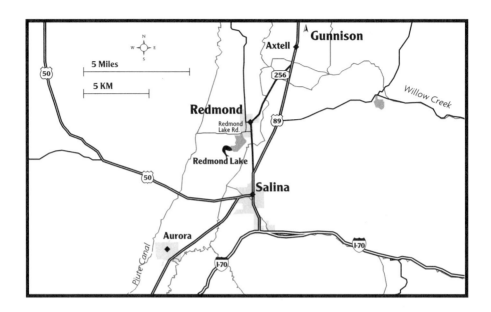

When to Go

This lake has many springs and stays open all winter. Best fishing for pike is from December through February. ◆

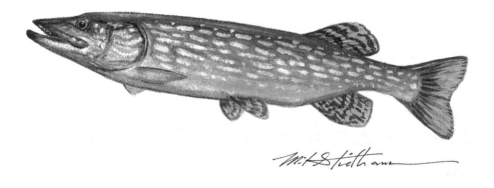

Pike. (ARTIST: MIKE STIDHAM)

Yuba Reservoir (Sevier Bridge)   JUAB COUNTY

Y uba Reservoir has suffered a collapse of the yellow perch forage due to heavy predation by walleye combined with angling pressure. The DWR is trying to maintain forage populations (yellow perch) by limiting harvest. To this end, there is a 10-fish limit on yellow perch. Some harvest of walleyes is desirable to maintain a balance between them and their forage.

Perch caught in deep water usually don't survive when released. It is recommended that perch anglers keep the first 10 perch they catch and then stop fishing. This will prevent waste of the perch resource and help to protect against another population collapse.

Because the perch are heavily preyed upon in this body of water, one can find some very large individuals, some exceeding 13 inches. Ray Johnson caught the state record here in 1984. It was a 15 1/8 inch specimen that weighed 2 lb. 11 oz.

Fish Species

Channel catfish, yellow perch, walleye, northern pike, and rainbow trout.

Special Regulations

❏ Yellow perch, limit 10.

❏ Walleye limit, 6; but only 1 over 20 inches.

❏ Dead yellow perch may be used as bait.

Yuba Lake is open to the use of two poles by anglers that purchase a second pole permit for $10.00 along with their regular fishing or combination license (see regulations).

Tactics

"Ice out" fishing can be exceptional, as walleye hungry from the winter prepare for the spawn. April, May, and June see spawning activity, with fish easier to locate. Fishing should remain good all through the summer and well into fall. Fish here prefer shallow cover, such as willows and moss beds. Don't be afraid to get hung up, just bring extra tackle. Perch-colored crankbaits, and night crawler harness work well, but jigs tipped with night crawler or plastic bodies are easier to fish in cover.

The best places for walleye are around Painted Rocks and Walleye Bay. The shoreline on either side of the dam can also be good.

Perch populations were strong in 1997 even though the spawn wasn't as success-ful. One should expect to find a good number of these panfish with some very large individuals — up to 13 inches. Small jigs and worms will be the best offer-ings. Fish will be in shallow water to spawn as soon as the ice goes out, probably in late March, depending on the year. Schools of perch will be in deeper water after April. Yuba can be a good ice-fishing destination as well. Anglers jig spoons and ice flies in water from 10 to 30 feet deep. Waxworms, perchmeat, and perch eyes are all good baits.

Several large pike have been taken here. Dean E. Johnson caught the current state record northern pike here in 1986. It was a 22 lb. fish over 44 inches long. Trolling or casting in the lake's shallow upper end is the best bet for pike. Be aware that there are only a few of these large predatory fish in Yuba Reservoir.

Several thousand catchable rainbow trout were planted here in the fall of 1998.

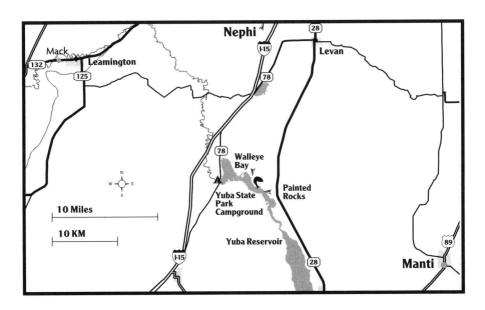

How to Get There

From Nephi, go south on I-15 for 23 miles to Exit 202. Go south 4 miles on Fourth Street (SR 78) to the Yuba Lake State Recreation Area.

An alternative is to leave I-15 at Exit 222 and get on SR 28. Go south 23 miles, then turn west at the sign for Painted Rocks State Park.

Accessibility

Main access points are the State Parks and a new "boat in" camping area that opened in 1998. Fishing from boats or other watercraft is preferred here, but there are many places to reach the water, with many dirt roads near the lake on the south shore.

GPS Coordinates

Yuba State Park Campground	N 39° 22' 46" W 112° 01' 29"
Painted Rocks (approximate)	N 39° 21' 13" W 111° 56' 42"
Walleye Bay	N 39° 22' 53" W 111° 58' 59"

Maps

USGS 1:24000   Mills, Skinner Peaks, Hells Kitchen Canyon SW, Scipio North, Hayes Canyon

Utah Atlas and Gazetteer   Pages 37, 45

When to Go

"Ice out" is arguably the best time to be on the Yuba with a rod in hand. Springtime is very active as well, but this reservoir is a good fishing option until it freezes. Ice-fishing for perch can be very good once there is enough ice for safety. ◆

Services

Camping:

Yuba State Park
Nephi
tel: (435) 758-2611
Reservations: (800) 322-3770
(In Salt Lake City, call 322-3770)

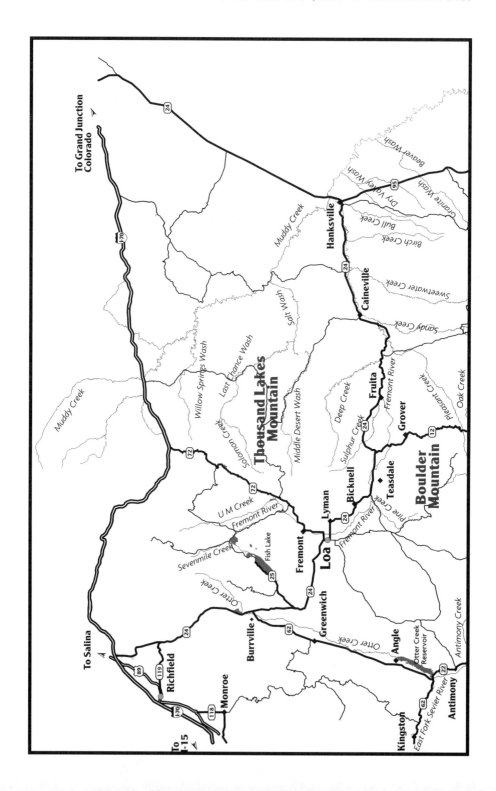

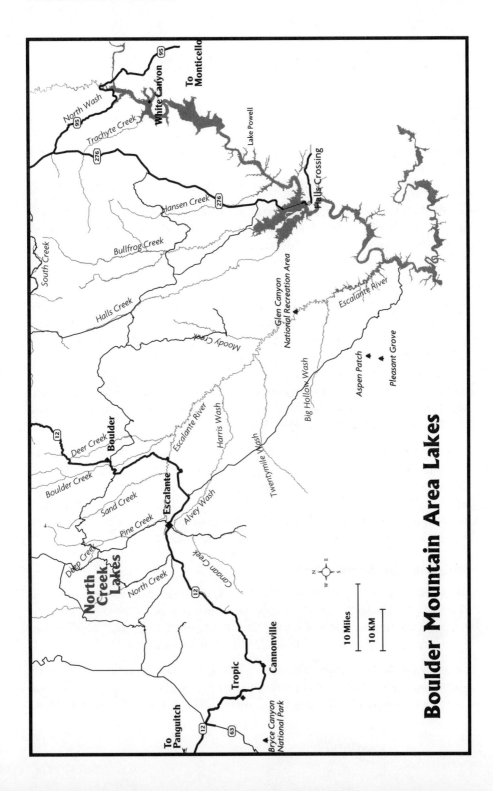

Boulder Mountain Area Lakes

Boulder Mountain Area Lakes

U tah is blessed with two remarkable high-elevation lake areas. The Uinta Mountains are much larger, but the Boulder Mountain area boasts several desirable characteristics of its own. One major difference is nearly 3 degrees of latitude, meaning that the Boulders are about 180 miles further south. This provides for a longer fishing season and a longer growing season for trout.

While the wilderness designation for most of the High Uintas preserves its pristine nature, it also means that to visit many of the remote lakes, anglers must commit to hiking or riding long distances. On the other hand, all the lakes in the Boulder Mountain area have road access or require less than 3 miles of walking to reach their shores.

All lakes are subject to change over time. They collect sediments on the bottom and become shallower, until they can no longer support fish. The forces of nature, grazing, logging, and road-use all combine to speed this process in the region. To help reduce erosion, some roads have been closed. Management of this area is moving towards a "Closed Unless Posted Open" policy. We can do our part by respecting road closures and supporting the DWR and the Forest Service in their efforts to protect our fisheries. Anglers gain little advantage by being able to drive to a lake that is too shallow to hold fish.

Dining on fresh trout around the campfire is a key part of the fishing experience for many. Keep in mind, though, that you will have less of an impact on the fishery if you harvest fish from lakes with large populations of smaller trout. Nature and the DWR can produce several small fish with relative ease. A trophy-sized brook trout is a rare thing. If carefully photographed and released, it can thrill anglers for years and pass its traits on to the next generation.

High Lake Geographic Areas

These high lakes are divided into three geographic areas in the following sections of this guide. The largest area is Boulder Mountain proper, followed by Thousand Lakes Mountain just north of Torrey, and the North Creek Lakes northwest of Escalante. Only lakes believed to sustain viable fisheries are listed.

Don't overlook the streams. They often hold good numbers of fish, particularly above and below lakes. Beaver ponds can provide excellent fishing as well. Look for more information in the chapter on Rivers and Streams of Southern Utah.

Special Regulations

Boulder Mountain Streams and Lakes (Wayne and Garfield counties) — *including the Dixie National Forest; Teasdale and Escalante Ranger Districts: general locations known as the North Boulder Slope, East Boulder Slope, South Boulder Slope, Griffin Top, Boulder Top, Escalante Mountain;* **except** *Pine Lake, Wide Hollow Reservoir and Lower Bowns Reservoir in Garfield County where statewide rules apply, and* **except** *Dougherty Basin in Garfield County, where separate specific rules apply:*

❑ Trout limit, 6; but only 2 over 13 inches.

Dougherty Basin Lake (Garfield County) — *Boulder Mountain:*

❑ Artificial flies and lures only.

❑ Brook trout limit, 4.

❑ **Closed** January 1 through 6 a.m. the second Saturday of July (July 10, 1999).

❑ **Closed** to the possession of cutthroat trout or trout with cutthroat marking.

Tactics

Each lake is uniquely different. When you arrive at your fishing destination, pause a moment to observe. Look for signs of where and how fish might be feeding and adapt your methods accordingly. Polarized glasses are your window into the underwater world of these high lakes. They can help you find drop-offs and other structures, especially if you take advantage of high points.

As most of these are small lakes that have road access or just require a short hike, they are ideal for anglers using float tubes and kick boats.

Many of these lakes grow large scuds (freshwater shrimp), which are excellent food sources for trout. Fly-fishers should try scud patterns in sizes 10-14 in orange, pink, and olive. These flies will be especially effective when trailed 3 feet behind a large, flashy wooly bugger fished on sink-tip or full-sink fly lines. When you find brook trout in smaller ponds, bead head and weighted nymph patterns cast with a floating line can be great. Try to cast in front of fish and slowly strip in the line when they approach your fly. Recommended wet-fly patterns for this area are wooly buggers, scuds, and prince nymphs. Expect Callibaetis hatches in spring followed by damselflies in summer. Black ants, elk hair caddis, and renegades are effective dry flies.

Spin-fishers can present flies behind a casting bubble. Brook and cutthroat trout both respond well to spinners (Mepps, Panther Martin and Vibrax) and small spoons. Splake (Blind Lake, Fish Creek, and Beaver Dam Lakes) prefer heavy spoons and jigs tipped with dead minnows. Tiger trout (Mooseman and Floating Island Lakes) are aggressive fish and respond well to flashy spinners.

Bait-fishers have good success for rainbows and brook trout by still-fishing with worms and Power Bait. Shallow beaver ponds can be effectively fished by using ultralight tackle to cast one half of a night crawler with no weight. Allow your bait to slowly settle to the bottom, then lift it and allow it to settle again.

How to Get There

From Salt Lake City, the most direct route is I-15 south to Exit 188 at Scipio. Proceed south on US 50 to Aurora, where you can pick up SR 24. Continue south to Loa, Bicknell, and Torrey. You can reach SR 12 just east of Torrey and follow it south to Boulder and Escalante.

Accessibility

Most of these lakes are above 9,000 feet. Extreme weather can move in quickly. Road conditions deteriorate rapidly. It is best to be prepared to overnight rather than risk a serious accident. Roads will usually dry out after a few days of good weather and there are several lakes accessible from SR 12 to occupy anglers while they wait.

Backcountry travelers should always be equipped with a good compass and topographic maps (1:24000 scale are best). The *Trails Illustrated* map of this area (Fish Lake North & Central Capitol Reef #707) is particularly good for road travel on Boulder and Thousand Lakes Mountains. The following sections include many positions that can be entered into GPS receivers to ease navigation, but this equipment is no substitute for maps, good navigational skills, and common sense. Most GPS units will only tell you the direction and distance to a destination. They do not warn of obstacles in your path, or display nearby trails or roads that will ease your journey. The best equipment is of no use without the skills to use it properly in the field. Take the time to practice before your trip.

When to Go

Spring comes a bit earlier here, with the lower elevation lakes becoming accessible some time in May. The higher-elevation areas open between mid-June and the first of July. Since this is dependent on snow pack and weather, it can vary quite a bit from year to year.

Fishing should remain good through the end of September. The large brook trout wear their brightest coloring for the spawning season in fall. Substantial snowfall is possible anytime after the first of October. ♦

Another nice trout succumbs to Paul Swan and his float tube. ▶
(PHOTO: JOHN CAMPBELL / WWW.OUTDOORSOURCE.NET)

Services

Food:

Cafe Diablo
599 W Main Street
Torrey, UT 84775
tel: (435) 425-3070
(*Exceptionally good food.*)

Guides & Outfitters:

Outdoor Source
HC 61, P.O. Box 230
Fremont, UT 84747
tel: (435) 836-2372
cell: (801) 558-7952
winter: (702) 795-1552
www.outdoorsource.net
info@outdoorsource.net

Lodging:

Boulder Mountain Guest Ranch
Salt Gulch
Boulder, UT 84716
tel: (435) 335-7480

Boulder Mountain Lodge
Junction of Burr Trail and SR 12
P.O. Box 1397
Boulder, UT 84716
tel: (435) 335-7460 / (800) 556-3446
fax: (435) 335-7461
www.boulder-utah.com
e-mail: bmlut@color-country.net

Boulder View Inn
385 W Main Street
Torrey, UT 84775
tel: (435) 425-3800 / (800) 444-3980

The Lodge at Red River Ranch
2900 W SR 24
P.O. Box 69
Teasdale, UT 84773
tel: (435) 425-3322 / (800) 20-LODGE
fax: (435) 425-3329
website: www.redriverranch.com
e-mail:thelodge@redriverranch.com

Boulder Mountain Lakes   WAYNE AND GARFIELD COUNTIES

 egend says the original name for this high plateau was Thousand Lake Mountain, until cartographers mistakenly switched names with the comparatively dry mountain to the north.

Boulder Mountain is home to some very large brook trout. Milton Taft caught a 7 lb. 8 oz. specimen here in 1971 that holds the current state record. Travis L. Clark holds the catch-and-release state record with a 23-inch brook trout caught in 1997. There are few moments in an angler's career that can surpass reaching into the water to cradle a jewel-bright slab of a brook trout in its full spawning glory.

A number of roads exist on the relatively flat mountaintop. Most of the lakes can be driven to and the rest can be reached by hiking less than 3 miles.

How to Get There

To drive up on top of Boulder Mountain, go southeast 2.5 miles from Bicknell on SR 24 and turn southwest on the paved road. Take the right fork at the sign for Boulder Top. Go 3 miles and take the left fork at the sign for Antelope Spring and Pollywog Lake. About 1 mile further, take the left fork for FR 178, which takes you up onto Boulder Mountain.

Near Bluebell Knoll you can turn south onto FR 782 and go 1.1 miles to Elbow Lake, which is at the center of Boulder Top. For this reason, Elbow Lake is used as the starting point for access to many of the lakes listed in the lake descriptions table beginning on page 494.

Accessibility

Navigation on Boulder Mountain, with its maze of old roads, is extremely challenging. Signs at many of the lakes have been removed, either as souvenirs or to confuse other anglers. Signs marking forest roads are present in most places. It is recommended that you bring a full array of navigational aids, including topographic maps, a compass, and a GPS system.

Closure of roads is being considered in several areas to prevent erosion. Please respect road closures. When planning a trip to Boulder Top, allow extra time for finding your way and be prepared to hike a reasonable distance if roads are closed.

Note: Access to Purple and Blue Lakes is currently possible on FR 491. This road will likely be closed in the near future. Anglers will then have to take FR 176 to Row Lakes and hike or drive east from there.

In the lake descriptions for the Boulder Mountain Area, the following abbreviations were used:

AT	= albino trout		NW	= northwest
BK	= brook trout		RA	= road access
BT	= brown trout		RT	= rainbow trout
CG	= campground		S	= south
CT	= cutthroat trout		SE	= southeast
E	= east		SP	= splake
ESE	= east southeast		SR	= state route
FK	= fork		SW	= southwest
FR	= forest road		TR	= trail
GR	= arctic grayling		Trhd	= trailhead
Lw	= lower		TT	= tiger trout
Mdws	= meadows		Up	= upper
N	= north		W	= west
NE	= northeast		WSW	= west southwest

Boulder Mountain beauty: Rim Lake (PHOTO: EMMETT HEATH / WESTERN RIVERS FLYFISHER)

Lake Descriptions

Lake / Species	GPS Coordinates / Comments
Beaver Dam ..... BK/SP	**N 38 09' 56" W 111 25' 58"** FR 179 to Green Lake, hike S 2 mi. (past Blind Lake). It is possible to use 4-wd to lake. Dam rebuilt 1996. 9,950-feet elevation. 2 mi. hike to the lake.
Bess .... BK	**N 38 08' 07" W 111 27'13"** 2.4 mi. SE on FR 782 from Elbow Lake, then N 0.7 mi. on FR 322. A small lake at 11,000 feet.
Big .... RT	**N 38 06' 27" W 111 25' 28"** Near Meeks. From Elbow Lake, 7.6 mi. SE on FR 782, then 0.9 mi. NE on 4-wd trail. May winterkill. 10,900 feet.
Blind .... RT/CT/BK/SP	**N 38 10' 40" W 111 26' 30"** FR 179 to Green Lake. Hike S 1 mi. Heavy use. Blind Lake covers 52 acres and is up to 57 feet deep. Float tubes are a great advantage here.
Black .... BK	**N 38 00' 06" W 111 32' 58"** Hell's Backbone Road to FR 566. Between Dry and McGath Lakes. A small lake at 9,600 feet.
Blue .... BK/CT	**N 38 05' 03" W 111 34' 10"** Near Purple. From Posey Lake Road, go E 8.6 mi. on FR 162 to FR 491, then N 3.4 mi. N of Purple Lake. A medium-sized lake at 10,500 feet. (See note on page 492 on road closures.)
Bullberry .... BK	**N 38 14' 41" W 111 30' 09"** From Coleman Lake, go S 1 mi. on trail. Many small brook trout. Small ponds. Can be very fast fishing.
Chuck .... BK	**N 38 08' 53" W 111 32' 21"** From Elbow Lake, go N 1.4 mi. on FR 782, then W 1.9 mi. on FR 178. Walk S 1.5 mi. on closed road, then W 1.2 mi. Subject to winterkill but does produce nice fish when they over-winter successfully.
Coleman .... RT/BK	**N 38 15' 13" W 111 29' 27"** From SR 12, take FR 521 3.6 mi. SW, then turn SW to Coleman Lake. Small lake with heavy use. Next to Flat Iron, which has no fish.
Cook .... RT	**N 38 10' 37" W 111 32' 20"** 5 mi. W of Elbow Lake and just N of FR178. 1 mi. N of Miller Lake. This is a 10-acre lake at 10,700 feet.

Lake / Species	GPS Coordinates / Comments
Crater .... BK	**N 38 06′ 23″ W 111 28′ 09″** From Elbow Lake, take FR 782 SE 1.5 mi. to FR 302. Go 1 mi. S to FR 304, then 2 mi. to Crater Lake. Road closed 0.2 mi. from lake. This lake is hard to find. It is 1 mi. N of Horseshoe Lake. FR 304 is very faint and hard to follow.
Crescent .... CT/BK	**N 38 04′ 36″ W 111 29′ 02″** FR 286 to Crescent is closed. Hike 2 mi. E from Spectacle or 2 mi. SW from Horseshoe. This 9-acre lake is at 10,900 feet and is as deep as 27 feet.
Deer Creek ...... BK/CT	**N 38 02′ 25″ W 111 22′ 60″** From SR 12 take FR 554 W 1.2 mi. to trailhead. Hike 3 mi. W on trail. This lake covers 26 acres at 10,000 feet.
Donkey .... BK	**N 38 12′ 13″ W 111 29′ 27″** Take FR 521 S from near Teasdale to Donkey Lake. Heavy use, subject to drawdowns.
Fish Creek .... BK/SP	**N 38 09′ 48″ W 111 26′ 14″** FR 179 to Green Lake, hike S 2 mi. (past Blind Lake). It is possible to drive 4-wd to lake. This 28-acre lake at 10,000 feet gets heavy use.
Green .... BK	**N 38 11′ 22″ W 111 26′ 55″** From SR 12 N of Grover, go W 11 mi. on FR 179. Near Blind Lake. Heavy use. This lake is 15 acres at 10,300 feet.
Halfmoon .... BK	**N 38 04′ 49″ W 111 28′ 25″** From Horseshoe Lake, go S 1 mi. on trail. 9 acres at 10,700 feet.
Honeymoon ..... BK	**N 38 09′ 47″ W 111 26′ 36″** Go 0.2 mi. W of Fish Creek Lake. A 1-acre pond at 10,250 feet.
Horseshoe .... BK	**N 38 05′ 16″ W 111 27′ 60″** From Elbow Lake, take FR 782 SE 1.5 mi. to FR 302. Go 4.5 mi. S. At 10,700 feet. 12 acres and 14 feet deep.
Lost .... BK	**N 38 13′ 39″ W 111 30′ 41″** From Coleman Lake, go 2.8 mi. SW on trail. Most remote lake on the mountain.
Lower Bowns ..... RT	**N 38 06′ 27″ W 111 16′ 13″** From SR 12, go E 4.2 mi. on FR 181. Small dirt boat ramp. Expect campground improvements in 1999.

Lake / Species	GPS Coordinates / Comments
McGath .... BK	**N 38 00' 02" W 111 34' 10"** Hell's Backbone Road to FR 566. W of Black Lake. Large lake of 43 acres at 9,370 feet.
Meeks .... BK	**N 38 06' 54" W 111 24' 02"** From Elbow Lake, go 3.2 mi. SE on FR 782, then NE 2.2 mi. on FR 321. Head SE 1.7 mi. on FR 313. May winterkill. Part or all of FR 313 may be closed to vehicles.
Miller .... RT/BK	**N 38 09' 27" W 111 32' 51"** 5 mi. W of Elbow Lake and just S of FR178. 1 mi. S of Cook Lake. A 6-acre lake at 10,650 feet. Up to 12 feet deep.
Moosman .... TT	**N 38 02' 32" W 111 23' 55"** 0.6 mi. W of Deer Creek Lake. A pond of 1.5 acres at 9,850 feet.
Oak Creek ...... BK	**N 38 04' 14" W 111 22' 27"** From SR 12, go SW 2 mi. on FR 567. Hike or 4-wd the last 0.5 mi. to the lake. A 27-acre lake at 10,100 feet. Up to 30 feet deep.
Pear .... BK	**N 38 10' 14" W 111 26' 28"** FR 179 to Green Lake, go S on hiking trail 1.5 miles. Just S of Blind Lake. Heavy use. This lake is 9 acres at 10,250 feet.
Pine Creek ...... BK	**N 38 12' 05" W 111 34' 02"** Hike 0.9 mi. NE from the Aquarius Guard Station on FR 178. A 3-acre reservoir at 9,100 feet. Depths to 11 feet.
Pleasant .... BK	**N 38 05' 39" W 111 24' 57"** From Elbow Lake, go SW on FR 782 7 miles. Go 0.1 mi. NE from stream crossing. Small lake at 10,500 feet on the E edge of mountain.
Posey (Posy) ..... RT/BK	**N 38 56' 12" W 111 42' 44"** From Escalante, go 17.9 mi. N on Posey Lake Road (Pine Creek Road). Popular lake with a campground.
Purple .... BK	**N 38 04' 28" W 111 34' 14"** From Posey Lake Road, go E 8.6 mi. on FR 162 to FR 491, then N 2.5 mi. 0.5 mi. S of Blue Lake. This is a 14-acre lake at 10,500 feet. Maximim depth is 16 feet. (See note on page 492 on road closures.)
Raft .... BK/CT	**N 38 09' 54" W 111 29' 34"** From Elbow Lake, go N 0.4 mi. on FR 782, then N 1 mi. on FR 177. May winterkill. This is an 18-acre lake at 11,000 feet.
Rim .... BK	**N 38 04' 25" W 111 30' 26"** From Elbow Lake, take FR 277 S 6.5 miles. This 8-acre lake is up to 19 feet deep.

Lake / Species	GPS Coordinates / Comments
Round .... BK	**N 38 12' 22" W 111 28' 23"** Near Donkey Lake. Take FR 521 S near Teasdale. Heavy use. Covers 6 acres at 10,000 feet.
Row .... RT	**N 38 04' 27" W 111 35' 10"** From Posey Lake Road, go E 7.2 mi. on FR 162 to FR 176, then N 1 mi. W of Purple Lake. Four shallow lakes in a row. They are 5 to 30 acres. Subject to winterkill.
Scout .... BK	**N 38 03' 47" W 111 21' 18"** From SR 12, go NW 2.8 mi. on FR 554. Heavy pressure. Covers 2.5 acres.
Solitaire .... BK	**N 38 11' 36" W 111 28' 59"** Go SSE 0.7 mi. from Donkey Reservoir. This is a 4-acre lake at 10,200 feet.
Spectacle .... BK/CT	**N 38 04' 57" W 111 30' 30"** From Elbow Lake, take FR 277 S 5.7 miles. Covers 34 acres when full. Subject to drawdown.
Surveyor .... BK	**N 38 08' 18" W 111 32' 53"** From Elbow Lake, go N 1.4 mi. on FR 782, then W 1.9 mi. on FR 178. Walk S 3 mi. on closed road. Subject to severe drawdown. This is a 5-acre lake at 10,850 feet.
Tule .... BK	**N 37 55' 55" W 111 42' 19"** Go 0.5 mi. SW of Posey Lake. Covers 7 acres at 9,100 feet.

Maps

USGS 1:24000	Torrey, Blind Lake, Grover, Lower Bowns, Deer Creek Lake, Jacobs Reservoir, Roger Peak, Posey Lake, Big Lake, Government Point
Utah Atlas and Gazetteer	Pages 27, 28
Trails Illustrated	Fish Lake North & Central Capitol Reef (#707)

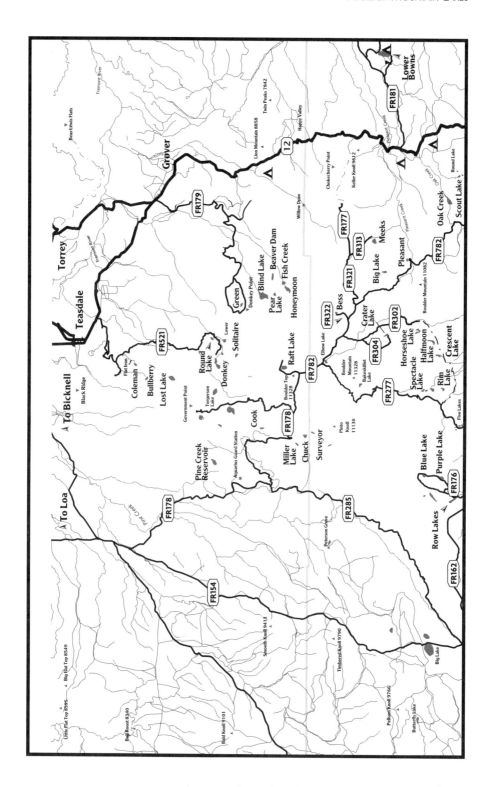

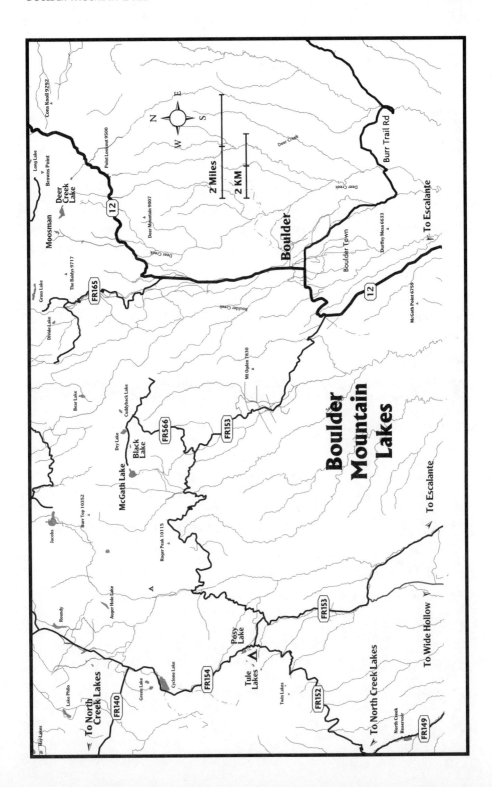

Boulder Mountain Lakes

North Creek Lakes

T he North Creek Lakes lie just under Griffin Top at the headwaters of North Creek. Barker and Lower Barker are accessible by road and Barker Reservoir has seven sites for primitive camping. The remaining lakes are all within easy hiking distance.

Dougherty Basin Lake will be used by the DWR to hold brood stock for native strain Colorado cutthroat trout. With the new regulations (see Special Regulations under Boulder Mountain Area Lakes), anglers can expect some larger fish here in the future. Be especially careful to release any cutthroat unharmed.

How to Get There

From Escalante, go west 5.5 miles on SR 12, then turn north onto North Creek Road (FR 149). Continue north and then west for 21 miles to reach Barker Reservoir.

Lake Descriptions

Lake / Species	GPS Coordinates / Comments
Barker .... RT / BK	**N 37 55′ 18″ W 111 49′ 37″** From SR 12 W of Escalante, go N on FR 149. 9,950 feet elevation. Primitive campground.
Barker (Lower) ... RT / BK	**N 37 55′ 27″ W 111 49′ 23″** From SR 12 W of Escalante, go N on FR 149. 0.7 mi. from Barker Reservoir Campground.
Blue .... BK / CT	**N 37 56′ 08″ W 111 49′ 26″** Near Yellow Lake. Hike 1.2 miles N from the trailhead at Lower Barker Lake. A few cutthroat trout. This is a very small lake. Just N of Yellow Lake.
Dougherty Basin .. CT	**N 37 55′ 17″ W 111 50′ 10″** 0.5 miles W of Barker Reservoir. See Special Regulations.
Flat .... BK	**N 37 55′ 55″ W 111 49′ 35″** Hike 1 mi. N from the trailhead at Lower Barker Lake. Elevation is 9,516 feet.
Joe Lay .... BK	**N 37 55′ 47″ W 111 49′ 10″** Hike 0.6 mi. N from trailhead at Lower Barker Lake. A small 3-acre lake at 9,500 feet.

Lake / Species	GPS Coordinates / Comments
Long Willow ..... **Bottom** BK / CT	**N 37 54′ 28″ W 111 50′ 45″** Hike SW 1.5 mi. from Barker Reservoir Campground. A 4-acre lake at 9,800 feet.
Round Willow .... **Bottom** BK	**N 37 54′ 21″ W 111 50′ 33″** Hike SW 1.5 mi. from Barker Reservoir Campground. A 7-acre lake at 9,800 feet.
Yellow .... BK	**N 37 56′ 04″ W 111 49′ 22″** Hike 1.1 mi. N from the trailhead at Lower Barker Lake. Some winterkill. This lake is 5 acres.

Maps

USGS 1:24000   Barker Reservoir

Utah Atlas and Gazetteer   Page 27

Angling may be said

to be so like

the mathematics,

that it can never

be fully learnt.

Izaak Walton (1593-1683)

PHOTO: BYRON GUNDERSON / FISH TECH OUTFITTERS

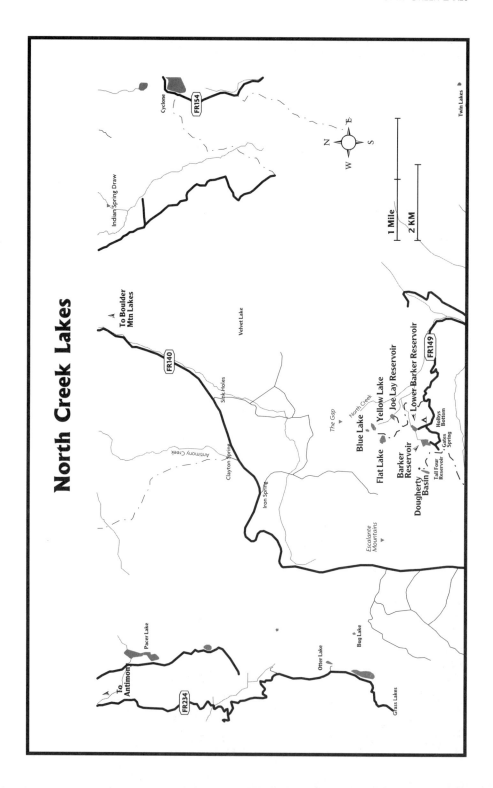

North Creek Lakes

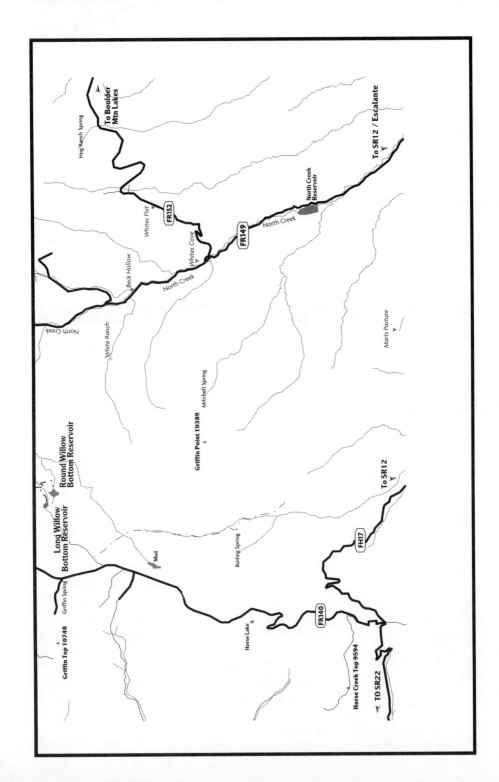

Thousand Lake Mountain   WAYNE COUNTY

T he terrain of Thousand Lake Mountain is very similar to Boulder Mountain. Most of the lakes are quite productive, though some may winterkill at times. All are accessible by road or a short hike, with the exceptions of Blind Lake and Neff Reservoir.

How to Get There

From Fremont, go northeast 8.5 miles on SR 72. Turn east onto FR 206 near Forsyth Reservoir. It is about 5 miles to the intersection of forest roads near Heart Lake. Elkhorn Campground is another 3.5 miles south on FR 206.

Lake Descriptions

Lake / Species	GPS Coordinates / Comments
Blind . . . . BK	**N 38 25′ 40″ W 111 30′ 42″** Walk 5.5 mi. SW from Elkhorn Campground on Neff Reservoir Trail. A small, remote lake at 10,000 feet.
Deep Creek . . . . . . BK	**N 38 26′ 01″ W 111 27′ 51″** From Elkhorn CG, go S 1.3 mi. on FR 206, SW 1.8 mi. on FR 209. Walk on trail 0.2 mi. W. Very pretty lake at about 10,550 feet.
Farrell . . . . RT / BK	**N 38 32′ 33″ W 111 27′ 27″** From FR 206 by Heart Lake, go 4 mi. NE on FR 020, W 3.4 mi. on FR 019, NW 0.4 on FR 568. Shallow and mossy, but many fish. 8,300 feet. Poor road last 0.4 mi.
Floating Island . . . . RT / BK / TT	**N 38 32′ 06″ W 111 27′ 27″** 0.4 mi. WSW on Meeks Lake. Short hike. State record tiger trout caught here in 1997. Elevation 8,460 feet.
Little Grassy . . . . . BK / CT	**N 38 26′ 08″ W 111 27′ 55″** Just NW from Deep Creek Lake. Shallow lake, but fish overwinter well.
Meeks . . . . RT / BK	**N 38 32′ 16″ W 111 27′ 01″** From FR 206 by Heart Lake, go 4 mi. NE on FR 020, W 3.4 mi. on FR 019, 0.1 mi. E from end of road. Fishing negatively affected by water fluctuations and many rough fish. 8,336 feet.
Morrell . . . . RT / BK	**N 38 32′ 49″ W 111 26′ 10″** From FR 206 by Heart Lake, go 4 mi. NE on FR 020, W 0.9 mi. on FR 019. Turn N 0.2 mi. Good for young anglers. Bring a float tube. You can drive right to this lake.

Lake / Species	GPS Coordinates / Comments
Neff . . . . BK	**N 38 26' 50" W 111 29' 37"** Walk 3.4 mi. SW from Elkhorn Campground on Neff Reservoir Trail. Scenic reservoir at 10,250 feet.
Round . . . . RT / BK / CT	**N 38 29' 41" W 111 26' 33"** From FR 206 by Heart Lake, go SE 0.7 mi. on FR 022. Go NE 1 mile on FR 211. Last mile is rough. Need high-clearance vehicle to reach lake. Elevation 8,800 feet.

Maps

USGS 1:24000	Flat Top, Lyman, Geyser Peak
Utah Atlas and Gazetteer	Pages 27, 28
Trails Illustrated	Fish Lake North & Central Capitol Reef (#707)

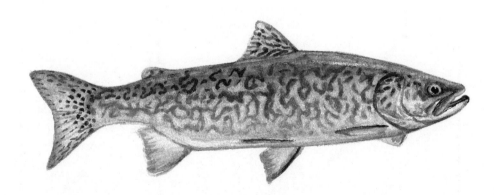

Tiger trout. (ARTIST: MIKE STIDHAM)

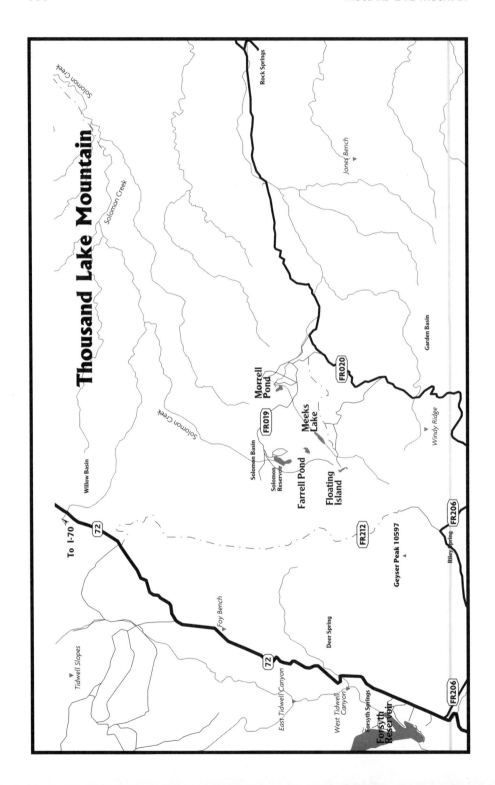

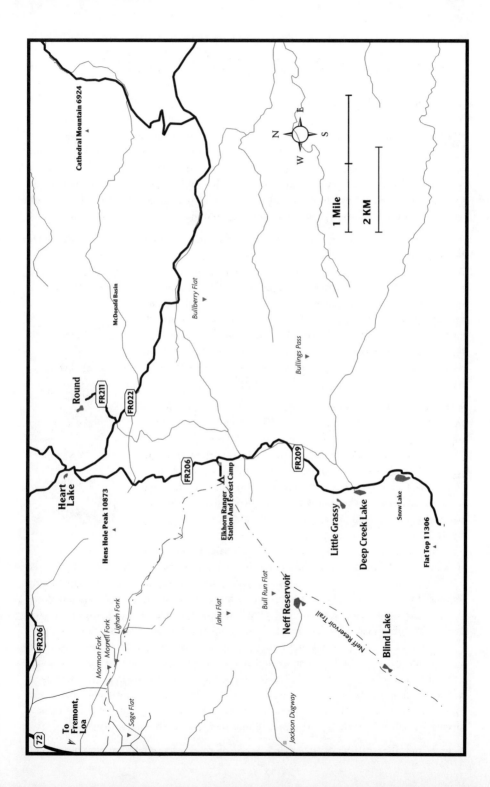

Fisheries Management in Utah

by Tom Pettengill, *DWR Sport Fisheries Coordinator*

H istorically, two subspecies of cutthroat trout (Bonneville and Colorado River) and three subspecies of whitefish (Mountain, Bonneville and Bear Lake) and the Bonneville cisco were the only game fish native to Utah. Only 27 of the 66 species of fish found in Utah today were native to Utah. Most of the sport fishing in Utah occurs for introduced species. Rainbow trout, brown trout, brook trout, lake trout, largemouth bass, smallmouth bass, walleye, bluegill, yellow perch, etc. were not native to Utah.

Utah is the second driest state in the nation. The only state with less water is Nevada. Since the settlement of Utah in the 1800s, water has been a valuable commodity. To provide food for the early settlers our streams were diverted for irrigation and reservoirs were built to hold snow melt for later use. These alterations of our streams had dramatic impacts on many of the native fish. Fish were also harvested to provide food for the early pioneers. Bonneville cutthroat trout were commercially harvested from Utah Lake and hauled by the wagon load to markets in Salt Lake City. Between over harvest of adults and loss of young cutthroat trout into fields by irrigation diversions many of Utah's fisheries were heavily depleted by the late 1800s.

Utah is the second driest state in the nation.

In the late 1800s fish culture and fish stocking was really getting under way all across the United States. The public was demanding improvement in declining fisheries and early fisheries managers and fish culturist's were eager to help. With the help of the transcontinental railway about every known species of fish or their eggs were shipped back and forth across the country and stocked into about every available water. This was when many new species were originally brought into Utah. Carp and brown trout were brought into the United States from overseas. Rainbow trout from the west coast. Brook trout from back east. Largemouth bass were brought in from the south. Salmon were brought in from the west coast and stocked in Utah Lake and Bear Lake. All these new species that hadn't evolved in Utah's waters had varying degrees of success in providing a fishery and varying impacts on the native fish populations. In Bear Lake, the salmon survived and grew but couldn't successfully spawn in diverted streams any more than native cutthroat. Runs eventually died out when stocking stopped. Some species like brown, brook and rainbow trout were successful. They were easily cultured in our hatcheries and were successful at spawning in our streams. Some populations were sustained by natural reproduction in the higher reaches of streams. The same areas still occupied by our native cutthroat trout. In many cases the newly introduced species out competed the native cutthroats. Between altered habitats and the introductions of new species our native cutthroats were almost eliminated from their natural habitats.

Many of our altered habitats, whether streams or reservoirs, could not support natural fisheries on there own and fish culture and fish stocking was important to maintaining sport fishing. Cutthroat trout have always been a difficult species to raise in hatcheries. Much more difficult than rainbow trout and because of that the rainbow trout became the trout of choice for stocking all across the United States. At first rainbow trout fry, 1 - 2 inch, newly hatched, fish were stocked. Millions of small fry were stocked all across Utah. Metal milk cans full of fry of various species were loaded on rail cars, wagons and horse back and stocked where ever biologists or anglers could get. Eventually it was learned that stocking larger fingerlings and eventually catchable sized fish was more productive. As fish size increased the numbers of fish stocked had to decrease.

In the early days fishing regulations were simple. Daily limits were high. Anglers were allowed 35 trout per day. But as our population grew so did angling pressure and even stocking couldn't keep up with the demand.

Over the last 100 years fisheries management and fishing regulations have become much more complicated and complex. Instead of a one-size-fits-all program, management and stocking today are tailored more towards the capabilities of specific waters. Public attitudes and needs have changed. Early settlers relied on natural resources to put food on their tables. Even 20 years ago most sport fish caught were harvested by the angler. Today it's cheaper to go to the supermarket and buy fish than it is to drive 50 or 100 miles each way to catch a mess of trout. A new "Conservation Ethic" is putting greater emphasis on conserving wildlife and managing for native species rather than just providing sport fisheries for harvest. Angling interests are much more diverse. Trout are still the most important species in Utah. Seventy-five percent of Utah anglers fish for trout and 75% of our angling is done on reservoirs and lakes. Today fisheries managers are expected to provide fisheries for fly fishers, trophy lake trout fishers, native cutthroat fishers, etc. No longer is a trout a trout. Some anglers still want to harvest lots of fish while others think every fish should be released. Some Utah residents don't think we should allow any fishing or harvest of fish. Utah has grown from a lightly populated western state to the sixth most urbanized state in the nation with a rapidly growing population. In spite of all the challenges that fisheries managers face today, fishing in Utah may have never been better overall than is has been in the 1990s.

Fisheries managers are going to continue to face challenges and changes in the new century. Greater emphasis on native species will mean more opportunities for anglers to catch Bonneville and Colorado River cutthroat trout. In the last 10 years, Utah's fisheries managers have been working hard to expand native cutthroat trout back into streams and lakes they historically occupied. Much more work needs to be done. Native non-game fishes are also getting much more attention. This will limit management options for fisheries managers. Some species of non-native game fish will not be stocked because of their impacts on recovery of native fishes. As our angling population continues to grow and attitudes about fishing and harvest change we'll see more waters managed for wild fish, and more waters with restrictions on fishing methods and harvest. But with Utah's altered and impounded streams many of our fisheries will continue to be sustained by stocking of hatchery raised fish. In spite of all the changes and challenges that fisheries managers face, the future of sport fishing in Utah remains bright. ◆

Game Fish of Utah

COOL/WARMWATER GAME FISH

Walleye. Prominent "canine" teeth distinguish this big perch from its smaller family member, the yellow perch. Color is brassy-olive buff, sometimes shading to yellowish sides and white beneath. Large, dark blotch at rear base of the first dorsal fin and the lower lobe of tail is white-tipped. The tail is moderately forked.

Smallmouth Bass. The snout is long and bluntly pointed, the lower jaw slightly longer than the upper jaw. Smallmouth bass vary in color with habitat, but are normally dark olive to brown on the back with the sides lighter and yellowish and the belly yellowish. There are eight to 15 (average nine) dark vertical bars on the sides which distinguishes them from the largemouth bass. Anterior dorsal fin has 10 spines, and is strongly joined in the soft dorsal. The anal fin has three spines.

Largemouth Bass. Head is large and long. Mouth is large and terminal with upper jaw reaching past the center of the eye in adults. The upper parts of the body and head are greenish with a silvery or brassy luster. The belly is white to yellow. There is an irregular dark stripe along the sides. Eyes are brown.

Northern Pike. Large toothy mouth of a predator. It has a very elongated torpedo-like body. They are dark green to dark brown along the back with light colored spots on the sides. They are uncommon in Utah, only found in Redmond Lake, the Sevier drainage and a few in the Green River.

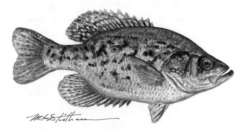

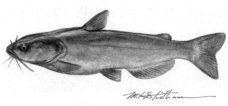

Striped Bass. Coloration is bluish-black to dark gray, or olive-green above, the sides are silvery, the belly white. Striped bass have seven to nine unbroken stripes along each side. The body is somewhat streamlined. Mouth is oblique and the lower jaw longer than the upper. The dorsal fins are clearly separated. The caudal is forked.

Channel Catfish. Distinguished from other catfishes by their long anal fin and deeply forked tail. The body is pale bluish-olive above and bluish-white below. They usually have spots but lose them when older. Both dorsal and pectoral fins have strong, sharp spines. The mouth is short, wide and horizontal with chin and snout barbels.

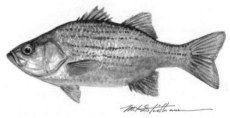

Black Crappie. The black crappie has two closely joined dorsal fins. Black crappie are silver-olive with numerous black or green splotches on the sides. Vertical bars, prominent in the young, are absent in adults. Sides are light, iridescent green to silvery. Belly is silvery to white. Pelvic fins are opaque with some black on the tips of the membranes, and pectoral fins are dusky and transparent. It is fairly abundant in Utah lowland warmwaters from Cache Valley to Lake Powell.

White Bass. Coloration on the back is gray or charcoal, green, with silvery sides and white belly. They have five to seven longitudinal stripes on each side. The body is deeper and less stream-lined that the striper. They are common in Utah Lake, where they dominate all other fishes.

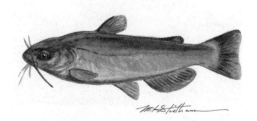

Black Bullhead. Adults are blackish, dark olive, or dark brown on the back. Belly is greenish-white or bright yellow. They are common in many warmwaters of Utah, and abundant in Utah Lake.

COOL/WARMWATER GAME FISH

NATIVE GAME FISH

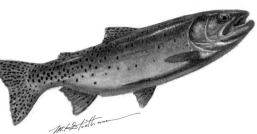

Green Sunfish. Body deep and laterally compressed but smaller than closely related bluegill. Long opercular flap with colored margin. Body brown to olive with an emerald sheen. Darker on top with light yellow green sides.

Cutthroat Trout. Two sub-species evolved from the only trout native to Utah. Cutthroats are best distinguished by their crimson slash along the lower jaw. They lack the iridescent pink stripe of the rainbow trout. The *Bonneville cutthroat* inhabited the Bonneville Basin and has sparsely scattered, very distinctly round spots over the upper body. They are clothed in subdued colors of silver-gray to charcoal upper body with subtle hues of pink on flanks during spawning. They, particularly the Bear Lake strain, often lack the bright crimson jaw slash that at times may be yellow.

Yellow Perch. Body is oval in cross section and snout is blunt. Dark green, olive or golden brown on dorsal surface. Dark stripes on flanks separated by yellow or light green. Yellow pectoral fins and eyes are yellow to green. These fish are important as forage in many Utah waters.

The *Colorado River cutthroat trout* evolved in the Colorado/Green River drainages and is noted for its brilliant coloration. The males, in spawning condition, have bright crimson stripes along their sides and their stomach is often crimson. Spotting is usually concentrated posteriorly.

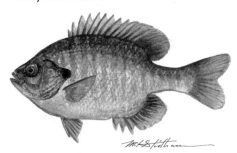

The *Yellowstone cutthroat* was introduced into Utah early in the 1900s and has been the predominant subspecies used in management programs throughout the state. It is lightly spotted with distinctly round spots concentrated toward the tail area. Today, the native strains are becoming more extensively used in the sport fisheries programs and are being reintroduced to many of their former habitats.

Bluegill. Very deep, compressed body. Head is deep with totally black opercular flap with no pale or colored margin. Green, olive or brown on top with vague vertical bands extending down sides. Breast may be yellow or copper orange.

NATIVE GAME FISH

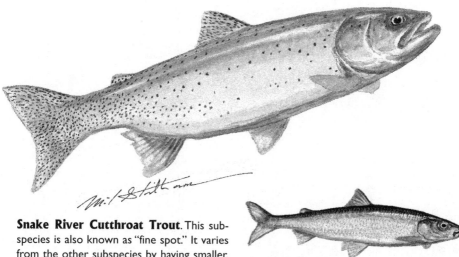

Snake River Cutthroat Trout. This subspecies is also known as "fine spot." It varies from the other subspecies by having smaller, more numerous spots.

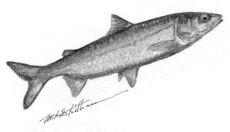

Bear Lake whitefish and Bonneville whitefish. These two fish are indistinguishable beyond 10 inches in length. The Bonneville whitefish (pictured) have gray-blue spots along their sides until they reach that size. These whitefish are elongate, relatively cylindrical fish. They are silvery-white along their sides grading into a charcoal gray to black on their backs. They have small delicate mouth parts that make them difficult to catch. They may reach four pounds in weight and grow to 20 inches. Both species occur only in Bear Lake, nowhere else in the world.

Bonneville Cisco. A diminutive fish found only in Bear Lake. The Bonneville cisco is a long, slender, pearly-silver fish that rarely grows beyond seven inches. It has a dusky blue black and a brassy band along its flanks at spawning time. The snout is sharply pointed. It is noted for its mid-winter spawning concentrations along a rocky beach on the east side of Bear Lake in mid-January where it is dipnetted in large numbers. It is a prolific fish that is an important forage for the predatory species in Bear Lake.

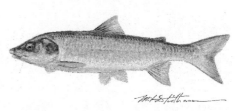

Mountain whitefish. Light brown on the back and fins and silvery to white on the belly and sides. Snout and lower jaw are short and blunt, with a flap on each nostril.

HYBRID GAME FISH

Wiper. A hybrid cross between a female striped bass and male white bass. Its appearance is intermediate between the two parents. It has six to eight dark horizontal stripes over a silver-white background with a dark charcoal to black back. It has two dorsal fins. The anterior with 8-10 sharp spines. It is slightly heavier bodied than the striped bass and grows up to 123 pounds in weight and 24 inches in length. The wiper was recently introduced into Willard Bay.

Tiger Muskellunge. A hybrid cross between a muskellunge and Northern pike with intermediate characteristics between the two parents. It has a very elongated torpedo-like body. Its most notable feature is the gray-green vertical bars along its sides. It thrives where there are good numbers of perch and sunfish for food. The tiger muskie was recently introduced into Pineview Reservoir. It can be expected to grow to 45 inches long and weigh 20 pounds.

Tiger Trout. Tiger trout, a cross between brown trout and brook trout has a unique, dark maze-like pattern over a brownish, gray body. The belly is yellowish orange as are the pectoral, pelvic and anal fins. The tall fin is square.

Splake Trout. A splake trout is the hybrid cross between lake trout and brook trout. It has a dark background with white spots. The tall fin is not as deeply forked as lake trout. The pectoral fins are easily distinguished from rainbow trout as splake have a dark background with white spots and rainbows have a lighter, silvery background with dark spots.

INTRODUCED TROUT

Lake Trout. These fish have a background color of gray-brown overlaid with light spots that vary in intensity with age and environment. The background color covers the back, sides and fins and serves to highlight the lighter gray spots. Trout in large lakes are sometimes so silvery that the spots are difficult to see. Spotting is usually more intense on small fish. The caudal fin is deeply forked. The mouth is large and terminal with strong teeth on both jaws. They are present in Fish Lake, Bear Lake and Flaming Gorge Reservoir.

Rainbow Trout. Colors vary greatly, with patterns depending on habitat, size, and maturity. Stream residents and migrant spawners are darker and have more intense colors than lake residents or non-spawners. Lake residents tend to be silvery. A mature rainbow is dark green to bluish on the back with silvery sides. The reddish horizontal band typifies the species. The belly may be white to silvery. Irregular black spots are usually present on the head, back and sides. Rainbow trout are heavily stocked in almost every coldwater drainage in Utah.

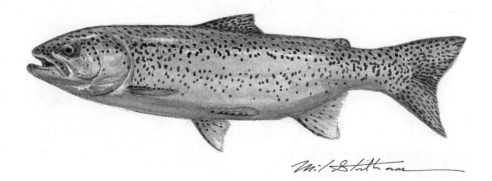

INTRODUCED TROUT

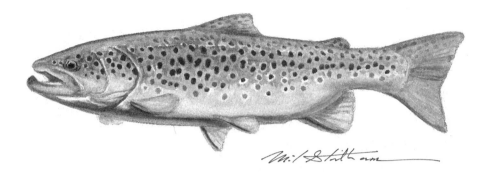

Brown Trout. It is a very hardy trout that competes well with other fishes and endures marginal water qualities better than most trouts. It generally has golden brown hues with yellow under parts. The males during spawning are often brilliantly splashed with crimson spots circled with blue halos. Its upper body is usually profusely dappled with large, irregular dark-chocolate spots. It is quite carnivorous and sports a stronger, sharper set of teeth than most trouts. Brown trout often grow to considerable sizes in excess of 10 pounds.

Kokanee Salmon. Kokanee *(not pictured)* are bright silvery fish with no definitive spotting pattern. Kokanee have a dark blue back with silvery sides. As the spawning season approaches, both male and female kokanee turn a deep red (shades from gold to orange to red) and the lower jaw of the male develops a characteristic hook common to the Pacific salmon. A deeply forked tail also distinguishes them from rainbow, cutthroat and brown trout. They are present in Flaming Gorge, Porcupine and Strawberry Reservoirs.

Grayling. Silvery to light purple colors on the sides and bluish-white on the belly are the distinctive colors of grayling. They are relatively slender and are most easily distinguished by their long, high, brilliantly-colored, bright purple, sail-like dorsal fin.

INTRODUCED TROUT

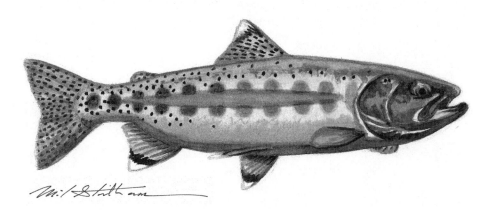

Golden Trout. One of the most colorful trout species *(pictured above)*. Dorsal surface brown to olive fading into yellow sides. They have the crimson slash along the lower jaw like cutthroat, with a diffuse pink stripe down the lateral line. Belly is crimson in spawning season and lavender oval par markings persist to maturity. Very uncommon in Utah with a few remaining in the Uinta Mountain Lakes.

Brook Trout. Exhibiting a wide range of colors, they may be olive to blue-gray on the back to white on the belly. Red spots, usually with bluish halos around them, are present on the sides. Characteristic light wavy marks on the back are a distinguishing feature. Obvious white and then black stripe along the fore edge of each of the lower fins aids in separating brook trout from most other trouts. Caudal fin is square or lightly forked.

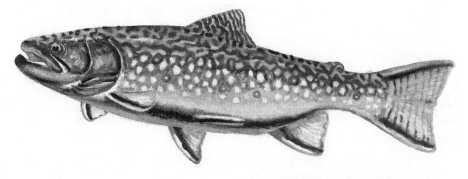

Current Catch-and-Release Record Fish
for the State of Utah

SPECIES	DATE	SIZE	FISHER	LOCATION
Bass, Largemouth	03/29/98	27 in.	Dennis Miller	Quail Lake
Bass, Smallmouth	04/18/97	17 ¼	Ray Johnson	Flaming Gorge
Bass, Striped	11/02/97	29 ½	Kent Erickson	Lake Powell
Bass, White	03/02/97	13 ¼	Ray Johnson	Utah Lake
Bluegill	04/18/98	9 ½	Steve Barney	Pond near Saltair
Bullhead, Black	06/15/97	13 ½	Shawn Clement	Kaysville Ponds
Carp	03/22/97	29 ½	Ray Johnson	Flaming Gorge
Catfish, Channel	07/03/97	33 ½	Wesley Schneider	Utah Lake
Chub, Utah	06/21/97	14 ¼	Sue McGhie Troff	Flaming Gorge Res.
Crappie, Black	01/10/99	13 ¾	Marty Peterson	Lake Powell
Grayling	09/06/97	14	Lawrence Mathis	Allen Lake - Uintas
Muskellunge, Tiger	11/28/98	53 ¼	Ray Johnson	Pineview Reservoir
Perch, Yellow	08/23/97	12 ¼	Vickie O'Farrell	Deer Creek Res.
Pike, Northern	06/13/98	49 ¾	Logan Hacking	Lake Powell
Salmon, Kokanee	05/30/97	23 ¾	Lisa Johnson	Flaming Gorge
Sucker, Utah	04/12/97	22 ¼	Ray Johnson	Jordan River
Sucker, White	04/26/97	19	Kirk Ray Johnson	Flaming Gorge
Sunfish, Green	11/03/97	9 ½	Kent Erickson	Lake Powell
Trout, Albino	11/21/97	18	David Curneal	Big Cottonwood Cr.
Trout, Brook	12/06/97	23	Travis L. Clark	Boulder Mountain
Trout, Brown	06/25/98	23 ½	Robert J. McNair	Green River ("A")
Trout, Brownbow	06/13/97	12 ¼	Kirk Johnson	Mill Meadow Res.
Trout, Cutthroat	03/09/97	20 ¾	Ray Johnson	Strawberry Res.

Current Catch-and-Release Record Fish
for the State of Utah (cont'd)

SPECIES	DATE	SIZE	FISHER	LOCATION
Trout, Lake	07/09/98	46 ½	Ray Johnson	Flaming Gorge
Trout, Rainbow	04/26/97	23 ¾	Jolene Johnson	Flaming Gorge
Trout, Splake	06/13/97	9 ¼	Lisa Johnson	Mill Meadow Res.
Trout, Tiger	06/14/97	16 ¼	Kirk Johnson	Mammoth Reservoir
Walleye	10/17/97	30	Wesley Schneider	Starvation Reservoir
Whitefish, Mtn.	11/28/97	23	Justin C. Bond	Provo River
Wiper	05/26/98	20 ½	Evan E. Day	Willard Bay Reservoir

Updated 1/19/99

Current Angling Record Fish for the State of Utah

SPECIES/LOCATION	YEAR	WEIGHT	SIZE	GIRTH	FISHER
Bass, Largemouth Lake Powell	1974	10 lb 2 oz	24 ¼	20	Sam Lamanna
Bass, Smallmouth Midview Res.	1996	7 lb 6 oz	22	16 ½	Alan Iorg
Bass, Striped Lake Powell	1991	48 lb 11 oz	45	31 ¼	Travis T. Jensen
Bass, white Utah Lake	1970	4 lb 1 oz			John R. Welcker
Bluegill Mantua Reservoir	1993	2 lb 7 oz	11 ½	14 ⅝	Jack Rask
Bullhead, Black Pineview Reservoir	1997	2 lb 13 oz	17	11 ½	Jake Rebmann
Carp Lake Powell	1993	32 lb 0 oz			Couger Elfervig

Current Angling Record Fish for the State of Utah (cont'd)

SPECIES/LOCATION	YEAR	WEIGHT	SIZE	GIRTH	FISHER
Catfish, Channel Utah Lake	1978	32 lb 8 oz	39 ¾	22	LeRoy Mortenson
Chub, Utah Starvation Reservoir	1987	1 lb 11 oz	13 ¼	11	Ray Johnson
Crappie, Black Quail Creek Reservoir	1993	3 lb 2 oz	17 ¼	14	Mike Flickinger
Grayling Big Dog Lake	1998	1 lb 12 oz	17 ¼	8 ¾	Terry J. Fieldsted
Muskellunge, Tiger Pineview Reservoir	1995	20 lb 7 oz	42	17 ½	Nathan Erwin
Perch, Sacramento Garrison Reservoir	1993	4 lb 5 oz	17	15	Harlan G. Thomas
Perch, Yellow Sevier Bridge Reservoir	1984	2 lb 11 oz	15 ⅛	9 ¾	Ray Johnson
Pike, Northern Sevier Bridge Reservoir	1986	22 lb 0 oz	44 ¼	17 ½	Dean E. Johnson
Salmon, Kokanee Strawberry Reservoir	1995	6 lb 0 oz	25	16	Todd Chikaraishi
Sucker, Utah Weber River	1988	6 lb 6 oz	24 ½	13	William Mehn
Sucker, White Flaming Gorge Res.	1992	2 lb 8 oz	19 ¼	9 ½	Ray Johnson
Sunfish, Green Lake Powell	1996	0 lb 15 oz	9 ¾	9	Eddie Goitia
Trout, Albino Joes Valley Reservoir	1989	9 lb 2 oz	24 ¾	17	Nick Manning
Trout, Brook Boulder Mountain	1971	7 lb 8 oz			Milton Taft
Trout, Brown Flaming Gorge Res.	1977	33 lb 10 oz	40	25	Robert Bringhurst

Current Angling Record Fish for the State of Utah (cont'd)

SPECIES/LOCATION	YEAR	WEIGHT	SIZE	GIRTH	FISHER
Trout, Cutthroat Strawberry Res.	1930	26 lb 12 oz			Mrs. E. Smith
Trout, Golden Atwood Creek	1977	0 lb 14 oz	14 ½		Breck Tuttle
Trout, Lake Flaming Gorge Res.	1988	51 lb 8 oz	45 ⅛	31 ¾	Curt Bilbey
Trout, Rainbow Flaming Gorge Res.	1979	26 lb 2 oz			Del Canty
Trout, Splake Fish Lake	1992	10 lb 12 oz	29	18	Joel Davenport
Trout, Tiger Floating Island Lake	1997	5 lb 13 oz	23	15	Scott Tanner
Walleye Provo River	1991	15 lb 9 oz	31 ¾	20 ¾	Jeffery Tanner
Whitefish, Bonneville Bear Lake	1982	4 lb 4 oz	21	13 ¾	Deon Sparks
Whitefish, Mountain Deer Creek Reservoir	1997	4 lb 12 oz	21 ½	14	Roy L. Montoya
Wiper Willard Bay	1998	5 lb 15 oz	22	16	Floyd Eggli

Updated July 17, 1998

New Record Fish Program

Beginning January 1, 1997, the Utah Division of Wildlife Resources began a new Catch & Release record fish program. This program has been initiated to allow anglers to be recognized for catching large fish without having to kill them. This program emphasizes the live release of the fish so they can be caught and enjoyed again in the future by some other lucky angler. If there is any information that the fish was overly stressed, detained, abused or transported from the capture site the application will be rejected. This program is somewhat of an "on your honor" system but each catch will have to be witnessed on the water and a color photograph of the fish must be submitted. Records will be based entirely on the total length of the fish. Fish should be measured to the nearest 1/4 inch. Measure the total length of the fish from the tip of its mouth to the tip of the tail with the tail squeezed lightly to its full extension. The same game species currently recognized in the "weight" state record program will be included.

If you plan to catch and release fish you should not fish with bait. Typically fish caught on bait suffer a much higher hooking mortality than those caught on flies or lures. Some fishing techniques where bait is fished on a tight line and the fish is hooked as soon as it takes the bait have lower hooking mortality than if the fish is allowed to take the bait deeper into its mouth or swallowed. If you do catch a large fish on bait that you want to release and it is hooked deep, cut the line close to the mouth. Eventually the hook will dissolve. Ideally if you plan to release a fish it should not be removed from the water. It should be brought to the surface or shallows where it can be photographed and unhooked without lifting it from the water. Fish caught from water 30 feet or deeper, except lake trout, probably cannot be released. The quick change in pressure coming from deep water to shallow causes the swim bladder to expand rapidly inside the fish and also blood chemistry changes. The fish may appear to swim off normally but it probably will not live. Also trout caught from water warmer than 70 degrees have a much higher mortality than fish caught in cooler water. Following some of these basic catch and release guidelines and taking only the fish you need for a meal or two (not always your limit) will mean better fishing for you and others the next time you get on the water.

Applications for the new program will be available from all Division of Wildlife Offices and on the Division's Internet website www.nr.state.ut.us/dwr/!homeypg.htm. Completed applications along with a color, side-view, photograph should be submitted to your nearest Division of Wildlife Resources Office or mailed to the Sport Fisheries Coordinator, Division of Wildlife Resources, 1594 West North Temple, Suite 2110, Box 146301, Salt Lake City, UT 84114-6301. Anglers who catch a record fish will receive a Catch & Release Record Fish Certificate. ◆

Guides & Outfitters

Alpine Anglers

310 West Main, Torrey, UT 84775
 tel: (435) 864-3473 / (888) 484-3331
fax: (435) 864-3112.
Guide Service for Fly-fishing and Pack trips
on Boulder Mountain. Our fly shop offers
top quality gear for both fishing and hunting. We also sell hunting and fishing licenses, t-shirts and hats. We offer one- or multi-
day trips for fly-fishing over 80 high-moun-
tain lakes.

Anglers Inn

2292 S. Highland Drive
Salt Lake City, UT 84106
tel: (801) 466-3921 / (888) 426-4466
www.anglersfly.com
Permittee Ashley National Forest
Fly-fishing on quality waters in Utah and
around the world.

Bill Dvorak's Kayaking and Rafting Expeditions, Inc.

17921 Hwy 285, Nathrop, CO 81236
tel: (719) 539-6851 / (800) 824-3795
fax: (719) 539-3378
www.dvorakexpeditions.com
e-mail: dvorakex@amigo.net
One-half to 12 day expeditions on eight of
the Southwest's major rivers: Colorado,
Green, Dolores, Arkansas, Gunnison, North
Platte, Rio Chama, Rio Grande.
Instructional kayak, raft, inflatable kayak
programs. Combination activities, including
rafting, 4-WD, horseback riding, mountain
biking, hiking, and custom float fishing.
Outfitters since 1969. Special family rates.

Boulder Mountain Flyfishing

P.O. Box 1403, Boulder, UT 84716
tel: (435) 335-7306.
Guided fly-fishing trips on Boulder
Mountain and the Aquarius Plateau. All
equipment and lessons provided.

Buckboard Marina

25 miles S of Green River, WY off Hwy 530
Open: year-round, 7:00am-8:00 pm
tel: (307) 875-6927 / (800) 824-8155
Permittee Ashley National Forest
Guided fishing and sightseeing tours
on Flaming Gorge Reservoir.

Cedar Springs Marina / Sport Fishing Adventures

P.O. Box 337, Dutch John, UT 84023
tel and fax: (435) 889-3795
cell: (435) 880-8200
www.cedarspringsmarina.com
Permittee Ashley National Forest
Two miles south of Flaming Gorge Dam.
Morning and evening trips, sport fishing
adventures, state-of-the-art equipment.
Open: April 15 - October 15,
8:00 am-6:00 pm.

Conquest Expeditions

tel: (435) 784-3370
Reservoir, 28' Sport Fisher, self contained,
up to six passengers. 24 hours daily.
March-December.

Cowpie Adventures

2837 Breeze Drive, Magna, UT 84044
Mailing address: Box 6, Magna, UT 84044
tel: (801) 250-8266 / 888-4-cowpie
Outfitters that take people camping, hiking,
fishing and biking on Boulder Mountain
(Dixie National Forest), Fishlake National
Forest and Thousand Lake. Cowpie supplies
transportation, camping gear and food.

Creative Fishing Adventures/ Eagles Nest Lodge

tel: (435) 784-3301
Reservoir: trophy lake trout. Open: March-
December, daily.

Dinosaur River Expeditions / Destination Sports

738 Main Street, Park City, UT
tel: (800) 345-RAFT
fax: (435) 649-8126
500 E Main Street, Vernal, UT
Permittee Ashley National Forest and Dinosaur National Monument
Fly-fishing on local waters or on the Green. Guided float trips through the famous canyons of the Green. Also combination float and mountain bike or float and horse rides. Whitewater trips on the Yampa and Green Rivers.

Eagle Outdoor Sports

1507 South Haight Creek, Kaysville, UT 84037
tel: (801) 451-7238
fax: (801) 451-RAFT
e-mail: wcgn57a@prodigy.com
River running and boat tours in Northeastern Utah/Dinosaur National Monument. Specialty trips for groups and families. Guided fishing on the Green River.

Expedition Fly Shop

tel: (435) 755-6800
Guides on private trout waters near Paradise, in Cache Valley. Source for information on Longan River and Blacksmith Fork.

Falcon's Ledge Lodge

P.O. Box 67, Altamont, UT 84001
tel: (435) 454-3737
fax: (435) 454-3392
e-mail: falcon@ubtanet.com .
An Orvis endorsed luxury lodge in the Uinta Mountains of northeastern Utah offering bed & breakfast getaways, fly-fishing, wingshooting, corporate retreats, falconry, hiking, gold panning and other guided wilderness adventures.

Fish Tech

6153 Highland Dr.
Salt Lake City, UT 84121
tel: (801) 272-8808
fax: (801) 272-6935

Flaming Gorge Lodge Guide Service

155 Greendale, US 191
Dutch John, UT 84023
tel: (435) 889-3773
fax: (435) 889-3788
www.fglodge.com
e-mail: lodge@fglodge.com
Permittee Ashley National Forest

Four Seasons Flyfisher

tel: (801) 288-1028 / (800) 498-5440
www.Utahflyfish.com
e-mail: info@utahflyfish.com
Fly-fishing Utah and Wyoming quality waters.

Green Rivers Outfitters

P.O. Box 200
Dutch John, UT 84023
tel: (435) 885-3338
fax: (435) 885-3370
www.utah-greenriver.com
e-mail: greenriver@cisna.com
Permittee Ashley National Forest

Jans Mountain Outfitters

1600 Park Ave., Park City, UT 84060
Mailing Address: P.O. Box 280, Park City, 84060
tel: (435) 649-4949 / (800) 745-1020
fax: (435) 649-7511
e-mail: sports@jans.com
www.jans.com
Jans Mountain Outfitters is a full-service fly tackle and accessory shop with full guide service, retail and rentals available. Let us show you Utah's hidden wonders in the high Uinta Mountain range or our high desert plateau. We offer both river and pond fly-fishing.

L.C. Ranch

P.O. Box 63, Altamont, UT 84001
tel: (435) 454-3750
www.lcranch.com
e-mail: lcranch@ubtanet.com
Fly-fishing resort, six lodges with catering. Great for honeymoons, anniversaries, business & family retreats. Guided catch and release fly-fishing only.

Lucerne Valley Marina and Campgrounds

tel: (435) 784-3483 / (888) 820-9225
www.flaminggorge.com
Permittee Ashley National Forest.
Guided fishing on Flaming Gorge Reservoir.
Seven miles east of Manila.
Open: March 30 - November 15,
7:00 am-9:00 pm, daily.

Mountain West Outfitters

tel: (801) 394-2769
Guides on Strawberry reservoir and private
waters.Fly-fishing classes.
Permittee USDA.

Old Moe Guide Services

P.O. Box 308
Dutch John, UT 84023
tel and fax: (435) 885-3342
www.quickbyte.com/oldmoe
e-mail: gwerning@union-tel.com
Permittee Ashley National Forest

Outdoor Source

H.C. 61, P.O. Box 230, Fremont, UT 84747
tel: (435) 836-2372
www.outdoorsource.net
e-mail: info@outdoorsource.net
The Outdoor Source runs fly-fishing and
hiking services in southern Utah: Capitol
Reef and Escalante-Grand Staircase
National Monument and on the Fremont
River and Boulder Mountain. Services: Day
trips, fly-fishing schools, University of Utah
Teen/Family programs, corporate outdoor
adventures and training.

Park City Fly Shop

2065 Sidewinder Dr., Park City, UT 84060
tel: (435) 645-8382 / (800) 324-6778
www.pcflyshop.com
Walking and float trips on the Provo River.

Red Pine Adventures

2050 W White Pine Canyon Road,
Park City, UT 84060
tel: (435) 649-9445 / (800) 417-7669
Guided horseback tours in the mountains
around Park City. Other areas by special
arrangement. Ride to fishing waters.

U-Bar Ranch

tel: (435) 645-7256 / (800) 303-7256
fax: (435) 649-2553
Permittee Ashley National Forest
Offer horse rides, pack trips and snowmobil-
ing. U-Bar is on the Uinta River adjacent to
the High Uinta Wilderness area and offers
pack trips to high lakes. Lodging is available.

Rocky Meadows Adventures

12000 West 1595 South, Bluebell, UT
84007-9711
Mailing Address: HC 65 Box 165, Bluebell,
UT 84007-9711
tel: (435) 454-3176
e-mail: awhite@ubtanet.com
Working cattle ranch vacations, hunting,
fishing, horseback riding, and camping near
High Uinta's and wilderness.

Spinner Fall Fly Shop

2645 East Parley's Way
Salt Lake City, UT 84109
tel: (801) 466-5801 / (800) 959-3474
fax: (801) 466-3029
www.spinnerfall.com
Permittee Ashley National Forest

Triangle G Service

P.O. Box 271
Manila, UT 84046
tel: (435) 784-3265
winter: (435) 882-1076
www.3gfish@aros.com

Trout Bum 2

4343 N SR 225, Suite 101
Park City, UT 84098
tel: (435) 645-6611 / (877) 878-2862

Trout Creek Flies

P.O. Box 247
Dutch John, UT 84023
tel: (435) 885-3355 / (800) 835-4551
fax: (435) 885-3356
www.fishgreenriver.com
e-mail: info@fishgreenriver.com

Permittee Ashley National Forest

Trout Creek Flies (cont'd)

Trout Creek Flies offers single- or multiple-day and overnight guided fly fishing trips. We use Mekenzie-style drift boats or walk/wade for Rainbow, Brown, and Cutthroat Trout on Utah's Green River below Flaming Gorge Dam. Scenic floats also available.

Western Rivers Flyfisher

1071 East 900 South
SLC, UT 84105
tel: (801) 521-6424 / (800) 545-4312
fax: (801) 521-6329
www.wrflyfisher.com
e-mail: westriv@xmission.com
Permittee Ashley National Forest
Guided fly-fishing trips to the Green River,
Provo River and the L.C. Ranch.

Wild Country Outfitters

tel: (801) 479-1194 / (888) 377-9453
www.wild_fit@msn.com
Guides for quality trout on private waters in northern Utah.

ARTIST: GREG PEARSON / WESTERN RIVERS FLYFISHER

Trout Unlimited

by Wes Johnson, *Chairman, Utah Council of Trout Unlimited*

"To conserve, protect, and restore North America's coldwater fisheries and their watersheds."

F orty years ago, July 1959, a group of trout fishers in Michigan got together to form a fishing club. But this club was different; instead of discussing their latest fishing exploits, these men were determined to do something about the declining trout fisheries in their local area.

Today, Trout Unlimited (TU) has grown to nearly 700 chapters across the nation with over 100,000 members. TU's members are composed of conservation minded individuals from all walks of life. We value coldwater fisheries as recreational resources that are threatened by polluted waters, unhealthy forests and rangelands, and a lack of biological diversity. TU's members are grassroots volunteers backed by a professional staff of scientists and resource advocates. As a preeminent conservation organization TU seeks to:

❐ Protect fish and their habitat through advocacy and conservation programs;

❐ Promote conservation through research publications, national and regional conferences, state and local meetings, and education programs;

❐ Restore habitat and critical resources through projects and public/private partnerships;

❐ Assist affiliates and other organizations that share TU's mission.

TU National has it main offices in Arlington, Virginia. There are also six state offices located in California, Colorado, Michigan, Montana, Washington, and Wyoming. Overseeing the business and professional operations of TU is a Board of Trustees. These 35 individuals assist in raising funds for critical resource issues identified by the grassroots volunteers. Individuals are selected to be on the Board based on their business experience and the skills the can contribute to further TU's mission. Members of the current Board is comprised of such names as Hemingway, Roosevelt, Armour, and Ford. Other Board members are associated with such companies as Sage, Orvis, Simms, GlenMorangie and Trask shoes.

In order to more effectively represent the grassroots efforts TU has divided the nation into ten regions. Each region has a chief volunteer officer known as the Regional Vice President. As members of the Board of Trustees, their role is to represent the grassroots component of TU and act as a link between TU's National Resource Board and the Board of Trustees. These Vice Presidents serve a vital link between these two boards. These Vice Presidents also coordinate activities between the various councils and chapters.

The National Resource Board (NRB) oversees resource initiative planning and provides input to TU nationals conservation agenda. Many of these members are professional biologists who have a very deep scientific understanding about our fisheries and how they should be properly managed. Each of the ten regions across the nation has three NRP members assigned to it.

In Utah there are currently six chapters associated with Trout Unlimited. These include one of the oldest chapters of TU in the nation, the Stonefly Society, TU chapter #048 in the Salt Lake Valley. High Country Fly Fishers, chapter #599, is centered in the Park City and Heber Valley area. The Utah Green River chapter, #620, is centered in Vernal. Color Country, chapter #636 is located in Cedar City. Cache Anglers is chapter #665 and is found in the Cache Valley area. Weber Basin Anglers is located in the Ogden area and is chapter #681. A new chapter in forming, at the time of this writing, in the Price area. We are looking forward to having other chapters form in various regions of the state.

These chapters and the Utah Council of Trout Unlimited (UTTU) act as "watchdogs" on various waters through out the state. Without the vigilance of the Stonefly Society and other groups, the Provo River would have been decimated by the Utah Department of Transportation reconstruction project. The loss of habitat, reduction in water quality, and potential excess effluent discharge into East Canyon Creek was brought to the attention of the Divisions of Wildlife Resources (DWR) and Water Quality by the council and High Country Fly Fishers. Cache Anglers have been very involved in the Bear River relicensing of various dams that affect its quality fishing. The council has been very active in monitoring the efforts of the Utah Reclamation Mitigation and Conservation Commission in restoring fishery habitat and acquiring angler access.

The UTTU is a signatory to various agreements with DWR, the U.S. Forest Service, the Bureau of Land Management and the U.S. Fish and Wildlife Service. As a cooperator with these agencies we have seen efforts to restore and enhance fisheries through out the state of Utah. These agencies have asked for and received our participation and criticism on numerous projects. We have responded to livestock issues, timber harvest, road construction, instream enhancements and restoration projects; all at the request of various state and federal agencies.

It was noted in recent years that the Utah Department of Agriculture (DoA) was very lackadaisical in their monitoring of the private aquaculture industry. We have seen the transport of whirling disease infected fish from a private hatchery to public waters (a Salt Lake City park) under the DoA authority. The monitoring efforts of the DoA were non-existent on numerous occasions. We also seen the DoA wanting to allow private hatcheries to put their fish in public waters. This could not be tolerated.

Through the combined efforts of all the chapters, the council, other angling organizations, and private businesses new legislation was drafted that would result in the formation of a new Fish Health Board. Trout Unlimited insisted that the board be balanced between the DWR and the DoA, with the chairperson being independent. The DoA was totally opposed to our efforts. However, when the legislative committee was presented with the facts and seen the support for the anglers legislation they had to listen to their constituents. Result: Our public waters and fisheries are now under the control of the DWR, not the DoA. The Fish Health Board is balanced, with a TU member siting on the Board. However, we must remain diligent to prevent any stocking by private hatcheries in our public waters.

An issue of vital concern to the UTTU today is the relentless stocking of hatchery raised fish in streams that could maintain viable wild populations. Hatcheries have become a necessity of life; mainly to provide a put-and-take fishery. This is mainly to satisfy the needs of those individual who feel that they have a right to catch as many fish as the law allows; and for some to kill more than the law allows. Decreased water quality, a possible result of poor management of our public lands, has lead to an increased demand to meet the general publics fishing needs through the hatchery system. If as much time, effort, and money was put into restoring and holistically managing our aquatic and riparian habitats as is put into hatcheries we would see more naturally sustainable populations of our fisheries.

An issue of vital concern to the UTTU today is the relentless stocking of hatchery raised fish in streams that could maintain viable wild populations.

Hatcheries do play a vital role. They can and are being used to provide restocking of native fish into their historical range. They can be used to supplement wild populations when adverse conditions occur that reduce their reproductive capabilities. Hatchery raised fish, catchables, are a great way to get today's kids interested in fishing; Hooked on Fishing — Not Drugs. Hatcheries also provide an angling opportunity to those areas where sustainable populations cannot be established.

Trout Unlimited here in Utah, and in other states, has used in-stream incubators to help establish populations with very little human intervention. At the request of DWR, the U.S. Forest Service (USFS), the Bureau of Land Management (BLM) we have used these incubators in various locations to enhance native trout populations. Some sites that have been selected include Little Dell Creek, Trout Creek, Sheep Creek and other locations. Most in-stream incubator projects have been very successful; few have failed, mainly due to outside factors. These incubators allow an egg to develop in a natural stream. Imprinting that stream in the trout's senses will encourage it to return to spawn future generations.

The Utah Council of Trout Unlimited (UTTU) not only coordinates activities between the various chapters, but it also acts as a bridge to TU national. By bringing local issues relating to coldwater fisheries to the attention of TU national, broader support can be attained. This is the case with Lost Creek and its reservoir. The rebuilding of the dam at Lost Creek caused a major impact on the fishery in the reservoir and below the dam. By working with the Divisions of Wildlife Resources and Parks and Recreation, we sent letters of support to Congressman Jim Hansen for funding of new facilities at the state park and angler access below the dam. When TU national was advised of the local support, they too commented directly to Congress to voice their support. Result: An additional $1,000,000 was requested to support the Lost Creek   project.

Through the UTTU, projects that may be of interest between two or more chapters can be coordinated. Also, the various Embrace-A-Stream (EAS) grants are coordinated through the council. These EAS grants can amount to thousands of dollars for habitat enhancement, education, and other projects that enhance coldwater fisheries. Here in Utah these funds have been used in City Creek above Salt Lake City, and in Little Dell and Lambs Canyon Creek to help restore the Bonneville Cutthroat Trout populations and imporve their habitat.

Thousands of dollars have been used as matching funds for Division of Wildlife Resources aquatic habitat projects. These include the Strawberry River, Trout Creek, Emigration Creek, Little Dell Creek and various other streams. Nearly $10,000 was spent on signs and other materials to educate the angling public about whirling disease and how to prevent its spread.

As a 501(c)(3) tax exempt organization TU is creating a land conservation program that will protect riparian corridors important to coldwater fisheries. By working with private land owners we can help reduce their liabilities through conservation easements, angler access agreements, and projects to protect their properties. TU seeks to cooperate with private landowners to complete habitat enhancement projects on their property that help prevent erosion and destruction of riparian zones. One important factor related to this is protecting the rights of the private land owner.

TU supports the private property rights of all land owners and feel that they should have a say in how angling is allowed on their lands. If a property owner wishes to open his riparian areas to anglers, he should be allowed to define what sort of angling shall be allowed. If a land owner is agreeable to allowing angler access for fly fishing only, catch-and-release/slot limit then they have a right to do so. How can an individual find out more about Trout Unlimited. One of the best sources is through the Internet: www.tu.org. From here all chapters have the ability to list their upcoming events in the "Chapter Newsletter" section. Most chapters post their meeting time, place and agendas in local newspapers or in the various sporting goods stores and fly fishing shops. Here in Utah we are establishing our own council web site, and the Stonefly Society has already completed theirs. The council will also publish a quarterly newsletter that will be available to non-members through various outlets.

What is the future of Trout Unlimited here in Utah? With growing membership and new chapters we seek to keep the public informed about the numerous issues relating to our cold water fisheries and their habitats. We seek cooperation with local land owners in preserving their riparian zones from erosion and allowing angler access under their terms. We seek the continued cooperation with and between ourselves, other conservation groups, state and federal agencies in numerous projects throughout the state. We seek the reestablishment of viable populations of native trout to their historical ranges. We seek the establishment of wild populations, not dependent on continued hatchery stocking. We seek water quality of a high enough standard to maintain trout fisheries.

The key thing to remember about Trout Unlimited is that it is a conservation organization. Our mission statement says it all: *to conserve, protect, and restore North America's coldwater fisheries and their watersheds.* By supporting TU you become a vital link in accomplishing this mission and ensuring the future of our fisheries. ◆

Rocky Mountain Anglers

by Ray Shelbe

R ocky Mountain Anglers (RMA) is a unique fishing club in Utah. The club's focus leans toward walleye fishing, but RMA's fishing interests encompass all freshwater fish. Club members represent a wide range of ages and occupations along the Wasatch Front. All share a love of fishing and a desire to improve themselves and fishing in general.

Education, service, and competition make up the foundations of RMA.

Education

RMA was formed by a group of anglers who wanted to learn more about Utah walleye and walleye fishing, and education has always been a major focus. Regular monthly meetings and a monthly newsletter help to keep members in touch and informed. Meetings frequently feature guest speakers, including officials from the Utah Division of Wildlife Resources. This promotes a dialogue between anglers and fisheries managers and helps club members better understand Utah fish management issues. Club members regularly report on issues and projects they are involved in. Education also plays a part in RMA service projects and in the club's competitive pursuits.

Service

RMA maintains a strong commitment to improving Utah's fisheries. The club has participated in service projects and donated funds to benefit a variety of fish species including walleye, catfish, tiger muskie, smallmouth bass, and wiper.

Also, a number of improvements in the Utah fishing proclamation over the years were enacted through club efforts.

The club's annual spring walleye seminars, co-sponsored by Utah Fishing and Outdoors Magazine, the Utah Division of Wildlife Resources, and others, have become a spring tradition on the Wasatch Front. The seminars always draw a large crowd of Utah walleye anglers. The discussion goes beyond fishing techniques to other subjects RMA considers important such as angler ethics and current issues affecting Utah walleye. Club members take great pride in being able to share what they have learned.

Competition

A slate of walleye-only and multi-species club tournaments throughout the year challenge participants' fishing skills and encourage an exchange of ideas on techniques, equipment, and strategies. Tournament locations include Starvation, Willard Bay, Lake Powell, Fish Lake, Redmond, Pineview, and many others. Club tournament contestants draw for partners and are awarded plaques. Points are scored by measuring the length of fish so they can be imediately released.

Over the years, the club has helped bring a more serious brand of competitive walleye fishing to Utah by working closely with officials of the Starvation Walleye Classic and, more recently, with the Utah Walleye Circuit. RMA members alsofish walleye competitions and circuits in other states as well.

Rocky Mountain Anglers celebrates its 10th anniversary in 1999. As the club has grown in size, so has its involvement with Utah fisheries. The next decade promises more of the same.

Anyone interested is invited to attend a meeting. For more information and for meeting times and locations, send a letter to Rocky Mountain Anglers, P.O. Box 926, Midvale, Utah, 84047-0926, or visit the club's site on the world wide web at www.utahfishing.com under the "clubs" directory. ◆

The browns get aggressive in the fall on the Green. (PHOTO: EMMETT HEATH / WESTERN RIVERS FKYFISHER

Index

Author with daughter Jess.

About the Author

Steve Cook holds a Bachelor's degree in Fisheries and Wildlife Management from Lake Superior State University in northern Michigan. He is an avid outdoorsman who has lived in and explored Utah for the past 15 years as a fly-fishing guide and instructor. When not in Utah, he works as a GPS surveyor in the remote areas of Alaska. This is his first book.